Fundamental Issues in Arch

Series Editors

Gary M. Feinman
Field Museum of Natural History, Chicago, IL, USA

T. Douglas Price
University of Wisconsin-Madison, Madison, WI, USA

For further volumes:
http://www.springer.com/series/5972

T. Douglas Price · Gary M. Feinman
Editors

Pathways to Power

New Perspectives on the Emergence
of Social Inequality

 Springer

Editors
T. Douglas Price
Department of Anthropology
University of Wisconsin-Madison
1180 Observatory Drive
Social Science Building
Madison, Wisconsin 53706
USA
tdprice@wisc.edu

Gary M. Feinman
Department of Anthropology
Field Museum
1400 S. Lake Shore Drive
Chicago, Illinois 60605-2496
USA
gfeinman@fieldmuseum.org

ISSN 1567-8040
ISBN 978-1-4419-6299-7 (hardcover)   e-ISBN 978-1-4419-6300-0
ISBN 978-1-4614-3303-3 (softcover)
DOI 10.1007/978-1-4419-6300-0
Springer New York Dordrecht Heidelberg London

Library of Congress Control Number: 2010931700

Printed on acid-free paper

Springer is part of Springer Science+Business Media (www.springer.com)

Preface

In 1992 the two of us were colleagues at the University of Wisconsin-Madison. We had lots of talks and debates about archaeology at lunch, between classes, and in each other's offices. Gary is interested in sociopolitical evolution and works primarily with state-level societies in highland Mexico and in eastern China. Doug is interested in hunter-gatherers and the origins of agricultural societies and works primarily in northern Europe. Our common interests often intersected at questions concerned with the origin and nature of social inequality. When does this major organizing principle in human society appear and what forms does it take?

Because of our friendship, shared interests, and these interesting questions, we decided to organize a symposium at the 1993 Society for American Archaeology annual meetings in St. Louis, Missouri. We invited colleagues who had investigated questions relating to status differentiation and social inequality—doing relevant fieldwork and/or probing the theoretical issues involved. Many of the papers from that symposium found their way into the volume *Foundations of Social Inequality*, published in 1995 by Plenum Press. The volume was well received—still used in university classes and found on the shelves of many archaeologists.

Much has happened in the intervening years. The millennium turned. Terror and war define most of this new era. Terms like deflation, bailout, depression take on meaning in our own lives. The Internet now permeates daily life. Gary Feinman moved to the Field Museum of Natural History in Chicago. Plenum Press was acquired by Springer.

The new archaeology editor at Springer, Teresa Kraus, spoke to us a few years ago about the success of *Foundations* and that it might be time to consider a revised edition. We thought about it for some time, uncertain whether a second version was appropriate. In the end, we decided that so much new information and so many new ideas have appeared in the intervening years that a new volume would in fact be a good thing to do. The topic remains timely and is one of the more interesting addressed through archaeological research. In fact, since the roots of inequality stem deep in the past, this issue is one most appropriately assessed by archaeologists.

We have followed much the same plan as that for the first volume. We organized a symposium at the 2007 Society for American Archaeology meetings in Dallas, Texas. We invited some of the authors from the original volume, along with several new scholars to join us in Dallas. It was a good session with generally excellent papers. Based on the large audience and the excellent discussion that took place at that meeting, it seems that interest in social inequality has only increased among archaeologists since the original volume was published.

The new volume is entitled *Pathways to Power* for a reason. We borrowed the volume title from the paper by Brian Hayden in *Foundations of Society Inequality*. We believe that this second volume provides much new perspective on questions concerning both the origins and the pathways along which social inequality develops. This phrase emphasizes not just the foundations—the origins—of inequality, but more so the forms, or paths, that it follows in prehistory.

This volume brings together a set of distinguished archaeologists and authors to present their thoughts on the rise and role of human inequality in past human societies. We have organized the volume to present these essays in a coherent and logical order. Our opening essay provides an overview of the topic and a brief look at the papers that follow. We emphasize the major themes that are the focus of the volume. Ken Ames provides an excellent introduction to the general subject of inequality in Chapter 2. Ken's chapter is followed by an important consideration of the degrees and kinds of inequality by Dick Drennan, Christian Peterson, and Jake Fox. This chapter sets the tone for the volume, emphasizing the evidence for pathways to power, using examples from a variety of prehistoric contexts. Mark Aldenderfer in Chapter 4 examines the role of ritual and religion in creating and maintaining inequality, a reminder that there are many facets to this topic. Brian Hayden and Suzanne Villeneuve consider an ethnographic case from Polynesia for heightened insight on inequality, and how it works. They ask a very pragmatic question: who benefits from status differentiation?

The volume then moves to a series of case studies from the Old World, arranged in chronological order from the Neolithic, to the Bronze, and ultimately the Iron Age. Price and Ofer Bar-Yosef raise again the question of the origins of inequality, arguing that agriculture and status differentiation appear almost simultaneously. Focus is on Southwest Asia and the changes from the Natufian to the PrePottery Neolithic. Kristian Kristiansen examines the Bronze Age of northern Europe and another expression of inequality. Tina Thurston takes a deep look at the European Iron Age and what power and kingship meant in that time of transition to state-level societies. Gary Feinman's paper is a formidable conclusion to the book, and a very different paper for an archaeology volume, bringing ideas and concepts from studying the past to a perspective on the modern world.

A book such as this one is the result and consequence of many efforts. Teresa Kraus, our editor at Springer, started the ball rolling. The participants in the SAA symposium in Dallas brought their ideas, knowledge, and time to bear on the issue of inequality. The authors of the papers in this volume have spent many hours writing, revising, and finalizing years of thought, laboratory, and field work. We owe a great debt of thanks for their efforts and accomplishment.

We very much hope you find the book to be of use, to inspire your perspectives and to encourage new research on questions regarding human inequality in the past. You will find a few answers, but many more questions. There is much to learn.

Contents

Contributors

Mark Aldenderfer School of Anthropology, University of Arizona, Tucson, AZ, USA, aldender2@gmail.com

Kenneth M. Ames Department of Anthropology, Portland State University, Portland, ME, USA, amesk@pdx.edu

Ofer Bar-Yosef Department of Anthropology, Harvard University, Peabody Museum, Cambridge, MA, USA, obaryos@fas.harvard.edu

Robert D. Drennan Department of Anthropology, University of Pittsburgh, Pittsburgh, PA, USA, drennan@pitt.edu

Gary M. Feinman Department of Anthropology, The Field Museum, Chicago, IL, USA, gfeinman@fieldmuseum.org

Jake R. Fox Department of Anthropology, Radford University, Radford, VA, USA, jake@sigmaxi.net

Brian Hayden Archaeology Department, Simon Fraser University, Burnaby, BC, Canada, bhayden@sfu.ca

Kristian Kristiansen University of Gothenburg, Gothenburg, Sweden, kristian.kristiansen@archaeology.gu.se

Christian E. Peterson Department of Anthropology, University of Hawaii at Manoa, Honolulu, HI, USA, cepeter@hawaii.edu

T. Douglas Price Department of Anthropology, University of Wisconsin-Madison, Madison, WI, USA, tdprice@wisc.edu

Tina L. Thurston Department of Anthropology, The University at Buffalo, State University of New York, Buffalo, NY, USA, tt27@buffalo.edu

Suzanne Villeneuve Archaeology Department, Simon Fraser University, Burnaby, BC, Canada, sp6074@sfu.ca

Chapter 1
Social Inequality and the Evolution of Human Social Organization

T. Douglas Price and Gary M. Feinman

This volume on the emergence of inequality brings a renewed perspective, through varied lenses, at questions surrounding the origins of modern human social organization. In 1995 we edited a volume entitled *Foundations of Social Inequality*, concerned with many of these same issues. Here we return to this fascinating subject, to unanswered questions, new ideas, and new directions of study and explanation.

Archaeology provides a unique perspective on this question because of the time depth available. Many aspects of our human condition evolved in the deep past and cannot be fully understood without the long vantage point of history and prehistory. This is certainly true for the fundamental principles of human organization—the structure and function of the operation of society—which have been present for thousands of years. The study of inequality is essentially a concern with the evolution of human society and in fact is a predominant issue in recent considerations of social evolution (e.g., Ames 2007, Earle and Johnson 2000, Marcus 2008, Pluciennik 2005, Rousseau 2006, Shennan 2008, Trigger 2003).

This chapter is intended to outline some of the major questions concerning inequality and to introduce the contents of this volume. We will do this first by considering a definition of social inequality and some of the evidence that has been used to identify this condition in the past. A subsequent section pursues key questions. Why are we still talking about these issues? Why does the emergence of social inequality matter, and what don't we know? There are three major issues in the archaeological study of inequality that relate to the questions of when, why, and how. When did inequality originate? Why did inequality emerge in human society? How did/does it operate? Are there different manifestations of inequality that structure human society? These questions are considered in our discussion and in the chapters that follow.

T.D. Price (✉)
Department of Anthropology, University of Wisconsin-Madison, Madison, WI, USA
e-mail: tdprice@wisc.edu

T.D. Price, G.M. Feinman (eds.), *Pathways to Power*, Fundamental
Issues in Archaeology, DOI 10.1007/978-1-4419-6300-0_1,
© Springer Science+Business Media, LLC 2010

A Definition of Social Inequality

There are few larger questions in the prehistory of our species than the emergence of social inequality. Social inequality, the organizing principle of hierarchical structure in human society, is manifested in unequal access to goods, information, decision making, and power. Status is the determinant of social position, and status differentiation is the foundation of inequality. A variety of human conditions are used in ordering social hierarchies and in determining status and access. These include age, gender, birth order, class, race, and a number of others. Social inequality is a characteristic of virtually every society on earth today and its history goes back thousands of years.

This structure of unequal relations, of status differentiation, is essential to higher orders of social organization and is basic to the operation of more complex societies. So, questions about inequality are intricately bound up with questions concerning human cooperation, leadership, and social differentiation both vertical (hierarchical) and horizontal. An understanding of the transformation from relatively egalitarian societies to more hierarchical organization is fundamental to our knowledge about the contemporary world. This volume is intended to examine some of the mechanisms, forces, and motivations involved in the shift in human societies from egalitarian to hierarchical and the relationship between these changes and inequality.

Why Are We Still Talking About Social Inequality?

A fair question might be raised at this point—why are we still talking about the emergence of social inequality? The simple answer is that we still don't know very much. The origin of inequality remains essential because there is no scholarly consensus. The jury is still out. Archaeologists working in vastly different time periods seem to suggest that inequality appears de novo in their particular part of time and space. Individuals working in the Iron Age or with state-level societies often write as though inequality was something new and previously unknown. Different forms of inequality may appear in social and political arrangements, but it is our distinct impression that status differentiation and inequality have been around for a very long time.

We do know that social inequality has been the dominant structuring principle in most human societies over the last 5,000 years or more. At the same time, we still do not know precisely when or why this principle became dominant, or how it operated in the past. How was inequality expressed in the past? Were there different trajectories to hierarchy?

At some point in the deep human past, the biological imperative for dominance behavior, common in our closest animal relatives, was dampened by a cultural mechanism. This mechanism, known as egalitarianism, reflects the importance of cooperative behavior in the emergence of culture, in learning and sharing knowledge, and in survival (e.g., Boehm 1993, 2000, Knauft 1991, Wiessner 2002). Human society operates within this didactic tension between dominance and equality, between hierarchical and egalitarian, between modes of behavior that feature or privilege the group to those that accent individuals.

A number of authors have written about the evolutionary value of cooperative behavior (e.g., Bowles 2006, Fehr and Fischbacher 2004, Henrich 2003, Maschner and Patton 1996, Nowak 2006, Smith and Choi 2007), in the face of the competition that is natural selection. Bowles, for example, argues that lethal conflicts between early human groups may have selected for more altruistic units. He suggests that practices such as food sharing beyond the family, monogamy, and other forms of reproductive leveling were crucial to this process and presume advanced cognitive and linguistic skills associated with fully modern humans.

The roots of cooperation and egalitarian behavior are probably linked to the evolution of groups and social cognition in the human species. Tomasello et al. (2005, see also Dunbar 1993) have proposed that the crucial difference between human cognition and that of other species is the ability to participate with others in collaborative activities with shared goals and intentions: a shared intentionality. The remarkable human capacity for cooperation thus seems to have evolved mainly for interactions within the group. It is because they are adapted for such collaborative activities that human beings are able to do so many exceptionally complex and impressive things (e.g., Tomasello 1999).

We suggest that a small degree of inequality in some form or another has always been present in human society, albeit largely suppressed among various groups of hunter-gatherers. At some point in time, perhaps with the rise of *Homo sapiens sapiens*, human relations must have been transformed by the rise of cooperation and egalitarian behaviors that were selected for learning and alliance building. We would argue that inequality and dominance behavior re-emerge in early farming societies (or perhaps earlier, see, e.g., Coupland et al. 2009, Hayden 2001) as human numbers increase and larger group size becomes common. Various causes for an increase in human numbers and group size with the advent of agriculture have been proposed (e.g., Armelagos et al. 1991, Cohen 1977, Sellen and Mace 1997, Spielmann 1989). Becker et al. (1990), for example, document a fascinating relationship between food costs and fertility in historical Europe. Group size apparently increased dramatically in the Neolithic, but again specific causality is not well understood (e.g., Adams and Kasakoff 1975, Bandy 2008, Bentley et al. 1993, Johnson 1982, Sussman 1972). Whatever the reason, there seems little doubt that human numbers increase dramatically during the Holocene, and specifically with the onset of the Neolithic (e.g., Boquet-Appel and Bar-Yosef 2008, Chesnais 1986).

The advent of larger group sizes and greater densities of interpersonal interactions likely was intertwined with new social arrangements. Boyd and Richerson (1988; Richerson et al. 2003) have demonstrated from game theory and computer simulation that reciprocal cooperation becomes more difficult as group size increases. In a very real sense, human society over the last 100,000 years or more may have been characterized by a fundamental tension between relations based on dominance, hierarchy, and kin altruism (part of our primate heritage) and new capacities for social cognition, cultural learning, alliance building, and cooperation, whether the latter behaviors were learned or part of recently acquired innate tendencies (Boehm 2000, Stone 2008: 79, Tomasello et al. 2005).

A major question we consider in this volume involves the different pathways or trajectories that the development of social inequality follows. We suggest that the tension between cooperation and dominance in human behavior is reflected in different paths of leadership and in the organization of inequality over time and space. Certainly there is a great deal of variation in inequality represented among the societies, both ancient and modern, encountered in the pages of this book. Some of that inequality is a matter of degree, but other differences relate to the nature or the specific ways in which inequality can be articulated. Blanton, Feinman, and others (Blanton et al. 1996, Feinman 1995, 2000, 2005) have described these latter trajectories as ranging between corporate and network (or exclusionary) modes of interconnection between leaders and followers. At one end of a range, leadership and inequality emphasize the group and the special roles within that group, while at the other end of the spectrum leadership is more directly linked to the amassing of wealth, and those individuals who hold power stand out ostentatiously from the rest of the population (e.g. Bender 1978, 1989, Hayden 1990, 2001).

The definition of this range of variation was influenced by Renfrew (1974), who contrasted group-oriented and individualizing chiefdoms, as well as by Lehman (1969), who contrasted different ways that power may be wielded. In more collective, corporately organized groups, leaders tend not to monopolize wealth in their own hands, but they do use their offices or special access to societal beliefs and rituals to wield their power and influence. For example, larger Puebloan societies in the past, as well as in more recent times, may have been organized in this way (Feinman 2000, Feinman et al. 2000, Mills 2000).

In contrast, the chiefdoms of prehispanic Panama generally were characterized by more individualizing chiefs, who derived considerable resources through exchange and warfare. Prestige goods, such as decorated metal objects, were both distributed to followers to encourage allegiance and worn and held by chiefs to display their own power, which often was passed down through lineal descent to their immediate kin (Fowler 1992, Helms 1976, 1979, Linares 1977). Clearly, both of these regions were internally heterogeneous, characterized by spatial and temporal diversity, but in an overarching sense, the bases of power were markedly different in accord with the contrast outlined above (see also Earle 1997).

The Chapters in This Volume

The following paragraphs provide an overview of the chapters in this volume in order of appearance. Our goal is to provide a brief summary to introduce the authors and their essays. We believe strongly that the chapters collected here provide an extraordinary statement on the study of inequality in human society and a starting point for breakthrough research in the future.

Ken Ames

Ken Ames (PhD, Washington State 1976, Professor, Portland State University) begins this series of contributed papers with an outstanding essay on the nature of and the relationship between dominance and cooperative behaviors in human society. Ken's deep background in hunter-gatherer studies brings important insight to the subject. He reminds us of the fact that both of these behaviors are present in all human societies. Ken argues that dominance behavior, rather than equality, is likely the norm in human society. We need to describe and document the nature of egalitarian societies, rather than prove the existence of inequality among hunter-gatherers and early farming societies in the archaeological record.

There are many cases of discordance between expectations for egalitarian behavior and visible evidence for hierarchy in the archaeological record: small-scale societies that exhibit some degree of inequality, but lack many of the other traits associated with complexity. Ames provides examples from several prehistoric North American cultures. Recognizing this variability in the archaeological record, Ames examines the foundations of our concepts regarding inequality. He visits a series of issues including the human propensity for inequality based on our primate heritage, conceptions of egalitarianism—including its origins and persistence, explanations for the long-term existence for prestige seeking, the evolution of prestige technologies, and the evolution of egalitarianism.

Important concepts in this consideration are external and internal constraints on cultural variation (Trigger 1991), dominance and prestige (Henrich and Gil-White 2002), and attention structures and costly signaling. The idea of attention structures and rank orders comes from ethological research with primates and pre-school age children. The frequency of being at the center of attention may be the best measure of status (Hold-Cavell 1996: 20). Attention structure also may complement costly signaling and conspicuous consumption, at least in terms of status dynamics. Costly signaling has been used to explain the seemingly irrational displays associated with high status (Bliege Bird and Smith 2005, Smith and Bliege Bird 2005). In terms of attention structure, costly signaling is what one does to attract and sustain attention. Ames' discussion leads to a conclusion that human inequality and egalitarianism may be aspects of the illusive quality of "modernity."

Dick Drennan, Christian Peterson, and Jake Fox

This chapter also considers the variation in manifestations of hierarchy present among archaeological cultures. The chapter is a thoughtful and deliberate consideration of the degrees and kinds of inequality from the minds of Robert D. (Dick) Drennan (PhD, University of Michigan, 1976, Professor, University of Pittsburgh), Christian Peterson (PhD, 2006, University of Pittsburgh, Assistant Professor, University of Hawai'i at Manoa), and Jake R. Fox (PhD, University of Pittsburgh, 2007, Assistant Professor, Radford University).

This chapter sets the tone for the volume, emphasizing the evidence for multiple pathways to power, using examples from a variety of prehistoric contexts. These authors take an objective approach to distinguishing levels of inequality, quantifying major variables like burial contents and construction, household differences in size and wealth, and amount of public architecture. Their aim is to develop methodology for comparing both kind and degree of hierarchy among early complex societies. In this chapter the focus is largely on chiefdoms, but the methods they are using can be applied across a broad range of human societies. Emphasis is on the empirical archaeological evidence. They point out that inequality may not be expressed in all categories of archaeological evidence and that it is thus essential to consider a range of information in such studies. They note for example that an archaeological culture may have a very homogeneous set of burials, but nonetheless possess hierarchical social organization that might be manifest in household wealth.

The authors use statistical analysis—multidimensional scaling—of data on variation in burial, household assemblages, and public construction to examine the organization of status, wealth, and economic and ritual specialization. These analyses tend to reveal differences in status versus wealth revealed in patterns of corporate versus individual structures for hierarchical organization. The results of their study point to several conclusions. There is substantial variability in how inequality is expressed among archaeological cultures. This variation is measurable and quantifiable and expressed in different kinds of archaeological evidence. Drennan, Peterson, and Fox argue that more quantitative investigations of hierarchical societies are needed to begin to better understand and explain this variation.

Mark Aldenderfer

Mark Aldenderfer (PhD, Penn State University, 1977, Professor, University of Arizona) in Chapter 4 examines the role of ritual and religion in creating and maintaining inequality, a reminder that there are many facets to this topic. Mark argues in his chapter that religion needs to be considered among the causal factors that led to the emergence and establishment of persistent inequality in the past. Religion is a vague and abstract concept in archaeology, so he focuses not on definition, but action—on what religion *does*.

He points out that actors of all kinds—aggrandizers, their followers, and their opponents—live in a context that is in part created and directed by religious practice and belief. Aldenderfer argues that religion is part of practice, of the *habitus*, in the social and economic world and cannot be understood outside of other aspects of human behavior. More specifically, in terms of the debate here, he argues that religion provides the sanctions for the emergence of persistent social inequality or creates resistance to it (Aldenderfer 1993, 2005: 30). The changes in human social behavior that we seek to understand likely involve important beliefs and practices that were key elements in the lives of the actors. In sum, Aldenderfer argues that we need to look for the material manifestations of religion in the archaeological record of societies experiencing the emergence of persistent social inequality.

Brian Hayden and Suzanne Villeneuve

The next contribution moves in a different direction, as Brian Hayden (PhD, University of Toronto, 1975, Professor, Simon Fraser University) and Suzanne Villeneuve (MA, University of Victoria, 2008) ask a very pragmatic question: who benefits from status differentiation? Their study of this question focused on the chiefdoms on Futuna, some 500 km northeast of Fiji. Futuna is a relatively small volcanic island, only 20 × 5 km. Today, 5,000 people live on the island, politically divided into two competing chiefdoms in a total of 14 villages. They examine the question of who benefits from the perspective of political ecology—the way in which resources (and in particular surplus resources) are used by certain members of pre-industrial communities to acquire practical, political, and economic benefits. It is important to note that pigs represent the consummate wealth item on Futuna, used for feasts, while bark cloth and mats were highly valued wealth items produced by women. Pigs represent a household's major investment of surplus food and labor.

The main points in this study by Hayden and Villeneuve are that feasting played a critical role in creating political complexity, that creating political hierarchies requires considerable supplemental resources beyond subsistence needs (Rambo 1991)—especially for the feasts and prestige goods required to make these systems function—and that the possibility of controlling some portion of community surpluses provided great potential for self-aggrandizement and the acquisition of power which consequently motivated ambitious individuals to create complex sociopolitical structures.

Hayden and Villeneuve argue that claims that chiefs served their communities to their own material detriment are untenable and inaccurate. Nor do traditional chiefs appear to take up their positions primarily out of a sense of duty. On the basis of their Futunan research, it seems clear that chiefly families were the main beneficiaries of the chiefdom political organization. Just as in transegalitarian societies, aggrandizers are the motivating force behind a number of social, political, and ideological changes. They use a range of strategies to achieve self-interested goals; they pander to common interests when necessary, they use economic leverage or coercion when they can, and they promote new ideological concepts as justifications for their endeavors or as a means of obtaining compliance. The ultimate motivation for developing and maintaining status inequality is the benefit conferred on those in power.

T. Douglas Price and Ofer Bar-Yosef

The volume then moves to a series of case studies from the Old World, arranged in chronological order from the Neolithic, to the Bronze, and ultimately the Iron Age. Price (PhD, University of Michigan 1975, Professor, University of Wisconsin-Madison, University of Aberdeen) and Ofer Bar-Yosef (PhD, Hebrew University, 1970, Professor, Harvard University) raise again the question of the origins of inequality, arguing that agriculture and status differentiation appear almost simultaneously. Focus is on Southwest Asia and the changes from the Natufian to the Pre-Pottery Neolithic. Their discussion involves a review of archaeological evidence from the time of the transition to agriculture in the ancient Near East. The context for this review is the emergence of social inequality and whether this phenomenon is associated with the beginnings of farming. The shift from hunting to farming takes place in the Levant and southern Anatolia between approximately 14,500 and 8,200 cal BP.

Their discussion begins with a consideration of social inequality and some of the arguments for the timing and nature of the shift from egalitarian to hierarchical society. Evidence from the Natufian and Neolithic periods is considered in detail as it relates to questions about status differentiation in human society. Attention is focused on burial practices and body decoration, household architecture and contents, exotic artifacts, monumental construction, and variation in site size and function. Price and Bar-Yosef suggest that indications of the emergence of inequality during the transition to agriculture are indeed present and can be used to argue for a strong association between social relations and subsistence behavior, two of the bigger changes that have taken place in the evolution of human society.

Kristian Kristiansen

Kristian Kristiansen (PhD, University of Aarhus, 1975, Professor, University of Gothenburg) examines the Bronze Age of northern Europe and another context of inequality. In this case, Kristiansen writes about the decentralized complexity that characterizes chiefdoms of the Bronze Age, distinct from more clear-cut, stratified cultures in the eastern Mediterranean at this time. More specifically, he writes about change over time in these societies that lasted from 1750 to 500 BC.

The arrival of the northern Bronze Age is characterized by the introduction and use of simple bronze tools, especially axes. At the same time huge longhouses for large (chiefly) households begin to appear. New tools, weapons, and ornaments made of bronze appear, together with a warrior elite. After 1500 BC, a distinctive Nordic Bronze Age culture appears, characterized by the construction of thousands of large barrows, a new material culture, and new more elaborate house architecture. Thousands of burial barrows marked long lines of communication and interaction across the landscape of southern Scandinavia. Barrows belonged only to members of chiefly clans, perhaps 15–20% of the population. These groups were highly diversified in terms of power and prestige, with the lowest ranks being close to commoners, as demonstrated by variation in burial wealth and the huge differences in farm sizes.

Kristiansen focuses on the analysis of political economy to understand how complex power structures operated in societies defined by the Germanic mode of production (Gilman 1995), wealth finance (Earle 1997), or a prestige goods system (Kristiansen and Larsson 2005, Kristiansen 1998). While the institution of ritual chiefs represented the highest level of chiefly power, only enjoyed by a relatively small group among the upper chiefly clans, access to the warrior groups was more open, and membership could probably be recruited from a larger segment of the chiefly clans. Kristiansen argues that the pastoral economy of Early Bronze Age Denmark was used as mobile wealth, linking production of cattle to the production and distribution of prestige goods and control over people. He follows Bourdieu's (1977) argument to explain how gift obligations among elite are transformed over time into tribute and slavery. For more than 1,000 years a relatively stable, complex, hierarchical, and decentralized society existed in southern Scandinavia without large settlements, concentrated population, or public works. Thus the Danish chiefdoms relied heavily on networked strategies, using systems of wealth finance to structure political hierarchies.

Tina Thurston

Tina Thurston (PhD, University of Wisconsin-Madison, 1996, Associate Professor, SUNY—Buffalo) takes a detailed look at the Iron Age and what power and kingship meant in that time of transition to state-level societies, again in the context of northern Europe, and particularly southern Scandinavia. Her title—"bitter arrows and generous gifts"—in many ways captures the nature of hierarchical society during the period between 500 BC and about AD 1075, including the Viking period during the last 250 years or so.

This contribution begins with a detailed look at the meaning of power and its use in archaeology. Thurston then considers various ways that power is expressed among hierarchical human groups. Thurston points to two ends of a range among such societies that reflect the network and corporate approaches we have discussed above. Visual differentiation characterizes network structures in terms of architecture, burial, and personal ornament. Chiefs and rulers rarely redistributed anything unless they are forced to do so by the power of their constituencies (e.g. Fisher 2000). On the other hand, there are the enigmatic examples like the Anasazi, Harappans, and Teotihuacanos that appear politically complex but show little evidence for typical indicators such as aggrandizement of individual rulers, centralized institutions, and markedly stratified social classes. Iron Age societies in southern Scandinavia follow a pattern similar to what is described for the Bronze Age (Kristiansen, this volume, Kristiansen and Larsson 2005). Her concern in this essay is that many Iron Age archaeologists have failed to recognize this range of variation and that the complexity of the Iron Age is often underestimated because of such oversight. She quotes Feinman et al. (2000: 450), who observed archaeologists "failed to recognize the potential for hierarchy and equality to coexist simultaneously in all human societies."

In this context, Tina's primary question becomes more than intriguing—what was a king in the Iron Age north of the Alps? Her focus is on political organization, its development, and the nature of political power. In the arena of the north, power was constituted as a shared responsibility or privilege. Thurston argues for a view of the northern European Iron Age as one in which decentralized power within a stratified society is manifest in heterarchic organization and political power is balanced between the warlord, and the assembly (or ting), and religious specialists who retain substantial power in their own realm. Kings they may be, but power is shared and negotiated.

Gary Feinman

Gary Feinman's (PhD, CUNY, 1980, Curator, Field Museum) contribution provides a conclusion to this volume, as well as a very different perspective—bringing ideas and concepts from the study of the past to bear on contemporary society. Feinman (1995, 2001, Blanton et al. 1996) has been at the fore of developing dual-processual theory, postulating exclusionary (or network) versus corporate strategies in hierarchical society. In the exclusionary mode, political actors endeavor to consolidate and monopolize sources of power. In the corporate mode, power is shared and divested in different groups or social segments.

A number of questions and counterarguments have been raised about this theory. In his essay here, Gary addresses those concerns though the use of the "metaphor" of modern American political economy. Metaphor is, of course, the wrong word because the modern American political economy is different only in scale in terms of many of the principles that also operated in ancient chiefdoms and states. Gary finds remarkable resonance between the implications of dual processual theory and the operation of American government. At the outset it is important to note as well that the corporate/exclusionary continuum in the way power was supported and implemented is, in a sense, orthogonal to the vertical dimension of hierarchical complexity (Feinman et al. 2000: 454). That is to say, both forces of this theory, corporate and network/exclusionary, operate in the same social and political context.

One of the advantages of considering modern history is the wealth of information, quantitative data, and tight chronological control. Using this rich historical database, Gary examines five key aspects of the corporate/network continuum: (1) the balance of power or shifts in the ways that political power is divided or shared, (2) the associated strategies of legitimation, (3) the relative importance of personal networks, (4) the broader economic underpinnings of power, and (5) shifts in the distribution of wealth and economic manifestations of inequality. The discussion of these dimensions is followed by a consideration of some of the factors, strategies, and global conditions that are thought to have fostered observed shifts. In conclusion, Feinman returns to implications for the study of change and inequality in the deeper archaeological past.

Pathways to Power

Selecting a title for a book is not an easy task. *Pathways to Power* is taken from the paper by Brian Hayden that appeared in the volume *Foundations of Social Inequality* in 1995. The title was chosen to indicate continuity with our earlier efforts. At the same time the subtitle—*New Perspectives on the Emergence of Social Inequality*—emphasizes that many new ideas have emerged in the last 15 years and that our understanding of the emergence of inequality has grown in that period.

The title also was selected to highlight the fact that this volume is indeed concerned largely with pathways, with the various ways that human societies have moved toward hierarchical structure and organization. The authors in the volume look at inequality from many different perspectives, a variety of angles—theoretical, ethnographic, ethnohistoric, typological, archaeological—and in many different times and places. Times and places include the ancient Near East, Bronze Age Europe, present-day islands in the South Pacific, and modern America. The vocabulary of concept and evidence used in the discussion of social inequality in the past is staggering: ritual and religion, biology, population and fertility, prestige technology, monumental construction, burial, household, feasting, agriculture, heterarchy, and many, many more. This is a large and complex question in archaeological research.

The goals of a new book also vary considerably. We put this volume together because of our common interest in the subject of social inequality as one of the truly big questions in archaeology. We asked friends and colleagues to join us in conference and authorship to share their knowledge and thoughts on this subject. It is our hope that the results, compiled in this volume, will inspire new discussions of the emergence of inequality and drive new research that will enlighten our understanding of hierarchy, and, more importantly, of the human condition in the deep past as well as for the present and future.

References

Adams, J.W., and Kasakoff, A.B. 1975. Factors Underlying Endogamous Group Size. In Nag, M. (ed.), *Population and Social Organization*, pp. 147–173. The Hague: Mouton.

Aldenderfer, M. 1993. Ritual, hierarchy, and change in foraging societies. *Journal of Anthropological Archaeology* 12: 1–40.

Aldenderfer, M. 2005. Preludes to Power in the Highland Late Preceramic Period. In Conlee, C., Ogburn, D., and Vaughn, K. (eds.), *Foundations of Power in the Prehispanic Andes*, pp. 13–35. Washington: Archaeological Papers of the American Anthropological Association, Paper No. 14.

Ames, K. 2007. The Archaeology of Rank. In Bentley, R.A., Maschner, H.D.G., and Chippendale, C. (eds.), *Handbook of Archaeological Theories*, pp. 487–514. Lanham: Alta Mira Press.

Armelagos, G.J., Goodman, A.H., and Jacobs, K.H. 1991. The origins of agriculture: Population growth during a period of declining health. *Population and Environment* 13: 9–22.

Bandy, M. 2008. Global Patterns of Early Village Development. In Bocquet-Appel, J.P. and Bar-Yosef, O. (eds.), *The Neolithic Demographic Transition and its Consequences*, pp. 333–357. New York: Springer.

Becker, G.S., Murphy, K.M., and Tamura, R.F. 1990. Human capital, fertility, and economic growth. *Journal of Political Economy* 98(5Pt. 2): pp. S12–37.

Bender, B. 1978. Gatherer-hunter to farmer: A social perspective. *World Archaeology* 10: 204–222.

Bender, B. 1989. The Roots of Inequality. In Miller, D., Rowlands, M., and Tilley, C. (eds.), *Domination and Resistance*, pp. 83–95. London: Unwin Hyman.

Bentley, R.G., Goldberg, T., and Jasienska., G. 1993. The fertility of agricultural and non-agricultural traditional societies. *Population Studies* 47: 269–281.

Blanton, R.E., Feinman, G.M., Kowalewski, S.A., and Peregrine, P.N. 1996. A dual-processual theory for the evolution of mesoamerican civilization. *Current Anthropology* 37: 1–14.

Bliege Bird, R., and Smith., E. 2005. Signaling theory, strategic interaction, and symbolic capital. *Current Anthropology* 46: 221–248.

Bocquet-Appel, J.P., and Bar-Yosef, O.(eds.). 2008. *The Neolithic Demographic Transition and its Consequences*. New York: Springer.

Boehm, C. 1993. Egalitarian society and reverse dominance hierarchy. *Current Anthropology* 34: 227–254.

Boehm, C. 2000. Forager Hierarchies, Innate Dispositions, and the Behavioral Reconstruction of Prehistory. In Diehl, M.W. (ed.), *Hierarchies in Action: Cui Bono?* pp. 31–58. Occasional Papers No. 27. Carbondale: Southern Illinois University.

Bourdieu, P. 1977. *Outline of a Theory of Practice*. Cambridge: Cambridge University Press.

Bowles, S. 2006. Group competition, reproductive leveling, and the evolution of human altruism. *Science* 314: 1569–1572.

Boyd, R., and Richerson., P.J. 1988. The evolution of reciprocity in sizable groups. *Journal of Theoretical Biology* 132: 337–356.

Chesnais, J.C. 1986. *La Transition Démographique: Etapes, Formes, Implications Économiques*. Paris: Presses Universitaires de France.

Cohen, M.N. 1977. *The Food Crisis in Prehistory: Overpopulation and the Origins of Agriculture*. New Haven: Yale University Press.

Coupland, G., Clark, T., and Palmer., A. 2009. Hierarchy, communalism, and the spatial order of Northwest Coast Plank houses: A comparative study. *American Antiquity* 74: 77–106.

Dunbar, R.I.M. 1993. Co-evolution of neocortex size, group size, and language in humans. *Behavioral and Brain Sciences* 16: 681–735.

Earle, T. 1997. *How Chiefs Come to Power*. Palo Alto: Stanford University Press.

Earle, T., and Johnson., A. 2000. *The Evolution of Human Societies: From Forager Group to Agrarian State*. Palo Alto: Stanford University Press.

Fehr, E., and Fischbacher, U. 2004. Social norms and human cooperation. *Trends in Cognitive Sciences* 8: 185–190.

Feinman, G.M. 1995. The Emergence of Inequality: A Focus on Strategies and Processes. In Price, T.D. and Feinman, G.M. (eds.), *Foundations of Social Inequality*, pp. 255–275. New York: Plenum Press.

Feinman, G.M. 2000. Corporate/Network: New Perspectives on Models of Political Action and the Puebloan Southwest. In Schiffer, M.B.(ed.), *Social Theory in Archaeology*, pp. 31–51. Salt Lake City: University of Utah Press.

Feinman, G.M. 2001. Mesoamerican Political Complexity: The Corporate-Network Dimension. In Jonathan, H. (ed.), *From Leaders to Rulers*, pp. 151–175. New York: Kluwer Academic/Plenum Publishers.

Feinman, G.M., 2005. The Institutionalization of Leadership and Inequality: Integrating Process and History. In Scarborough, V. (ed.), *A Catalyst for Ideas: Anthropological Archaeology and the Legacy of Douglas W. Schwartz*, pp. 101–121. Santa Fe: School for American Research Press.

Feinman, G.M., Lightfoot, K.G., and Upham, S. 2000. Political hierarchies and organizational strategies in the puebloan southwest. *American Antiquity* 65: 449–470.

Fisher, W.H. 2000. *Rainforest Exchanges: Industry and Community on an Amazonian Frontier*. Washington: Smithsonian Institution Press.

Fowler, W.R., Jr. 1992. The Historiography of Wealth and Hierarchy in the Immediate Area. In Lange, F.W.(ed.), *Wealth and Hierarchy in the Intermediate Area*, pp. 357–377. Washington: Dumbarton Oaks Research Library and Collection.

Gilman, A. 1995. Prehistoric European Chiefdoms: Rethinking "Germanic" Societies. In Price, T.D. and Feinman, G.M. (eds.), *Foundations of Social Inequality*, pp. 235–254. New York: Plenum Press.

Hayden, B. 1990. Nimrods, piscators, pluckers and planters: The emergence of food production. *Journal of Anthropological Archaeology* 9: 31–69.

Hayden, B. 2001. Richman, Poorman, Beggarman, Chief: The Dynamics of Social Inequality. In Feinman, G. and Price, T.D. (eds.), *Archaeology at the Millennium*, pp. 231–272. New York: Plenum Publishing.

Helms, M.W. 1976. Competition, Power, and Succession to Office in Pre-Columbian Panama. In Helms, M.W. and Loveland, F.O. (eds.), *Frontier Adaptations in Lower Central America*, pp. 25–35. Philadelphia: Institute for the Study of Human Issues.

Helms, M.W. 1979. *Ancient Panama: Chiefs in Search of Power*. Austin: University of Texas Press.

Henrich, J. 2003. Cooperation, punishment, and the evolution of human institutions. *Science* 312: 60–61.

Henrich, J., and Gil-White, F. 2002. The evolution of prestige: Freely conferred deference as a mechanism for enhancing the benefits of cultural evolution. *Evolution and Human Behavior* 22: 165–196.

Hold-Cavell, B. 1996. The Ethological Basis of Status Hierarchies. In Wiessner, P. and Schiefenhovel, W. (eds.), *Food and the Status Quest: An Interdisciplinary Perspective*, pp. 19–31. Providence: Berghahn Books.

Johnson, G. 1982. Organizational Structure and Scalar Stress. In Renfrew, C., Rowlands, M., and Segraves, B.A. (eds.), *Theory and Explanation in Archaeology*, pp. 389–421. New York: Academic Press.

Knauft, B.M. 1991. Violence and sociality in human evolution. *Current Anthropology* 32: 391–428.

Kristiansen, K. 1998. The Construction of a Bronze Age Landscape. Cosmology, Economy and Social Organisation in Thy, Northwest Jutland. In Hänsel, B. (ed.), *Mensch und Umwelt in der Bronzezeit Europas*, pp. 281–293. Kiel: Oetkers-Voges Verlag.

Kristiansen, K., and Larsson., T. 2005. *The Rise of Bronze Age Society. Travels, Transmissions and Transformations*. Cambridge: Cambridge University Press.

Lehman, E.H. 1969. Toward a microsociology of power. *American Sociological Review* 34: 453–465.

Linares, O.F. 1977. *Ecology and the Arts in Ancient Panama: On the Development of Social Rank and Symbolism in the Central Provinces*. Washington: Dumbarton Oaks Research Library and Collection.

Marcus, J. 2008. The archaeology of social evolution. *Annual Review of Anthropology* 37: 111–130.

Maschner, H., and Patton., J. 1996. Kin Selection and the Origins of Hereditary Social Inequality. In Maschner, H. (ed.), *Darwinian Archaeologies*, pp. 89–108. New York: Plenum Press.

Mills, B. (ed.). 2000. *Alternative Leadership Strategies in the Prehispanic Southwest*. Tucson: University of Arizona Press.

Nowak, M.A. 2006. Five rules for the evolution of cooperation. *Science* 314: 1560–1563.

Pluciennik, M. 2005. *Social Evolution*. London: Duckworth.

Rambo, A.T. 1991. Energy and the Evolution of Culture: A Reassessment of White's Law. In Rambo, A. and Gillogby, K. (eds.), *Profiles in Cultural Evolution*, pp. 291–310. Ann Arbor: University of Michigan Press.

Renfrew, C. 1974. Beyond a Subsistence Economy: The Evolution of Social Organization in Prehistoric Europe. In Moore, C.B. (ed.), *Reconstructing Complex Societies: An Archaeological Colloquium*, pp. 69–85. Cambridge: American Schools of Oriental Research.

Richerson, P.J., Boyd, R.T., and Henrich., J. 2003. The Cultural Evolution of Human Cooperation. In Hammerstein, P. (ed.), *The Genetic and Cultural Evolution of Cooperation*, pp. 357–388. Cambridge: MIT Press.

Rousseau, J. 2006. *Rethinking Social Evolution*. Montreal: McGill-Queen's University Press.

Sellen, D.W., and Mace., R. 1997. Fertility and mode of subsistence: A phylogenetic analysis. *Current Anthropology* 38: 878–889.

Shennan, S. 2008. Evolution in archaeology. *Annual Review of Anthropology* 37: 754–791.

Smith, E.A., and Bliege Bird., R. 2005. Costly Signaling and Cooperative Behavior. In Herbert G., Samuel B., Robert B., and Ernst F. (eds.), *Moral Sentiments and Material Interests: On the Foundations of Cooperation in Economic Life*, pp 115–148. Cambridge: MIT Press.

Smith, E.A., and Choi., J.-K. 2007. The Emergence of Inequality in Small-Scale Societies: Simple Scenarios and Agent-Based Simulations. In Kohler, T.A. and Van der Leeuw, S.E. (eds.), *Model-Based Archaeology of Socionatural Systems*, pp. 105–120. Sante Fe: SAR Press.

Spielmann, K.A. 1989. A review: Dietary restrictions on hunter-gatherer women and the implications for fertility and infant mortality. *Journal of Human Ecology* 17: 321–345.

Stone, B.L. 2008. The evolution of culture and sociology. *The American Sociologist* 39: 68–85.

Sussman, R.W. 1972. Child transport, family size, and increase in human population during the Neolithic. *Current Anthropology* 13: 258–259.

Tomasello, M. 1999. *The Cultural Origins of Human Cognition*. Cambridge: Harvard University Press.

Tomasello, M., Carpenter, M., Call, J., Behne, T., and Moll, H. 2005. Understanding and sharing intentions: The origins of cultural cognition. *Behavioral and Brain Sciences* 28: 675–735.

Trigger, B.G. 1991. Distinguished lecture in archaeology: Constraint and freedom – A new synthesis for archaeological explanation. *American Anthropologist* 93: 551–569.

Trigger, B.G. 2003. *Understanding Early Civilizations*. Cambridge: Cambridge University Press.

Wiessner, P. 2002. The vines of complexity: Egalitarian structures and the institutionalization of inequality among the Enga. *Current Anthropology* 43: 233–269.

Chapter 2
On the Evolution of the Human Capacity for Inequality and/or Egalitarianism

Kenneth M. Ames

Introduction

Many theories of the evolution of human social inequality are based on the necessity of overcoming the inertia of egalitarianism, which rests in turn on the assumption that egalitarianism is our default social organization at least in small groups (e.g. Smith and Choi 2007). Wiessner (2002: 234) has described this assumption as a "slate of simplicity" upon which a variety of forces acts to create inequality. She is critiquing agency theory approaches to inequality, but the assumption is much broader. Its roots lie in the concept of the tabula rasa: the notion that "people are so widely malleable by their social environment that the very concept of human nature must be rejected" (Gintis 2006: 377). While varying in language and formulation, it shapes theory building, explanations and expectations of the archaeological record (Wason 1994), especially for hunter-gatherers. It is also the basis of archaeological methodologies for determining the presence of inequality; inequality has to be proven, egalitarianism does not. The absence of evidence for rank is evidence for egalitarianism (Ames 2007a). However, it is reasonable to hypothesize that human inequality is at least in part due to a pan-Primate order propensity for social differentiation, dominance, and subordination. Those can take highly variable forms from primate to primate species and perhaps from hominin to hominin species. It follows from this that there is no general "inertia of egalitarianism" to overcome, or that it is weak. In other words, inequalities are always present in human societies, as is the potential for more formal systems of rank.

I do not try to prove such a propensity exists, although I think it does, but explore some of its ramifications. This is not to advocate biological determinism, but that we must understand the creature we are. I wish to avoid and have my readers avoid the "naturalistic fallacy" (Moore 1903) : the idea that "natural" behaviors, whatever those may be, are therefore inherently "good" and moral or must be accepted as

K.M. Ames (✉)
Department of Anthropology, Portland State University, Portland, OR, USA
e-mail: amesk@pdx.edu

T.D. Price, G.M. Feinman (eds.), *Pathways to Power*, Fundamental
Issues in Archaeology, DOI 10.1007/978-1-4419-6300-0_2,
© Springer Science+Business Media, LLC 2010

inevitable. Richerson and Boyd (1999) show how societies, through what they term "work-arounds," deal with human nature, and as Ruse puts it, "On many occasions, that which is right involves fighting that which has evolved rather than supporting and promoting it" (Ruse 2006: 239). No alleles for prestige competition have been identified. Proof will be difficult to come by; it will ultimately be indirect and take the form of a consilience of inductions and arguments to the best explanation (Ruse 2006).

Permanent social inequality is almost universally seen as a major attribute of social complexity among humans. Complexity, of course, can mean many things, including having many interrelated parts (e.g. Price 1981). As with simultaneous hierarchy (Johnson 1982), differentiation (McGuire 1983) and even heterarchy (Crumley 1995) this does not explicitly require political hierarchy or permanent inequality. However, this is not the common meaning of "complexity." When the concept of "complex hunter-gatherers" was first developed (Price 1981), inequality was one among an array of social, economic, technological and demographic traits that differentiated complex hunter-gatherers from generalized hunter-gatherers (e.g. Kelly 1995). These traits include relatively high population densities, semi to full sedentism, intensive subsistence economies moderately to heavily dependent on food storage, corporate groups, some degree of occupational specialization and so on. Substantive and theoretical research over the ensuing years has decoupled inequality from many of those initially associated traits (Ames 2007a, Arnold 1996, Sassaman 2004). Despite this decoupling, inequality is often seen as the last of these traits to emerge, or as not emerging without some or all of them being present as causes or preconditions. Theories about the origins and evolution of permanent inequality are often also theories about the origins and evolution of political economies. Earle defines political economy as "... *the material flows of goods and labor through a society, channeled to create wealth and to finance institutions of rule*" (Earle 2002: 1, *italics* his). Political economies institutionalize and pay for permanent inequality (e.g. Clark and Blake 1994). Recently, there has been discussion whether complexity, broadly defined, can exist without inequality (Ames 2007b). The issue in this paper is whether inequality can exist without social complexity, including a political economy.

This question arises as the known archaeological record expands, revealing small scale societies who seem to exhibit some degree of inequality but lack many of the other traits associated with complexity. For example, in the southeastern USA, large and elaborate earthworks were constructed in the Middle Holocene (e.g. papers in Gibson and Carr 2004) by societies that lacked many of the normal attributes of complexity, such as sedentism, high population densities, and surplus production (Sassaman 2004, Saunders 2004). Watson Brake, the most famous of these, was apparently constructed during a short period of time around 5400 and 5300 cal BP (Sassaman and Heckenberger 2004, Saunders et al. 1997). However, it was part of a more extensive system of works and a cultural pattern that persisted for centuries that to some researchers indicates "enduring inequalities" in the absence of economic and political institutions (Sassaman 2004, 2006, Sassaman and Heckenberger 2004).

My own example of this comes from the interior Pacific Northwest of the USA between ca.10,600 BC and perhaps as late as 3500–2500 BC, a period spanning the Paleoarchaic and portions of the Archaic in the region (Ames 2000). The region's Paleoarchaic and Archaic people were generally mobile foragers, although Paleoarchaic people were somewhat more logistically organized than later Archaic groups (Ames 1988). Available evidence suggests Paleoarchaic and Archaic group territory sizes ranged between 8,000 and 10,600 km^2 (e.g. Connolly 1999, Hess 1997, Reid and Chatters 1997) with "long-term" land use estimates of territories ranging between 70,000 and 500,000 km^2 (Hess 1997). The former territories are large enough to support a small, mobile band (Reid and Chatters 1997), while the long-term estimates encompass a group's movements over a generation or more (e.g. Binford 1983).

High mobility seems to have been coupled with mortuary practices that tied people to fixed points in the landscape, marked by burial grounds with no associated residential sites. Grave goods accompanying these burials suggest some differences in access to wealth and status. Minimally, at least, there were people who were buried in these places and those who were not.

Elements of this pattern are present with the region's earliest known burial ca. 10,500 BC (Green et al. 1998) at Buhl, Idaho. Better-known examples were recovered at the Marmes Rockshelter in southeastern Washington (Ames 2000, Rice 1969). Twenty-two inhumations were excavated there, in addition to a large cremation hearth containing remains of five individuals. The cremation hearth is the oldest evidence of funerary ritual at Marmes and may date as old as 9500 BC. Of the 22 burials, five pre-date ca. 5700 BC and 15 span the period from 5700 BC to at least 2200 BC.

There are differences among the burials in the cost of the mortuary treatment. Although the cremations may not seem costly, Schulting (1995) suggests cremations are expensive forms of mortuary ritual, since they require the accumulation of the fuel. The five inhumations dating between ca. 9500 and 5700 BC have *Olivella* shell beads, projectile points, bifaces, cobbles, and bone and other chipped stone tools associated with them. The *Olivella* shells are from the Pacific Coast, at least 480 km west. While some burials had only two of these, others had 50 or more. In addition to the grave goods listed above, post-5700 BC grave goods included milling stones, stone beads, bone pendants, ochre, atlatl weights, and bear canines. Burial #9 is a good example of a rich interment. The individual was accompanied by 54 olivella shell beads, a cobble tool, an anvil stone, two bear canines (one grooved), an antler point, and red ochre. Several individuals were also associated with organic materials, including choke cherry seeds (Rice 1969).

The Marmes mortuary program was part of a broader regional pattern Pavesic (1985, 1992) terms the Western Idaho Archaic Burial Complex (WIABC). Other examples include the DeMoss site in west-central Idaho and several sites in southern Idaho. The DeMoss site dates to ca. 5000–4700 BC and yielded the skeletons of 22 individuals. In addition to the skeletal materials, 236 large well-made bifaces and biface fragments were also recovered. Many of these are of sufficient artisanship to suggest they were made to be placed in the graves (Green et al. 1986,

Pavesic et al. 1993). Open WIABC sites are dated as early as 5000 BC by radiocarbon dates on human and dog bones (Yohe and Pavesic 2000). Dates derived from obsidian hydration analyses indicate an age between 3200 and 2500 BC, although Pavesic feels those dates are too young (Max Pavesic personal communication). In any case, the WIABC disappears after these dates. The mortuary program includes flexed burial positions, commonly in sandy knolls overlooking large rivers. Red ocher and *Olivella* shells are common grave goods, as are a variety of large well-made bifaces, including so-called turkey-tailed blades, large side-notched points, and caches of bifaces and blanks. Much less common grave goods are canid skulls, bone and shell beads, pipes, hematite crystals, and bone, chipped stone and ground stone tools, including pumice shaft straighteners. Technologically, the DeMoss and SWIBC bifaces are linked. As noted above, the burial sites are not associated with residential sites (Green et al. 1986, Pavesic 1985).

Reid and Chatters (1997) argue these practices are the result of communal reburial by small, dispersed groups. Pavesic (Max Pavesic personal communication 2000) strongly disagrees with these conclusions, arguing the cemeteries are associated with large, stable residential groups. There is empirical support for Pavesic's views. Radiocarbon dates from the oldest documented house structure in the general region overlaps with WIABC radiocarbon dates. The pithouse, recovered in the north central Oregon uplands, was an oval structure of about 5 × 4 m, and 30–50 cm deep (Pettigrew and Schalk 1995). It is dated by four dates, the oldest of which is 5500–4300 BC (Pettigrew and Schalk 1995). Three other associated dates are considerably younger and are closer to 3800 BC. The Givens Hot Spring site (Green 1993) on the Snake River in southwest Idaho is a residential site within the general vicinity of WIABC cemeteries. House 2 there is dated by six dates on charcoal and may date as early as ca. 4000–3600 BC. There are a number of other early houses on the Plateau, most of which date between 3500 and 2500 BC, although a few are somewhat earlier (Ames 2000).

Similar to the Southeastern mounds, the SWIBC can be interpreted to reflect enduring inequalities in access to ritual, in this case mortuary ritual, as well as to markers of wealth and/or status. The pattern persists for millennia and seems associated, for several millennia, with high mobility levels. It disappears in the southeastern Plateau after collector mobility strategies, semi-sedentism, intensive economies and storage became well established in the region around 1800 BC (Ames 2000, Chatters 1995).

The inequality hinted at by these data was probably never strongly expressed, perhaps even invisible on a daily basis. The differential flows of material indicated by the grave goods were likely not the result of a formal political economy but rather consequences of the kinds of behaviors described below. This is not what Arnold (1993, 1996) and others mean by inequality and this paper is not about that inequality. It is rather about the social and economic organization from which that inequality evolved.

There are other cases like these (e.g. Glassow 2004), where indications of prestige differentials far less substantial than the Watson Brake mounds twinkle on and off in the archaeological record with no accompanying evidence of affluence or complexity, just as there are cases in which affluence is obvious but the evidence for inequality frustratingly ephemeral [e.g. the Japanese Jomon (Ames 2007a)]. There is little in the record of the southeastern Plateau suggesting the presence of affluent foragers or complex hunter-gatherers before ca. 1800 BC and aside from the mortuary practices, nothing that would even lead them to be classed as transegalitarian. The burial data would not support claims of permanent inequality in the form of ranking. On the other hand, the Idaho data, like the southeastern mounds, intimate long-term persistent patterns of differentials of prestige and material flows not readily accommodated either to our ethnographically based notions of either egalitarianism or inequality, or to our ideas about how inequality evolves from egalitarianism.

Several distinctions and concepts are basic to this chapter. These include external and internal constraints on cultural variation (Trigger 1991), dominance, and prestige (Henrich and Gil-White 2002), and attention structures and costly signaling (see below). The rest of this section discusses these ideas. The sections following examine a series of issues including the possibility that a human propensity for inequality rests on our primate heritage, conceptions of egalitarianism including about its origins and persistence, explanations for the long-term persistence for prestige seeking, the evolution of prestige technologies, and the evolution of egalitarianism. These discussions suggest that human inequality and egalitarianism may be aspects of the illusive quality of "modernity" and briefly review the relevant archaeological record.

Constraints and Freedom

Over the past decade or more Bruce Trigger engaged in a vast intellectual project: accounting for cross-cultural continuities and similarities, sources of local variation and the interplay between them to explain the course of history (e.g. Trigger 1991, 1998, 2003). For Trigger, variation in human culture and behavior is limited by external and internal constraints. He identified three sets of external constraints: first, ecological, technological and economic constraints; second, humanity's biological nature, including our brain, a product of biological evolution; and thirdly, systemic constraints: e.g. there are only so many ways to successfully organize human societies. Keen's analysis of the interplay of ecological and social factors in limiting the development of social hierarchies in Australia exemplifies the actions of the first and third constraints (Keen 2006). Johnson (1982) and Kosse's (Kosse 1990) suggestions that the structure of human short- and long-term memory processing contribute to hierarchy formation exemplify the second kind of constraint, which also, for Trigger (2003) includes an evolved human nature with a propensity toward inequality. Trigger (2003), saw the first constraint contributing to cross-cultural variability, and the last two contributing to cross-cultural regularities.

Trigger's internal constraints are

> Knowledge (or lack of knowledge), beliefs, values, and culturally conditioned habits. In this case...the main challenge is ...the need for patterns or structural principles that provide some degree of coherence and meaning to the inexhaustible variety of concepts that the human mind is capable of inventing and manipulating (Trigger 1991: 557–558).

In addition to coherence and meaning, these patterns or principles have to have "some reasonable congruence to objective reality" (Trigger 1991: 555) for them to persist. Following Childe, Trigger argued that culture is free to vary in content, within the limits set by external and internal constraints and objective reality. Another internal constraint, although not mentioned by Trigger, would be cultural transmission and selection (Boyd and Richerson 1985, Durham 1991).

Prestige, Dominance, Attention Structure, and Costly Signaling

According to Henrich and Gil-White (2002), prestige is given or awarded to individuals by others in their social group while dominance is enforced through agonistic behavior and fear. People to whom prestige is awarded are honored; they are *"listened to*, their opinions are heavily weighed (not obeyed) because the person enjoys credit, estimation or standing in general opinion" (Henrich and Gil-White 2002: 168, *emphasis* theirs). Prestige may or may not carry authority, the ability to channel the behavior of others in the absence of power (Fried 1967). High status is usually invested with moral worth (Berremen 1981), although the source of worthiness may vary considerably. Moral worthiness is generally attached to prestige but can justify dominance. It is also possible for dominant individuals or groups to have low moral worth. However, human systems of inequality as we know them are inevitably invested with meaning. This is one fundamental way in which they differ from those of hominin kin.

Wiessner's distinction between repressive and affiliative strategies for gaining status or rank (Wiessner 1996a) parallels Henrich and Gil-White's distinction. She claims non-human primates rely most commonly on "aggression or repression to dominate and displace competitors, while in human societies nurturant and affiliative 'prosocial behavior'—initiating and organizing activities, protection or sharing—plays a greater and, in the long run, a more effective role" (Wiessner 1996a: 6–7). She also notes, however, that the latter behaviors also occur among chimps and bonobos. Among humans then those who behave in a "nurturant and affiliative" way are awarded moral worth and prestige by other people.

Wiessner distinguishes between status and rank or rank order. Status seeking, according to Wiessner, is "part of a complex of behaviors in which individuals strive to be in the focus of attention in order to improve their position in the rank hierarchy of a group" (Wiessner 1996a: 2). By this definition, relative status is measured by the extent to which an individual is the center of attention in a group; by how much attention that person receives. In this sense, high status is given by others. This is similar to the awarding of prestige in Henrich and Gil-White's thinking. However, attention need not carry symbolic meaning while prestige does. Rank orders result from the interplay of individual status-seeking strategies. For some, being of subaltern or even low status may be a viable strategy: "a lower position may have its own rewards ... include[ing] avoidance of conflict, predictability of relations, protection, the benefits of organization, and other factors that also increase reproductive success" (Wiessner 1996a: 3).

The concepts of attention structures and rank orders come from ethological research with primates and pre-school age children. Hold-Cavell (1996) and Grammer (1996) argue that the frequency of being at the center of attention (Hold-Cavell 1996: 20) is a better measure of relative status in a group than are simple linear dominance hierarchies and their associated behaviors. Attention structures are essentially what animals pay attention to and how often. An individual's status is measured by the frequency with which other animals pay attention to it. There are two foci of attention: "One focus was based on positive relations, such as social grooming and proximity, where dominance or status is maintained through display, and the other was based on negative relations such as attack and threat" (Hold-Cavell 1996: 22).

An example of attention structure and status familiar to academics occurs at professional meetings. In a large and spatially dispersed discipline such as anthropology, we wear name tags at conferences so we can identify and be identified by individuals who may know us only by our name on publications and not by face. We are all familiar with talking with people who constantly scan the passing name tags, focusing their attention elsewhere and then often going off in pursuit of a higher status name as well as with the common circumstance of a room filling when a famous scholar presents her paper and then emptying like the tide going out when the unknown graduate student follows regardless of the presentation's quality. The name tags have one important departure from the kinds of attention structures described by Hold-Cavall (1996) and others. Those attention structures are based on propinquity and regular interaction. The names on the tags attract attention, but they also allow for the preservation of stable rank orders from annual conference to annual conference, although the actual personnel in the orders change through time.

An example of attention focused on attack or threat occurred to me when I was 13 years old. My family moved to a new town where I attended 8th grade in a large junior high school in which the students were drawn from a large catchment, thus the prestige structures were very unstable. During my first week there, the school's most infamous bully bodily picked me up, crammed me into my school locker and closed the door on me. He made his point. After that, I scrupulously avoided him (negative attention), and he paid no further attention to me. His subalterns, however, tormented me unmercifully for the rest of the year with little fear of direct retribution; the threat of his physical force being always there. This event illustrates several features observed among small children: status competition peaks at the beginning of the school year and, once the rank order is established, it becomes invisible unless disrupted by some event, such as vacation. After vacation, competition again peaks and then disappears. Competition of course can go underground and boil up from below. In my case, at the beginning of the year, I was a big, new, outsider male with no allies. I made friends as the year progressed but we were all low status in the school's hallways and common areas and had to pay close attention to where this person and his myrmidons were.

Because attention structure is a measure of status given by others paying attention, the concept of attention structure parallels Henrich and Gil-White's definition of prestige (Henrich and Gil-White 2002). People with prestige are attended to, the

prestige = attention

more attention, the greater the prestige. With prestige, the paying of attention carries symbolic meaning—that of worthiness. Not all attention inevitably does so. My tracking with my 8th grade bully did not confer prestige or worthiness on him, although it was a measure of his dominance.

Attention structure also may compliment costly signaling at least in terms of status dynamics. According to a definition of costly signaling,

> [Costly signaling theory] proposes that communication between individuals with conflicting interests can be evolutionarily stable if the signal honestly advertises an underlying quality of interest to observers. Advertising is kept honest and thus mutually beneficial to both signaler and observer as long as the cost or benefit of advertisement is so closely tied to the quality of the signaler that faking it costs more than the signal is worth (Bliege Bird et al. 2001).

This latter aspect about "faking it" is termed as the handicap principle. Boone (2000) explains it succinctly:

> Costly signaling operates as a handicap to the sender because it costs something—time, energy, or risk—to undertake: the higher the level of extravagance of the display, the higher the absolute cost of the display. . .the costly aspect of advertisement will act as a guarantor of the honesty of the display only if those of higher underlying quality pay *lower marginal costs per increment unit of display* than those of lower quality (and not, it should be emphasized, because they get more benefit per incremental unit of display) (Boone 2000: 86).

In anthropology, costly signaling has been used to explain the seemingly irrational costly displays associated with high status. In particular it has been applied to male hunting among foragers (e.g. Bliege Bird and Smith 2005, Bliege Bird et al. 2001, Hawkes and Bliege Bird 2002) as well as to cooperative behavior among humans (Gintis et al. 2001, Sugiyama and Sugiyama 2003). The key issues here are the nature of the signal and of the benefits accruing from the signal. Some signals may be only information, albeit expensive information, but just information. The benefit to the displayer is based on how the recipient of the information behaves toward the displayer. However, the signal may also benefit the audience. In a Northwest Coast potlatch, the person holding the potlatch has their status confirmed or increased, while the attendees receive gifts and attend an often sumptuous feast. The signaler may also receive benefits from the signal's recipients that can take a variety of forms (Bliege Bird and Smith 2005). It has been suggested that costly signaling can, under some circumstances, explain altruism, in that altruism can be a strong signal since it handicaps the sender and provides benefits for the receiver (Roberts 1998). Further, altruism can be maintained when altruists compete for the attention of other altruists (Robert 1998). However, in terms of attention structure, costly signaling is what one does to attract and sustain attention.

The Origins of Inequality or of Egalitarianism

Social scientists have formulated diverse explanations for the origins and evolution of inequality, some of which I list elsewhere (Ames 2007a). Currently many explanations focus on the actions of "aggrandizers." Aggrandizers are "aggressively ambitious" individuals acting to advance themselves, their close relatives and perhaps supporters. Hayden (1995: 191) describes them as "AAA-type personalities" who "regularly arise in small numbers in all societies." The explanatory appeal of aggrandizers crosscuts theoretical orientation (e.g. Clark and Blake 1994, Maschner 1991, Maschner and Patton 1996), since aggrandizer "theory" emphasizes the actions and intentions of a few individuals. It also carries ironic echoes of the "Great Man" theory of history in which all history results from the actions of a few individuals such as Julius Caesar and Napoleon. However, I do not pursue that here. Although not developed anywhere in the literature, the notion of aggrandizers as a universal, albeit perhaps relatively rare, personality type carries the implication that other, less ambitious and even perhaps anti-ambitious personality types are also universal to humans. Put another way, inherent to aggrandizer theories is the assertion that there are dominant and subordinate human personality types. Aggrandizer theories tend to ignore subdominance and subordination as active social strategies. Rather, people tend to be acted upon by aggrandizers. In any case, the assertion that there are universal personalities begs the fundamental questions of whether that is true, and if so, where they come from.

There is an emerging but still ill-defined body of theory that indicates there is at least some truth to this claim and that human inequality is based on propensities deriving from our primate heritage if not on personality types. It is clear for example, that Trigger (2003) is correct in some instances in calling egalitarianism "social engineering" (Cashdan 1980, Wiessner 1996b). He actually makes several claims about universal human propensities: that inequality is due at least in part to what he terms "a general acquisitiveness ... deeply embedded in human nature" (Trigger 2003: 670) and to a universal human tendency to interpret conspicuous consumption as evidence of political power (Trigger 2003: 677). The latter can be restated that humans invest costly signaling with symbolic meaning, especially relating to prestige and power (see below). He also saw our sociability and competitiveness as primate legacies. Maschner (1991, Maschner and Patton 1996) sees prestige competition as an innate tendency. Wiessner (1996b) has a somewhat different list of human behavioral dispositions: social and spatial territoriality, possessiveness and respect for norms of possession, reciprocity to create bonds, incest avoidance, creation of in and out groups, and the quest for status or high regard. Richerson and Boyd (2001) argue for humans having two sets of innate social predilections: an older set that is part of our primate heritage and a newer set they call the "tribal instincts" that evolved as part of biological-cultural convolution. Among the ancient instincts is the quest for status; among the tribal instincts are cooperation in large groups, and reciprocity. They hypothesize that our hyper-sociality is supported by these instincts and attribute what they see as our ambivalence toward leadership and exploitation to the consequence of contradictory tendencies from these different sets of instincts.

Among scholars accepting the idea of a primate legacy shaping human behaviors, this legacy generally includes bonding, competition and aggression; dispute settlement, reassurance and some limited food sharing; dominance and social control; subordination and flight as strategies in dominance relationships; coalition

formation and strategic behavior; and individual personalities and social roles associated with sex and age (Masters 1991). If this is correct, it implies that humans are
likely to develop dominance relationships and hierarchies as a matter of course,
unless constrained from doing so. The pressing theoretical issue then becomes
explaining not inequality, but egalitarianism.

Egalitarianism

Conceptions of egalitarianism vary widely. In some cases, it just means absence of
permanent ranking (Woodburn 1982). It is often used to refer to acephalous societies
in which certain individuals may be equals but have to compete very hard to gain
the prestige of being equal, competition in which there are winners and losers. In
Fried's classic definition, egalitarian societies are those in which "there are as many
positions of prestige in any given age/sex grade as there are persons capable of filling them" (Fried 1967: 715). Leadership is informal and leaders are chosen for their
abilities in certain circumstances and their leadership does not carry over. In such
societies individuals also have equal access to the means of production; reciprocity
and generosity are valued. Fried's definition recognizes the existence of prestige and
the potential for differences in prestige. Woodburn (1982: 432) defines egalitarian
societies as immediate return societies that "systematically eliminate distinctions-
other than those between the sexes-of wealth, of power and of status. There is here
no disconnection between wealth, power and status, no tolerance of inequalities in
one of these dimensions any more than in the others." He goes on to argue that this
is accomplished by social means that as he puts it "systematically disengage people
from property." Individuals have direct access to cultural, social and environmental
resources. Helliwell (1995) suggests Woodburn (1982) may conflate ideas of individual autonomy with egalitarianism and that while personal autonomy may be one
strategy of maintaining egalitarian relations, ideals of autonomy are not incompati-
ble with inequality. Brunton (1989) uses Woodburn's focus on individual autonomy
to argue egalitarian societies essentially lack institutions and the capacity to transmit
culture across generations. As a consequence, such societies will be short lived. This
idea has interesting implications for the long-term resilience of egalitarian societies.

In some ways, Hawkes' (2000) description of egalitarianism among the Hadza
(among whom Woodburn also conducted field work) mirrors that of Woodburn. She
suggests that hunting is a logical avenue for competition among men for prestige,
especially given its dietary and ideological importance to the Hadza. However, the
inherent unpredictability of hunting undercuts any sustained claim to high status
based on hunting success. In this case, egalitarianism is a very unstable, fluid rank
order, rather than an institution repressing prestige competition.

Boehm (1993, 1999, 2000) posits that egalitarianism does not exist; rather he
postulates a "reverse dominance hierarchy" in which coalitions of subdominant individuals prevent normally alpha individuals from exercising dominance. Importantly,
for Boehm this is a learned behavior while prestige seeking is part of our primate

heritage. He also stresses the ideological aspects of egalitarianism, that it represents a moral order. In some ways, he seems more interested in the evolution of moral orders than in egalitarianism per se. Erdal and Whiten (1994, 1996) reject his notion of a reverse dominance hierarchy, preferring "counter-dominance." They see counter-dominance evolving from a positive feedback loop between prestige competition and the continued evolution of social intelligence in humans. The social intelligence is also part of our primate heritage, in their view. But, over the course of human evolution, it has ratcheted up and at some point, the social dynamics and manipulations required for maintaining dominance became too expensive; it was energetically cheaper to resist dominance (counter-dominance) and ensure a fair share of resources via sharing than expending energy to control resources. They see sharing as having some innate basis.

In contrast, Wiessner argues egalitarianism is the outcome of complex institutions and ideologies created and maintained by cultural means that empower coalitions of the weaker to curb the strong (see also Cashdan 1980, Kelly 1995). Egalitarian coalitions vary as greatly in configuration, composition, scope, and nature as do hierarchical power structures, producing a wide variety of paths to and outcomes of the institutionalization of inequality in different societies (Wiessner 2002: 234). She (Wiessner 1996b) describes the range of sanctions employed in a sample of 27 foraging societies to prevent the accumulation of prestige by successful hunters. She concludes such sanctions are virtually universal among egalitarian foragers, although diverse in form. Their ubiquity suggests to her that status seeking is a universal human disposition that can be repressed but not eradicated. She explains the necessity for these measures by arguing they are part of long-term pooling of risk—not just hunting risk, but "an extraordinarily wide range of risks must be pooled over the long-term through reciprocal relationships" (Wiessner 1996b: 186). This explanation for egalitarianism is perhaps the most widely accepted by anthropologists and archaeologists (e.g. Ames 2004), although it is challenged, sometimes on sharply differing grounds (e.g. Hawkes et al. 2001, Sassaman and Heckenberger 2004).

A number of theorists suggest egalitarianism is part of the prosocial human instincts and behaviors ensuring high levels of cooperation within small human groups despite "low levels of genetic relatedness among group members" (Bowles and Gintis 2004). They postulate a proximal mechanism that they call "strong reciprocity: where members of a group benefit from mutual adherence to a social norm, strong reciprocators obey the norm and punish its violators, even though as a result they receive lower payoffs than other group members" (Bowles and Gintis 2004: 17). The emphasis here is on cooperation, and so includes reciprocity as risk reduction. More importantly, however, these models rest on the postulates that strong reciprocity requires modern human cognitive abilities (Bowles 2006), and on prosocial instincts or tendencies that evolved through gene-culture coevolution (Richerson and Boyd 2005).

These theories and others vary in the degree to which they stress the absence of prestige-seeking behavior (e.g. Boehm 1993, 1994, 1999, Knauft 1991, 1994) or the active repression of prestige-seeking behavior (e.g. Wiessner 1996b, Woodburn

1982) and the degree to which that requires institutions or sanctions to accomplish (e.g. Brunton 1989, Wiessner 1996b). They also vary somewhat in the societies included in their ethnographic samples, which in turn shapes their results, producing some controversy (e.g. Erdal and Whiten 1996, Knauft 1991, 1994). This variance probably also reflects variability in what constitutes what is labeled egalitarianism in actual practice. It seems to conflate an array of social practices from weak, unstable or stable rank orders with no repression of prestige competition to active repression of competition and a strong egalitarian ethos. When the distinction is necessary here, I term the latter option formal egalitarianism. There is similar variation in the mechanisms scholars propose to overcome the inertia of egalitarianism (Ames 2007a).

Whatever mechanisms are proposed, they assume that all Pleistocene societies, or at least Late Pleistocene societies, were egalitarian despite possible evidence to the contrary (e.g. Soffer 1985, Vanhearen and d'Errico 2005). This assumption is made a self-fulfilling prophecy by archaeological methodology. Egalitarianism in the archaeological record is demonstrated by negative evidence—the absence of evidence for inequality. Inequality has to be proven; egalitarianism does not (Ames 2007a). Because the evolution of permanent inequality is widely seen to be a major Rubicon in human history, archaeologists have developed a large armorium of methods for investigating its presence and variation in ancient societies (e.g. Ames 2007a, Wason 1994). We have no equivalent methods for positively demonstrating the presence of egalitarianism, nor are such methods generally thought to be necessary. Scholars often apply Yoffee's rule: if you have to argue whether it is, it isn't (Ames 2005, Pauketat 2007, Yoffee 1993): if it is possible to debate whether a particular ancient society had inequality, then it did not, which means, *ipso facto*, it was egalitarian, especially if it was a small society of mobile hunter-gatherers. As a consequence, the seemingly lengthy archaeological record of egalitarianism is a record of cases assumed to have been egalitarian on the grounds of "default egalitarianism" or which failed Yoffee's rule. Even the concept of "transegalitarian" societies which was proposed (Clark and Blake 1994) to encompass the typological murkiness between egalitarian and stratified societies requires demonstration of "emerging" inequalities. This is not to recommend less rigorous standards (see Ames 2007a) rather to stress that a failure to demonstrate ranking is not the same as demonstrating egalitarianism and that without positive evidence, the case is unproven. To paraphrase Lieberman (2008: 56): to establish whether an ancient society is egalitarian or ranked should be equally burdensome in terms of rejecting a hypothesis. There also may be more alternatives from which to pick.

These issues aside, the origins of egalitarianism are generally placed either in the more remote human past, in the Lower Paleolithic (Wiessner 2002) or as much as two million years ago (Hayden 2001). Other estimates date it to ca. 100,000 years ago (e.g. Boehm 1999, Gintis et al. 2003, Richerson and Boyd 1998). These latter estimates link egalitarianism and human forms of inequality to modern human cognition regardless of whether the behavior is learned or part of recently acquired innate tendencies. Egalitarianism then becomes part of the package of cognitive and behavioral traits comprising "modernity," which distinguishes modern *Homo sapiens sapiens* from all other hominids including not so modern *Homo sapiens*. For others (e.g. Hayden 2001), egalitarianism either predates modernity, or modernity predates modern *Homo sapiens sapiens* (e.g. Barham 2007, Hayden 1993, Zilhão 2007). The first of these possibilities is unproblematic if egalitarianism is our default form of organization or if Hawkes (2000) and Erdal and Whiten (1996) are correct, since their theories do not require culturally based norms. The second possibility is a matter of intense debate and well beyond the scope of this paper.

The persistence of egalitarianism, regardless of when it originated, is generally seen as the consequence of the balanced, reciprocal social, and economic relationships egalitarianism is thought to maintain among individuals and social groups. These ties are believed to have been essential to survival in the high-risk environments of the Pleistocene (e.g. Hayden 1995, 2001, Wiessner 2002). This explanation has been challenged. Hawkes et al. (2001) use Hadza data to argue that the meat sharing thought to be central to these reciprocal relationships represents costly signaling rather than reciprocity. Additionally, egalitarianism is not necessary to maintain widespread reciprocal social ties that give access to resources (e.g. Hadja 1984, Suttles 1960) and the environments occupied by the classic egalitarian groups may not be as high risk as generally thought (Porter and Marlow 2007). But that is not the immediate issue here. Rather, the issue addressed here arises from the claim that modern human inequality rests upon tendencies in human nature rooted in our primate heritage: if egalitarianism was the norm for hominin societies for some 100,000–2,000,000 years, how and why did our innate tendencies toward inequality persist? Put another way, if egalitarian behavior was advantageous over many millennia, why did natural selection not work against the more competitive, dominance-seeking individuals. If it can build "prosocial" tendencies, including egalitarianism (Bowles and Gintis 2004, Boyd et al. 2003, Boyd and Richerson 2006, Gintis et al. 2003, Richerson and Boyd 1998, 1999, 2001, Richerson et al. 2003), why not work against prestige seeking? Knauft (1991) seems to suggest that it did exactly that over much of the Pleistocene until increasing population density and economic production revived hierarchical organization in the Late Pleistocene/early Holocene. Erdal and Whiten (1994, 1996) are quite explicit on this point. In their "Machiavellian Intelligence" model, egalitarianism, as resistance to dominance, develops as the less costly alternative to dominance seeking. One ensures his or her own fair share of resources (meat in their model) while preventing others from getting more is cheaper than trying to get the most resources via prestige competition. This seems to describe a circumstance in which selection might work against individuals with innate tendencies toward prestige seeking.

The Persistence of Prestige Seeking

Frankly, at some level, asking why an innate tendency toward inequality would persist seems like a stupid question, but it leads in some interesting directions. There are a few answers: the tendency could be so deeply engrained in our genome (similar to having five fingers or binocular vision) that it would be exceedingly difficult for selection to eliminate. More narrowly for humans, Heinrich and Gil-White (2002) suggest that the granting of prestige by humans facilitates and speeds cultural transmission. A more obvious answer is that it is simply biologically good to have high prestige; benefits accrue to high prestige individuals, including better health, access to resources and ultimately relatively higher reproductive fitness, even among apparently egalitarian foragers (e.g. Maschner and Patton 1996, Smith 2004). These benefits are well documented and widespread among social animals (Sapolsky 2004). Further, they may accrue within very finely graded systems of ranking.

In a series of studies of health status among British civil servants, Marmot demonstrates significant health differences even between immediately adjacent ranks (Marmot 2004). These are not the obvious differences in health between lower and upper class individuals but are differences among members of the same social class who differ narrowly in their civil service rank. Marmot (2004) has extended this analysis beyond Britain to encompass other industrialized countries in what he terms the "status syndrome." He explains these differences proximately as a consequence of less individual autonomy at lower ranks, even between immediately adjacent ranks and ultimately to mind–body interaction. Be that as it may, what is important here is that these differences exist between individuals who differ only slightly in their status and in ways that might be invisible to all but the best informed observer. Therefore, it is plausible that differences in health status might accrue within otherwise apparently egalitarian societies that have a stable prestige rank order, even where the difference seem slight or invisible. Speth (1990) argues that these slight or seemingly invisible differences can have important health and nutrition consequences, particularly during annual periods of food stress. He documents these consequences for women in forager societies but raises the possibility that there may be status consequences as well.

A study of dental health among three Pygmy groups lends supports for these inferences. The three groups—the Efe, Aka, and Mbuti—are generally archetypes of egalitarian organization. Walker and Hewlett (1990) examined the dental health of members of all three groups as a proxy measure of overall health. Dental health varied along two dimensions: gender and status. Women had poorer dentition than men. Men who were leaders (i.e. with higher prestige) had significantly better teeth than those who were not leaders. Additionally, Aka leaders are on average 3 cm taller than the average Aka male (Hewlett 1988). They propose that gender differences reflect women having more carbohydrates in their diets. There are no visible prestige-based dietary differences. However, the likelihood is that the prestige-related differences reflect greater amounts of meat in the diet. They propose two alternative explanations. Good teeth are prized in these societies and thus men with better teeth are more likely to become leaders, or men with higher prestige have wider social networks that give them greater access to meat. Kent (1991) proposes a third explanation: that good hunters have more meat in their diets and therefore have better teeth, and good hunters (or men with good teeth) become leaders. A key issue in all three explanations is that whatever is causing the good dental health has to be sustained over time, since the leaders in the survey were middle-aged men, years past when their adult teeth erupted.

Walker and Hewlett (1990) place little credence in their first explanation (men with good teeth become leaders because good teeth are prized) since it does not explain how good teeth are maintained over a lifetime. In their response to Kent (Hewlett and Walker 1991, Kent 1991), they develop their second hypothesis more fully in arguing against her hunting hypothesis. They note that there are three leadership positions among the three groups, one of which is clearly based on hunting prowess. These individuals are generally elephant hunters but are also active in spiritual affairs. There is usually one of these individuals for every two or three camps. Although the other two leadership positions are held by the oldest active hunters in a camp, hunting or spiritual abilities are not leadership factors; rather, it is the ability to "calmly and thoughtfully mediate disputes." Additionally, they observe these individuals come from the largest patrilineages present in a camp. The resulting greater "kinship resources" affect a range of other resources, including marriages. They hypothesize that the larger kin network would give individuals lifelong access to a relatively greater range of foods, including meat, which would contribute to sustained dental health. While they do not develop the point, this seems to carry the implication that leadership positions are associated with particular kin groups and therefore may have some degree of ascription (see also Hewlett 1988).

Kent's hunting hypothesis (Kent 1991) would require that an individual have access to a regularly successful hunter while their permanent dentition was coming in, and then themselves became a regularly successful hunter in turn. This seems to necessitate a level of hunting success higher than what the ethnographic record indicates for hunters generally. It also requires access to the meat gained in the hunt. Even if one invokes Marmot's autonomy explanation, that sense of autonomy would need to exist even before the person became a leader to account for the good dentition.

Sugiyama and Sugiyama (2003) postulate that higher prestige may bring health benefits in the form of greater care in a health crises. They argue that giving health care is costly to the provider and ask what benefits does the provider accrue when giving care and how does one ensure in turn they will get the care they need when it is needed. They argue this is done through the cultivation of valued and essential skills, i.e. costly signaling that benefits the audience, in fact, that needs to benefit the audience. The cultivation of skills brings prestige (see also Olaussen 2008).

Walker and Hewlett's (1990) empirical study has not been duplicated (which is different from saying their results have not been duplicated). Thus extrapolating just from their sample (albeit with its three but related populations) to all egalitarian foragers and human evolution is risky. However, their results combined with Speth's (1990) and Marmot's (2004) show that higher status and prestige can differentially benefit their holders even in situations where the differences in prestige are slight to invisible and the causes of the differentials in benefits difficult to perceive. A number of studies have shown that among foragers hunting success leads to increased prestige, which positively affects fitness (Smith 2004). Given that good health should also positively affect fitness, Walker and Hewlett's (1990) study raises the possibility that the size of social networks impacts fitness. However, the point here is that even in ostensibly formal egalitarian societies, there are a number of avenues along which natural selection would maintain a human predilection for status differentials and competition. Taking this point further, these subtle but likely persistent differentials occur in the absence of any overt control of resources.

This returns the discussion to the notion of "altruistic competition" (Roberts 1998) and the nature of status competition in egalitarian societies. My father was a protestant minister, and I grew up in the Baptist church (although anyone familiar with Baptists will know there is no Baptist "church"). Churches, their congregations and individuals within congregations compete for prestige and control along any number of avenues. The members of church music committees, for example, can compete over the tempo at which hymns are played during services by the church organist, themselves often a volunteer and member of the committee. This competition may seem pathetic, but the person who controls the pace of music controls the tone of the service (e.g. slow, reverential, and funereal vs. upbeat and cheerful) and markedly affects the experience of the congregation. A protracted battle can even drive out a minister. Congregations can also compete among themselves via relative piety. In my childhood, at least, Baptist churches and services were quite austere; the buildings had few decorations and embellishments; the services were equally plain. This was originally a reaction to the rich decorations and elaborate rituals of Catholicism. However, Baptist churches and congregational factions also vied among themselves to be the more austere as a reflection of greater piety. This competition required little in the way of material resources; in fact it made a virtue of apparent relative poverty. The less one displays, the greater one's piety or purity. In formal egalitarian societies, high prestige accrues to those who exemplify egalitarian values, humility, generosity, and what might be termed altruism. In the same way that congregations can compete via the relative austerity of their services and churches, foragers can compete via being more humble. In fact, I would suggest that's exactly what an aggrandizer with a Machiavellian intelligence would do: humble him or herself all the way to high prestige.

While austere piety may not be materially costly, it is hard work and has marginal costs. Austere piety requires continual vigilance and enforcement; individuals who stray need to be identified and punished, sometimes by being severed from the church. This is not unlike the work required to maintain egalitarianism through what Boyd et al. (2003) term altruistic punishment; the punishment of non-cooperators in group situations where the punishment costs both the punisher and non-cooperator. The ongoing costs of norm enforcement and punishment are borne by the group and by the individuals who enforce group norms both on themselves and others (Gintis 2006).

From this it follows that one of the effects of egalitarianism may not be the elimination of status competition, but making it materially cheap. The material costs of costly signaling via humility may be very low even if the signal provides some benefit to the audience (Gintis et al. 2001). I am not suggesting this as an explanation for egalitarianism, merely that this may be one of its effects. Henrich and Gil-White

(2002) compare what they term the ethology of dominance among chimpanzees and of prestige among humans. None of the human prestige-granting behaviors they list carry much if any cost. Feinman and Nietzel (1984) enumerate high-status markers in a sample of middle-range societies. Among these are special houses, multiple wives and elaborated mortuary ritual, all of which might be costly. However, they also list several that are not costly, including obeisance, special language, and services. All of these considerations taken together suggest that, like our close primate relatives, it is possible humans and our ancestors have had rank orders conveying differential biological and social benefits over long periods of time without what Hayden calls "prestige technologies" (1998) or visible political economies.

On the Evolution of Prestige Technologies

The discussions of attention structures and costly signaling are the basis for suggesting two parallel hypotheses for the evolution of prestige technologies and for the maintenance of rank orders and dominance hierarchies in hominin societies. Attention structures require regular propinquity to maintain rank orders. They can be sustained by periodic aggressive enforcement as with the reassertion of dominance in school groups at the beginning of a new year or after a holiday. Primate data also show that rank orders require renewing and reorganization when new individuals join the group or others leave. According to Dunbar (1997, 2003), mutual grooming, an intimate, tactile form of attention, is a primary means by which primate rank orders are acted out and created on the fly as it were and is the glue holding most primate societies together. Humans, of course, do not socially groom. Dunbar (1997, 2003) argues language evolved to replace grooming in the large, spatially dispersed groups that characterize humans.

Gamble (1998) postulates a scalar ordering of hominid social networks, identifying four such ego-based networks and linking them to the famous "magic numbers" of hunter-gatherer social demography. The networks are the intimate network with perhaps five to seven people, the effective network has six to perhaps 34 people; the extended network encompasses 100–400 people; and the global network that has an upper limit of about 2,500 people. These demographic thresholds have appeared in other guises (e.g. Kosse 1990). Gamble argues the global network is unique to modern humans, while the other three are general primate networks. He operationalizes them archaeologically by distinguishing among locales, where individuals interact, local-scale networks, which are the intimate and effective networks, and the social landscape, which encompasses the demographically largest global network and is itself a set of linked local networks. The smaller networks have regular face-to-face interaction and are the scale at which mutual grooming works. At their level, dominance hierarchies and rank orders could be maintained by on-going reinforcement of attention structures. Overt dominance might be rare. However, this would not be possible at the large demographic and spatial scale of social landscapes. It is at this level, for example, that symbolic signaling of group membership, status, etc., would come into play (Wobst 1977). Such signaling would be unnecessary at more intimate scales where the individual is known. Indeed, for Gamble (1998, 1999), symboling makes social landscapes possible and he places the appearance of social networks between 100,000 and 60,000 years ago, a time he sees marked by greatly increased mobility and expanded networks. He calls this the "escape from proximity."

Beads and other forms of personal adornment, especially ochre (Barham 2002, Marean et al. 2007, Watts 2002), are among the very earliest items often thought to mark the appearance of modern cognition, or at least symbolic capacities. The specific symbolic meaning of beads and arrangements of beads can be extremely difficult if not impossible to establish (d'Errico et al. 2003, Kuhn and Stiner 2007). However, from the standpoint of attention structure, their ancient meaning is actually irrelevant. They materialize attention, capturing and focusing it on the wearer in the same way name tags do at academic conventions. They store attention structures (Donald 1991) while at the same time providing new avenues for competition. In populations that were mobile and dispersed, and/or participating in Gamble's (1998) social landscape, a materialized attention structure would stabilize rank orders across space and time. Their appearance in the archaeological record could mark circumstances where proximity-based rank orders were increasingly difficult to maintain and increasingly fluid with expanding social networks and increasing mobility.

In its broadest form, costly signaling theory is about natural and sexual selection building expensive organic structures or behaviors. Among humans, it is generally applied to hunter-gatherer hunting and modern "conspicuous consumption," which is costly signaling via material culture, either through making or consuming things requiring labor, time, and/or skill. Costly signaling does not require symboling. It is unlikely peacock hens symbol, and, among hominins, it can convey information in small face-to-face networks as well as in large social landscapes. Given its ubiquity among animals, it likely has great antiquity among hominids (e.g. O'Connell et al. 2002).

It is also plausible, even likely, that as symboling evolved, however and whenever that happened, it co-opted costly signaling, or costly signaling co-opted it, via mutual reinforcement. The same would hold for attention-getting devices such as beads and red ochre. Human prestige is attention giving with an overlay of symbolic meaning that reinforces the original behavior and gives it an ideological significance that it did not originally have. For example, if O'Connell et al. (2002) are correct about hominin males competing for prestige via meat acquisition at the Plio-Pliestocene boundary, meat's role in hominid status construction is far more ancient than its current wide spread symbolic meaning as a prestige food.

The discussion in the preceding two sections suggests that differential access to resources including food, health, and reproduction can persist in egalitarian societies in the absence of an overt or visible political economy. Intense competition via competitive altruism or competitive humility can occur using non-material resources. Even costly signaling may have no material consequences. This latter point is not to suggest that resources and differential resource flows are irrelevant. Seemingly minor differences in health and fertility can have long-term evolutionary consequences. However, it is to suggest that differential access to resources and unequal benefit from resources can exist without an overt political economy. Inequality, at least in the form of persistent rank orders, does not require complexity.

At the same time, costly signals, attention structures and existing rank orders, when coupled with symboling, can literally materialize. This materialization does not necessarily mean their emergence or origin but the material manifestation and perhaps intensifying of preexisting rank orders. The same holds for political economies; they evolve from preexisting differential resource flows rather than from some blank economic slate.

The Evolution of Egalitarianism

Paleontological and DNA evidence together suggests anatomically modern humans evolved in Africa perhaps 200,000 years ago and subsequently dispersed out of Africa (Balter 2002, Mellars 2006). When modernity develops is much more difficult to date as is what constitutes modernity. The evolution of "modernity" is a greatly vexed subject, especially since there is no agreement on what it is (e.g. Clark 2002, Henshilwood and Marean 2003, Milliken 2007, Wadley 2001, papers in Mellars et al. 2007). There are debates over what the criteria should be, whether the current ones are universal, Eurocentric, or should be Afrocentric (Henshilwood and Marean 2003). The issue is made more complicated by the likelihood that the evolution of modern cognitive abilities was a multistage process involving the evolution of not only symboling (e.g. Deacon 1997, Donald 1991) but memory and neural processing capacities as well (e.g. Coolidge and Wynne 2001, Dunbar 1997, 2003, Wynne and Coolidge 2003). Henshilwood and Marean's definition is

> Modern human behavior is ... behavior ... mediated by socially constructed patterns of symbolic thinking, actions, and communication that allow for material and information exchange and cultural continuity between and across generations and contemporaneous communities. The key criterion for modern human behavior is not the capacity for symbolic thought but the use of symbolism to organize behavior (see Wadley 2001) (Henshilwood and Marean 2003: 635).

They suggest the "use of symbolism to organize behavior" might be recognizable in "the complexity of . . . general behavioral systems" and that egalitarianism may be an example of such a system. Wadley (2001) suggests, following Deacon (1997) that we look for evidence of extrasomatic storage of symbols. She sees artwork, jewelry, and other forms of personal adornment and the social use of space as such evidence. Establishing "the use of symbolism to organize behavior" with small samples of inevitably fragmentary data is methodologically extremely difficult (e.g. d'Errico et al. 2003, Zilhão 2007).

Watt's analysis of red ocher used in the Middle Stone Age of southern Africa illustrates these problems (Watt 2002). He examines some 4,000 possible pieces of pigment from MSA sites to test two hypotheses: that the pigments were used ritually or for hide preservation (Wadley 2001). Ultimately he suggests that pigment use is an example of costly signaling, which as he notes, and as I have above, does not require symbolic capacity. However, he argues that symbolism is indicated if it can be shown the objects were used in collective ritual (he regards ritual as costly signaling so that individualized ritual, e.g. the performance of a single peacock, is not evidence for symboling); if there is also evidence for consistency of form; and if functional explanations can be eliminated.

Watt's discussion is salient to both beads as markers of symboling and as attractors of attention/costly signaling. He stresses that such objects have to have what he terms visual salience—people need to be drawn to them. He, therefore, is at pains to demonstrate that humans are optically wired to be visually drawn to the red color of ochre. In any case, costly-signaling theory and visual salience provide an explanation for the proximal mechanisms for why humans invest certain kinds of objects with meaning. Costly signaling also muddies the theoretical waters because it does not require symboling to work. Costly signaling may account for many of the objects put forward as evidence for symboling before the Upper Paleolithic. While Watt's concept of collective ritual may provide a route out of this difficulty, as might methods employed by Vanhearen and d'Errico (2005), Kuhn and Stiner's (2007) approach is more useful.

They argue that while actual meanings of beads or pigments is impossible to know, they can be analyzed as information technology (an approach rooted in Wobst 1977) using performance characteristics. They identify six performance characteristics for beads: durability, standardization and formal redundancy, expression of quantity, expression of investment differential, transferability, and cost. They suggest that beads score moderately to high along these dimensions, while pigments score low (e.g. pigments are not very durable, they can be standardized but not necessarily, they have limited capacity to express quantity or amount of investment, they are not transferable and are not as good as beads in indicating cost). They suggest pigments functioned best at carrying short-term information in face-to-face circumstances and use of pigments was intended to "increase an individual's visual impact ... a way to stand out and express individual uniqueness." They further suggest

> The widespread appearance of beads in the late (Middle Stone Age/Early Upper Paleolithic) implies that different kinds of information were being conveyed through body ornamentation and to a different scale of audience as well. The fact that beads and beaded objects are lasting and physically transferable frees communication from a complete dependence on direct interaction, allowing the same information to be transferred, or expressed over larger spatial and temporal domains (Kuhn and Stiner 2007: 51).

They hypothesize this change in the scale and complexity of social interactions could be a consequence of cognitive evolution or of demographic factors including population growth that increased the need to convey more messages to more people. The current consensus based on African evidence seems to be that modernity evolved in a gradual, mosaic fashion rather than suddenly (e.g. Klein 1995, 2000). McBreaty and Brooks (2000) see evidence for some aspects of modern behavior in Africa as much as 280 kya including expanded territorial ranges (McBreaty and Brooks 2000). Marean et al. (2007) date it in southern Africa to as early as ca.

164 kya based on evidence for the use of littoral resources coupled with the use of pigment and the presence of small blades. Other crucial evidence includes over 8,000 pieces of ochre, of which two are engraved and some 39 perforated shell beads from Blombos Cave in South Africa. The engravings are dated to ca. 77 kya and the shell beads to 76 kya (Henshilwood et al. 2004, 2008). The possibility of shell beads dating as early at 100–135 kya in Israel and Algeria (Vanhaeren et al. 2006) remains unsettled (Zilhão 2007). There is also an interesting gap in the South African bead record between ca. 76,000 and 35,000 years ago (Zilhão 2007).

In a recent synthesis of the fossil, genetic and archaeological data, Mellars (2006) proposes a mosaic, multistep model of the evolution of modern humans in which anatomically modern humans appear between ca. 150 and 200 kya, with clear expression of symboling present by ca. 110–90 kya. He sees southern Africa subject to rapid climatic and environmental changes between 80 and 70 kya, which is accompanied by major technological, economic, and social changes that he sees as equivalent to the later more famous changes in Europe that mark the Upper Paleolithic. These changes are initially limited to southern and eastern Africa. This is followed by these populations expanding first in Africa between 60 and 70 kya and thence out of Africa by 60 kya.

This model will be highly controversial in how Mellars reads the African evidence (e.g. McBrearty 2007), the place of Neanderthals in the evolution of modern cognition (Clark 2002, Hayden 1993, Zilhão 2007) and so on. However, it provides a basis for discussion. If we assume egalitarianism evolved as part of a package of behavioral, mental, and morphological traits (Finlayson 2004, Richerson et al. 2005) associated with modern humans, then presumably it might have evolved in Africa sometime between 200 and 60 kya, a period marked by increasingly unstable global climate conditions with rapid climatic fluctuations at time scales of much less then a millennium (Alley 2000). Finlayson (2004) suggests that African hominids during that period responded to the rapid changes and the resulting increased risk by expanding the temporal and spatial scale of their activities with greater "dispersal capacity." Interestingly, Leiberman (2008) speculates that changes in the human face marking anatomically modern *Homo sapiens* may, in part, be the result of selection for improved running as opposed to walking. As argued above, expanded home ranges and greater dispersal across the landscape would make it more difficult to maintain social dynamics and ties based on propinquity. These would include enduring attention-based rank orders, social ties as well as, perhaps, social transmission, at least in the absence of language. Dispersal here is not the same as mobility patterns, referring rather to the temporal and spatial scales at which organisms are distributed. Greater mobility would also create the kinds of conditions outlined by Kuhn and Stiner (2007) for the shift from pigments to beads as the likelihood of encountering and interacting with others would increase.

Egalitarianism could arise in this context in several ways. It might have been the simple consequence of an increased inability to maintain rank orders either because of rapid dispersal, frequent failure of prestige-seeking activities (e.g. Hawkes 2000) or the kind of Machiavellian competition and repression of dominants postulated by Erdal and Whiten (1994). This does not account for its ideological or "social

engineering" aspects nor does it require modern cognition. It could have been positively selected along with cooperation and other leveling mechanisms, either as a
behavior or an instinct, under conditions in which group level extinction was frequent (Bowles 2006, Choi and Bowles 2007). Extinction could be due to rapid
environmental shifts and high subsistence risk and/or intense inter-group competition and warfare. Bowles finds high levels of interpersonal violence among modern
hunter-gatherers, which is at variance with Knauft's conclusions (Knauft 1991).
Bowles' models (Bowles 2006, Choi and Bowles 2007) also positively link strong
intra-group prosocial behaviors with "parochialism," i.e. ethnocentricism. A third
alternative is Trigger's third constraint, the organizational one: small, highly mobile
human groups do not persist for long without actively repressing status competition
or minimizing its costs (e.g. competitive humbleness) regardless of what the natural or social environments are doing. These latter two possibilities are not exactly
the same: the former stresses biocultural selection for affiliative, prosocial behaviors
and the latter stresses functional limits on what small societies can tolerate and still
persist. Either of these options account for the social engineering.

It is at least plausible that egalitarianism, especially formal egalitarianism,
evolved multiple times in the Late Pleistocene and Holocene, a possibility not generally anticipated in anthropological and archaeological thinking given the assumption
of default egalitarianism. Similar ideas are central to the so-called revisionist critique (e.g. Hallpike and Wilmsen 2002, Wilmsen 1989) of interpretations of San
egalitarianism (Ames 2004, Cashdan 1980, Lee 1981). San foraging and social
organization, including its egalitarianism, is seen as relatively recent and more generally modern hunter-gatherer social organization, which is argued to result from
their encounter with colonialist expansion (Sassaman and Heckenberger 2004). The
notion here is somewhat different. Formal egalitarianism, like permanent rank, could
be the result of convergent evolution with different starting points and historical
trajectories. In some places, Holocene social and cultural environments may have
mirrored the Late Pleistocene structurally but not in content (e.g. rapid and extreme
changes but not necessarily climatic ones). These might include but not be limited to the colonial expansion of the last 500 years. For example, there is a reason
to think that Holocene hunter-gatherer demography may have been subject to bot-
tlenecks and boom and bust cycles (Boone 2002, Excoffieri and Schneider 1999).
Perhaps groups with formal egalitarianism might have been more likely to persist
under these circumstances.

This argument could be extended to contemplate whether formal egalitarianism,
at least of the kind described by Hayden (2001) and Wiessner (1996b) with institutionalized repression of competition, has never been particularly common. Perhaps
over much of the last 100,000 years the majority of human societies were small,
with prestige competition and fluid rank orders, with a minority of formally egalitarian societies and another minority with stable, sometimes materially visible rank
orders or perhaps even formal ranking. Over the relatively short spans of centuries,
societies shifted back and forth across these social forms; over millennia, they went
extinct, giving the archaeological record of the last 100,000 years or so its flickering
character.

Summary and Conclusions

This chapter explores the possibility that the "default human social organization" is not egalitarianism, but is marked by rank orders maintained by competition for prestige and dominance based to some degree on innate primate propensities. The rank orders have varying degrees of fluidity, permanence, and explicitness, but there will always be individuals of high prestige. Prestige competition via costly signaling may take visible forms, e.g. male hunting, or it may involve non-corporeal resources. Differential access to resources may not be visible but social and economic practices produce differential benefits that have cross-generational effects. Status is measured via attention structures, thus hominin rank orders in the absence of symboling require some degree of regular face-to-face interaction to maintain.

Such societies are "egalitarian" in that they lack formal institutions of rank and because the anthropological concept of egalitarianism lacks precision. Formal egalitarian societies are those that act on egalitarian mores to actively repress prestige competition, although competition is likely to continue *sub rosa*. The evolution and persistence of such societies requires archaeological explanation as much as does that of so-called complex societies: those with permanent systems of rank.

Archaeological methodology makes this task difficult since it assumes small scale societies are formally egalitarian unless permanent ranking can be demonstrated. Archaeologists lack methodologies for establishing whether an ancient society was egalitarian. I strongly suspect that to do so will require using modeling, including agent-based modeling, which assumes some degree of inequality to explore the pay offs for actively repressing competition and what the consequences of that might be.

Both egalitarianism and permanent inequality as usually understood by anthropologists require modern human cognitive capacities in the form of symboling. However, maintaining rank orders via attention structures and costly signaling does not. Thus the appearance of prestige technologies in the archaeological record does not necessarily indicate the evolution of prestige competition and rank orders. It may initially indicate the evolution of symboling and the materialization of persistent dynamics via material culture.

Increased mobility and expanded social networks, coupled with increasingly rapid, short-cycle climatic fluctuations during the past 200,000 years may have selected for formal egalitarian organization, or just made maintaining rank orders more difficult, hence prestige technologies. It is also possible that small-scale human societies work better and are more likely to persist if prestige competition is repressed, regardless of what is happening in the socio-natural environment.

This explains neither the development of permanent inequality nor political economies. It does suggest that many of the instances of the "origins of inequality" hailed by archaeologists are simply the visible crystallization of preexisting patterns. However, like the apparent appearance and disappearance of beads in Middle Stone Age Africa, these crystallizations seem to twinkle on and off across millennia suggesting there may be social, demographic, or economic thresholds, depending on

circumstances, where attention structures and rank orders materialize and demateri-
alize. It also suggests that permanent differentials in access to resources and material
flows do not need to be invented out of whole cloth by conniving aggrandizers; the
necessary raw material in the form of economic and social relations is always at
hand.

References

Alley, R. 2000. *The Two-Mile Time Machine: Ice Cores, Abrupt Climate Change and Our Future.*
Princeton: Princeton University Press.

Ames, K. 2007a. The Archaeology of Rank. In Bentley, R.A., Maschner, H.D.G., and Chippendale,
C. (eds.), *Handbook of Archaeological Theories*, pp. 487–514. Lanham: Alta Mira Press.

Ames, K. 2007b. Whither affluently complex hunter-forager-gatherers: a review of: 'Beyond affluent foragers: rethinking hunter-gatherer complexity'. *Before Farming: The Anthropology and
Archaeology of Hunter-Gatherers.* Online 2006/4: Paper 8.

Ames, K. 2005. Intensification of Food Production on the Northwest Coast and Elsewhere. In Deur,
D. and Turner, N.J. (eds.), *Keeping It Living: Traditions of Plant Use and Cultivation on the
Northwest Coast of North America*, pp. 67–100. Seattle: University of Washington Press.

Ames, K. 2004. Supposing hunter-gatherer variability. *American Antiquity* 69(2): 364–374.

Ames, K. 2000. *Kennewick Man: Cultural Affiliation Report, Chapter 2: Review of the
Archaeological Data.* Washington: National Park Service, September 10, 2007; http://www.
nps.gov/archeology/kennewick/AMES.HTM

Ames, K. 1988. Early Holocene Forager Mobility Strategies on the Southern Columbia Plateau.
In Willig, J.A., Aikens, C.M., and Fagan, J. (eds.), *Early Human Occupation in Western North
America*, pp. 325–360, Anthropological Papers No. 21. Carson City: Nevada State Museum.

Arnold, J. 1996. The archaeology of complex hunter-gatherers. *Journal of Archaeological Method
and Theory* 3: 77–126.

Arnold, J. 1993. Labor and the rise of complex hunter-gatherers. *Journal of Anthropological
Archaeology* 12: 75–119.

Balter, M. 2002. What made humans modern? *Science* 295: 1219–1225.

Barham, L. 2002. Systematic pigment use in the middle Pleistocene of South-Central Africa.
Current Anthropology 43: 181–190.

Barham, L. 2007. Modern Is as Modern Does? Technological Trends and Thresholds in the
South-central African Record. In Mellars, P., Boyle, K., Bar-Yosef, O., and Stringer, C.
(eds.), *Rethinking the Human Revolution: New Behavioral and Biological Perspectives on
the Origins and Dispersal of Modern Humans*, pp. 165–176. Cambridge: MacDonald Institute
Monographs.

Berreman, G. 1981. Social Inequality: A Cross-Cultural Analysis. In Berreman, G.D. (ed.), *Social
Inequality: Comparative and Developmental Approaches*, pp. 3–40. New York: Academic
Press.

Binford, L. 1983. *In Pursuit of the Past.* London: Thames and Hudson Ltd.

Bliege Bird, R., and Smith, E. 2005. Signaling theory, strategic interaction, and symbolic capital.
Current Anthropology 46: 221–248.

Bliege Bird, R., Smith, E., and Bird, D. 2001. The hunting handicap: costly signaling in human
foraging strategies. *Behavioral Ecology and Sociobiology* 50: 9–19.

Boehm, C. 1993. Egalitarian behavior and reverse dominance hierarchy. *Current Anthropology* 34:
227–254.

Boehm, C. 1994. Reply (to Erdal and White). *Current Anthropology* 35: 178–180.

Boehm, C. 1999. *Hierarchy in the Forest: The Evolution of Egalitarian Behavior.* Cambridge:
Harvard University Press.

Boehm, C. 2000. Forager Hierarchies, Innate Dispositions, and the Behavioral Reconstruction of Preshistory. In Diehl, M.W. (ed.), *Hierarchies in Action: Cui Bono?* pp. 31–58, Occasional Papers No. 27. Carbondale: Southern Illinois University.

Boone, J. 2002. Subsistence strategies and early human population history: an evolutionary ecological perspective. *World Archaeology* 34: 6–25.

Boone, J. 2000. Costly Signaling, Social Power, and Lineage Survival. In Diehl, M.W. (ed.), *Hierarchies in Action: Cui Bono?* pp. 84–110, Center for Archaeological Investigations Occasional Paper No. 27. Carbondale: Southern Illinois University.

Bowles, S. 2006. Group competition, reproductive leveling, and the evolution of human altruism. *Science* 314: 1569–1572.

Bowles, S., and Gintis, H. 2004. The evolution of strong reciprocity: cooperation in heterogeneous populations. *Theoretical Population Biology* 65: 17–28.

Boyd, R., and Richerson, P. 2006. Culture and the Evolution of the Human Social Instincts. In Enfield, N.J. and Levinson, S.C. (eds.), *Roots of Human Sociality: Culture, Cognition and Interaction*, pp. 453–477. Oxford: Berg.

Boyd, R., and Richerson, P. 1985. *Culture and the Evolutionary Process*. Chicago: The University of Chicago Press.

Boyd, R., Gintis, H., Bowles, S., and Richerson, P. 2003. The evolution of altruistic punishment. *Proceedings of the National Academy of Sciences* 100: 3531–3535.

Brunton, R. 1989. The cultural instability of egalitarian societies. *Man (NS)* 24: 673–681.

Cashden, E. 1980. Egalitarianism among hunter-gatherers. *American Anthropologist* 82: 116–120.

Chatters, J. 1995. Population growth, climatic cooling, and the development of collector strategies on the Southern Plateau, Western North America. *Journal of World Prehistory* 9: 341–400.

Choi, J.-K., and Bowles, S. 2007. The coevolution of parochial altruism and war. *Science* 318: 636–640.

Clark, G. 2002. Neanderthal archaeology—implications for our origins. *American Anthropologist* 104: 50–67.

Clark, J.E., and Blake, M. 1994. The Power of Prestige: Competitive Generosity and the Emergence of Rank Societies in Lowland Mesoamerica. In Brumfiel, E. and Fox, J.W. (eds.), *Factional Competition and Political Development in the New World*, pp. 17–30. Cambridge: Cambridge University Press.

Connolly, T.J. 1999. *Newberry Crater: A Ten-Thousand-Year record of Human Occupation and Environmental Change in the Basin-Plateau Borderlands*. Salt Lake City: University of Utah Anthropological Papers. University of Utah.

Coolidge, F., and Wynn, T. 2001. Executive functions of the frontal lobes and the evolutionary ascendancy of homo sapiens. *Cambridge Archaeological Journal* 11: 255–260.

Crumley, C. 1995. Heterarchy and the Analysis of Complex Societies. In Ehrenreich, R., Crumley, C., and Levy, J. (eds.), *Heterarchy and the Analysis of Complex Societies*, pp. 1–6, Archaeological Papers of the American Anthropological Association, No. 6. Washington: American Anthropological Association.

Deacon, T. 1997. *The Symbolic Species: The Co-Evolution of Language and the Brain*. New York: W.W. Norton & Company.

d'Errico, F., Henshilwood, C., Lawson, G., Vanhaeren, M., Tillier, A.-M., Soressi, M., Bresson, F., Maureille, B., Nowell, A., Lakarra, J., Backwell, L., and Julien, M. 2003. Archaeological evidence for the emergence of language, symbolism, and music—an alternative multidisciplinary perspective. *Journal of World Prehistory* 17: 1–71.

Donald, M.W. 1991. *Origins of the Modern Mind*. Cambridge: Harvard University Press.

Dunbar, R. 2003. The social brain: mind, language, and society in evolutionary perspective. *Annual Review of Anthropology* 32: 163–181.

Dunbar, R. 1997. *Grooming, Gossip and the Evolution of Language*. Cambridge: Harvard University Press.

Durham, W. 1991. *Coevolution: Genes, Culture and Human Diversity*. Stanford: Stanford University Press.

Earle, T. 2002. *Bronze Age Economics: The Beginnings of Political Economies*. Boulder: Westview Press.

Erdal, D., and Whiten, A. 1994. On human egalitarianism: an evolutionary product of machiavellian status escalation. *Current Anthropology* 35: 175–183.

Erdal, D., and Whiten, A. 1996. Egalitarianism and Machiavellian Intelligence in Human Evolution. In Mellars, P. and Gibson, K. (eds.), *Modeling the Early Human Mind*, pp. 139–150, MacDonald Institute Monographs. Cambridge: MacDonald Institute for Archaeological Research.

Excoffier, L., and Schneider, S. 1999. Why hunter-gatherer populations do not show signs of pleistocene demographic expansions. *Proceedings of the National Academy of Sciences* 96: 10597–10602.

Feinman, G., and Neitzel, J. 1984. Too Many Types: An Overview of Prestate Societies in the Americas. In Schiffer, M.B. (ed.), *Advances in Archaeological Method and Theory*, Vol. 7, pp. 39–102. Orlando: Academic Press.

Finlayson, C. 2004. *Neanderthals and Modern Humans: An Ecological and Evolutionary Perspective*. Cambridge: University of Cambridge Press.

Fried, M. 1967. *The Evolution of Political Society: An Essay in Political Anthropology*. New York: Random House.

Gamble, C. 1999. *The Paleolithic Societies of Europe*. Cambridge: Cambridge University Press.

Gamble, C. 1998. Paleolithic society and the release from proximity: a network approach to intimate relations. *World Archaeology* 29: 426–449.

Gibson, J.L., and Carr, P.J. (ed.). 2004. *Signs of Power: The Rise of Cultural Complexity in the Southeast*. Tuscaloosa: The University of Alabama Press.

Gintis, H. 2006. Moral sense and material interests. *Social Research* 73: 377–404.

Gintis, H., Smith, E.A., and Bowles, S. 2001. Costly signaling and cooperation. *Journal of Theoretical Biology* 213: 103–119.

Gintis, H., Bowles, S., Boyd, R.T., and Fehr, E. 2003. Explaining altruistic behavior in humans. *Evolution and Human Behavior* 24: 153–172.

Glassow, M. 2004. Identifying Complexity During the Early Prehistory of Santa Cruz Island, California. In Arnold, J.E. (ed.), *Foundations of Chumash Complexity*, pp. 17–24. Los Angeles: Costin Institute of Archaeology, University of California.

Grammer, K. 1996. Systems of Power: The Function and Evolution of Social Status. In Wiessner, P. and Schiefenhovel, W. (eds.), *Food and the Status Quest: An Interdisciplinary Perspective*, pp. 69–85. Providence: Berghahn Books.

Green, T.J. 1993. Aboriginal Residential Structures in Southern Idaho. *Journal of California and Great Basin Archaeology* 15(1): 58–72.

Green, T.J., Cochran, B., Fenton, T.W., Woods, J.C., Titmus, G.L., Tieszen, L., Davis, M.A., and Miller, S.J. 1998. The buhl burial: a paleoindian woman from Southern Idaho. *American Antiquity* 63: 437–456.

Green, T., Pavesic, M., Woods, J., and Titmus, G. 1986. The demoss burial locality: preliminary observations. *Idaho Archaeologist* 9: 31–40.

Hajda, Y. 1984. *Regional Social Organization in the Greater Lower Columbia, 1792–1830*, PhD Dissertation. Ann Arbor: University of Washington, University Microfilms.

Hallpike, C.R., and Wilmsen, E.N. 2002. Comment: primitive mentality. *Journal of the Royal Anthropological Institute* 8: 571–572.

Hawkes, K. 2000. Hunting and the Evolution of Egalitarian Societies: Some Lessons from the Hadza. In Diehl, M.W. (ed.), *Hierarchies in Action: Cui Bono?* pp. 59–83, Center for Archaeological Investigations Occasional Paper No. 27. Carbondale: Southern Illinois University.

Hawkes, K., and Bliege Bird, R. 2002. Showing off, handicap signaling, and the evolution of men's work. *Evolutionary Anthropology* 11: 58–67.

Hawkes, K., O'Connell, J.F., and Blurton Jones, N.G. 2001. Hadza meat sharing. *Evolution and Human Behavior* 22: 113–142.

Hayden, B. 2001. Richman, Poorman, Beggarman, Chief: The Dynamics of Social Inequality. In Feinman, G. and Price, T.D. (eds.), *Archaeology at the Millenium: A Sourcebook*, pp. 213–268. New York: Kluwer Academic Publishers.

Hayden, B. 1998. Practical and prestige technologies: the evolution of material systems. *Journal of Archaeological Method and Theory* 5: 1–55.

Hayden, B. 1995. Pathways to Power: Principles for Creating Socioeconomic Inequalities. In Price, T.D. and Feinman, G.M. (eds.), *Foundations of Social Inequality*, pp. 15–86. New York: Plenum.

Hayden, B. 1993. The cultural capacities of Neandertals: a review and re-evaluation. *Journal of Human Evolution* 24: 113–146.

Helliwell, C. 1995. Autonomy as natural equality: inequality in 'Egalitarian' societies. *The Journal of the Royal Anthropological Institute* 1: 359–375.

Henrich, J., and Gil-White, F. 2002. The evolution of prestige: freely conferred deference as a mechanism for enhancing the benefits of cultural evolution. *Evolution and Human Behavior* 22: 165–196.

Henshilwood, C.S., and Marean, C.W. 2003. The origin of modern human behavior. *Current Anthropology* 44: 627–651.

Henshilwood, C., d'Errico, F., Vanhaeren, M., van Niekerk, K., and Jacobs, Z. 2004. Middle Stone Age shell beads from South Africa. *Science* 304: 404.

Henshilwood, C., d'Errico, F., Yates, R., Jacobs, Z., Tribolo, C., Duller, G., Mercier, N., Sealy, J., Valladas, H., Watts, I., and Wintle, A.G. 2008. Emergence of modern human behavior: Middle Stone Age engravings from South Africa. *Science* 295: 1278.

Hess, S.C. 1997. *Rocks, Range and Renfrew: Using Distance-Decay Effects to Study Late Pre-Mazama Period Obsidian Acquisition and Mobility in Oregon and Washington*, Ph.D. dissertation. Ann Arbor: Washington State University, University Microfilms.

Hewlett, B. 1988. Sexual Selection and Paternal Investment among Aka Pygmies. In Betzig, L., Burgerhoff Mulder, M., and Turek, P. (eds.), *Human Reproductive Behavior*, pp. 263–276. Cambridge: Cambridge University Press.

Hewlett, B., and Walker, P. 1991. Social status and dental health among the Aka and Mbuti Pygmies. *American Anthropologist* 93: 943–944.

Hold-Cavell, B. 1996. The Ethological Basis of Status Hierarchies. In Wiessner, P. and Schiefenhovel, W. (eds.), *Food and the Status Quest: An Interdisciplinary Perspective*, pp. 19–31. Providence: Berghahn Books.

Johnson, G. 1982. Organizational Structure and Scalar Stress. In Renfrew, C., Rowlands, M., and Seagraves-Whallon, B.A. (eds.), *Theory and Explanation in Archaeology*, pp. 389–421. Orlando: Academic Press Inc.

Keen, I. 2006. Constraints on the development of enduring inequalities in late holocene Australia. *Current Anthropology* 47: 7–38.

Kelly, R. 1995. *The Foraging Spectrum: Diversity in Hunter-Gatherer Lifeways*. Washington: Smithsonian Institution Press.

Kent, S. 1991. Cause and effect of dental health, diet, and status among foragers. *American Anthropologist* 92: 942–943.

Klein, R. 1995. Anatomy, behavior, and modern human origins. *Journal of World Prehistory* 9: 167–198.

Klein, R. 2000. Archaeology and the evolution of human behavior. *Evolutionary Anthropology* 9: 17–36.

Knauft, B. 1994. Reply (to Erdal and Whiten). *Current Anthropology* 35: 181–182.

Knauft, B. 1991. Violence and sociality in human evolution. *Current Anthropology* 32: 391–428.

Kosse, K. 1990. Group size and societal complexity: thresholds in the long-term memory. *Journal of Anthropological Archaeology* 9: 275–303.

Kuhn, S., and Stiner, M. 2007. Body Ornamentation as Information Technology: Towards an Understanding of the Significance of Early Beads. In Mellars, P., Boyle, K., Bar-Yosef, O., and Stringer, C. (eds.), *Rethinking the Human Revolution: New Behavioral and Biological Perspectives on the Origins and Dispersal of Modern Humans*, pp. 15–20. Cambridge: MacDonald Institute Monographs.

Lee, R. 1981. Is there a foraging mode of production? *Canadian Journal of Anthropology* 2: 13–19.

Lieberman, M. 2008. Speculations about the selective basis for modern human craniofacial form. *Evolutionary Anthropology* 17: 55–68.

Marean, C., Bar-Matthews, M., Bernatchez, J., Fisher, E., Goldberg, P., Herries, A., Jacobs, Z., Jerardino, A., Karkanas, P., Minichillo, T., Nilssen, P., Thompson, E., Watts, I., and Williams, H. 2007. Early human use of marine resources and pigment in South Africa during the middle Pleistocene. *Nature* 449: 905–908.

Marmot, M. 2004. The *Status Syndrome: How Social Standing Affects Our Health and Longevity*. New York: Henry Holt and Company.

Maschner, H. 1991. The emergence of cultural complexity on the Northern Northwest Coast. *Antiquity* 65: 924–934.

Maschner, H., and Patton, J. 1996. Kin Selection and the Origins of Hereditary Social Inequality. In Maschner, H. (ed.), *Darwinian Archaeologies*, pp. 89–108. New York: Plenum Press.

Masters, R. 1991. Conclusion: Primate Politics and Political Theory. In Schubert, G. and Masters, R.D. (eds.), *Primate Politics*, pp. 221–250. Carbondale: Southern Illinois University Press.

McBrearty, S. 2007. Down with the Revolution. In Mellars, P., Boyle, K., Bar-Yosef, O., and Stringer, C. (eds.), *Rethinking the Human Revolution: New Behavioral and Biological Perspectives on the Origins and Dispersal of Modern Humans*, pp. 133–152. Cambridge: MacDonald Institute Monographs.

McBrearty, S., and Brooks, A. 2000. The revolution that wasn't: a new interpretation of the origin of modern human behaviour. *Journal of Human Evolution* 39: 453–563.

McGuire, R.L. 1983. Breaking Down Cultural Complexity: Inequality and Hetereogeneity. In Michael B.S. (ed.), *Advances in Archaeological Method and Theory*. vol. 6. Academic Press, New York.

Mellars, P. 2006. Why did modern human populations disperse from Africa ca. 60,000 years ago? A new model. *Proceedings of the National Academy of Sciences* 103: 9381–9386.

Mellars, P., Boyle, K., Bar-Yosef, O., and Stringer, C. (eds.). 2007. *Rethinking the Human Revolution: New Behavioral and Biological Perspectives on the Origin and Dispersal of Modern Humans*. Cambridge: MacDonald Institute Monographs.

Milliken, S. 2007. Neanderthals, anatomically modern humans, and 'modern human behaviour' in Italy. *Oxford Journal of Archaeology* 26: 331–358.

Moore, G. 1903. *Principia Ethica*. Cambridge: Cambridge University Press.

O'Connell, J.F., Hawkes, K., Lupo, K.D., and Blurton Jones, N.G. 2002. Male strategies and plio-pleistocene archaeology. *Journal of Human Evolution* 43: 831–872.

Olausson, D. 2008. Does practice make perfect? craft expertise as a factor in aggrandizer strategies. *Journal of Archaeological Method and Theory* 15: 28–50.

Pauketat, T.R. 2007. *Chiefdoms and Other Archaeological Delusions*. Lanham: Altamira Press.

Pavesic, M.G. 1992. Death and Dying in the Western Idaho Archaic. In Goldsmith, A.S., Garvis, S., Selin, D., and Smith, J. (eds.), *Ancient Thought: The Archaeology of Ideology*, pp. 289–293. Calgary: Department of Archaeology, University of Calgary.

Pavesic, M.G. 1985. Cache Blades and Turkey Tails: Piecing Together the Western Idaho Archaic Burial Complex. In Plew, M.G., Woods, J.C., and Pavesic, M.G. (eds.), *Stone Tool Analysis: Essays in Honor of Don E. Crabtree*, pp. 55–89. Albuquerque: University of New Mexico.

Pavesic, M.G., Miller, S.J., Gamel, P.A., and Green, T.J. 1993. DeMoss site: a material culture and faunal update. *Idaho Archaeologist* 16(1): 3–15.

Pettigrew, R.M., and Schalk, R.F. 1995. Site 35-JE-51B (The Johnson Site). *In* Schalk, R.F., Pettigrew, R.M., Lebow, C.G., Moratto, M.J., and Atwell, R.G. (eds.), *Archaeological Investigations PGT-PG&E Pipeline Expansion Project Idaho, Washington, Oregon, and*

California. Volume IIB, Book 1 of 2, Summary Reports: Prehistoric Sites Oregon, pp. 8-1–8-87, M. J. Moratto (general ed.). Fresno: INFOTEC Research, Inc.

Porter, C.C., and Marlowe, F.W. 2007. How marginal are forager habitats. *Journal of Archaeological Science* 34: 59–68.

Price, T.D. 1981. Complexity in "Non-complex" Societies. In Van der Leeuw, S.E. (ed.), *Archaeological Approaches to the Study of Complexity*, pp. 55–99. Amsterdam: Universiteit van Amsterdam.

Reid, K.C., and Chatters, J.C. 1997. *Kirkwood Bar: Passports in Time Excavations at 10IH699 in the Hells Canyon National Recreation Area, Wallowa-Whitman National Forest*. Rainshadow Research Project Report No. 28 & Applied Paleoscience Project Report No. F-6. Pullman: Wallowa-Whitman National Forest.

Rice, D.G. 1969. *Preliminary Report, Marmes Rockshelter Archaeological Site*. Pullman: Washington State University.

Richerson, P.J., and Boyd, R.T. 2005. Not By Genes Alone: How Culture Transformed Human Evolution. Chicago: The University of Chicago Press.

Richerson, P.J., and Boyd, R.T. 2001. The Evolution of Subjective Commitment of Groups: A Tribal Instincts Hypothesis. In Nesse, R.M. (ed.), *The Evolution of Commitment*, pp. 186–220. New York: Russel Sage Foundation.

Richerson, P.J., and Boyd, R.T. 1999. Complex societies: the evolutionary origins of a crude superorganism. *Human Nature* 10: 253–289.

Richerson, P.J., and Boyd, R.T. 1998. The Evolution of Human Ultra-sociality. In Eibl-Eibesfeldt, I. and Salter, F.K. (eds.), *Indoctrinability, Ideology and Warfare*, pp. 71–96. New York: Berghahn Books.

Richerson, P.J., Bettinger, R.L., and Boyd, R.T. 2005. Evolution on a Restless Planet: Were Environmental Variability and Environmental Change Major Drivers of Human Evolution? In Wuketits, F.M. and Ayala, F. (eds.), *Handbook of Evolution Volume 2: The Evolution of Living Systems (including Hominids)*, pp. 223–242. Weinheim: Willey—VCH Verlag GmbH & Co.

Richerson, P.J., Boyd, R.T., and Henrich, J. 2003. The Cultural Evolution of Human Cooperation. In Hammerstein, P. (ed.), *The Genetic and Cultural Evolution of Cooperation*, pp. 357–388. Cambridge: MIT Press.

Roberts, G. 1998. Competitive altruism: from reciprocity to the handicap principle. *Proceedings: Biological Sciences* 265(1394): 427–431.

Ruse, M. 2006. *Darwinism and Its Discontents*. Cambridge: Cambridge University Press.

Sapolsky, R.M. 2004. Social status and health in humans and other animals. *Annual Review of Anthropology* 33: 393–418.

Sassaman, K.E. 2006. Comment. *Current Anthropology* 47(1): 25–26.

Sassaman, K.E. 2004. Complex hunter-gatherers in evolution and history: a North American perspective. *Journal of Archaeological Research* 12: 227–280.

Sassaman, K.E., and Heckenberger, M.J. 2004. Crossing the Symbolic Rubicon in the Southeast. In Gibson, J.L. and Carr, P.J. (eds.), *Signs of Power: The Rise of Cultural Complexity in the Southeast*, pp. 214–233. Tuscaloosa: The University of Alabama Press.

Saunders, J. 2004. Are We Fixing to Make the Same Mistake Again? In Gibson, J.L. and Carr, P.J. (eds.), *Signs of Power: The Rise of Cultural Complexity in the Southeast*, pp. 146–161. Tuscaloosa: The University of Alabama Press.

Saunders, J.W., Mandel, R.D., Saucier, R.T., Allen, E.T., Hallmark, C.T., Johnson, J.K., Jackson, E.W., Allen, C.M., Stringer, G.L., Frink, D.S., Feathers, J.K., Williams, S., Gremillion, K.J., Vidrine, M.S., and Jones, R. 1997. A mound complex in Louisiana at 5400–5000 years before the present. *Science* 277: 1796–1799.

Schulting, R.J. 1995. *Mortuary Variability and Status Differentiation on the Columbia-Fraser Plateau*. Burnaby: Archaeology Press.

Smith, E.A. 2004. Why do good hunters have higher reproductive success? *Human Nature* 15: 343–364.

Smith, E.A., and Choi, J.-K. 2007. The Emergence of Inequality in Small-Scale Societies: Simple Scenarios and Agent-Based Simulations. In Kohler, T.A. and Van der Leeuw, S.E. (eds.), *Model-Based Archaeology of Socionatural Systems*, pp. 105–120. Sante Fe: SAR Press.

Soffer, O. 1985. *The Upper Paleolithic of the Central Russian Plain*. Orlando: Academic Press.

Speth, J.D. 1990. Seasonality, resource stress, and food sharing in so-called "Egalitarian" foraging societies. *Journal of Anthropological Archaeology* 9(2): 148–188.

Sugiyama, L.S., and Sugiyama, M.S. 2003. Social roles, prestige, and health risk: social niche specialization as a risk-buffering strategy. *Human Nature* 14: 165–190.

Suttles, W. 1960. Affinal ties, subsistence, and prestige among the coast salish. *American Anthropologist* 62: 296–305.

Trigger, B.G. 2003. *Understanding Early Civilizations: A Comparative Study*. Cambridge: Cambridge University Press.

Trigger, B.G. 1998. Archaeology and epistemology: dialoguing across the Darwinian chasm. *American Journal of Archaeology* 102: 1–34.

Trigger, B.G. 1991. Distinguished lecture in archaeology: constraint and freedom—A new synthesis for archaeological explanation. *American Anthropologist* 93: 551–569.

Vanhaeren, M., and d'Errico, F. 2005. Grave goods from the saint-germain-la-riviere burial. *Journal of Anthropological Archaeology* 24: 117–134.

Vanhaeren, M., d'Errico, F., Stringer, C., James, S.L., Todd, J.A., and Mienis, H.K. 2006. Middle paleolithic shell beads in Israel and Algeria. *Science* 312: 1785–1788.

Wadley, L. 2001. What is cultural modernity? A general view and a South African perspective from Rose Cottage Cave. *Cambridge Archaeological Journal* 11: 201–221.

Walker, P.L., and Hewlett, B.S. 1990. Dental health and social status among Central African foragers and farmers. *American Anthropologist* 92: 383–398.

Wason, P.K. 1994. *The Archaeology of Rank*. Cambridge: Cambridge University Press.

Watts, I. 2002. Ochre in the middle stone age of Southern Africa: ritualized display or hide preservative. *South African Archaeological Bulletin* 57: 1–14.

Wiessner, P. 2002. The vines of complexity. *Current Anthropology* 41(2): 233–269.

Wiessner, P. 1996a. Introduction: Food, Status, Culture, and Nature. In Wiessner, P. and Schiefenhovel, W. (eds.), *Food and the Status Quest: An Interdisciplinary Perspective*, pp. 1–18. Providence: Berghahn Books.

Wiessner, P. 1996b. Leveling the Hunter: Constraints on the Status Quest in Foraging Societies. In Wiessner, P. and Schiefenhovel, W. (eds.), *Food and the Status Quest: An Interdisciplinary Perspective*, pp. 171–191. Providence: Berghahn Books.

Wilmsen, E.N. 1989. *Land Filled With Flies: A Political Economy of the Kalahari*. Chicago: University of Chicago Press.

Wobst, H.M. 1977. Stylistic Behavior and Information Exchange. In Cleland, C.E. (ed.), *Papers for the Director: Research Essays in Honor of James B. Griffin*, pp. 317–342, Anthropological Papers no 61. Ann Arbor: Museum of Anthropology, University of Michigan.

Woodburn, J. 1982. Egalitarian societies. *Man (NS)* 17: 431–451.

Wynn, T., and Coolidge, F.L. 2003. The role of working memory in the evolution of managed foraging. *Before Farming: The Archaeology and Anthropology of Hunter-Gatherers (Online)* 2: 1–16.

Yoffee, N. 1993. Too Many Chiefs? (or Safe Texts for the '90s). In Yoffee, N. and Sharrett, A. (eds.), *Archaeological Theory: Who Sets the Agenda*, pp. 60–78. Cambridge: Cambridge University Press.

Yohe, R.M.I., and Pavesic, M.G. 2000. Early Domestic Dogs from Western Idaho. In Crockford, S.J. (ed.), *Dogs Through Time: An Archaeological Perspective*, pp. 93–104, BAR International Series 889. Oxford: Archaeopress.

Zilhao, J. 2007. The emergence of ornaments and art: an archaeological perspective on the origins of "behavioral modernity". *Journal of Archaeological Research* 15: 1–54.

Chapter 3
Degrees and Kinds of Inequality

Robert D. Drennan, Christian E. Peterson, and Jake R. Fox

Much recent archaeological literature has stressed the variety of forms that early non-egalitarian societies may take. This variety has been characterized as "horizontal" variation (Drennan 1996, Feinman 2000) in contrast to the "vertical" dimension of social ranking most emphasized in the traditional cultural evolutionary literature. Much of cultural evolutionary thinking has, of course, a strongly unilineal character, and refocusing on horizontal variation has enabled fuller recognition of the very multilineal character of the emergence of hierarchical societies. This has provided much richer views of the origin and development of hierarchical societies. At the same time, however, it has made dealing with the vertical dimension considerably more complicated.

The distinction between corporate and network modes of organization (Blanton et al. 1996), for example, has been described as a horizontal axis that crosscuts the vertical dimension of increasing hierarchy (Feinman 2000). The classic archaeological manifestations of institutionalized social inequality, such as burials with impressive offerings, elaborate residences for leaders, etc., are specifically connected with the network mode, while the alternate corporate mode is said to be just as hierarchical but leaves much less conspicuous archaeological evidence. This concept has been offered, for example, as a resolution to the debate over just how hierarchical Puebloan societies were. The absence of conspicuous signs of social ranking has been taken to indicate, not an absence of hierarchical organization, but rather fully developed hierarchical organization of the less obvious corporate sort (Earle 2001, Feinman 2000). This does provide a way of reconciling seemingly contradictory evidence about the degree of hierarchy represented by Puebloan societies, but, finally, it begs the question of just how hierarchical these societies were.

Rautman (1998) offers another solution to the problem of how complex Puebloan societies were. She suggests that they were heterarchical, and that this characterization obviates the question about hierarchy. She is explicit in arguing that it is misguided, not only to pose the question as a dichotomy—a choice between

R.D. Drennan (✉)
Department of Anthropology, University of Pittsburgh, Pittsburgh, PA, USA
e-mail: drennan@pitt.edu

T.D. Price, G.M. Feinman (eds.), *Pathways to Power*, Fundamental
Issues in Archaeology, DOI 10.1007/978-1-4419-6300-0_3,
© Springer Science+Business Media, LLC 2010

egalitarian and hierarchical—but even to attempt to position a society along a continuum between the two extremes. She advocates discarding the question of how hierarchical they were and focusing instead on qualitatively different forms of complex organization. By identifying Puebloan societies as heterarchical, she lays aside the notion of hierarchy, moving in what seems the opposite direction from the corporate/network scheme. The corporate/network approach to Puebloan societies makes them no less hierarchical than other agreed-upon examples of complex societies, but only less recognizably so because of the less conspicuous corporate form of their hierarchy. Rautman makes them no less complex but not hierarchical at all. And finally McGuire and Saitta (1996; Saitta and McGuire 1998), to whose initial paper Rautman's was a reaction, also makes Puebloan societies complex, but both hierarchical *and* egalitarian.

All these approaches avoid imagined implications of inferiority from ranking Puebloan societies "lower" on a scale of either hierarchy or complexity than some others. They shift our attention from scales of measurement to qualitative and even typological differences, according Puebloan societies a "separate but equal" status. It is undeniably true that recognizing such differences in forms of organization is essential to understanding the developmental dynamics of the societies involved. Such recognition, however, must not come at the expense of addressing the very real differences in degrees of complexity and hierarchy to be observed among prehistoric societies. Efforts to study the emergence and development of social hierarchy in comparative perspective demand consistent ways not only of distinguishing between different kinds of hierarchy but also of assessing differences in the degree of hierarchy. Our aim in this paper is to experiment with means of comparing both kinds and degrees of hierarchy in early complex societies. The cases we compare are mostly chosen from those that might be described as chiefdoms—at least if we take an extremely broad definition of "chiefdom"—but we have sought to include a substantial amount of variety so as to put some minimally hierarchical or even non-hierarchical societies alongside agreed-upon "classic" chiefdoms or even "paramount" chiefdoms. The variety we examine here falls into three categories of evidence: burials, household artifact assemblages, and public works.

Burial Evidence

Burials are, of course, the archetypal if controversial source of archaeological information about social ranking (Binford 1971, Brown 1981, Cannon 1989, Carr 1995, Hodder 1982, O'Shea 1984, Parker Pearson 1999, Saxe 1970, Tainter 1978). This fundamental idea has been deeply imbedded in archaeological interpretation since long before even the term "social ranking" became popular, and the general principle that mortuary differences reflect social differences remains sound. Here we take a bottom-up approach beginning with empirical archaeological observations.

Sitio Conte in central Panama is a classic case of elaborate burials taken to indicate social differentiation from the time of their initial discovery (Hearne and

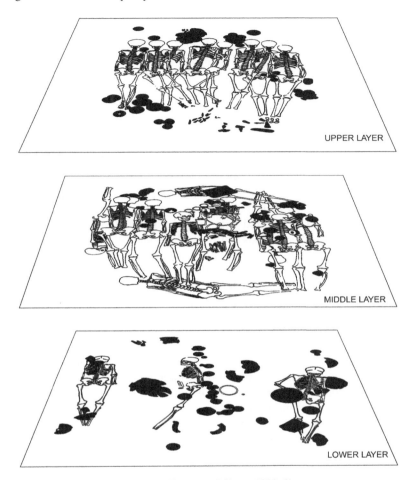

Fig. 3.1 Burial 11 at Sitio Conte (after Hearne and Sharer 1992: 9)

Sharer 1992, University of Pennsylvania Museum Archives 1999). These remarkable graves date to between AD 400 and 900. The most elaborate, No. 11, consisted of a circular pit 3 m across and 4 m deep. It contained a total of 23 adult skeletons, mostly males, deposited in three layers (Fig. 3.1). The most spectacular grave goods were of gold, including, according to the field notes, at least 8 plaques over 20 cm in diameter; 10 cuffs, wristlets, and anklets; 91 ear and nose ornaments; 57 bells; 3,089 beads; 153 other ornaments; 16 chisels; and 65 figures of wood, bone, or resin inlaid with gold. Also found in the grave were 121 monochrome and 32 polychrome ceramic vessels; 163 celts and adzes; 20 bone points; 1,584 flaked stone points; 2 copper ornaments; teeth of rabbit, dog, shark, and whale; feline claws; stingray spines; and 1 ceramic whistle. So much of the gold was associated with the central skeleton in the middle layer that this is taken to be the principal individual interred. It has been speculated that the other 22 individuals were purposely killed in order to accompany the principal individual in death.

Pueblo Bonito, in Colorado's Chaco Canyon, has been at the heart of much debate about hierarchy in the Puebloan Southwest (see, for example, Cameron and Toll 2001)—debate which sometimes seems to have become quite disconnected from the empirical evidence. Pueblo Bonito's richest burial was excavated in the early twentieth century (Akins 2001, Pepper 1920). Two adult men (burials 13 and 14) were laid on a layer of clean sand and wood ash beneath a plank floor in Room 33 of the great house itself. The skeleton of Burial 14 showed evidence of a violent death. Associated with this individual were a total of 13,861 beads (mostly turquoise, but also shell and stone), 632 pendants and other ornamental items (again mostly of turquoise), 1 red stone and 4 jet inlays, 41 shell bracelets, 1 shell trumpet, 2 baskets covered with turquoise mosaics, and a few other items. Burial 13 had a total of 5,893 beads and 14 pendants and larger ornaments. Arranged around the two individuals beneath the plank floor were an additional 1,822 beads, pendants, and other ornamental pieces (mostly turquoise), 43 pieces of malachite, 3 reed arrows, 1 bone bracelet, 1 shell bracelet, 1 jet inlay, and 2 ceramic vessels. The disarticulated remains of 14 or 15 other individuals (men, women, and at least one infant, who may have been sacrificed) were found above the plank floor, along with 14 ceramic vessels, 26,976 turquoise and shell beads, 963 pendants and other ornaments (mostly turquoise), 1,052 pieces of turquoise mosaic, 198 other shell ornaments and pieces of worked shell, 173 inlays of jet and stone, 1 jet ring, and 2 iron pyrite ornaments. In any context other than the US Southwest, the presence of such burials would immediately be taken to indicate substantial social inequality. Such an interpretation might well be incorrect for Pueblo Bonito, but any comparative analysis must depart from a recognition that burials with lavish offerings are not absent from Pueblo Bonito.

Elaborate burials at the Middle Formative (800–400 BC) Olmec center of La Venta on Mexico's southern Gulf Coast, like those of Sitio Conte, suggest the presence of powerful leaders. Several monumental tombs were excavated in a complex of plazas and platforms extending some 400 m north to south (Drucker 1952, Drucker et al. 1959). The highest platform at the southern extreme of the complex was over 30 m in height. Two smaller mounds located along the complex's central axis rose 3 or 4 m above the surrounding plaza. Under one of these smaller mounds was a tomb built of 44 natural basalt columns 2–3 m long (Fig. 3.2, top). Above the stone slab floor of the tomb were two bundle burials coated with red cinnabar pigment. One bundle contained two jade figurines, one jade pendant, five jade beads, five other small jade decorative objects, two polished obsidian disks, and a hematite mirror. The other bundle contained two jade figurines, four jade beads, six other small decorative jade objects, one shark tooth, one jade stingray spine, and a number of real stingray spines. Under the other of the two smaller mounds was a tomb measuring 5 × 2 m with floor, walls, and roof made of dressed sandstone slabs (Fig. 3.2, bottom). In the center of the tomb was a thick bed of cinnabar in a roughly elliptical shape about 2 m long and 1 m wide. Beneath the cinnabar were a jade

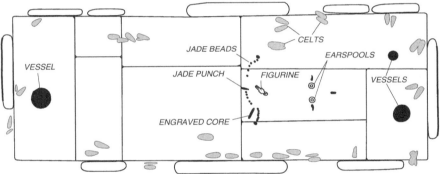

Fig. 3.2 Columnar basalt tomb (*top*, as removed and reconstructed out of context) and sandstone slab tomb (*bottom*, after Drucker 1952: 69) at La Venta

tube, 2 incised jade earspools with pendants, and 110 tiny jade beads, pendants, and other objects, all polished and perforated as for sewing onto clothing. These objects clearly indicated the central extended burial of a single individual of whose skeletal remains no trace was preserved in the acidic soils. A serpentine figurine with obsidian insets for eyes, a jade punch, an incised obsidian core, a curved line of 64 jade beads, and a jade turtle carapace completed the accouterments of this central burial. Further scattered around this individual were 28 jade and 9 serpentine celts, as well as 3 elaborate ceramic vessels. At least three other only slightly less impressively furnished tombs were located along the central axis of the complex.

Tomb construction as well as grave goods at La Venta represent a remarkable quantity of resources invested in burial ritual—although perhaps not quite as remarkable as the most elaborate known burials at either Sitio Conte or Pueblo

Bonito. Clearly, only a very few individuals in any society could receive such elaborate burial treatment, and both sets of burials have long been cited as spectacular archaeological indicators of early chiefly power. The nature of this power may not be entirely clear, but one cannot escape concluding that these two societies featured dramatic social inequalities.

In Colombia's Alto Magdalena, during the Regional Classic period (AD 1–800), important people were buried in monumental tombs covered with earthen mounds up to perhaps 5 m in height (Duque and Cubillos 1979, 1983). The tomb chambers for principal individuals, placed at the centers of their mounds, measured up to about 2 by 3 m and were constructed of large stone slabs; occasionally, designs painted on the slabs are preserved. Sometimes bodies were placed in rough stone sarcophagi. Smaller tombs were placed in non-central locations in the mounds as well as in the areas around the mounds. Statues, sometimes over 2 m high, and often depicting obviously supernatural themes, accompanied these central burials (Fig. 3.3). While architecturally and sculpturally elaborate, these tombs appear not to have contained such rich offerings as those already described. It is difficult to be certain, because the largest known monumental tombs had been excavated by looters before archaeologists were able to record information about them, but an intact subsidiary tomb chamber in one quite substantial mound was accompanied by one small statue and contained two small beads in the form of fish covered with gold, another fish-shaped bead without gold covering, one tubular stone bead, several tiny gold beads, and one polishing stone. The general pattern for the Alto Magdalena does seem to involve fairly small amounts of grave goods. Relatively large slab tombs found intact consistently have offerings limited to a maximum of three or four ceramic vessels, polished stone celts, beads, and a few very small gold ornaments; some apparently intact slab tombs have no goods at all. Investment of resources in the burials of important people in the Alto Magdalena clearly was less than at Sitio Conte or La Venta and probably Pueblo Bonito. The investment in the Alto Magdalena was concentrated largely in architecture and sculpture; even

Fig. 3.3 Alto Magdalena tomb (Mesita A)

the most elaborate tomb chambers appear to have contained offerings representing only a tiny fraction of the investment in grave goods seen in some La Venta, Sitio Conte, or Pueblo Bonito graves. The same kinds of modest offerings are also sometimes found with burials in the Alto Magdalena that have little in the way of formal tomb architecture, are not within mounds, and have no association with sculpture. It is, then, the monumental architectural and sculptural elaboration of their tombs, not the kind or quantity of grave goods, which distinguishes a very small group of especially important individuals from the rest of the population of the Alto Magdalena.

The western Liao Valley of northeastern China was home to the Hongshan "culture" between 4500 and 3000 BC, and, like some of the regions discussed thus far, is famous precisely for its burials and associated architecture and artifacts (Childs-Johnson 1991, Guo 1995, 2005). The burials that have attracted most attention were dug into the fill of platforms 1–3 m high. Platforms often had a central burial in a stone-lined cist roughly 1 by 2 m and up to 5 m deep; as many as 27 other cists were sometimes arranged around the central burial. The construction of a single platform could incorporate hundreds of bottomless painted pottery cylinders 20–50 cm in diameter and up to 1 m high. The signature offerings in these burials were carved and incised jades, often representing animals and supernatural themes (Fig. 3.4). They came in the form of plaques as much as 20 cm across, smaller figures, bracelets, pendants, earrings, discs, tubes, and beads. The two known graves with the most abundant jade artifacts contained 20 and 15, respectively. Like the individuals buried in monumental tombs in the Alto Magdalena, those in platforms with jade objects in the western Liao Valley represent a very small group of important people, sharply set off from the rest of society. For the western Liao, though, the distinction is marked not only by tomb architecture but also by the kinds of offerings. Non-platform graves do not include carved jades, except for a very occasional bead or ornament. Instead, grave goods consist primarily of utilitarian objects of

Fig. 3.4 Location of Hongshan central tomb in platform in the western Liao Valley (Niuheliang Locality 2)

kinds virtually never found in platform burials (Guo 1997). These include coarse cooking pots, finer serving vessels, lithic cores, flake tools, axes, chisels, plows, shovels, grinding stones, bone tools, and shell ornaments. A "rich" grave in this group might include as many as a dozen artifacts of this sort in a stone cist; many are simple earthen pits containing no goods at all.

Like other Mississippian societies in the southeastern US (and continuing along the lines of the discussion above), Moundville is especially well known for elaborate burials placed in earthen mounds, dating primarily between AD 1300 and 1450. The collection of mounds at Moundville served both residential and burial functions; two mounds, in particular, have been described as the burial places of "paramount chiefs" (Knight and Steponaitis 1998). These mounds, at about 5 m high, were not the largest mounds at the site, but between them, they contained nearly 100 burials, including the most richly furnished ones (Peebles 1974). The individuals buried in mounds are taken, as a group, to represent the Moundville elite, but, unlike La Venta, the Alto Magdalena, or Hongshan, principal individuals are not sharply set off in each mound by central location and elaborate stone tomb construction. "The Great Chief of Mound C," as the individual in one of these burials was labeled in a magazine article at the turn of the twentieth century (Knight and Steponaitis 1998: 18), was buried with a copper axe, bracelets and anklets of copper-covered beads (61 altogether), three sheet-copper gorgets, a sheet-copper hair ornament with a bison-horn pin, an amethyst human head pendant, and a pearl necklace. This set of grave goods clearly represents an investment of resources far less than that required for the extravagant offerings in Burial 11 at Sitio Conte or Burials 13 and 14 at Pueblo Bonito; it is nonetheless worth noting that materials obtained from long distances away were used for all the artifacts included in this burial from Moundville Mound C.

Most Early and Middle Formative period (1500–500 BC) burials in the Valley of Oaxaca, in the southern highlands of Mexico, occurred in and around the residences of the deceased (Drennan 1976, Flannery and Marcus 2005, Whalen 1981). None were distinguished as burial monuments in any way, and few contained many offerings. The most elaborate burial known was that of a 60-year-old woman buried with 4 ceramic vessels and 55 polished stone beads (Fig. 3.5). This burial was not at the principal regional central place of San José Mogote, but rather at the small peripheral village of Fábrica San José. It is conceivable that more elaborate burials at San José Mogote were destroyed when a central portion of the site was extensively reconstructed about 600 BC; at least one burial dating to after this time was placed in a shallow stone-lined grave, a practice that had not previously existed, but the small size of this grave (1.3 by 0.5 m) would not have allowed for the inclusion of very many offerings. While the woman from Fábrica San José probably does not represent the very highest ranking members of Middle Formative society in the Valley of Oaxaca, it is unlikely that any higher ranking people were much more elaborately buried.

These last four examples, taken together (Alto Magdalena, western Liao, Moundville, and Oaxaca), form a group where "elite" burials are readily recognizable, but contained far less elaborate offerings than those of Sitio Conte, Pueblo

Fig. 3.5 Middle Formative
burial from Oaxaca (Burial
39 at Fábrica San José)

Bonito, or La Venta. As with Sitio Conte, Pueblo Bonito, and La Venta, it is difficult to reconcile the burial data for the Alto Magdalena, Hongshan, Moundville, and Oaxaca with any suggestion that these societies lacked social hierarchy. At least as far as the mortuary manifestation of such hierarchy is concerned, however, elites in these latter four cases would not seem to have been as dramatically set off from other people as in the Sitio Conte, Pueblo Bonito, and La Venta examples.

We conclude this review of an array of burial practices with two examples usually taken to show very little reflection in mortuary custom of social differentiation. Jenné-Jeno in the Middle Niger was (around AD 800) a settlement with a large and compact enough population that it has often been called "urban" (McIntosh and McIntosh 1993, McIntosh 2005). Burial practices were complicated, frequently involving cremation, interment in arrangements of multiple ceramic vessels, and secondary burial (McIntosh 1995: 353). There is, however, little about the variation in burial practice to suggest social ranking. The large ceramic burial urns represent a certain amount of investment, but their use is not restricted to a selected few burials, making them poor markers of special elite status. Apart from the ceramic containers, offerings are extremely scarce; two burials, each with two iron bracelets, are reported (McIntosh 1995: 66). Iron was undoubtedly a valuable material at Jenné-Jeno, but it was widely used for tools and weapons—more so, in fact, than for ornamental purposes, although bracelets occurred in a number of residential contexts. These bracelets, then, seem not to mark the burials of elites strongly set off from the rest of the population. The Wankarani complex of the Bolivian altiplano (1800 BC–AD 200), in sharp contrast to the large and compact settlement at Jenné-Jeno, consisted of extremely small compact villages (Ponce 1970). Burial practices did have their complexities, with cemeteries at Chuquiña, for example, apparently separated by sex (Estévez and Bermann 1996, 1997, Fox 2007, Fox et al. 2004). No more elaborate offerings, however, are known than a single, whole, utilitarian olla at the head, as occurred in two burials at Pusno (Fox 2007).

Both Wankarani and Middle Niger societies have been characterized as lacking social hierarchy, and there is certainly nothing in the burial evidence to suggest much ranking. Simple inhumations in pits without any offerings at all are the least elaborate burials for all seven regions previously described, and this marks the zero point from which the distance to the most elaborate known burials has been assessed. The most elaborate known Wankarani burials represent only the most trivial departure from this zero point. While Middle Niger burials as a group may represent more investment than Wankarani ones, only the most minimal social differentiation could be argued from them. A region or period that produces a very homogeneous set of burials, of course, might nonetheless possess hierarchical social organization, even though it was not expressed in mortuary practice. It might be expressed in such evidence as household artifact assemblages, to which we turn in a later section.

Burials and Social Inequality

The burial practices reviewed above, then, clearly represent varying degrees of inequality of investment in funerary ritual. In the organization of these descriptions we began with three cases where such inequality seems quite pronounced, continued with four where inequality was unmistakable but not as dramatic, and finished with two where little inequality at all was recognizable. This, then, comprises a scale of high, medium, and low inequality of investment in burial ritual. A scale consisting only of high, medium, and low is obviously a blunt instrument of measurement, but it is nonetheless an instrument of measurement, and not as blunt a one as a dichotomy. The path toward a more precise and refined scale of measurement is not, in principle, particularly complicated. Its inspiration is in a common way of measuring economic inequalities in modern societies. In 1968, for example, the richest 5% of households in the United States collected 16.6% of the country's total income. It is taken as a substantial increase in income inequality that by 1998 the top 5% had increased its share of the total income to 21.4% (Jones and Weinberg 2000). In similar fashion, one could calculate what proportion of total investment in mortuary equipment was lavished on the most elaborate 5% of the graves. This would require a good sample of burials, but this already exists for at least some cases. At Moundville, for example, over 2,000 burials have been excavated, and those usually classified as "elite" (because they are in or near mounds and contain artifacts made of exotic imported materials) comprise about 5% of the population. Approximations of the amount of labor expended in acquiring exotic raw materials, manufacturing goods, and constructing mounds could be made so as to calculate what proportion of the total effort was represented by the top 5% of burials.

The proportional distribution of investment in burial equipment we have focused on could be assessed more comprehensively and precisely with the Gini coefficient, as has, in fact, previously been suggested for archaeological applications by McGuire (1983) and Smith (1987). Our characterization of burial investment amounts to a rough Gini coefficient: it would be accurate to say that, as far as investment in burial is concerned, the Gini coefficient of inequality for Sitio Conte, Pueblo Bonito, and La Venta seems high; that for the Alto Magdalena, the western Liao Valley, Moundville, and the Valley of Oaxaca is medium; and that for Wankarani and the Middle Niger is low. The burial sample for Moundville would permit calculation of the actual value of this Gini coefficient, but this seems unnecessary, at least for present purposes. Our real interest here is in degrees of social inequality, and inequality of investment in burial is, at best, a rough indicator of social inequality. Investing considerable effort in exact measurement of a rough indicator seems likely to produce only false precision. For now, then, it seems sufficient to conclude that burial investment suggests some considerable differences in the degree of social inequality shown in these societies. These differences occur not only between societies that might be called "egalitarian" and "ranked;" there are also substantial differences in degree of inequality among "rank societies" or "chiefdoms." Some seem, at least on the basis of burial investment, considerably more hierarchical than others, and one of the members of the top rank in this comparison (Pueblo Bonito) has often been considered non-hierarchical or "essentially egalitarian" (Renfrew 2001: 14).

In seeking to clarify differences in degree of hierarchy we by no means aim to diminish the importance of investigating different forms or aspects of hierarchy. The goal we pursue is, instead, to weave together analyses of degrees and kinds of inequality. It is useful to begin that effort with the same line of evidence we have just been using: burials. Burials have figured prominently in identifying the opposing extremes of some popular dichotomies of kinds of social organization. It is burials focused on glorifying particular individuals and their exalted social positions that are most often the evidence cited for a strongly developed "network" mode of organization (as opposed to a "corporate" one). This way of using the evidence reduces the corporate/network concept from a package of interrelated variables to nothing more than Renfrew's (1974) distinction between individualizing and group-oriented societies. Since nothing more than this is really often meant when the terms "corporate" and "network" are used, and since this is the concept we would like to focus on in any event, we just use Renfrew's terms instead. The burial practices in the nine examples we have discussed can also be ordered with regard to how strongly individualizing these societies were.

The burial monuments of the Alto Magdalena show a strong and very public focus on particular individuals. The burial mounds occur in clusters in a number of locations on the landscape, associated with monumental sculpture but no other monumental architecture. It is the burial monuments themselves that are the raison d'être for these complexes, with the consequence that the ritual spaces created are single-mindedly focused on constructions whose whole purpose is the veneration of specific individuals. Sitio Conte represents a similarly strong focus on individuals, although in a different and less permanently visible form. Although multiple individuals were involved in the lavish burials of Sitio Conte, in each case one principal individual is easily distinguished as the central focus of the entire ritual, a ritual for which the other individuals may actually have been sacrificed. Hongshan ritual spaces in the western Liao Valley, like those in the Alto Magdalena, are organized around what are specifically burial monuments with principal individuals. The burials at Moundville are, of course, also of important individuals, but the overall monumental design of the ritual space emphasizes the position of the elite group as a whole more strongly than of particular individuals. Mounds C and D contained the burials identified as most elite, but neither mound had a central principal burial nor any particular one or few that stood strongly apart from the others in terms of offerings. Other mounds were largely residential in function. As impressive as the burials of important individuals at La Venta were, they formed only a minor constituent of a massive complex of temples, platforms, plazas, and non-mortuary offerings. The burials of important people were incorporated into the complex but were not the focus of its design. Some of the monumental sculpture, however, did memorialize particular individuals. Pueblo Bonito's most elaborate burial was integrated into the great house, and not as conspicuously monumental as some of the other cases. We might rank these six societies roughly in this order from more to less individualizing, but particular leaders of some sort were strongly present in all six.

Whatever the nature of leadership in the other three cases was, it was much more "faceless and anonymous" (Renfrew 1974). Formative Oaxaca elite burials were usually associated with residences; they were not monumental or visible. Essentially the same can be said for all Middle Niger burials. Wankarani burials were grouped in cemeteries, but again did not involve permanent visible monuments. It is collective social groups that were emphasized in all three cases rather than outstanding individuals. Thus these three cases would score low on an individualizing society dimension; that is, they are at the group-oriented end of this dimension.

Ranking these nine cases in terms of their individualizing tendencies produces a ranking similar to the previous ranking according to degree of social hierarchy as inferred from burial evidence. This is not surprising given that both are based on burial evidence. The corporate/network or individualizing/group-oriented dimension has been posed as a variable independent of and cross-cutting degree of hierarchy (Feinman 2000). But it may not be as easy to separate individualizing tendencies from social ranking as the archaeological literature sometimes would lead us to believe. This is partly a problem of archaeological evidence, and partly one of conceptual overlap. Strongly developed hierarchy is likely to bring individuals strongly to the fore, because it is individuals or their immediate families that are very often the social units ranked. Individualizing tendencies often seem weak precisely because social hierarchies are not much developed. Among these cases, Pueblo Bonito's richest burial suggests considerable social inequality, but Pueblo Bonito has often been considered less individualizing than conventionally recognized strongly hierarchical cases. It is no coincidence that this case has been especially controversial in this regard. The application of the "corporate" label to it (Earle 2001, Feinman 2000, Peregrine 2001) tends to obscure the remarkable richness of these burials; it also ignores the fact that many of these goods were long-distance imports. The minimal monumental commemoration of individual burials, however, precludes calling it "network." Dealing adequately with non-individualizing hierarchies thus requires considering different aspects of hierarchy and looking at evidence other than burials.

Household Evidence

While archaeologists have not been analyzing household artifact assemblages for as long as they have paid attention to burials, such analysis has become relatively common practice. The differences between the assemblages of artifacts recovered from different household units are taken to reflect differences in social status, wealth, and economic and other activities (Hirth 1993, Smith 1987). Some of these things, of course, are also reflected in burials, as discussed above. Individuals, however, the epitome of burial analysis, are virtually invisible in household artifact assemblages. The artifact assemblages in household garbage, on the other hand, are much more directly connected to the differing patterns of family life. In contrast to the momentary symbolic statement made by burial ritual, household garbage is not itself a symbolic statement at all, and offers the possibility of time averaging that can facilitate reconstruction of long-term patterns. Analysis of household assemblages requires a substantial sample of households from a community, since the objective is to delineate the similarities and differences between roughly contemporaneous households that interacted with each other over a span of generations. Such similarities and differences cannot be adequately identified in a sample of two or three households. To the extent possible, in the analyses whose results are presented below, we have sought samples of artifacts from archaeological contexts that can reliably be interpreted as household garbage—that is, midden deposits. Such samples of artifacts can be large enough for statistical analysis and are more likely to accurately represent the average run of garbage produced by a household than, for example, the artifacts recovered from house floor contexts. It is not necessary that the remains of house structures be associated with such midden deposits, only that they be recognizable as domestic refuse and that there be sufficient spatial separation between samples to assure that they were produced by different households. It follows that even the fieldwork of excavators unconcerned with the identification of household units may well produce suitable samples of artifacts. Under some conditions, such samples can even come from surface collections.

   The results of household artifact assemblage analysis for five of the nine societies whose burials were discussed above are presented in Fig. 3.6. The variables in each

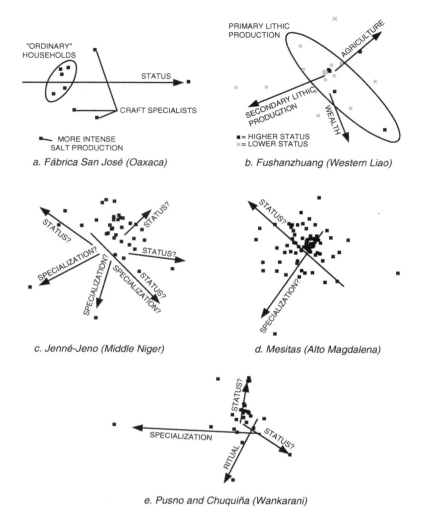

a. Fábrica San José (Oaxaca)

b. Fushanzhuang (Western Liao)

c. Jenné-Jeno (Middle Niger)

d. Mesitas (Alto Magdalena)

e. Pusno and Chuquiña (Wankarani)

Fig. 3.6 Multidimensional scaling plots of household artifact assemblages. Each square represents an individual household (or at least a specific location in a residential zone)

of the five analyses are counts of artifacts and ecofacts, expressed as percentages or ratios to compensate for differing sample sizes. Artifact and ecofact numbers were summed for a number of separately excavated archaeological contexts, providing good-sized samples that gave an aggregate view of the domestic activities in a particular set of locations in a community, averaged over time. The cases in the analyses, then, are those different locations in their respective communities, each taken to represent a particular household (or perhaps a few adjacent ones). For each of the five analyses, similarities were measured between each such "household" and each of the others in the data set, using Euclidean distance on standardized variables. The Euclidean distances were the basis of a non-metric multidimensional scaling analysis. The plots in Fig. 3.6 are pairs of dimensions from the configurations produced by the scaling, chosen to show the patterns of relationships among household assemblages as clearly as possible. Points that are close together in the plots represent assemblages composed of very similar proportions of their constituent artifacts and ecofacts; those that are farther apart in the plots are assemblages with more strongly differing proportions. The interpretations concerning economic and other kinds of activities, as well as household status and wealth, are based on an examination of which variables (i.e. artifact types) the assemblages in particular parts of the plots have in common. For example, a region in a plot where all the assemblages have high proportions of spindle whorls, weaving tools, and bone needles presumably represents a concentration of textile work in these households. The artifact types and ecofacts that are the variables must, of course, be different for each of these regions, reflecting the very different archaeological records they present us with. We compare the analyses for different regions in regard to the kinds of patterns that can be recognized and the strength and clarity with which they emerge.

Fábrica San José was a Middle Formative village of only about a dozen households near the chiefly center of San José Mogote in the Valley of Oaxaca (Drennan 1976). The scaling of its household assemblages (Fig. 3.6a) shows a clear dimension related to social status and/or wealth. Households toward the right in the figure, culminating in one extreme case, have increasing proportions of decorated pottery, serving vessels, preferred foods such as deer meat, and other artifacts that can similarly be related to higher social standing or material well-being. Three households have high proportions of artifacts related to several kinds of craft production (bone awls and needles, shell debitage, etc). These three are all relatively highly ranked, suggesting a connection between these craft specialties and higher social standing. "Ordinary" households, without evidence of economic specialization, rank still lower, but the lowest ranking household of all is one with evidence of fairly intensive specialization in the production of salt from saline springs that emerge at the site. Both status/wealth and economic specialization are principles of differentiation between household assemblages at Fábrica San José that emerge clearly and strongly from the scaling analysis.

Fushanzhuang was the central community in a western Liao Valley polity, although a relatively small and peripheral one as Hongshan polities go. About 30 households were defined and artifact assemblages were recovered through intensive surface collection (Peterson 2006). The scaling of its household assemblages (Fig. 3.6b) shows specialization in the production of lithic tools and several households with particularly high proportions of tools related to agricultural production. Households separated from the main group toward the lower right in the scaling plot seem wealthier than others, as indicated by higher proportions of finer and better-finished ceramics. An additional dimension perpendicular to those shown in Fig. 3.6b distinguishes what appear to be higher status households, and these are represented as darker symbols in the figure. The wealthiest household is among the higher status ones, but overall there is no relationship between status and wealth, suggesting a social pattern in which status and wealth were two separate and unrelated dimensions of recognizable social ranking (Drennan and Peterson 2006).

Jenné-Jeno is a much larger community, with a population numbering well up into the thousands, the central place for its region in the Middle Niger. Excavation units scattered across the site provide samples of artifacts from different locations within it (McIntosh 1995). High proportions of artifacts that might well be related to status and/or wealth (metal ornaments, glass artifacts, figurines) do occur in certain assemblages. These high values do not, however, consistently lie in any particular direction in the scaling, but instead are scattered broadly across the upper right sector of Fig. 3.6c. Unlike other scalings, in which modest numbers of highly ranked households are separated from a larger cloud of more "ordinary" ones, this sector of the scaling consists of a large and relatively undifferentiated cloud of points, with a high value for one or another artifact type scattered here and there. Toward the lower left in Fig. 3.6c two assemblages are sharply set off from the pack. The high proportions that pull these two assemblages out in this way are crucibles and furnace fragments in one instance and spindle whorls and iron slag in the other. These are obviously all related to craft production, but the patterns of association are peculiar and ambiguous. It is not at all clear why one household should have especially high proportions of crucibles and furnace fragments but not slag, while the other presents the reverse pattern. Both have a high proportion of spindle whorls, which, while obviously not related to iron working, do reflect craft specialization. The closest thing to an overall trend through the scaling plot runs toward the lower right. The artifacts that occur in higher proportions toward the lower right are decorated pottery and iron implements. It is not clear whether this might relate to social standing or specialization or both. Various kinds of goods used at Jenné-Jeno require somewhat complicated technology for their manufacture (McIntosh 2005: 151–157). Some may have been brought from elsewhere, although clearly craft production occurred at Jenné-Jeno, especially iron working. Patterns of specialization in this production, however, do not emerge as strongly and clearly in the analysis of spatial variation in artifact assemblages at Jenné-Jeno as they did in the scalings of assemblages from other communities discussed above. The indications of social status and wealth are even less clear. Although the artifact assemblages contain artifact types often taken to indicate such things, a pattern of high values for several artifact types together does not coalesce. Nor is there any sign of a distinction between status and wealth as there was in the Fushanzhuang scaling.

Mesitas was a very dispersed community of around 70 households during the Regional Classic in the Alto Magdalena (González 2008). Several indicators of wealth or status (decorated pottery, plates, bowls, pendants) occur in higher proportions in households generally toward the upper left in the scaling plot (Fig. 3.6d), although the trends are not unequivocal. Toward the lower left are assemblages with higher proportions of sherd disks, flaked stone implements, polishers, and miscellaneous polished stone artifacts. All these things could be related to several kinds of craft specialization, although, again, the trends are equivocal.

The Wankarani household assemblages analyzed date to the Middle Formative, about 1100–300 BC, and come from excavation units scattered across two settlements (Pusno and Chuquiña) neither of which contained more than a handful of families (Fox 2007). As at Jenné-Jeno, artifacts possibly connected with status (decorated pottery, copper ornaments, bone spoons, shell and other ornaments, more desirable camelid meat portions) appear in higher proportions in different places at the right and at the top of the scaling plot (Fig. 3.6e). A substantial number of artifacts related to textile specialization (awls, needles, weaving tools, spindle whorls, sherd disks) have higher proportions at the left, although this pattern is produced almost exclusively by the one household that is widely separated from the others in this direction. The trend toward the bottom of the plot is a somewhat more general one, suggesting a concentration of ritual activities (ceramic trumpets, ceramic spoons, ceramic plaques, stone effigy heads). For Wankarani, status is highly ambiguous; textile specialization seems fairly clear, although represented essentially by a single household; the strongest trend in the scaling plot is probably increasing concentration of ritual activities toward the bottom.

These multidimensional scaling analyses of household assemblages, then, show differences between the communities analyzed in terms of the organization of status, wealth, and economic and ritual specialization. Fábrica San José shows the strongest and clearest patterns, even though it was only a small subsidiary community in its region. The patterns it shows, moreover, are those often taken as prototypical of chiefdoms: a single clear dimension of social ranking, unequivocal craft specialization, and a connection between the two in that most craft specialist households had relatively high status. At Fushanzhuang, several different kinds of productive specialization are clear but not as strongly developed as those of Fábrica San José. Two principal indicators of ranking show clear but separate trends to suggest two separate hierarchies, one of wealth and an uncorrelated one of social status. Wealth seems connected to specialization, but status does not. The patterns of community organization indicated for Fushanzhuang can thus be said to be qualitatively different from those at Fábrica San José. At the same time both specialization and ranking (in both its dimensions) at Fushanzhuang are quantitatively less strong. It is thus legitimate (and necessary for adequate comprehension) to identify Fábrica San José not only as differently developed but also as more developed than Fushanzhuang in terms of economic specialization and social hierarchy. Jenné-Jeno has by far the largest population of all five communities analyzed here, but household assemblages do not show any clear patterns of status or wealth differentiation, consistent with what has previously been written about it (McIntosh 2005). Both textile work and iron-making are clearly in evidence, although the artifact assemblage evidence of craft specialization must be counted as weaker than at the very small communities of Fábrica San José or Fushanzhuang. Specialization and social hierarchy are both present in the household assemblages from Mesitas, but they seem weakly developed, despite the impressive burials of the Alto Magdalena. This kind of surprise did not emerge from the household assemblage analysis for the two extremely small Wankarani communities; the weakness of evidence for social ranking in the artifact assemblages parallels the conclusion drawn from the burial evidence. At least one household, however, is very easy to identify as a locus of specialized craft, and ritual activities were also clearly more concentrated in some households than others.

For the Middle Niger and for Wankarani, then, the conclusions drawn about social ranking from the household assemblage analysis are exactly what the burial evidence would lead us to expect: there was little social hierarchy in either case. The implications of household assemblage analysis and the burial evidence also fit together well for Hongshan society. Household assemblages suggested two uncorrelated hierarchies: social status or prestige on the one hand and wealth or material well-being on the other. And there were fundamentally two (internally ranked) groups of rather different Hongshan burials—those in platforms with carved jades, and those in cemetery or residential contexts with varying amounts of mostly utilitarian goods (Guo 1997). The former burials may well correspond to the higher status but not especially wealthy households identified in the artifact assemblage analysis; the latter burials, to the wealthier but not especially high-status households (Drennan and Peterson 2006). Both burials and household assemblages, then, suggest a fairly complex pattern of ranking in Hongshan society involving the two separate and uncorrelated dimensions of status and wealth. The Alto Magdalena and Oaxaca cases, however, are somewhat surprising; the household assemblage analysis seems to contradict the burial evidence. The monumental burials of the Alto Magdalena are the epitome of archaeological evidence for social hierarchy, but the household assemblages show very little such differentiation. Rather than being a contradiction, however, what this situation suggests is that the social hierarchy of the Alto Magdalena was one of status or prestige, without implications for wealth accumulation or differences in standard of living. In effect, the Alto Magdalena appears to have a system of social ranking that resembles the social status system of Hongshan society, but without the uncorrelated wealth hierarchy. This interpretation is consistent with previous observations that, despite their architectural and sculptural elaboration, the most impressive burials of the Alto Magdalena contain little in the way of offerings interpretable as wealth (Drennan 1995). In the Alto Magdalena, then, ranking was extremely strong with regard to status but only very poorly developed in its economic aspects. The apparent contradiction between household and burial evidence in the Valley of Oaxaca is the inverse of that for the Alto Magdalena. Status and wealth are, as far as we can tell, intertwined in Oaxaca; and this integrated system of ranking emerges strongly from the household evidence. Middle Formative burials, however, while not inconsistent with this notion, are much less impressive than those of other chiefdoms. This could be interpreted as a system of social ranking whose economic and symbolic aspects were correlated, but where the element of economic control (wealth accumulation) was much more strongly developed than it was in the other cases examined here. The relatively lower importance of the symbolic component may be related to the lack of emphasis on the public statements made by the burials of specific important individuals in Oaxaca, and it is this characteristic that has led some to label Middle Formative Oaxaca as a "corporate" society (Blanton et al. 1996). It does, at least, appear to be less individualizing than Alto Magdalena or Hongshan societies.

As we have seen, household artifact assemblages in the same community may differ from each other in several ways. Some kinds of differences appear strongly in one region but only weakly or not at all in others. With this recognition that several qualitatively different principles may be involved, it may be useful to look at the overall magnitude of differentiation to be seen in the household assemblages of different regions. A simple way to do this that derives directly from the analyses above is to focus on the magnitude of the calculated Euclidean distances that were the first step in those analyses. These distances are comparable for the analyses in different regions since they were based on standardized variables (variables expressed as number of standard deviations above or below the mean). If the matrix of distances between household assemblages for a region contains many large numbers, then the household assemblages for that region are, indeed, quite highly differentiated. One could compare matrices in this regard, then, by averaging all the distances in each and comparing means. At least this procedure would work if all the data sets contained the same number of variables. Since Euclidean distances receive a contribution from each variable, other things being equal, distances based on more variables are larger. This can be counteracted by dividing the mean Euclidean distance for a matrix by the number of variables in the analysis.

Figure 3.7 compares the mean Euclidean distances (divided by the number of variables) for each of the five household assemblage analyses. The results are highly consistent with the interpretations of the individual scaling analyses. As expected, the Wankarani assemblages have the lowest mean distance and can thus be considered the least differentiated of the five. This is the society that has traditionally been regarded as the "simplest" or least differentiated in the set. Indeed, Wankarani society is so obviously small scale and non-hierarchical (i.e. "egalitarian") that its inclusion in this comparison may seem strange. It was included intentionally, however, so as to have a baseline for the comparative analyses. If these measures for comparing chiefdoms are to provide useful discrimination between ones that are more or less "developed" in one way or another, then egalitarian societies should come out at the bottom of the scale. This is certainly where Wankarani society landed in terms of the burial evidence and in the household assemblage analysis as well, at least insofar as social ranking was concerned, even though craft specialization and concentration of ritual activities were (perhaps surprisingly) manifest.

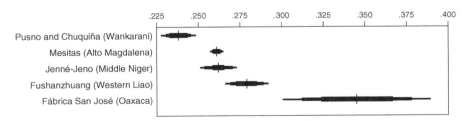

Fig. 3.7 Mean Euclidean distances between household assemblages divided by the number of variables in each analysis. Error ranges are shown for 80, 95, and 99% confidence

Wankarani is, nonetheless, still at the bottom of the scale with regard to overall mean differentiation of household assemblages. There is a modest but highly significant difference between the mean Euclidean distance for Wankarani household assemblages and those for Mesitas and Jenné-Jeno, the two of which are statistically indistinguishable from each other (Fig. 3.7). It thus seems meaningful to say that the overall degree of household assemblage differentiation for these two cases is quite similar, even though different principles of differentiation are at work in the two. In a higher position on this differentiation scale is Fushanzhuang, showing a highly significant difference from Mesitas and Jenné-Jeno. And finally, a very large step up the scale, comes Fábrica San José. Although it is represented by only a small sample of households, resulting in large error ranges in Fig. 3.7, Fábrica San José is different enough from the other communities in this regard for the difference to be very highly significant. It is worth observing in particular that the two most strongly differentiated sets of household assemblages are from communities that are relatively small and peripheral in their own cultural context—Fábrica San José as a small village subsidiary to San José Mogote and Fushanzhuang as the central place in a relatively small and marginal Hongshan polity. That overall household differentiation at these two communities is so strong indicates this as a pervasive characteristic of Middle Formative Oaxaca and Hongshan western Liao Valley societies. The spread shown in Fig. 3.7 from Mesitas to Fábrica San José is much larger than the difference that separates Mesitas from egalitarian Wankarani society. The variability in household assemblage differentiation that Fig. 3.7 shows among the four "complex" societies is thus much greater than the gap that separates "simple" from "complex."

Public Works Evidence

Another of the classic sources of archaeological evidence for complex societies is the construction of large-scale public works, which often remain conspicuous on the landscape for millennia. The labor requirements of such construction projects have been connected to leadership and complex organization via notions of management, mobilization, and power. And such public works are another arena in which early complex societies vary substantially.

All nine of the societies whose burial patterns were discussed above engaged in public works construction of one sort or another on what, in local context at least, seems a monumental scale. The burials themselves were often large scale public monuments, irrespective of the quantity and nature of offerings included in them. To varying degrees, the burials described above for the Alto Magdalena, central Panama, the western Liao Valley, Moundville, and La Venta all fall in this category. Large-scale public construction took a number of other forms as well among these nine societies. As Fig. 3.8 makes quite clear, the scale of these construction efforts varied considerably. Estimating the labor required for monumental-scale construction has long been a popular archaeological pastime, although it has not often been done systematically for comparison. We have made labor estimates for each of the nine societies in the usual way—applying ethnographically derived estimates of the person-days required for various tasks to the amount of such work involved in the construction of monuments of the size documented for each of these regions (cf. Abrams 1994, Erasmus 1965, Lekson 1986, and many others). There is, of course, a fairly wide range in the estimates available of the amounts of labor required to accomplish particular tasks. We have not let that worry us too much. Since our purpose here is very specifically that of comparison, we have concentrated less on the accuracy of absolute numbers and more on using compatible approaches to each of the sets of monuments. Our conclusions about which monuments required more (or vastly more) labor than which others are thus more reliable than the absolute numbers of person-days estimated in each case.

The size of the labor force available for such construction varied substantially across these nine societies as well. The available labor pool was calculated from population estimates for the likely sustaining regions of the centers where the monuments were built. In some instances these estimates are based on systematic regional settlement study; in others they are educated guesses, usually by regional specialists. We have assumed that in all cases, one-third of the population was available to labor in such projects, so one-third of the regional population estimate was multiplied by the span of time over which the monuments were constructed to estimate the total available labor pool in person-years. The relationship between available labor pool and overall construction effort can be examined by calculating the approximate "tax rates" which sustaining populations would have been subjected to in order to accomplish the construction. The total estimated labor investment (in person-days) was divided by the available labor pool (in person-years) to arrive at the tax rate (number of days' labor per year per available laborer required for construction). These estimates of tax rates for monumental construction are seen in Fig. 3.9 (and, of course, do not include the costs of a variety of other activities for which additional resources were clearly mobilized by elites in these societies).

La Venta's massive complex of civic-ceremonial buildings created truly large-scale public spaces (Drucker 1952, Drucker et al. 1959), and it comes as no surprise that this is by far the largest public construction effort examined here, requiring some 5,400,000 person-days of labor. Most of this labor was dedicated to earth moving for the construction of the vast array of platform mounds (up to more than 30 m high) and plazas shown in Fig. 3.8a. The moving and carving of large basalt sculptures and the acquisition of serpentine in huge quantity for burying as "massive offerings" were also substantial efforts. The result was a classic ceremonial center: structured space for ritual performance. The burials of important individuals, as described above, were part of this architectural complex but were by no means its major focus. Important people were more conspicuously present for posterity in sculptural form. As might well be guessed from Fig. 3.8h, Moundville comes next in terms of labor investment, requiring about 1,600,000 person-days. Again, most of the labor went into earth moving for the creation of tall platform mounds, although the arrangement of the mounds lacks the formal spatial organization of La Venta. At least some mounds seem to have served residential purposes, and large numbers of

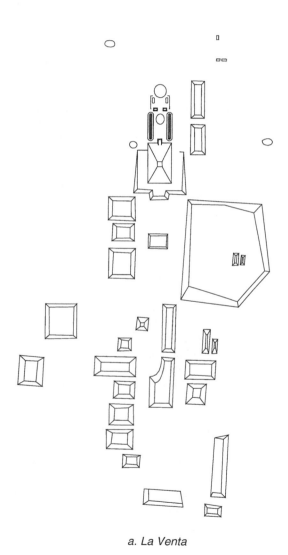

a. La Venta

Fig. 3.8 Monumental construction from different societies, all to the same scale

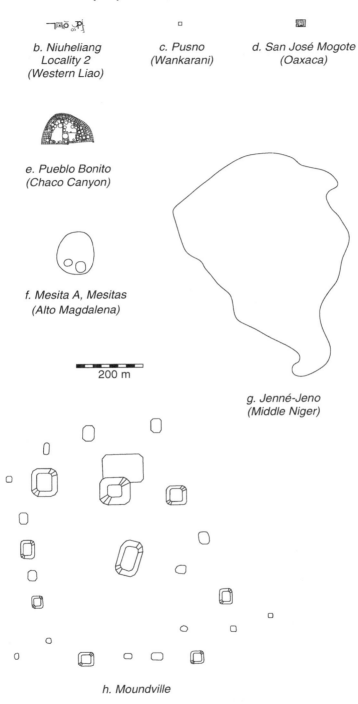

b. Niuheliang
Locality 2
(Western Liao)

c. Pusno
(Wankarani)

d. San José Mogote
(Oaxaca)

e. Pueblo Bonito
(Chaco Canyon)

f. Mesita A, Mesitas
(Alto Magdalena)

200 m

g. Jenné-Jeno
(Middle Niger)

h. Moundville

Fig. 3.8 (continued)

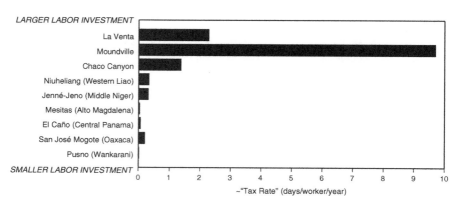

Fig. 3.9 Estimated tax rates for monumental construction in different societies

people of varying ranks were buried in and around them. Impressive as it was, the palisade that surrounded Moundville required considerably less construction effort than the mounds themselves. La Venta and Moundville also had the highest tax rates for public construction (Fig. 3.9), but, surprisingly, Moundville's tax rate was several times higher than La Venta's. This heavy burden was produced not just by a modest amount of available labor and substantial construction effort, but especially by the extreme rapidity with which most of the mounds and associated palisades were constructed—a mere 50 years.

The labor required for the construction of Pueblo Bonito in Chaco Canyon (Fig. 3.8e) was around half that required for Moundville (some 700,000 person-days). This was a very different sort of construction, though, providing substantial amounts of living space; only the kivas were truly ceremonial, and they represent only about one-sixth of the estimated construction effort. On the other hand, there were about a dozen such great houses in Chaco Canyon, as well as another whole public works effort in the form of a network of "roads" covering large distances. These roads were, in places, substantial raised causeways, but comprehensive data for estimating labor requirements are not available. So, while the nature and purposes of monumental construction in Chaco Canyon were rather different from either Moundville or La Venta, the magnitude of the labor invested clearly puts this case in the top ranks of this set of nine. The tax rate required for such construction in Chaco Canyon (Fig. 3.9) was probably also several times higher than those of the societies we have not yet discussed.

Niuheliang, the largest complex of Hongshan public monuments in the western Liao Valley, consists of 16 localities separated by distances of up to a few km (Chaoyang and Liaoning 2004, Liaoning 1986, 1997). Locality 2, shown in Fig. 3.8b, is the most thoroughly investigated and perhaps the largest concentration of ceremonial platforms. The central tombs in some of these platforms made them funerary monuments, although not all platforms had tombs. The central purpose of monumental construction was the creation of ceremonial space, as at

La Venta. Altogether, however, the construction effort for the 16 localities did not exceed 200,000 person-days, more than a full order of magnitude less than the labor requirements for La Venta. Although regional sustaining populations were probably not large, the construction was spread through an extremely long period, producing a tax rate vastly lower than those already discussed (Fig. 3.9).

Public construction effort at Jenné-Jeno was dedicated to a strikingly different purpose from any of the other cases discussed here—a massive wall surrounding much of the community (Fig. 3.8g), possibly for defensive purposes but perhaps more likely for control of commercial access (McIntosh and McIntosh 1993: 632). It required somewhat more than half the total construction labor needed for the Hongshan monuments at Niuheliang (about 110,000 person-days), but, because it was accomplished in a shorter period of time, the average tax rate works out very similar to that at Niuheliang. The monumental tombs of Mesitas, surrounded by stone statues, were monuments of more wholly funerary character than those considered above. The two modest mounds of Mesita A shown in Fig. 3.8f are only one of the four principal locations of monuments at Mesitas; altogether the construction effort, at some 87,000 person-days, was only slightly less than that of Jenné-Jeno. The tax rate, however, was a full order of magnitude lower than Jenné-Jeno's or Niuheliang's because of higher sustaining populations than Niuheliang's and a much longer period through which the monumental construction was spread than at Jenné-Jeno. Central Panama's monuments, exemplified by the burial mounds and associated sculpture of El Caño (Verrill 1927, Lleras and Barillas 1985), seem quite like those of the Alto Magdalena, although the massive and lavish offerings included with the Sitio Conte burials were a sharp contrast to the very modest ones in Alto Magdalena tombs. It is not entirely clear that Sitio Conte had monumental construction like that which is better preserved at El Caño, but there were at least arrangements of columnar basalt monoliths of similar nature. The monumental construction at El Caño was on a smaller scale than at Mesitas, but the sustaining population was probably also smaller, resulting in a tax rate somewhat higher than the Alto Magdalena's (Fig. 3.9).

Monumental construction at Rosario phase San José Mogote (Fig. 3.8d) was mostly ceremonial in character, although one lavish elite residence is included in the calculations as well (Flannery and Marcus 2005). Construction effort in any event was small, but the population of the San José Mogote chiefdom was even smaller by comparison, resulting in a higher tax rate than other cases that fall at the low end of the construction effort scale (Fig. 3.9). Wankarani public construction in the settlement system at La Joya was truly minimal (Fig. 3.8c), consisting of a single elevated platform and one adobe-walled structure at Pusno (Fox 2007), but the total regional population was very low. Consequently, the tax rate for public works construction in this "egalitarian" society, while the lowest of all the societies considered here (Fig. 3.9), was not so different from those of central Panama or the Alto Magdalena, which we are quite accustomed to considering "classic" chiefdoms. Taken together, "chiefly" central Panama or Alto Magdalena and "egalitarian" Wankarani, then had similarly low tax rates, strikingly different from those of even the western Liao Valley or the Middle Niger, not to mention Chaco Canyon, Moundville, or La Venta.

Although the two largest construction efforts were for creating ceremonial spaces, no one kind of public monumental construction is consistently associated with particularly high or particularly low tax rates in this sample of early complex societies. The least complex case of all (Wankarani) does not have a tax rate that sets it off much from several cases regarded as "classic" chiefdoms, including central Panama with its spectacular "chiefly" burials at Sitio Conte. The populations of central Panama did, of course, have to provide the skilled labor to acquire and/or make the goods included with such burials as offerings, and this investment is not included in monument construction. The same caveat applies to the western Liao Valley with its labor-intensive carved jade burial offerings, but not to the Alto Magdalena, where offerings included with even very elaborate burials were minimal. It is tempting to speculate that the soaring tax rate for monumental construction at Moundville (which is due to the rapidity of its construction) may have been partly responsible for Moundville's short florescence—population evidently flooded into the central place during the 50-year period of intensive construction and then dispersed, with regional "decline" following not long thereafter. Symbolic or religious bases for social hierarchy have sometimes been characterized as expensive (they require psychological reinforcement through massive monument construction) and of limited efficacy (in part because of the burden of those expenses). La Venta and Moundville are usually thought of as based largely on symbolic means of integration; their tax rates do indeed seem to have been high and their stability relatively low—at least both disintegrated politically, although La Venta managed 400 years of stability first. In the Alto Magdalena, where political integration was also largely based on symbol systems, though, the tax rates were low and stability higher—at least 900 years of persistence followed by political change that cannot be described as disintegration. In Oaxaca, where economic means of social control seem much more important, tax rates were also fairly low. This may have led to considerable persistence through a millennium of political growth and demographic stability in the Middle Formative. This was followed, not by disintegration, but by a major surge of development that produced an expansive conquest state—the only example among all the cases discussed here that led to such a regional development.

Conclusions

The early complex societies we have discussed demonstrate yet again what surely by now needed no further demonstration: there is not just one unilineal evolutionary pathway that all societies follow. Our consideration has been largely synchronic, but it is impossible to imagine all (or perhaps any) of these societies as on the same developmental trajectory. They vary in too many complicated ways. Developmental or evolutionary differences have been thought of as "vertical," and if development or evolution is to be thought of as multilineal, we must think of multiple "vertical" dimensions or axes of variability. There is not just *more developed* and *less developed* (and not just *developed differently*), but rather more and less developed in a variety of different ways. Or, in simpler, and perhaps less value-loaded language, there are varying quantitative values on a number of different scales that matter. We have discussed several such scales above, and placed several synchronic snapshots of different societies in their relative positions on them. Middle Formative Valley of Oaxaca ranks high in terms of degree of household economic specialization; the Alto Magdalena ranks low in this regard. Sitio Conte and Pueblo Bonito rank very high in terms of social differentiation expressed in burial offerings; Moundville ranks lower on this scale; the Alto Magdalena still lower; then Oaxaca. Wankarani or Jenné-Jeno mark what is effectively the zero point on this scale. La Venta and Moundville rank very high in terms of investment in monumental public works; Jenné-Jeno and Mesitas, substantially lower, but not as low as San José Mogote or Wankarani. The per capita burden for monumental construction was extremely high at Moundville and La Venta, much lower at Jenné-Jeno and San José Mogote, and extremely low at all the others examined here.

These dimensions of variability are among those that people have thought of as "vertical"—ones that reflect degree of hierarchical development. Other dimensions have been characterized as "horizontal," for example, the degree to which leadership was "individualizing" (as opposed to "group oriented"). On a scale of individualizing leadership, the Alto Magdalena and central Panama would both rank very high, Moundville probably a bit lower, Oaxaca much lower, and Wankarani or Jenné-Jeno lowest of all. Burials 13 and 14 at Pueblo Bonito would superficially, at least, suggest strongly individualizing organization, persistent efforts to label it "corporate" notwithstanding. What is not clear is how this scale is less vertical and more horizontal than the others. It does not represent qualitative, as opposed to quantitative, variation: societies are readily ranked along it. It certainly does not correspond at all well to overall degree of development, but it shares this characteristic fully with each of the "vertical" dimensions discussed in the previous paragraph. It is not at all clear just what the difference is between some dimensions of variability that are called vertical and some others that are called horizontal. The distinction has helped us recognize that the phenomenon we seek to understand is empirically more complicated than just degree of development, but it is now time to abandon it in favor of a fuller and richer recognition of the nature of variability in early complex societies and of the patterning in it. Without the vertical–horizontal dichotomy, we are left with a potentially goodly number of interesting dimensions of variability whose relationships can be *both* theorized about *and* investigated empirically. This means that relationships between these dimensions of variability are not simply assumed at the outset because they seem to make sense, but rather that relationships between dimensions of variability are posed as hypotheses for empirical evaluation. Before such work can be undertaken, however, the axes of variability must be defined and delineated, and means of using archaeological evidence to at least rank societies along them must be developed. It is this largely "bottom-up" approach that this and several earlier papers have taken (Drennan and Peterson 2005, 2006, 2008, Peterson and Drennan 2005).

We have attempted here and elsewhere to delineate dimensions of variability that are amenable to measurement along a scale. This actually provides an alternative to creating dichotomies or typologies, which everyone seems to hate without somehow being able to move beyond. It is certainly possible to provide means of true measurement along such scales by assigning numbers to things in different positions along them. This is what we have done, for example, with labor investment figures and estimates of tax rates. The differences that matter between societies on this scale are so huge that worries about how precisely archaeological information enables us to measure such social variables simply disappear. Often, in any event, it is more than adequate for our purposes to simply rank cases along these scales. Even simple rankings provide a much more sophisticated device for initial characterization of variability than a dichotomy or a set of types. And the wealth of new information on archaeological sequences in many parts of the world has clearly outstripped the abilities of the traditional apparatus for characterizing it. The popularity of notions like heterarchy or the contrast between corporate and network modes of organization is a testament to widespread recognition of this problem. The solution is not, however, new ways of oversimplifying. We see no way to avoid recognizing and dealing simultaneously with many dimensions of variability, even though it is conceptually much more difficult than reducing complexity to a few dichotomies or typologies.

One way to integrate the information encapsulated in numerous scales of variability is to think in terms of the correlations between dimensions. If high values on some dimensions correspond to consistently high (or low) values on others, these dimensions form "packages," and knowing that such packages exist gives us patterns to try to make sense of by building theoretical constructs to account for them. To the extent that existing theory implies the existence of such packages, they can be sought in the archaeological evidence as a means to evaluate the theoretical models. The former (bottom-up) way of working by no means contradicts the latter (top-down) approach. They are complementary. Both bring our knowledge of what happened in prehistory together with the theoretical notions that help us understand how it came to happen that way; they come together in the act of empirical evaluation of theoretical models.

Another approach to integrating the information from numerous scales of variability is to think in terms of social profiles. A society that ranks very high on one scale, low on another, and in the middle on a third has a different profile from a society that ranks low on the first scale, low on the second, and middle on the third. Its profile is, however, not as different from that society as it is from a third that ranks low on all three scales. Such social profiles, in effect, take the place of what has been thought of as "horizontal" variation—different patterns not clearly or necessarily related to overall degree of development. If quite similar social profiles occur repeatedly, such groups of very similar profiles can be accurately characterized as a type or category. If there is not such a recurrence of similar profiles, this in itself is an interesting empirical finding. It means that there are simply not useful societal types to be found.

Finally, of course, understanding social change requires giving such conceptualizations a diachronic and dynamic component. Here, we have treated all the cases we have looked at as synchronic snapshots. They are all, of course, actually moments in a trajectory of change, and comparing such synchronic snapshots by any means is only the first step toward comparative study of change. The sorts of correlations between variables we have discussed above, of course, have diachronic implications, since they can only hold generally true if change along one of these scales implies change along another. Otherwise none would be correlated. Recurring social profiles also have implications about change. Such a situation suggests that particular imaginable profiles are relatively untenable, and societies in process of change would move through such configurations relatively rapidly in a major transition toward a more stable configuration. If this turned out to be the case, it might give considerable comfort to die-hard proponents of traditional cultural evolutionary schemes. If the results of empirical investigation were otherwise, it would provide a powerful new argument against such schemes. And this, finally, is the point. These and other much more sophisticated issues are not questions to be resolved with social philosophy but rather with empirical documentation of what people actually did in prehistory. This paper has been an effort to contribute to our ability to characterize, on the basis of archaeological evidence, what human social organization was like in the past, focusing on how the societies of one region differed from those of another, or from those that preceded or followed them. We consider it empirical work, not in contrast to theoretical work, but in pursuit of theoretical objectives.

References

Abrams, E.M. 1994. *How the Maya Built Their World: Energetics and Ancient Architecture*. Austin: University of Texas Press.

Akins, N. 2001. Chaco Canyon Mortuary Practices: Archaeological Correlates of Complexity. In Mitchell, D.R. and Brunson-Hadley, J.L. (eds.), *Ancient Burial Practices in the American Southwest: Archaeology, Physical Anthropology, and Native American Perspectives*, pp. 167–190. Albuquerque: University of New Mexico Press.

Binford, L.R. 1971. Mortuary Practices: Their Study and Their Potential. In Brown, J.A. (ed.), *Approaches to the Social Dimensions of Mortuary Practices*, pp. 6–29, Memoirs of the Society for American Archaeology, no. 25. Washington: Society for American Archaeology.

Blanton, R.E., Feinman, G.M., Kowalewski, S.A., and Peregrine, P.N. 1996. A dual-processual theory for the evolution of mesoamerican civilization. *Current Anthropology* 37: 1–14.

Brown, J.A. 1981. The Search for Rank in Prehistoric Burials. In Chapman, R., Kinnes, I. and Randsborg, K. (eds.), *The Archaeology of Death*, pp. 25–37. Cambridge: Cambridge University Press.

Cameron, C.M., and Toll, H.W. 2001. Deciphering the organization of production in Chaco Canyon. *American Antiquity* 66: 5–13.

Cannon, A. 1989. The historical dimension in mortuary expressions of status and sentiment. *Current Anthropology* 30: 437–457.

Carr, C. 1995. Mortuary practices: their social, philosophical-religious, circumstantial, and physical determinants. *Journal of Archaeological Method and Theory* 2: 105–200.

Chaoyang Shi Wenwubu and Liaoning Sheng Wenwu Kaogu Yanjiusuo. 2004. *Niuheliang Yizhi*. Beijing: Xueyuan Chubanshe.

Childs-Johnson, E. 1991. Jades of the Hongshan Culture: the dragon and fertility cult worship. *Arts Asiatiques* 46: 82–95.

Drennan, R.D. 1976. *Fábrica San José and Middle Formative Society in the Valley of Oaxaca*. Ann Arbor: Memoirs of the Museum of Anthropology, No. 8, University of Michigan.

Drennan, R.D. 1995. Mortuary Practices in the Alto Magdalena: The Social Context of the "San Agustín Culture". In Dillehay, T.D. (ed.), *Tombs for the Living: Andean Mortuary Practices*, pp. 79–110. Washington: Dumbarton Oaks.

Drennan, R.D. 1996. One for All and All for One: Accounting for Variability without Losing Sight of Regularities in the Development of Complex Society. In Arnold, J. (ed.), *Emergent Complexity: The Evolution of Intermediate Societies*, pp. 25–34. Ann Arbor: International Monographs in Prehistory.

Drennan, R.D., and Peterson, C.E. 2005. Early Chiefdom Communities Compared: The Settlement Pattern Record for Chifeng, the Alto Magdalena, and the Valley of Oaxaca. In Blanton, R.E. (ed.), *Settlement, Subsistence, and Social Complexity: Essays Honoring the Legacy of Jeffrey R. Parsons*, pp. 119–154. Los Angeles: Cotsen Institute of Archaeology, UCLA.

Drennan, R.D., and Peterson, C.E. 2006. Patterned variation in prehistoric chiefdoms. *Proceedings of the National Academy of Sciences* 103: 3960–3967.

Drennan, R.D., and Peterson, C.E. 2008. Centralized Communities, Population, and Social Complexity after Sedentarization. In Bouquet-Appel, J.-P., and Bar-Yosef, O. (eds.), *The Neolithic Demographic Transition and Its Consequences*, pp. 359–386. New York: Springer.

Drucker, P. 1952. *La Venta, Tabasco: A Study of Olmec Ceramics and Art*. Smithsonian Institution, Bureau of American Ethnology, Bulletin 153, Washington.

Drucker, P., Heizer, R.F., and Squier, R.J. 1959. *Excavations at La Venta, Tabasco, 1955*. Smithsonian Institution, Bureau of American Ethnology, Bulletin No. 170, Washington.

Duque Gómez, L., and Cubillos, J.C. 1979. *Arqueología de San Agustín: Alto de los Idolos, Montículos y Tumbas*. Bogotá: Fundación de Investigaciones Arqueológicas Nacionales del Banco de la República.

Duque Gómez, L., and Cubillos, J.C. 1983. *Arqueología de San Agustín: Exploraciones y Trabajos de Reconstrucción en las Mesitas A y B*. Bogotá: Fundación de Investigaciones Arqueológicas Nacionales del Banco de la República.

Earle, T.K. 2001. Economic support of Chaco Canyon society. *American Antiquity* 66: 26–35.

Erasmus, C. 1965. Monument building: some field experiments. *Southwestern Journal of Anthropology* 21: 277–301.

Estévez Castillo, J., and Bermann, M.P. 1996. *Reporte Preliminar de la Temporada 1996: Proyecto Arqueológico Oruro*. La Paz: Unpublished report to the Instituto Nacional de Arqueología.

Estévez Castillo, J., and Bermann, M.P. 1997. *Reporte Preliminar de la Temporada 1997: Proyecto Arqueológico Oruro*. La Paz: Unpublished report to the Instituto Nacional de Arqueología.

Feinman, G.M. 2000. Corporate/Network: New Perspectives on Models of Political Action and the Puebloan Southwest. In Schiffer, M.B. (ed.), *Social Theory in Archaeology*, pp. 31–51. Salt Lake City: University of Utah Press.

Flannery, K.V., and Marcus, J. 2005. *Excavations at San José Mogote 1: The Household Archaeology*, Memoirs of the Museum of Anthropology, No. 40. Ann Arbor: University of Michigan.

Fox, J.R. 2007. *Time and Process in an Early Village Settlement System on the Bolivian Southern Altiplano*, Ph.D. dissertation. Pittsburgh: University of Pittsburgh.

Fox, J.R., Castellón Campero, W., Pérez Arias, A., and Pérez Arias, M. 2004. *Proyecto Orureño Formativo: Reporte Preliminar de la Temporada 2003*. La Paz: Unpublished report to the Dirección Nacional de Arqueología y Antropología.

González Fernández, V. 2008. *Prehispanic Change in the Mesitas Community: Documenting the Development of a Chiefdom's Central Place in San Agustín, Huila, Colombia*. University of Pittsburgh Memoirs in Latin American Archaeology, No. 18.

Guo, D. 1995. Hongshan and Related Cultures. In Nelson, S.M. (ed.), *The Archaeology of Northeast China: Beyond the Great Wall*, pp. 21–64. London: Routledge.

Guo, D. 1997. Understanding the Burial Rituals of the Hongshan Culture through Jade. In Rosemary, S. (ed.), *Chinese Jades*, pp. 27–36. London: Percival David Foundation of Chinese Art.

Guo, D. 2005. *Hongshan Wenhua*. Beijing: Wenwu Chubanshe.

Hearne, P., and Sharer, R.J. (eds.). 1992. *River of Gold: Precolumbian Treasures from Sitio Conte*. Philadelphia: University Museum of Archaeology and Anthropology, University of Pennsylvania.

Hirth, K. 1993. Identifying Rank and Socioeconomic Status in Domestic Contexts: An Example from Central Mexico. In Santley, R.S. and Hirth, K.G. (eds.), *Prehispanic Domestic Units in Western Mesoamerica*, pp. 249–273. Boca Raton: CRC Press.

Hodder, I. 1982. The Identification and Interpretation of Ranking in Prehistory: A Contextual Perspective. In Renfrew, C. and Shennan, S. (eds.), *Ranking, Resource and Exchange: Aspects of the Archaeology of Early European Society*, pp. 192–218. Cambridge: Cambridge University Press.

Jones, A.F., Jr., and Weinberg, D.H. 2000. *The Changing Shape of the Nation's Income Distribution*. Washington: US Department of Commerce, Economics and Statistics Administration, US Census Bureau.

Knight, V.J., Jr., and Steponaitis, V.P. 1998. A New History of Moundville. In Knight, V.J., Jr. and Steponaitis, V.P. (eds.), *Archaeology of the Moundville Chiefdom*, pp. 1–25. Washington: Smithsonian Institution Press.

Lekson, S. 1986. *Great Pueblo Architecture of Chaco Canyon*. Chaco Canyon Studies, Publications in Archaeology 18B, National Park Service.

Liaoning Sheng Wenwu Kaogu Yanjiusuo. 1986. Liaoning Niuheliang Hongshan Wenhua "Nushenmiao" yu Jishi Zhong Qun Fajue Jianbao. *Wenwu* 8: 1–17.

Liaoning Sheng Wenwu Kaogu Yanjiusuo. 1997. *Niuheliang Hongshan Wenhua Yizhi yu Yuqi Jingcui*. Beijing: Wenwu Chubanshe.

Lleras Pérez, R., and Barillas Cordón, E.A. 1985. *Excavaciones Arqueológicas en el Montículo 4 de El Caño*. Panama: Instituto Nacional de Cultura, Dirección Nacional de Patrimonio Histórico, Centro Restauración OEA-INAC.

McGuire, R.H. 1983. Breaking down cultural complexity: inequality and heterogeneity. *Advances in Archaeological Method and Theory* 6: 91–142.

McGuire, R.H., and Saitta, D.J. 1996. Although they have petty captains, they obey them badly: the dialectics of prehispanic western pueblo social organization. *American Antiquity* 61: 197–216.

McIntosh, S.K. (ed.). 1995. *Excavations at Jenné-Jeno, Hambarketolo, and Kaniana (Inland Niger Delta, Mali), the 1981 Season*, University of California Publications, Anthropology, Vol. 20. Berkeley: University of California Press.

McIntosh, R.J. 2005. *Ancient Middle Niger: Urbanism and the Self-Organizing Landscape*. Cambridge: Cambridge University Press.

McIntosh, S.K., and McIntosh, R.J. 1993. Cities without Citadels: Understanding Urban Origins along the Middle Niger. In Shaw, T., Sinclair, P., Andah, B., and Okpoko, A. (eds.), *The Archaeology of Africa: Food, Metals, and Towns*, pp. 622–641. London: Routledge.

O'Shea, J.M. 1984. *Mortuary Variability: An Archaeological Investigation*. Orlando: Academic Press.

Parker Pearson, M. 1999. *The Archaeology of Death and Burial*. College Station: Texas A & M University Press.

Peebles, C.S. 1974. *Moundville: The Organization of a Prehistoric Community and Culture*, Ph.D. dissertation. Santa Barbara: University of California.

Pepper, G.H. 1920. *Pueblo Bonito*. Anthropological Papers of the American Museum of Natural History, Vol. 27. New York: American Museum of Natural History. (1996 reprint edition, Albuquerque: University of New Mexico Press).

Peregrine, P.N. 2001. Matrilocality, corporate strategy, and the organization of production in the Chacoan world. *American Antiquity* 66: 36–46.

Peterson, C.E. 2006. *"Crafting" Hongshan Communities? Household Archaeology in the Chifeng Region, Eastern Inner Mongolia, PRC*, Ph.D. dissertation. Pittsburgh: University of Pittsburgh.

Peterson, C.E., and Drennan, R.D. 2005. Communities, settlements, sites, and surveys: regional-scale analysis of prehistoric human interaction. *American Antiquity* 70: 5–30.

Ponce Sanguinés, C. 1970. *Las Culturas Wankarani y Chiripa y su Relación con Tiwanaku.* La Paz: Academia Nacional de las Ciencias, Vol. 25.

Rautman, A.E. 1998. Hierarchy and heterarchy in the American Southwest: a comment on Mcguire and Saitta. *American Antiquity* 63: 325–333.

Renfrew, C. 1974. Beyond a Subsistence Economy: The Evolution of Social Organization in Prehistoric Europe. In Moore, C.B. (ed.), *Reconstructing Complex Societies: An Archaeological Colloquium*, pp. 69–85, Supplement to the Bulletin of the American Schools of Oriental Research, No. 20. Cambridge: American Schools of Oriental Research.

Renfrew, C. 2001. Production and consumption in a sacred economy: the material correlates of high devotional expression at Chaco Canyon. *American Antiquity* 66: 14–25.

Saitta, D.J., and McGuire, R.H. 1998. Dialectics, heterarchy, and western Pueblo social organization. *American Antiquity* 63: 334–336.

Saxe, A.A. 1970. *Social Dimensions of Mortuary Practices*, Ph.D. dissertation. Ann Arbor: University of Michigan.

Smith, M.E. 1987. Household possessions and wealth in agrarian states: implications for archaeology. *Journal of Anthropological Archaeology* 6: 297–335.

Tainter, J.A. 1978. Mortuary practices and the study of prehistoric social systems. *Advances in Archaeological Method and Theory* 1: 105–141.

University of Pennsylvania Museum Archives. 1999. Sitio Conte, Panama 1940. 1999, http://www.museum.upenn.edu/SitioConte/index.html

Verrill, A.H. 1927. Excavations in Coclé Province, Panama. *Indian Notes (Museum of the American Indian, Heye Foundation)*, 4(1): 47–61.

Whalen, M.E. 1981. *Excavations at Santo Domingo Tomaltepec: Evolution of a Formative Community in the Valley of Oaxaca, Mexico.* Ann Arbor: Memoirs of the Museum of Anthropology, No. 12, University of Michigan.

Chapter 4
Gimme That Old Time Religion: Rethinking the Role of Religion in the Emergence of Social Inequality

Mark Aldenderfer

Even a moment's reflection on the daily news informs us of the powerful ability of religion to shape and transform the world in which we live, whether it is a war waged for religious purposes or the deliberations of a local school board. But when it comes to thinking about a more distant past, one in which pronounced social inequalities either did not exist or were on a pathway to becoming, we archaeologists suffer a mental disconnect. Religion falls by the wayside, words like "ideology" or "ritual" dominate our discourse when we do think about it, and almost inevitably, we return to our materialist roots and seek some sort of economic first cause or foundation for the emergence of social inequality.

As I argue in this paper, it is time that religion is brought back into the mix of causal factors that led to the emergence and establishment of persistent inequality in the past. I shall focus upon the idea not of what religion is, but instead on what religion *does*. I do not intend this discussion to be a return to a sterile functionalism, but instead as a recognition that actors of all kinds, be they aggrandizers, their followers and their opponents, live their lives within a framework in part created and directed by religious practice, and in some sense, belief. Putting it a different way, religion is part of practice, habitus if you will, in the wider social and economic world, and cannot easily be disaggregated from other aspects of cultural practice. I further argue that religion ultimately provides the sanction for the emergence of persistent social inequality or creates resistance to it (Aldenderfer 2005:30). In the remainder of this paper I examine this assertion in detail, and offer some insights into how to see the action of religion in the archaeological record of emerging inequality.

In the predecessor volume to this, *Foundations of Social Inequality*, Brian Hayden (1995:20–23) spells out the fundamental economic dimensions of early inequality. Among the assumptions he uses to guide his thinking are

> Some forms of inequality based on sex, age, *ritual knowledge* [emphasis mine] and other skills have always existed. . .but where these inequalities do not have an economic base, their effects on overall community complexity are limited to ephemeral.

M. Aldenderfer (✉)
School of Anthropology, University of Arizona, Tucson, AZ, USA
e-mail: aldender2@gmail.com

T.D. Price, G.M. Feinman (eds.), *Pathways to Power*, Fundamental Issues in Archaeology, DOI 10.1007/978-1-4419-6300-0_4, © Springer Science+Business Media, LLC 2010

Also,

> ... pronounced inequalities and cultural complexity... are directly related to economic production and the control of economic surpluses.

His argument is strongly supported by a very large body of ethnographic research on transegalitarian peoples, and this has led most anthropologists who have studied the emergence of inequality to agree with the assumption that persistent, multi-generational inequality is to be found exclusively within conditions of resource abundance. But does resource abundance "explain" the emergence of inequality? Although we might be able to identify it as an Aristotelian ultimate cause, what is needed is a sense of more proximate causes that had direct and tangible effects on the lives of people in the past. Indeed, this leads us to reconsider one of Hayden's other assumptions phrased in the form of a query:

main ?

> The most critical question to be asked is how some individuals manage to convert economic surpluses into power or other benefits and how they induce other community members not only to produce surpluses but also to surrender control over those surpluses.

Here we are in agreement: this is *the* question we must address as we consider the emergence of inequality. So just how do some individuals get others to relinquish the fruits of their labors? Those who rely upon economic assumptions generally argue that the way some individuals come to dominate others is via the generation of debt (Aldenderfer 2005:13–14). That is, because of the demands of balanced reciprocity in transegalitaraian societies, aggrandizers or entrepreneurs, working in self-interest, use their ability to generate wealth to create social obligations of debt, frequently by offering feasts. Those unable to repay in kind must provide labor, sub-sistence resources, or other valuables to the aggrandizer, thus increasing his wealth and creating a group of potential followers. Other ethnographically observed means by which debts are created include marriage (use of women as a gift or commodity),

2–4

bride wealth, and gift giving, among others (Hayden 1995).

But how is it that individuals and groups come to accept that their debt is a "natural" condition? Again, those who espouse economic determinants for the emergence of inequality argue that both aggrandizers and their potential debtors and followers make decisions under the assumption of economic rationalism. As Hayden (1995:69) puts it:

why people accept oppression

> the mere act of giving wealth away does not result in increased power for the giver. To be effective, wealth must be given away in contexts that generate recognized and binding obligations or other expected practical benefits.

In this line of thought, no one would act against their economic self-interest sim-ply to obtain status or esteem that is not tied directly and obviously to a "practical" benefit. This also explains why some individuals or groups might willingly enter into debt or obligation in the service of successful aggrandizers because of explicit promises of material gain. As Hayden and others who espouse this approach to inequality note, although people frequently make bad decisions on who to follow (the promises of aggrandizers are not kept, for example), this does not invalidate the core assumption of economic rationality as a foundation for the acceptance of inequality.

There really is no doubt that people frequently do make decisions that are consistent with economic rationality, but it is equally clear from ethnography as well as the challenge to neoclassical economics from so-called behavioral economics (Camerer and Lowenstein 2003) that people do in fact make decisions that seem to fly in the face of economic rationality. Marshall Sahlins (1976) was one of the first anthropologists in recent times to challenge the assumption of the universal existence of a western-style rationality by contrasting what he called "practical" versus "cultural" logic. The latter is a logic based upon history, custom, convention, and practice. According to this view, rationality as it is meant in western society is modified by these conventions. Thus, regimes of value, social honor, conceptions of social status and rank, and other areas of salience when we think of how to conceptualize inequality may not necessarily correlate well or even at all with a purely economic framework. Even one of the founding figures of neoclassical economics, Adam Smith, in his first book *The Theory of Moral Sentiments* (1759:1) argued:

> How selfish soever man may be supposed, there are evidently some principles in his nature, which interest him in the fortunes of others, and render their happiness necessary to him, though he derives nothing from it, except the pleasure of seeing it.

Throughout the book, Smith showed that so-called psychological principles or the emotional states of respect, sentiment, shame, and pride, among others, influenced economic decisions of all kinds. While it is not wise to use Smith's thinking as a definitive guide to human nature, we can nevertheless gain from it an appreciation of the potential power of cultural logic.

If we cannot fully rely upon economic rationality as a basis for the extension or acceptance of inequality, what remains? Thomas Hobbes, in the seventeenth century, suggested that willing acceptance of authority on the part of those seeking to avoid conflict and war was a possibility. That is, individuals and groups would enter into a social contract whereby rights would be surrendered to a protector who would defend them. A key assumption, however, was that the arrangement was to be between equals in status. And if the potential protector defaulted on his obligations but still required submission, this was labeled by Hobbes as injustice. Again, while there are numerous examples from ethnography that reflect this process, Hayden (1995:31) notes that this is an expensive strategy, and one not likely to persist given its high cost and significant drawbacks (see also Aldenderfer 2005:15–16 for an extended discussion of this issue).

Ethnography also makes it clear that attempts to extend inequality by strictly economic means are fiercely resisted in most hunting and gathering and transegalitarian societies (Boehm 1999, Lee 1990, Mitchell 1988). Wiessner and Tumu (1998: 376–377), in a discussion of why Enga big men were unsuccessful at creating persistent leadership despite their significant wealth derived through feasting and ceremonial exchange, write

> There is, however, another set of tasks that arise when unbridled socioeconomic competition collides with egalitarian ideals: altering social and economic values, setting new directions

and standards, bringing about their acceptance, establishing objectives of competition, and mediating the consequences. Until *ideological integration* (emphasis mine) is achieved... new forms of intergroup social integration via exchange cannot come about...

To my mind, although Wiessner and Tumu use the term ideology, what I believe they are saying is that we are left with religion to resolve these issues and create a context for persistent inequality to emerge. While I grant this thesis places me in perilous ground, there is a good reason for archaeologists to remember that religion really does exist in every society and it has a powerful influence on all social actors.

Religion and What It Does

Religion is hard to define. Many have lamented that there is no universally applicable definition of it, but upon reflection, it is easy to see why that is the case. In part, definitions almost always emerge from a theoretical stance, either explicit or implicit. And since theories have limited domains of relevance, no single definition of religion can necessarily or easily capture what some other theoretical stance might propose.

But a more fundamental problem is simply that there is real, not simply theoretical, disagreement, uncertainty, and unease about what religion is and whether it is a universal element of the human experience. Most anthropologists agree that some sort of "spiritual experience" is a cultural universal (Brown 1991:139), but that religion "proper" is not to be found in simpler societies. This of course reflects a bias toward definitions of religion that describe highly formal, ecclesiastical spiritual practice found within hierarchical polities (Insoll 2001:3–10). But it is the case that religion as a highly systematized body of knowledge and practice is hard to identify in relatively simple, non-hierarchical, or transegalitarian societies. Although people "have" religion, finding it presents real challenges to the ethnographer, not to mention the archaeologist.

But as I argue, not fully understanding what religion is does not make it impossible to understand what it does. Indeed, if we pull together the threads of previous attempts to define religion, we can begin to get a sense of what roles it can play within any society, be it simple or complex. For Edward Tylor, religion was "belief in spiritual beings"; he argued that religion was best seen as an attempt by people to understand the world in which they live (Tylor 1871). For Emile Durkheim, religion was a so-called social fact and served as a "unified system of beliefs and practice relative to sacred things, that is to say, things which are set apart and forbidden— beliefs and practices which unite into one single moral community called a church, all of those who adhere to them" (Durkheim 1995 [1912]:44). He also believed that religion was essential to social cohesion and social solidarity, and in this manner, he anticipated a functionalist view of religion. Bronislaw Malinowski (1954 [1925]) also saw religion as promoting social solidarity, but within an emotive context in which religious ritual was not so much about effecting a solution to a crisis but was more about enhancing group solidarity in the face of crisis. Elsewhere, he saw religion as a powerful moral force, one that defined right conduct. In the same vein, Anthony F. C. Wallace (1966:25–29), while emphasizing the role of religion as the fundamental societal force for social control, identity formation, and value definition, also portrayed it as a means by which social contradictions could be rationalized and justified. He also suggested that in some contexts, religion could be seen as a source of inspiration for social change, a topic I return to shortly. Clifford Geertz (1973:90) saw religion as a set of symbols that created "pervasive moods and motivations in men..." which conceptualized the nature of existence. Finally, Maurice Bloch (1992) sees religion and politics inextricably intertwined across all levels of sociocultural complexity, but notes that relationships between symbols, religion, ritual, politics, and action can be extremely complex. That is, a ritual event sanctioned by religious belief may remain constant and unchanging through periods of dramatic socioeconomic transformations. Here, religion may appear conservative, but through its use in novel and new contexts by emerging leaders, a traditional form is used to justify new social circumstances (Wengrow and David 2003).

Summarizing these perspectives as well as those of other theorists of religion, we can say that religion does at least the following: provides an explanation for the existence of the world, its form and content, and the place of people within it; offers significant opportunity for the development of a sense of group cohesion, social solidarity, or communal feeling, especially for the members of small-scale, face-to-face societies; explains, at least in part, the nature of social relationships within and between societies, and provides a justification for the shape of social norms and rules; creates an emotional and psychological context for the evaluation of daily experience and how it articulates with rules, roles, and norms; creates a basis for the formation of individual and group identity; identifies non-human actors as elements of existence and provides mechanisms whereby they can be addressed; creates set of procedures or processes—such as ritual—that can be used to influence the course of events; presents a set of symbols—material, linguistic, and cognitive—that conceptualize, reflect, capture, and represent the nature of existence; and finally, may become a kind of tool used by individuals to create new social and political spaces or resist their appearance.

In effect, religion can be seen as an *enabler*: it can be used by agents to maintain tradition, conservatism, and egalitarian rules and roles. It can also be transformative, however, and challenge those egalitarian rules by appropriation of traditional identities, roles, or symbols cast into new forms with new meanings, or even the introduction of wholly new ones. The problem, of course, is to determine the circumstances under which religion is traditional or becomes transformative, and how the material aspects of religion reflect (or fail to reflect) societal change and the appearance of more robust and persistent forms of social inequality.

Under What Circumstances Are Religions Traditional or Transformative?

Actors change culture, including religion. The old days of systems thinking, as helpful as they were to move archaeology into a more scientific paradigm, have been replaced by a much richer body of thought and theory that situates agents and actors as active participants in their cultures, and which provides them with the motivation and the tools wherein cultural change can be effected. But this is obviously problematic for the archaeologist since we seldom work at a scale suitable to see how decisions are made and played out over relatively short time frames. We can, however, examine broader societal, economic, and ecological contexts that would seem to promote the maintenance of traditional forms of religious practice as well as those in which religion could become transformative. In so doing, we are seeking more proximate, rather than ultimate, causes, although I grant that we often are not successful in this effort.

Religion in small-scale societies is never static and unchanging, but neither is it prone to dramatic transformations of content and structure under most circumstances. Aspects of religious belief and practice can be exchanged, replaced, dropped, or even forgotten, but core beliefs and principles of that practice remain intact and recognizable over generations even though specific meanings may in fact change. Aspects of ritual practice within a religious context may reflect existing power relationships between individuals or kin groups, and as these change and the fortunes of these actors wax and wane, thus the specifics of the ritual itself may vary or new meanings may appear based on these societal dynamics. But the ritual itself does not vanish, nor does the motivation to perform the ritual since it is sanctioned as "traditional" practice. Beidelman (1971) provides an interesting example how this plays out in one East African group; an annual ritual for the reification of land claims and spiritual rejuvenation of land ownership is performed via the medium of ancestral spirits. However, as a group wanes in power, a new set of ancestors are addressed. Content, not form, is changed.

Two very general contexts seem to be critical for looking at religion as an enabler for cultural change: circumscription and contradiction, which are often highly interconnected. Circumscription has long been suspected as a necessary condition for the emergence of social inequality (Aldenderfer 1993, Brown and Price 1985, Carneiro 1970, 1988). For both foragers and cultivators, circumscription is characterized by reduced residential mobility albeit at different scales and with varied periodicity. Circumscription has multiple causes ranging from the historically contingent and highly local to more global factors. Among the Yanomamo, one way for a small lineage to avoid constant exploitation by larger, perhaps better organized ones, is to make a long distance move to a less hostile environment (Chagnon 1997:74–81). However, as the number of neighbors grows, the number of suitable gardening locations also diminishes, and such a move becomes either impossible or is undertaken only with the greatest reluctance. When movement is too costly in both psychological and material terms, these smaller lineages have little choice but to submit to their more powerful neighbors or to seek new alliances. In highland New Guinea, Wiessner and Tumu (1998:150–152) note that while migration to avoid war was possible for a number of generations after the introduction of the sweet potato, the amount of unoccupied land diminished over time, resulting in the creation of new ways of dealing with population growth and the consequences of warfare, such as reparations payments. As these examples suggest, circumscription constrains options available to actors, thus creating contexts for increased social tension, potential for violence, and, of course, contradiction regarding social roles, rules, and perceptions.

Contradiction is a context wherein religion can enable actors to justify ongoing social changes or resist them. Contradiction describes situations in which existing social roles and rules become blurred, traditional relationships are threatened, and differences between people are exacerbated. As noted previously, this is a serious problem in small-scale societies which prize an egalitarian ideology and strongly resist efforts to subvert it. Actors see opportunity to effect changes that may benefit themselves or their kin group, and these may be at the expense of others, as in the case of the Yanomamo example cited previously. At least for a time, these efforts are not seen as threatening by others especially if these actors make efforts to display their generosity via feasts or gift giving. Religion, since it is a source of moral teaching, right behavior, and identify formation, may be pressed into service by those who wish to justify their emerging differences with their fellows. Many cultures appear to have ample tolerance for contradiction, and indeed, many within them are willing to tolerate a rupture of the egalitarian ethos if they receive direct benefits from it or are not threatened by it. This is especially true if mobility or movement remains an option. Although previously I have suggested this situation can be seen as a variant of a cost-benefit problem, wherein the costs of cooperation are balanced against those of resistance (Betzig 1986:60, Aldenderfer 1993:13), I have come to believe that such a formulation seriously devalues the psychological and emotive power of religion as an enabler of cooperation and tolerance, but also resistance. Douglas (1970) has argued that individuals seek consonance, which is the attempt to create personal reconciliation between the experiences of daily practice, religious beliefs, and the actions of others. This is a powerful emotive force, and one that at least for some individuals may provide a motivation for resistance to societal changes they perceive as excessive. Indeed, as societal changes become more intense and challenge more forcefully existing norms of behavior and moral obligations, resistance to them may also intensify, and those who are threatened by change may turn to religion as a means by which to confront aggrandizing actors.

When contradiction reaches a crisis state, if ever, is difficult to determine and is highly contingent on historical and local factors. However, it is possible to generalize to an extent and posit that small-scale societies that fall into the orbit of larger, more complex groups either through conquest, assimilation, or intensive economic contact are likely to experience crises that may find an outlet in the transformation of religious belief. Varied forms of religious resistance to change include revitalization, millenarian, and nativist movements (Wallace 1966). The cargo cults that appeared in Melanesia during the twentieth century are good examples of revitalization movements (Billings 2002, Jebens 2004), while the Ghost Dance of the late nineteenth century in the American West is best seen as a millenarian movement that had tragic consequences (Mooney 1896). As Linton (1943) observed, the Ghost Dance drew upon existing apocalyptic beliefs while selectively borrowing, then forging together, different strands of Plains Indian religion into a new synthesis. Yet another example of a nativistic movement created within a context of intensive culture contact was the emergence of the Midewiwin medicine society in the eighteenth and nine-teenth century among the Chippewa in the upper Great Lakes (Aldenderfer 1993, Hickerson 1970, Ritzenthaler 1978:19–22).

Although these examples are interesting and important, they are not likely to be representative of the historical trajectories of early social inequality. A more useful scenario for modeling the way in which religion enables transformation and resis-tance to social change is once again found in highland New Guinea and the crisis created by the growing wealth, power, and influence that big men achieved after the introduction of the sweet potato.

Maintaining, if Not Extending, Emerging Inequality

In their masterful analysis of warfare, exchange, and ritual in highland New Guinea, *Historical Vines*, Wiessner and Tumu (1998:353–384) describe at length how the introduction of the sweet potato led to a series of profound transformations in the lives of the peoples of Enga that bear directly on the ways in which inequality was created and resisted. The book provides fascinating insight into how agents worked within the constraints and opportunities of their culture to fashion new social roles as well as to strive for cooperation and the maintenance of traditional values. Not surprisingly, religion, via the cult, played a significant role in this nexus of change. Although much of what I describe is historically local to the cultures of this region, what matters in this discussion is not so much the specifics but instead the description of the distinct players in this drama, their motivations, and the varied instruments and outcomes of their interaction. As I hope to show, the complexity of this unfolding should both caution and encourage us: caution us to realize that sim-ple explanations for the emergence of complexity are likely to be inadequate, but encourage us to know that religion, via ritual and the materialization of symbols, can be seen as an active participant in this process.

The pre-sweet potato Enga were clan based, land holding groups that depended upon taro as the primary subsistence cultigen (Wiessner and Tumu 1998:99–100). Kinship through descent and marriage fixed an individual's place within society, and intragroup relationships had an ideology of egalitarianism, although differences in wealth could be generated by a favorable geographic location in the trade network of non-agricultural products. Wealth generated through this trade and a low level of economic intensification, focused primarily upon pigs, created competition for women via marriage and alliance formation. However, greater prestige was granted on the basis of the distribution of wealth and not on its accumulation. And while leadership was influenced by status and wealth, it was also low key and was gener-ally in the hands of classic big men, senior adult males who through their actions attracted followers by their overt generosity, oratorical skills, and persuasive abil-ities. While status competition was tolerated, it was tempered by the egalitarian ethos.

Ancestor cults formed the basis of pre-sweet potato religion in the eastern por-tions of the Enga domain, while in the west, while ancestors were important, a wider variety of cults was present (Wiessner and Tumu 1998:194–195). In the east, elder men directed the veneration of the ancestors via feasts, while in the west, cult and religious practice were directed by specialists, who were widely feared. These cults emphasized connections to the spirit world and were sources of mystery and anxiety. Religious specialists in the west never assumed the role of big man and apparently did not use their positions to garner wealth.

Although the date of the introduction of the sweet potato is not known, the effects of its appearance included rapid and substantial population growth, increased population density, and clan fissioning and movement. Over time, the sweet potato laid the foundation for the massive growth of pig populations, and thus pigs became a currency in the exchange and ceremonial systems of the region's peoples. Boundary maintenance and increased levels of warfare were observed in areas of the highest levels of population density, but it was ubiquitous and unrelenting across all of highland New Guinea. Potatoes and pigs provided existing big men with new opportunities for the generation of wealth that were significantly greater than could ever have been created in pre-sweet potato times. But the increased wealth in the hands of a limited few began to create a series of serious social problems within Enga society. As I noted previously, rampant competition collided with the prevailing egalitarian ethos, and contradiction regarding roles, right behavior, and notions of prestige and status began to emerge. In the east, where clan leaders, not cult specialists, were more important, emerging big men turned to primarily economic strategies to deal with these emerging contradictions, although over time they too turned to cults to justify increasing social differences. In the west, however, traditional forms of religious belief and their expression with the ancestor cults became the primary vehicle for the resolution of contradiction.

As Wiessner and Tumu (1998:179–213) show, cults became an effective tool in the hands of big men to create an ideological justification for their obvious wealth. Numerous cults were found across the highlands, and through the extensive trade networks that existed, the contents of different cults became widely known. Big men and clan leaders purchased cults that presented messages they wished to impart to their followers and the values, ideals, and symbols they wished to emphasize. Ritual specialists and leaders of these cults were imported to teach the essential content of the cult to local specialists, but aside from cooperation with these ritual specialists, the big men apparently never took active roles in directing the cult.

The Kepele cult is a good example of how a traditional cult format in the west of the Enga region was transformed by big men intent on justifying their emerging wealth after the introduction of the sweet potato. The cult had its origins as a boys' initiation ceremony in which they were told the essential secrets of the spirit world. But as the sweet potato transformed many aspects of Enga life, so too did the Kepele cult witness its own transformations. Instead of remaining simply an initiation cult (although this aspect of it was maintained), it was expanded to serve a number of social ends. Through varied means, it served to emphasize regional harmony and cooperation within kin lines as well as across those created by marriage so that sufficient financing of ceremonies was accomplished. And behind it, of course, were the big men. The cult was used to justify their increasing wealth

ex. of cult that maintains and extends inequality

while simultaneously re-casting and re-emphasizing the importance of cooperation and the reduction of social tension.

Among the religious ideas that were added to the cult was an explicit combination of agricultural fertility with a mythical story of the wandering fertility women (Wiessner and Tumu 1998:198), who were said to have introduced the sweet potato to the Enga. This recognition was materialized by the creation of so-called sacred stones, which were seen as the literal representation of the wandering women. Over time, a male symbol was added to the cult, and rituals involved the mating of male and female symbols within specially erected cult houses, which over time became larger, more elaborate, and more central to the community. As the time for the ceremony grew near, ritual and cult leaders created a bounded sacred space within the village. Each clan was expected to contribute a specific building material for the house. In some communities, multiple cult houses were built and distinct rituals, such as boys' initiation, were played out within them. Feasting and dancing was done outside the confines of the sacred space. Activities within the cult houses, especially that of the mating between the male figure and the sacred stones, were closed and private. The mating cult house was often burned after the completion of the ceremony, while the other structures were abandoned and left to rot.

In this instance, a traditional religious form—an initiation cult—was transformed by wealthy men so as to justify their continued acquisition of wealth. While aspects of the traditional ritual practice were maintained, these diminished in importance as the cult emphasized a mythical, but direct, representation of agricultural fertility, a female principal, and the increasing generation of wealth. Importantly, much of this wealth was reinvested, in a sense, through the sponsoring of feasts, dances, and other performances. While the cult may not have extended hierarchy in the sense of allowing big men to take on new social roles, it served as a justification for their continued violation of the egalitarian ethos. Ultimately, this allowed them to extend their efforts to participate in regional trade networks and to finance other major ceremonial events related to warfare and war reparations, among other things.

A Cultic Reaction to Increasing Inequality

The Ain cult, in contrast, is an example of a cult that appears to have been created at least in part as a response to pronounced differences in wealth. The cult has been described as a millenarian movement (Gibbs 1977, Meggitt 1973), and while it contains many features consistent with that interpretation, Wiessner and Tumu (1998:383–384) suggest that the cult was also a response to the stresses created by rampant competition between big men, including massive pig sacrifices, the increasingly expensive acquisition of ceremonial objects for the vast trade network in them, and intensifying warfare and the growing loss of life, especially of young men, as a result of the demands on overproduction to support the activities of big men and their allies. Other factors believed to have contributed to the expansion

ıX: cults as result to inequality

of this cult include a series of years in which agricultural production was substantially diminished by freezes followed by droughts, the rapid spread of epidemic disease of both humans and pigs, and a growing recognition of the importance of white intruders—Australians—and their panoply of desirable material possessions (Meggitt 1973:18–20). All of these factors appear to have created substantial contradiction between the ideological foundations of Enga society, particularly between the massive wealth of the most successful big men and the demands placed upon their followers.

The cult was created by four brothers, said to be men of "substance and reputation" (Meggitt 1973:20), but not big men. The ghost of their father visited them, and told them that since the traditional rituals, especially ancestor worship and the Kepele cult, had not protected the people from the serious problems they were facing, they should perform new rituals that the ghostly father had learned from a giant kangaroo. The sun was to be worshiped through new ritual to be conducted by the "shaking men," so named because they stared into the sun, which would induce them to shake violently as they chanted new sacred spells. The shaking men proclaimed that the sacred stones and cult houses of the Kepele should be abandoned, a new cult house with a special platform should be constructed at the dance ground by each clan segment, pigs should be sacrificed on the platform and not on the ground, ritual participants should bathe every day over the course of a month, men should give up warfare, and they should also stop participating in the ritual activities of the bachelor cult. Although Meggitt (1973:23) suggests that the cult, at least in its original incarnation, was not meant to last since the world would be "restored" and the problems afflicting the Enga would vanish if they followed the cult, it did indeed persist.

Any man regardless of status could become a shaking man, and Meggitt reports that sometimes even women and children could shake with the sun. However, traditional big men tended not to participate in the cult, and there are clear reasons for this. Most of the prescriptions of the cult can be seen as direct challenges to the "way things are" and the ways in which traditional religious practice supported the position of the big man. The rejection of both the Kepele cult and the bachelors cult cut away at the ideological justification of the big man's ability to generate wealth. In the case of the Kepele, the Ain rejected the connection between agricultural production, female fertility, and the big man via the initiation rites for boys. Similarly, since the bachelors cults were manipulated by big men and clan leaders alike to justify the accumulation of wealth by instructing young men in secret ceremonies that emphasized personal purity and harmonious behavior so as to attract good trading partners and favorable marriages (Wiessner and Tumu 1998:243), the Ain cult told its followers to ignore any restraint on sexual behavior with their wives so as "... to beget many children" (Meggitt 1973:23). Asking men to give up warfare can also be seen as a response to the power of the big man, for it is the follower that is enjoined to fight the big man's wars of boundary maintenance, access to land, or other provocations. Lavish pig sacrifice to the sun, another important element of the Ain cult, can also be seen as a rejection of traditional religious belief since the pig had become central to the big man's rise to power (Wiessner and Tumu 1998:383).

As an example, one of the cult prophets exhorted its followers to "continue killing pigs for the sun and eating meat until all are consumed; the sky people will replace them" (Meggitt 1973:34). Instead of alliances, hard work, and exploitation, wealth would be created simply by belief.

An even more dramatic challenge to the traditional order came as the Ain cult spread to neighboring groups. In a number of groups, the acquisition of wealth by *any* clansman became the central feature of cult practice. Gibbs (1977:21) notes that among the Ipili, a neighbor of the Enga, the cult came to represent a potential source of valuables, including shells, large pigs, and steel axes. Shells and pigs, of course, are the traditional instruments of wealth used by big men. Other rituals directed cult followers to dig large, deep holes around the margins of the dance ground, and at the appropriate time, the descent of a dark cloud over the village, cult followers were to retire to the Ain cult house. After the cloud dissipated, the holes would be filled with wealth that would be given to the cult members by the shakers (Meggitt 1973:35). In yet another example, cult prophets washed their ritual objects (obtained as pay in great part from their hosts intent on joining the cult) as new cult members bathed downstream, and as the "essence" of these objects touched the bathers, they would become wealthy and be able to become big men (Meggitt 1973:37). Not surprisingly, the Ain cult ultimately failed in great part because it could not live up to its promises that things would change for the better and that all followers would become big men. But active resistance by existing big men helped as well (Wiessner and Tumu 1998:383).

The Ain cult provides an example of how individuals used religious belief to enable resistance to changes in their world created by the increasingly destructive activities of the big men and their ceaseless competition. There is no question that the believers of the Ain cult were seeking a return to the egalitarian ethos that existed prior to the appearance of the sweet potato. Old forms of religion, such as the veneration of sacred stones, were rejected, and many of the messages of right and proper behavior transmitted by traditional religion via big man-sponsored cult practices were overtly challenged. New ritual practices and venues were constructed and new symbols created.

Religion, Persistent Inequality, and Persistent Leadership

These two examples show that while religion can play a significant role as an enabler of inequality or resistance to it, it also has limitations as well. It is clear that religion enabled big men to extend, then maintain, their accumulation of wealth. Religion served as the ideological core of a belief system that promoted the ideals of egalitarian behavior but which also justified why certain individuals could be allowed to accumulate wealth. But actions, not just belief, matter as well. If big men did not readily return some of their wealth to their followers through generosity, contradiction about social roles and their justification might have occurred earlier than it did in highland New Guinea. These examples answer, I think significantly, Hayden's original question cited previously:

The most critical question to be asked is how some individuals manage to convert economic surpluses into power or other benefits and how they induce other community members not only to produce surpluses but also to surrender control over those surpluses.

I would argue that religion does it. And importantly, religion enables some to resist the growth of inequality, although this too has limits. Going back to a simpler time through the manipulation of religious ideology, which is always a goal of a millenarian movement, always fails because at some point, the unrealistic promises of the cult never materialize.

But it remains the case that the New Guinea big men, despite their manipulation of religion, could not create a basis for persistent leadership using it:

On first glance, the brilliant performances of the big men of the twentieth century obscure to some extent what they could not change: the fundamental alterations in Enga social and political structure lagged behind economic and ritual developments. Individual and collective action restructured the economic base, ritual repertoire, and even aspects of cosmology, but rights that were essential for prosperity and reproduction were staunchly defended: rights to land, the products of labor equal status, and symmetrical reciprocity... It appears that only sustained quantitative growth, both demographic and economic, might have tipped the balance toward more enduring social inequalities by making the social rules and orientations of generations past no longer compatible with existing institutions (Wiessner and Tumu 1998:372).

Or put a slightly different way, although big men were able to bend the rules rather substantially for a very long period of time, through the use of religion, they were never able to make the qualitative leap from "power to" to "power over."

Religion, then, used by clever agents, enables them to maintain persistent inequality, but appears to be limited as an enabler of persistent leadership. This is a critical distinction. The New Guinea examples show that people have a real tolerance for persistent inequality as long as it does not lead to a crisis of contradiction. When contradiction reaches a crisis state, religion in the hands of other actors seeks to re-impose balance, and may be successful in so doing, at least for a time.

How then, does religion serve as an enabler for agents seeking persistent leadership, that which is passed down the generations? In the New Guinea examples discussed above, ritual specialists appear to have little secular power. They do accumulate wealth, but it does not seem to have been at the same scale as most big men. Big men have little direct power over the ritual process. By direct, I mean that the big men do not themselves direct religious rituals, nor do they appear to have special access to ritual objects or paraphernalia. But they do influence religion through their personal participation in traditional, mainstream cults like the Kepele or the bachelors cults as well as their financing of new, imported cults that they use to manipulate cooperation with and acceptance of their unequal status. Their motivations, however, are similar—both manipulate religious rituals and practice to obtain wealth. Note that in no sense am I challenging the presumed sincerity of their beliefs in their religious activities. Instead, I simply call attention, as I have argued in this paper, to the necessity of looking at what agents *do* with religion as part of practice.

If religion is part of the mix in the emergence of persistent leadership, and the evidence is strong that it is important in many trajectories to complexity, what seems to be necessary is that either the ritual practitioners obtain secular power, secular leaders obtain direct religious ritual power, or that some middle ground be reached between them. Gregory Johnson (1982) discussed the process at length, at least in theoretical terms, of how foragers move from so-called sequential hierarchies (where one individual has authority in a single domain of society) to simultaneous hierarchies (when multiple hierarchies are controlled by a single individual). In principle, it seems that a religious ritual specialist, since they had control of how meaning is presented, may have greater success in so doing, and I once argued this (Aldenderfer 1993:32–33). Winkelman (1990:344–347) made a similar argument via a cross-cultural analysis of how so-called magico-religious specialists are correlated with different levels of sociocultural complexity. He suggested that shamans could become "priests" (i.e. secular and religious leaders) with real "power over" but he never made a convincing case of what causal forces may have been involved aside from a weak functional argument. However, it seems clear from the New Guinea examples that religious ritual specialists may have distinctly different social and personal motivations than big men and, despite their abilities to control categories of social meaning, may not use their position to in fact extend themselves directly into more secular affairs.

Although New Guinea big men did not have direct religious authority, similar actors in other societies do:

> The Chippewa chief exercised moral authority through possession of 'sacred power' and was able to enhance his prestige through the wise use of that moral authority through persuasion and example and sponsorship of the annual Feast of the Dead. The chief, then, sat atop two distinct sequential hierarchies: one based upon his position as elder male of a lineage and the other based upon his control of sacred power (Aldenderfer 1993:27).

The sacred power in question is the possession of a bundle of religious objects of significance and importance. Winkelman (1990:346) reports a similar role for the Creek chief. In both cases, religious authority rested with these individuals, but neither had "power over." Aside from the control of a powerful source of religious authority, they are very much like the New Guinea big man. So at least in some contexts, then, big man-like agents were in fact invested with religious authority. How this happens is unclear, but is probably due as much to historical circumstance and accident (recall the regional difference in New Guinea between the eastern and western Enga in terms of the turn to secular or religious leadership after the introduction of the sweet potato that were attributed by Wiessner and Tumu to different resource configurations) as well as the statistical tendency for lineage heads to be the leaders of ancestor cults that are so common in sedentary, land holding and defending transegalitarian societies (Hayden 2003:230–233).

Ethnography shows, however, that in some groups, a level of cooperation existed between secular leaders and religious ritual specialists that goes beyond a merely economic arrangement as is seen in highland New Guinea. One of the most dramatic examples of such an arrangement is that of the Gabrileño of southern California. In pre-contact times, the Gabrileño were a complex foraging people characterized by ranked, non-localized clans each with its own headman; the headman of the highest ranking clan was the "chief" of the village. Numerous pathways to wealth and influence existed, but at the apex of the social hierarchy were the chiefs, who possessed sacred bundles which helped to legitimize their social positions. These bundles could be passed on from father to son, but this did not necessarily imply that the son would become chief himself. Chiefs had considerable social power, but like their New Guinea counterparts, they had to demonstrate their generosity through the sponsoring of feasts, ritual, and other public events (Blackburn 1974).

The religious specialist among the Gabrileño was the shaman, a figure feared and viewed with suspicion. Often a personal friend of the chief, the shaman was the nominal supernatural protector of the village, safeguarded the sacred bundles of the chief, and led public rituals. Some ethnographies speak of an "unholy alliance" of chief and shaman, who often cooperated to maintain their personal positions at the expense of others. The shaman, however, did not act in a public venue and what wealth he was able to obtain was not translated into other social domains (Aldenderfer 1993, Blackburn 1974:23–24).

Wealthy Gabrileños were invited to become members of the *toloache* cult, which was a repository of secret lore and had responsibility for the financing and organization of public rituals (Blackburn 1974:104). The cult had considerable social influence within the village given its composition and control of aspects of religious knowledge. The shaman, interestingly, was not typically a member of this cult. The *toloache* does not appear to have a parallel in highland New Guinea, and thus appears to represent an integration of secular power with some aspects of religious authority that the Enga big men were never able to accomplish. We also see in the *toloache* the cooperation of shaman, secular chiefs, and other wealthy individuals that clearly had converging interests.

Despite the influence of the cult and its members, however, we still do not have a basis for "power over." For the Gabrileño, this came with the advent of intensive contact with the Spanish, and its appearance provides us with a way to think about how one trajectory to "power over" may emerge. As Gabrileño society suffered under Spanish rule and the devastating effects of epidemic disease, the *Chingichgnish* cult was created. Best seen as a kind if nativistic cult (Bean and Vane 1978:669), the shamanic hero Chingichgnish appeared to certain members of the toloache and instructed them in a new body of beliefs, which included heightened obedience to authority and self-sacrifice within a new context of a threat of sanction by a body of avenging spirits. Not surprisingly, the members of the new cult were those of the toloache, and it seems obvious that the cult was created by holders of wealth and social power to create a new foundation for their unequal access to wealth, diminished though it may be.

This emphasis on sanction is new, and I think significant. Boyd and Richerson (1985:229–230) note that it is never in one's self-interest to punish others, and always better to find a third party to do so. What better third party than to invoke non-human agents! But human actions still matter, and as I have argued elsewhere:

> With the development of the Chingichgnish cult and its ideology of punishment, fear, and sanction, however, the chief gained more direct access to the coercive power of the shaman. ... The cult essentially redefined the basis of the moral authority of the chief by publicly permitting his use of the shaman to punish those who failed to live up to the new moral code (Aldenderfer 1993:29).

Although this cult did not persist for long, what matters in this example is the attempt to use religion as a basis for sanction for "power over." What is also apparent in this example is the crisis of contradiction within Gabrileño society that created a context for this attempt to extend secular leadership into a wholly new realm. Such crises in highland New Guinea, even those events that led to the creation of the nativistic Ain cult, were not suitably weighty to lead to an overt attempt to find a basis for sanction. Indeed, the failure of this cult as well as other avenues to persistent leadership through trade or warfare only serve to heighten the observation by Wiessner and Tumu (1998:300) "that centralized, stratified societies developed independently only rarely in history out of unusual circumstances, while others formed out of competition with or domination by more complex societies." But of those trajectories that do lead to persistent leadership, it is likely that religion and its manipulation is necessary for such a transition to succeed. Further, it is very likely that the medium within which religion can enable change of this magnitude (or to offer resistance to it) is the cult, which has become of late a fashionable topic of study (Barrowclough and Malone 2007).

Fashionable or not, I think cults are key to understanding the emergence of social inequality and the ways in which religion is used by actors to extend their differences with their fellows or to level them. This means that archaeologists are going to need to pay far more attention to cults and how to recognize them archaeologically. It is not just ritual that we are looking for, but instead contexts within which cults might be observed and the ways in which new rituals, old rituals, or something in between is being created. But the ethnographic examples described in this paper give us an idea of just how hard this is going to be. For example, we have seen new ritual structures and venues created (the post-sweet potato Kepele cult and its larger, more central cult house), new ritual actions contrasted with those of a previous activity (the burning of the new Kepele cult house after the ceremony rather than allowing it to rot as were old initiation cult houses), wholly new materializations of religion created (the sacred stones of the Kepele cult), discarding of old symbols (the removal of sacred stones from the Kepele cult house as well as its abandonment in the face of the Ain nativistic cult), and the increasing intensity of ritual performance (the massive pig slaughter of the Ain cult). Without ethnography, it would be very hard, maybe even impossible, to know that first three examples were attempts to justify increasing inequality while the latter two were within contexts of resistance to the extension of inequality. We will also have to be successful at reading contexts for circumscription and contradiction and to determine if the notion of the crisis of contradiction can be recognized in the archaeological record.

Final Remarks

In this paper, I have argued that despite formidable methodological problems, we need to actively seek the material manifestations of religion in the archaeological record of societies undergoing social and economic transformations leading to the emergence of persistent social inequality. We need to remind ourselves that we are looking at and for religion, not disembodied ritual, and that the changes we seek to identify were created by actors working within the context of belief systems and practices, while difficult to visualize, nevertheless were key elements of their lives.

Despite its real importance, however, the ethnographic examples I have offered in this paper show that religion in and of itself does not appear to be capable of creating a lasting foundation for persistent inequality. This foundation can only be created by a combination of religious authority and leadership and some form of secular power. Religion enables aggrandizers in their pursuits, but does not guarantee their success. Wealth and other forms of social power still matter. Nevertheless, religion must be re-situated in the causal mix of factors that lead to the appearance and maintenance of, as well as resistance to, attempts to create persistent inequality if we are to craft more plausible interpretations of its appearance in the past.

References

Aldenderfer, M. 1993. Ritual, hierarchy, and change in foraging societies. *Journal of Anthropological Archaeology* 12: 1–40.

Aldenderfer, M. 2005. Preludes to Power in the Highland Late Preceramic Period. In Vaughn, K.J., Ogburn, D.E., and Conlee, C.A. (eds.), *Foundations of Power in the Prehispanic Andes*, pp. 13–35. Archaeological Papers of the American Anthropological Association Number 14.

Barrowclough, D., and Malone, C. (eds.). 2007. *Cult in Context: Reconsidering Ritual in Archaeology*. Oxford: Oxbow Books.

Bean, L., and Vane., S. 1978. Cults and their Transformation. In Heizer, R. (ed.), *Handbook of North American Indians, Vol. 8, California*, pp. 662–672. Washington: Smithsonian Institution.

Beidelman, T. 1971. *The Kaguru: A Matrilineal People of East Africa*. New York: Holt, Rinehart, and Winston.

Betzig, L. 1986. *Despotism and Differential Reproduction: A Darwinian View of History*. Hawthorne: Aldine.

Billings, D. 2002. *Cargo Cult as Theater: Political Performance in the Pacific*. Lanham: Lexington Books.

Blackburn, T. 1974. Ceremonial Integration and Social Interaction in Aboriginal California. In Bean, L. and King, T. (eds.), *Antap: California Indian Political and Social Organization*, pp. 93–110. Ramona: Ballena Press.

Bloch, M. 1992. *Prey into Hunter: The Politics of Religious Experience*. Cambridge: Cambridge University Press.

Boehm, C. 1999. *Hierarchy in the Forest: The Evolution of Egalitarian Behavior*. Cambridge: Harvard University Press.

Boyd, R., and Richerson, P. 1985. *Culture and the Evolutionary Process*. Chicago: University of Chicago Press.

Brown, D.E. 1991. *Human Universals*. Philadelphia: Temple University Press.

Brown, J.A., and Price, T.D 1985. Complex Hunter-Gatherers: Retrospect and Prospect. In Price, T.D. and Brown, J. (eds.), *Prehistoric Hunter-Gatherers: the Emergence of Cultural Complexity*, pp. 436–442. New York: Academic Press.

Camerer, C., and Lowenstein., G. 2003. Behavioral Economics: Past, Present, and Future. In Camerer, C., Lowenstein, G., and Rabin, M. (eds.), *Advances in Behavioral Economics*, pp. 1–23. Princeton: Princeton University Press.

Carneiro, R. 1970. A theory of the origin of the state. *Science* 169: 733–738.

Carneiro, R. 1988. The circumscription theory—challenge and response. *American Behavioral Scientist* 31(4): 497–515.

Chagnon, N. 1997. *Yanomamo: The Fierce People*, 5th Edition. Ft. Worth: Harcourt Brace College Publishers.

Douglas, M. 1970. *Natural Symbols: Explorations in Cosmology*. New York: Pantheon.

Durkheim, E. 1995 [1912]. *The Elementary Forms of Religious Life*, Translated by K. Fields. New York: The Free Press.

Geertz, C.B. 1973. *The Interpretation of Cultures*. New York: Basic Books.

Gibbs, P.J. 1977. The cult from Lyeimi and the Ipili. *Oceania* 48(1): 1–25.

Hayden, B. 1995. Pathways to Power: Principles for Creating Socioeconomic Inequalities. In Price, T.D. and Feinman, G.M. (eds.), *Foundations of Social Inequality*, pp. 15–86. New York: Plenum.

Hayden, B. 2003. *Shamans, Sorcerers, and Saints: A Prehistory of Religion*. Washington: Smithsonian Books.

Hickerson, H. 1970. *The Chippewa and their Neighbors: A Study in Ethnohistory*. New York: Holt, Rinehart, and Winston.

Insoll, T. 2001. Introduction: The Archaeology of World Religions. In Insoll, T. (ed.), *Archaeology and World Religion*, pp. 1–32. London: Routledge.

Jebens, H. (ed.). 2004. *Cargo, Cult, and Culture Critique*. Honolulu: University of Hawaii Press.

Johnson, G. 1982. Organizational Structure and Scalar Stress. In Renfew, C., Rowlands, M., and Seagraves, B. (eds.), *Theory and Explanation in Archaeology*, pp. 389–421. New York: Academic Press.

Lee, R.B. 1990. Primitive Communism and the Origin of Social Inequality. In Upham, S. (ed.), *The Evolution of Political Systems: Sociopolitics in Small-Scale Sedentary Societies*, pp. 225–246. Cambridge: Cambridge University Press.

Linton, R. 1943. Nativistic movements. *American Anthropologist* 45: 230–240.

Malinowski, B. 1954 [1925]. *Magic, Science, and Religion in Society*. Garden City: Doubleday.

Meggitt, M.J. 1973. The sun and the shakers: a millenarian cult and its transformations in the new guinea highlands. *Oceania* 44(1): 1–37.

Mitchell, W. 1988. The defeat of hierarchy: gambling as exchange in a sepik society. *American Ethnologist* 15: 638–657.

Mooney, J. 1896. The Ghost Dance Religion and the Sioux Outbreak of 1890. *Proceedings of the 14th Annual Report of the Bureau of American Ethnology for the Years 1892–1893*. Part 2, Washington.

Ritzenthaler, R. 1978. Southern Chippewa. In Trigger, B. (ed.), *Handbook of North American Indians, Vol. 15, Northeast*, pp. 708–724. Washington: Smithsonian Institution.

Sahlins, M.D. 1976. *Cultural and Practical Reason*. Chicago: University of Chicago Press.

Tylor, E.B. 1871. *Primitive Culture: Researches into the Development of Mythology, Philosophy, Religion, Art, and Custom*. London: Murray.

Wallace, A.F.C. 1966. *Religion: An Anthropological View*. New York: Random House.

Wengrow, D. 2003. Machiavellian moments: a discussion with Maurice Bloch. *Journal of Social Archaeology* 3: 299–311.

Wiessner, P., and Tumu, A. 1998. *Historical Vines: Enga Networks of Exchange, Ritual, and Warfare in Papua New Guinea*. Washington: Smithsonian Institution Press.

Winkleman, M.J. 1990. Shamans and other "magico-religious" healers. A cross-cultural study of the origins, nature, and social transformations. *Ethos* 18(3): 308–352.

Chapter 5
Who Benefits from Complexity?
A View from Futuna

Brian Hayden and Suzanne Villeneuve

> *The reason that I expended all this effort on the Northwest Coast is that people have been saying that exploitation may exist elsewhere, but not on the Northwest Coast. I suggest that the ethnoenergetic model be applied elsewhere, especially to Polynesia.*
>
> (Ruyle 1973:627)

Introduction

Who benefits from complexity? Is it the general populace as systems theorists and functionalists would have it, or is it the elites as Marxists would have it? And if the latter, is it the warriors? the priests? the political big men or chiefs? This issue is critical for understanding the origins of socioeconomic inequality, one of the most important theoretical issues in archaeology being discussed today. There is a major rift among archaeological theorists as to whether political complexity and socioeconomic inequality emerged to serve the common good especially in enhancing defense, production, and distribution (Diehl 2000, Johnson 1982, Pebbles and Kus 1977, Saitta and Keene 1990:213–214, Saitta 1999, Suttles 1968), whether they emerged as a means of promoting elite self-interests or even exploitation by leaders (Diehl 2000, Earle 1977, 1978, 1997, Gilman 1981, Roscoe 2000), or whether they emerged from religious beliefs or other cultural values (as argued in Chapter 4 by Aldenderfer 1993, this volume, Cauvin 2000, Hollimon 2004:60, Lewis-Williams and Pearce 2005:165–167, 248, 288, Pauketat and Emerson 1997, Potter 2000:301, Rousseau 2001:119, Van Dyke 2004). Similarly, explanations for the collapse of complexity (as exemplified by the Olmec, Mississippian, Mayan, and Chacoan cases) vary from economic or environmental causes to social revolts, to loss of

B. Hayden (✉)
Archaeology Department, Simon Fraser University, Burnaby, BC, Canada
e-mail: bhayden@sfu.ca

T.D. Price, G.M. Feinman (eds.), *Pathways to Power*, Fundamental
Issues in Archaeology, DOI 10.1007/978-1-4419-6300-0_5,
© Springer Science+Business Media, LLC 2010

faith in chiefly ideologies (the latter views being expressed by Chazan 2007:353, Drennan 1976:360–364, Heizer [*Excavations at La Venta*] 1963, Smith [*Myths and the Moundbuilders*] 1995, Van Dyke 2004). The exchange of prestige objects is also sometimes viewed as the result of ideological factors (rather than materialist factors), for example in order to move artifacts of power from craftsmen who had spiritual powers to those who sought such power (Brookes 2004:112, Goldman 1970:496, Rousseau 2001:119).

In all of these models, the role of chiefs occupies a central position; and it will be important to determine whether chiefs were obeyed primarily because people believed in their claims of ancestral sacredness and mana, because they served the common good, or because of more political or practical reasons–supported or justified, to be sure, by ideological claims. While we are mainly concerned with the general nature of chiefdoms and their dynamics, we use a specific case study from the island of Futuna to exemplify many points since some colleagues maintained that power in Polynesian chiefdoms was based far more on ideological beliefs than in simpler transegalitarian societies. We explore these issues from a political ecology perspective in which the ultimate motivation for developing chiefly roles and ideologies is the benefit that can be conferred on those in power.

Using this political ecological approach, we investigated the feasting and corporate kinship groups that Futunan chiefs rely on to create relatively complex sociopolitical systems. By political ecology, we specifically refer to the study of the way in which resources (in particular surplus resources) are used by certain members of pre-industrial communities to acquire practical, political, and economic benefits. Our approach is distinct from traditional cultural ecology, which has focused on subsistence resources, foraging strategies, and nutritional requirements (Campbell 1983, Vayda 1969, Winterhalder and Smith 1981). Our approach is also distinct from modern political ecology that studies contemporary national elites and the ways that they exploit national resources for political and economic gain (e.g. Anderson 1994, Greenberg and Park 1994, Kottak 1999, Stott and Sullivan 2001, Wolf 1972,). Similar approaches to the one we employ here have been long advocated by Earle (1978, 1997) who described the "political economy" of chiefdoms, and more recently by Bliege Bird and Smith (2005) who explain many of the practices we address in terms of "signaling theory." We differ from Bleige-Bird and Smith, however, in viewing such practices as feasting not only as signaling behavior (which it is), but behavior that also entails real reciprocal contracts and debts that are used to create sociopolitical structures.

Some of the main points that we wish to make are (1) that feasting played a critical role in creating political complexity and achieving practical goals; (2) that creating political hierarchies requires considerable supplemental resources beyond subsistence needs (Rambo 1991), especially for the feasts and prestige goods required to make these systems function; (3) that it is unrealistic to try to base enduring and costly institutional leadership roles on practices or values that do not confer any practical advantages on leadership; and (4) that the possibility of controlling some portion of community surpluses provided great potential for self-aggrandizement and the acquisition of power, which consequently motivated ambitious individuals to create complex sociopolitical structures. Such motivation and opportunities created pressures over time to develop ever more complex sociopolitical systems wherever resource production could be augmented. We suggest that economic factors such as the control of irrigation, highly productive land, trade, or other resources provided the key leverage necessary to achieve sustained acceptance of new ideologies or values useful to aggrandizers and to consolidate socioeconomic inequalities and political power. While ideological belief systems can provide important support and justification for other, more practically grounded strategies, we doubt that ideological strategies on their own could ever constitute a sufficient or principal basis for the enduring development of centralized political control. It is our contention that in order to achieve widespread compliance with ideological claims, practical consequences must be brought to bear.

Transegalitarian Studies Provide a Prelude to Studying Chiefdoms

Because models of transegalitarian community dynamics played a critical role in formulating our approach, we begin our analysis with a summary of pertinent conclusions from this research from the Maya Highlands and Southeast Asia (see Hayden and Gargett 1990). Earlier Functionalist-oriented researchers had argued that in village societies like those of the Maya Highlands, New Guinea, and the Amazon, "leveling" devices prevented political leaders from benefiting from their roles. Ideas such as "limited good" impelled community members to exact expenditures from prosperous families (via expenses involved in public office holding) in order to curtail excessive accumulations. Within these models, sociopolitical structures like Melanesian big men networks and the Mesoamerican cargo system were viewed as functioning to curtail inequalities. In return for depleting their wealth, officeholders were supposed to acquire prestige and respect in their communities (Carrasco 1961, Foster 1967:123–124, Kirkby 1973, Nash 1958, Price 1972). It was argued that Big Men "must shoulder responsibility and produce a surplus of wealth for distribution among his dependants, temporary assistants, and ceremonial partners ... [and] By his own achievements he must constantly validate his preeminence and ... maintain the prestige of his clan" (Kaberry 1971:62). Political institutions were therefore "designed to take from the rich and give to the poor ... the principal instrument used to achieve this is the cargo" (Kirkby 1973:31). In this vein, Cancian (1965) portrayed the cargo system as primarily serving a community integrative function. Consequently, these communities have frequently been viewed as "egalitarian" societies, views that still dominate archaeological thinking (Roscoe 2000:114, Wiessner 2002).

In an attempt to obtain a better idea of the role of village level elites, Hayden traveled to remote Maya Highland villages in 1990. Aside from some loose national bureaucratic ties, these villages appeared to have operated essentially as independent traditional transegalitarian communities until the creation of a national road system in the 1950s and 1960s and therefore made a suitable study area for understanding transegalitarian community dynamics. Having adopted a communal, processual, systems approach similar to those discussed above, Hayden was convinced that political leaders would provide systemic advantages for everyone in times of crisis and that it was important to obtain ethnographic validation for this perspective (Hayden and Gargett 1990). However, it was a great surprise when none of the expectations for systemic benefits materialized from his ethnographic interviews in the Maya Highlands. Instead of benefits conferred on the community by the elites during times of crises (when benefits would have been most critical), there was blatant opportunism, exploitation of situations, and an almost total lack of assistance by elites in any form for less fortunate villagers (ibid).

For Hayden, this demonstrated that the great majority of village elites or political leaders were *not* motivated by ideals of serving their communities, but instead were involved in leadership roles in order to advance their own self-interests, sometimes in surprisingly unabashed fashions. Such clearcut results led to his abandonment of explanations based on idealized functional or systems paradigms. Instead, the "political" model that emerged from this reorientation closely resembled the perspectives that Timothy Earle (1977, 1978) had developed for Hawaii and that Patrick Kirch had formulated (1991:129) for the Marquesas where stored food was used to ensure the survival of elites while the poor starved.

While Hayden concluded from his Mesoamerican experiences that officeholders in transegalitarian communities were materially benefiting from their positions, the lip service given by the Maya (and most transegalitarian societies) to egalitarianism made it difficult to determine precisely how this was occurring in non-crisis situations. Hayden therefore decided to undertake a research program among Southeast Asian tribal groups to further examine such dynamics. The goals of the Southeast Asian program involved determining whether important inequalities existed within societies that had previously been categorized as "egalitarian," whether individuals in key positions obtained material advantages, how this was accomplished under the watchful gaze of those who wanted to defend their own self-interests and more "egalitarian" relations, and whether "aggrandizers" played a key role in dynamics involved in unequal material benefits.

In order to understand some of the critical dynamics involved in the disbursement of wealth, the Southeast Asian programs began to focus on the kinds of support networks that underlie costly feasts or office holding and the kinds of implicit or explicit reciprocal debts, political arrangements, and access to key resources they entail.

It was therefore critical to examine whether feasts really are economic drains, or if costly office holding or feasting can sometimes be practically beneficial for individuals. Feasts, with the publicly proclaimed motives of obtaining spiritual blessings for individuals, certainly do occur, but there are also often underlying agendas as Clarke (1998, 2001) has demonstrated. Mauss (1925), Firth (1959:423), Reay (1959), and Sillitoe (1978) all refer to the public façades that aggrandizers employ to camouflage their self-interested schemes (similar to the "false consciousness" of Marxists). As Sahlins (1963:289) phrases it: "Their ostensible interest in their supporters' general welfare hides a more profound measure of self-interest, entrepreneurial acumen, and economic calculation." Dynamics surrounding feasting systems that emerged from a more political-ecology-oriented analysis in these communities demonstrated the frequent façade of "egalitarian ethos" (Adams 2004, Clarke 2001, Hayden and Cannon 1984, Hayden 1996). Instead, feasts generally served to create and maintain social networks essential for mobilizing economic and political ambitions (Clarke 2001). Any wealth-leveling function of administrative roles or the egalitarian characterization of the communities seemed unlikely since substantial inequalities in resource ownership, wealth, and power typify these and other so-called egalitarian societies (e.g. Cancian 1965:140, Feil 1987:111–117).

From our perspective the term "egalitarian" is best applied to simple hunter/gatherers or other immediate-return societies, where there is no significant private ownership, no economically based competition, few wealth differences, and usually few prestige items as among Western Desert Australian Aborigines (Barnard and Spencer 1996:301). Where significant ownership of resources, economically based competition, and wealth differences occur but are not institutionalized as class distinctions, we refer to such societies as "transegalitarian" societies.

After examining the situation on Futuna, we suggest that the dynamics deduced to be important in transegalitarian societies were also fundamental to the organization of simple chiefdoms. We suggest that the Futunan case study probably represents a much more general pattern in the development of chiefdom-level sociopolitical complexity in the world. One of the key concepts in understanding the development of transegalitarian and chiefdom organizations is the role of the "aggrandizer."

Futuna sheds light on general transegalitarian development

Aggrandizers

We define "aggrandizers" as individuals who are strongly motivated to promote their own self-interests, typically at the expense of others. Aggrandizers tend to be aggressive, ambitious, and accumulative and so we sometimes refer to them as "Triple A" personality types. They constitute a special case of "agency" models that epitomize Margaret Mead's supposed dictum: "Never doubt that a small group of thoughtful, committed citizens can change the world." However, she undoubtedly had much more idealistic goals in mind than the self-serving motivations of aggrandizers.

While everyone needs to defend their own interests to some extent to survive, there is a wide range of actual behavior related to self-interest. At one end of the spectrum, some people are altruistically oriented and seem constantly alert for any situation in which they can be helpful to others. At the other end of the spectrum are people who are much more self-centered. These aggrandizing personalities seem to be constantly alert for any situations that will benefit themselves. In the most *extreme* cases, such individuals exhibit psychopathic behavior.

Many aggrandizers gravitate to political and entrepreneurial positions, although not everyone who becomes an administrator or entrepreneur in traditional societies is necessarily an aggrandizer. Sometimes the people that come to fill key roles, such as lineage heads, genuinely have the interests of their supporters at heart. They typically come to their roles simply by dint of birth or age rather than ambition, skill, or merit. However, where there are fixed rules of accession such roles are often figureheads that lack real power. In these cases, power generally resides with the members of councils, elder kin, or with "adjunct" administrators who are more likely to be ambitious and astute organizers and attain their positions by skillful maneuvering and achievement.

The role of the institutional figurehead is often simply to announce the decision of the power holders, often conferring an aura of sanctity upon it due to their ritual role, as in the case of the Akha *dzuma* (Clarke 2001:146). In Maori chiefdoms, Firth (1959:132) explicitly states that chiefs who were inept were relegated to ceremonial roles while their "aides" who were more intensely pragmatic took care of lineage or village business. Similarly, in Tonga, a formal division between the sacred and secular power of a paramount chief was established in 1470 with the creation of two paramount chiefs with different roles (Evans 2001:31–32)—a situation not unlike the largely ceremonial role of Futunan paramount chiefs and Territorial executive administrators today.

In Hayden's data from Southeast Asia, aides were often the real power brokers of some social groups and appeared to conform much more closely to the aggrandizer types of personalities, while in situations where kin group elders formed councils, it was the most successful achievers/aggrandizers who appeared to have the most influence in council decisions (Clarke 2001:150). Similarly, in Polynesia and Melanesia, opinions of the wealthy carried most weight (Grijp 2002:28, Roscoe n.d.). Among the Kpelle of West Africa, as well, "only a very wealthy man of advanced years could hope to pass initiation into the higher degrees ... the executive council and tribunal of the [secret] society decided policy and was the court of final appeal" (Little 1965:359). As Izikowitz (1951:117, 139) bluntly put it for the Lamet: the rich decide everything of importance.

It is our contention that a number of the ideological beliefs and values as well as sociopolitical organizations (such as corporate groups with their administrative or religious positions) can be viewed as having been created by aggrandizers, so that they could benefit from leadership roles whenever they could maneuver themselves into these (or key controlling) positions using various strategies. Although they serve other functions, their ultimate purpose is to ensure that positions exist which provide greater access to, or control over, certain resources.

In contemporary and traditional societies alike, we see that in order to achieve their goals, aggrandizers amass wealth, resources, wives, ritual knowledge, and other commodities in a variety of strategies developed to manipulate people. Hayden (2001b:258–262) documents the use (in varying combinations) of 13 basic strategies to achieve these goals (not including brute force). These include feasts, the use of surpluses in the establishment of prestige items (used to certify alliances or agreements in the acquisition of mates through payments–typically bride prices or dowries in the form of domestic animals or prestige items), and in the augmenting of children's worth through training or feasts so that marriage wealth exchanges could be increased, as well as other strategies. However, many of these strategies were undoubtedly as subtle and manipulative as the strategies that modern administrators, salesmen, and proselytizers use today. These more subtle strategies have been described in detail by social psychological studies of techniques that people use in order to obtain compliance of target populations (Perloff 2003:247–262, Trenholm 1989:311–315). One of the most common strategies used by aggrandizers in traditional societies is the appeal to the common good and the hosting of feasts. Dietler (2001) and Wiessner (2001) have both emphasized the ways that feasts can serve as important venues for manipulating community values and obtaining the compliance of community members (although various kinds of feasts obviously serve other functions as well). Thus aggrandizers are able to transform important social norms, beliefs, values, and practices by using several different strategies.

Hayden and several students spent nearly a decade exploring these various strategies and trying to determine who benefits from feasts and political positions in transegalitarian societies in Southeast Asia (Adams 2001, 2004, 2005, Clarke 1998, 2001, Hayden 2001a, b). The results were unambiguous. The leaders of powerful factions in Hill Tribe communities used feasts, bride prices, and other strategies to create and sustain their factional support both within and between kinship groups, while the factions themselves had important influences on the success and even survival of constituent households. In contexts where conflicts between households and between villages were endemic, being part of a powerful faction could spell the difference between well-being and enslavement, between good social status and ostracism, and between victory and rout in armed conflicts (see also Hakansson 1994:261, Izikowitz 1951:117, 139).

Conflicts occurred for many reasons: stealing of pigs, livestock, or wives; damage to crops from one's animals; transgressions of local traditions or taboos; illicit relationships; stealing or unauthorized use of property; injuries from dogs; boundary disputes; and disputes about inheritances or unpaid debts of deceased family members. Those individuals or families that lacked substantial support could be heavily fined, evicted from the community, driven to suicide, or enslaved (Condominas 1977:123, 139, 151, 156, 338–339). Individuals from powerful families might get off with light reprimands or fines due to "extenuating" circumstances. "Litigation" over these issues was constantly underway in the less pacified Hill Tribes in Southeast Asia, and it was the lineage heads of the most powerful factions in the communities who decided the outcomes (Condominas 1977, Leach 1954:183).

In other complex traditional societies, the same political dynamic often resulted in different penalties for members of different classes as exemplified by the protohistoric Celts (Ross 1986:89), the Maori (Firth 1959:348), West Africans (Little 1965:358), the Natchez (Swanton 1911:102–105), native British Columbians (Emmons 1991:46), Californians (Kroeber 1953:33), and the Sumerians (Westbrook 2003). Moreover, the most powerful factions in Southeast Asian Hill Tribes managed to appropriate the most productive economic resources for themselves, whether in the form of good land, livestock, or sources of trade items. These resources, in turn, were used to underwrite the creation of lineages and lineage factions through feasting and other strategies that created even greater power to control resources and local politics (Hayden 2001b).

Our research among transegalitarian societies suggests that it was aggrandizers who promoted the creation of important roles (such as lineage or clan heads, village political positions, and well-paid ritualists) and a variety of new ideological norms (such as many taboos, private ownership, inheritance, primogeniture, bride prices, reciprocal debts, ancestors' influences on the living, and costly funeral displays). Consistent with Sahlins' (1963) and others' observations, all of these roles and norms could be portrayed to fellow villagers as benefiting larger kin or residential groups (often with the initial underwriting provided by aggrandizers). However, these norms and roles often also had the effect of maximizing aggrandizers' interests. Once these new roles and values were adopted, they created a framework or structure that provided aggrandizers with the tools necessary to achieve self-interested goals as described by Roscoe (n.d.) for New Guinea. Achieving these goals was never a guaranteed outcome, only a potential one. These potentials were not fulfilled by every ambitious individual or everyone in a leadership role. The important point is that when aggrandizer personalities did move into leadership roles or more covert power roles, either by right or by manipulation, the roles and the associated values necessary for successfully implementing their strategies were in place and ready to be actively used to promote aggrandizer self-interests. The critical step was establishing the framework.

Not every leader, every faction, or every village was a success story, just as not every business venture is a success today. However, those that did use aggrandizer strategies successfully ensured that the tradition persisted. As Murphy (1980:204) concluded from his work among the simple chiefdoms of West Africa: "The resulting image of Kpelle elders is not one of benevolent wise old men ... Rather it is one of calculating elders who keep the young under their thumbs." While the specific strategies and ideologies employed by individual aggrandizers may vary according to their abilities, personalities, and historical circumstance, the patterns that transcend generations and communities must be the most successful ones that resonate the most with general conditions and people's concerns.

Some supporters of aggrandizers were undoubtedly motivated to provide support due to their own ambitions to rise as high as they could in the fledgling economic and political organizations. Others undoubtedly provided support simply to avoid falling prey to rapacious community members or falling into the marginalized and disadvantaged "rubbish" categories of society. Still others were probably tricked into contractual agreements involving debts, marriages, protection, or other ruses with unanticipated consequences—just as unscrupulous entrepreneurs today lure people into contracts with hidden consequences. As documented below (see Village Feasts, Fines and Penalties, and Role of Kindred), many villagers were also undoubtedly pressured or even physically coerced into supporting chiefly aggrandizers and their schemes. In traditional oral accounts and some early historical accounts, it would appear that aggrandizer Futunan and Polynesian chiefs did not hesitate to employ force and intimidation tactics to get their way (Dening 1980:67, 102, 231–232, Frimigacci 1990:173, Kirch 1991, Piazzi et al. 1991:14–16, Sahlins 1983, Stevens 1996:235–236, Viala 1919:237, 240). Indeed, one must wonder what amount of leverage must have been necessary to get people to adopt the figurative traditional greetings to chiefs such as: "Eat me" (Sahlins 1983:78–79). Elite members of chiefly secret societies elsewhere in the world often did not hesitate to terrorize or kill individuals or groups in order to obtain compliance (Little 1965:353). The same strategies were ruthlessly employed in complex chiefdoms and rudimentary states simply to manifest elite claims to power and ensure compliance with their wishes (Dickson 2006).

Thus there would have been many reasons for actively supporting strong leaders or factions. Some of the political and practical benefits that aggrandizers obtained in these transegalitarian sociopolitical systems included:

- The ability to broker the best bride prices or dowries for their own children;
- The greatest wealth exchanges with the most desirable families;
- The use of corporate wealth items (nominally held "in trust" for their social groups) for their own ends;
- Consuming the best foods and wearing the most opulent garments in all public displays;
- The potential to manipulate group finances to promote one's own interests (via demands for feasts or other group undertakings);
- The ability to own or exploit the best resources within or beyond the village territory;
- Elevated decision-making power within their group and the community;
- A greater ability to survive crises (such as famines, illness, accidents, litigations, and threats of attack); and
- The ability to obtain more desirable mates and more of them, as well as the ability to produce more children and be assured of a secure old age, a strong power base in the community, and perhaps increased prestige (also discussed by Boone 2000, Roscoe n.d.).

Roscoe (n.d.) documents many of the same benefits listed above as character-istic of the "huge men" (big men verging on becoming chiefs) in traditional New Guinea societies. Supporters within the kin or social group could expect to obtain many of these same benefits (to varying degrees) through active support of a suc-cessful aggrandizing leader, a point emphasized by Lindstrom and White (1997:9). Individuals who did not actively support group feasts or other undertakings could be delisted from genealogies of their kinship unit (as among Torajans in Sulawesi), prevented from marrying, marginalized in terms of all the above benefits, and essen-tially relegated to poverty, or even enslaved by their own kin or others as reported by Condominas.

In sum, aggrandizers are a strong motivating force behind a number of social, political, and ideological changes in transegalitarian societies. They use a range of strategies to achieve self-interested goals; they pander to common interests when necessary, they use economic leverage or coercion when they can, and they promote new ideological concepts as justifications for their endeavors or as a means of obtaining compliance.

A Prelude to Chiefdoms

Timothy Earle (1997), Jeanne Arnold (1996), and others have summarized the major theories about how chiefs come to power. Aside from cognitive factors, the major contenders are circumscription, warfare, trade and wealth financing (control over political economies), control over staple production, population pressure, the systemic advantages of central administration or redistribution, and extortion. A number of reviewers and commentators maintained that ritual and ideology were much more entrenched and powerful in chiefdoms than in transegalitarian societies, and that chiefs were obeyed primarily because of people's belief in their claims to ancestral sacredness and spiritual power. Such qualities were certainly promoted by elites in traditional Futunan chiefdoms and in Polynesian society in general, and it will be important here to examine to what degree people supported chiefs on the basis of ideology and belief systems.

The importance of ideas, values, and belief systems in structuring societies has a long history in anthropology, from Weber to Parsons, Sapir and Whorf, Foucault, Pauketat, Giddens, and Bourdieu. Recently, some archaeologists have maintained that it was "a particular suite of ideas [that] was central to the creating of large-scale social order" (Hodder 2007:114), while others argue that "ideological functions lie at the heart of aristocratic rule in all centralized non-industrial societies" (Helms 1999). Political and economic forms of power are considered by some to be lacking in some early chiefdoms like the Nasca, thus leaving ideology as the basis of power, notably through the manipulation of symbols (Vaughn 2005:116, 126). In other chiefdom contexts like Buganda, top positions of hierarchy are seen as being established by demonstrating "direct, effective, and/or tangible contact with cosmological primacy" (Helms 1999). Other archaeologists argue for the predominant importance of the role of sacred knowledge in the creation of chiefdoms and early states (Emerson et al. 2003, Gell 1993:240, Helms 1994:58–59, 1999, Joyce and Winter 1996, Lewis-Williams and Pearce 2005:165–167, 248, 288, Chazan 2007:308, Pauketat and Emerson 1997, see also Cauvin 2000). In these cases, "The critical question is the degree to which the elites managed society by ... religious authority" (Chazan 2007:308, 353).

While cognitivist models of cultural dynamics are often different from functionalist views, they share a common focus on cultural values and commonly held beliefs as the major determinants of behavior and sociopolitical institutions, notably in the power of ideology and beliefs in maintaining and supporting chiefly authority. Like, cognitive models, functionalist explanations for the roles of community institutions have a distinguished history in anthropology beginning with Enlightenment philosophers and embellished by Durkheim, Radcliffe-Brown, Malinowski, systems theorists, and ecologists. From a functionalist perspective, chiefly prestige or sacredness was seen as balanced by, or even the result of, leveling traditions and the need for chiefs to be generous, to the extent that they sometimes did not materially benefit from their position or were perennially in the poorhouse. Burrows (1936:89), the principal ethnographer for Futuna in Polynesia, wrote, "chieftainship leads to poverty." In a similar vein, Firth (1959:133, 298, 429) emphasized that chiefly power among the Maori required generous giving to supporters as well as lavish feasting and hospitality which drew on a chief's resources "to a serious extent" and often "drained him of food supplies." Similar notions are found among chiefdoms outside Polynesia. Sapir (cited by Rosman and Rubel 1971:90) observed that on the Northwest Coast, "potlatching makes one poor, not rich" and Beynon (2000:145) noted, "chiefs never used anything for their own ends, but for the benefit of their people." While some functionalist views may no longer be considered valid, there are a number of variants that continue to be popular such as the communitarian models advocated by Saitta (1999) and complex adaptive systems models. Some researchers would go so far as to say that functionalist views (in which people voluntarily subjugate themselves to leaders because hierarchies benefit everyone) are currently the most influential models in archaeological thought (Roscoe 2000:114).

There is truth in the observation that chiefs must be, or must appear to be, generous in order to retain power. They must also represent interests of their constituency if they are to stay in power. Moreover, it was not the gross amount given away that was important, rather it was the balance between incoming goods and expenditures, the net amount under one's control, and the net debts and benefits. As discussed below, it seems likely that chiefs who went too far in either direction quickly lost support and were toppled. Perhaps investments may have temporarily impoverished them, just as modern industrial entrepreneurs become heavily indebted, especially in the early stages of their investment careers.

From our own investigations in Futuna, and other researchers' observations, we suggest that both the cognitive and functionalist paradigms have focused too exclusively on commonly held beliefs as sources of power and as motivations for supporting positions of power. They have been misleading in terms of not demonstrating where the resources for expenditures originate, the reciprocal or investment nature of many expenditures, the material benefits of elite positions, the use of physical/economic/social coercion, and the way that expenditures are manipulated for elite self-interests. We view the cognitive and functionalist paradigms as overgeneralizations about the actual dynamics taking place in chiefdoms.

How people are convinced to adopt, or acquiesce to new ideological proposals is a critical issue that is usually not addressed by cognitivists. Whether the promotion of new beliefs and value systems provides enough leverage to implement changes in a social system has been a contentious issue for decades. The current situation concerning how to avert catastrophic climate changes provides a case in point. Will belief in the threat of climate change be effective in reducing people's consumption of fossil fuels, or will measures such as increasing the price of carbon fuels be a necessary requirement to implement effective changes? In the case of chiefdoms, political ecology leads us to question some of the received notions about the ideological basis of chiefs' powers and to probe more deeply the actual dynamics underlying those beliefs and power. Political ecology also seeks to determine whether practical costs and benefits are provided to chiefs and their supporters, and to what degree these provide incentives for acquiring political positions.

Traditional and Modern Chiefdoms in Polynesia

Since critical details of feasting and sociopolitical dynamics were not always obtainable from ethnographic sources, we undertook research in the Pacific in 2003 and 2004 to determine if it was possible, even at this advanced state of world economic impacts, to obtain indications concerning who benefited in traditional chiefdom societies and how they benefited. To successfully undertake such research, we reasoned that a study of the most traditional chiefdom societies would be the most useful. The professional advice we received indicated that the chiefdoms on Futuna, some 500 km northeast of Fiji were among the best suited for these purposes. The degree to which there has been continuity from "traditional" culture to the present is a topic of considerable debate, with Gailey (1985), Dening (1980) and others arguing for profound early transformations, while Evans (2001), Grijp (2004), Stephens (1996) and others argue for many basic continuities. Democracy and democratic ideologies have generally been imposed in the region by churches and national administrations; chiefs' powers have been diminished by outlawing labor duties to them and transferring some of their powers to new administrative roles; mass education has promoted desires for consumer goods; cash and market economics have entered the islands; and increasing populations have created landless households (Evans 2001, Grijp 2004, Lockwood 1993, Stevens 1996). Thus, it was initially uncertain as to whether enough of the traditional political and social structure would have been maintained to say anything meaningful about traditional chiefly roles and benefits.

Despite the contact influences just noted, the effects of these developments have not been uniform in Polynesia. Where the potential has been high for developing cash economies as on Tahiti, Hawai'i, and Fiji, there have been strong pressures to commodify land and alienate it from corporate kinship control. This has led to increased individual self-reliance, a diminution of corporate kinship groups, the breakup of reciprocal support networks, and the elimination of needs for elaborate (and costly) gift exchanges to create those networks. In these cases, the basis of political authority has shifted from alliances of corporate kinship groups managed by heads who held title to land (the elders and chiefs), to individual-based democratic types of political alliances based on individual interests (Grijp 1993:227, 2002:20, 29, 2004:13, Stevens 1996:188). In these situations, the destruction of the traditional political structure has been almost complete.

However, where the potential for developing commodity market economies has been low, people have been forced to rely to a significant degree on their own ability to produce food for survival. In these cases, the control over access to land has remained a key feature of life, and this control has often remained vested in the hands of corporate kinship groups even despite legislation to the contrary. The heads of these land-based corporate groups traditionally used their control over access to land as the key to structuring political power in a hierarchical fashion. Where reliance on subsistence agriculture has remained strong, there has been great resistance to abolishing corporate land tenure since it guaranteed corporate members subsistence and reproduction security (Grijp 2004:189, Lockwood 1993:29).

As a result, the importance of "family," kinship networks, and corporate land tenure have remained strong in some areas, although the sizes of corporate kinship groups has generally been reduced due to other economic factors. Thus, on many smaller islands, corporate kinship groups have remained the basis for local organization and social life (Grijp 2004:189–190, Lockwood 1993:29, Stevens 1996:198). In these cases, the major influences and decision makers are still the heads of the corporate kinship groups who create alliances and factions largely through reciprocal feasts and gift exchanges. In this system, traditional chiefs have also retained varying degrees of influence by creating political factions among corporate kinship heads resulting in a hierarchical kinship/political system in which gift exchanges (largely of agricultural produce) still dominate the economies, with goods and labor flowing asymmetrically upward (Evans 2001:36–38, 52–58, 81, 96, 152, Grijp 1993:226, 2002:189, Stevens 1996:155, 173, 198).

Where these basic structural relations have persisted (as is the case on Futuna and similar small outlying islands in the Society Islands and the Tongan archipelago— Evans 2001, Lockwood 1993, Stevens 1996), many of the traditional customs associated with this sociopolitical structure also have persisted. These include:

– Use of formal ceremonies to display and give away wealth (Evans 2001:56, 152, Stevens 1996:155).
– Use of feasts and wealth exchanges as the primary means of creating social groups and alliances, generally focused on life transitions of members and political events (Evans 2001:44, 50, 127ff, Grijp 2004:189).
– Use of pigs, taro, mats, and bark cloth as major wealth items in feasts and exhchanges (Evans 2001, Stevens 1996:634).
– Some provisioning of traditional local chiefs (generally with strong kinship ties to the community) and paramount figureheads (whether chiefs, church, or administrative officials) with produce and help/labor (Grijp 1993:226, 2002:56).
– A major preoccupation of chiefs with the realignment of corporate kinship group coalitions and rank positions (Evans 2001:34–35).
– The maintenance of well-defined chiefly lineages (versus the more amorphous bilateral optative memberships of most kin groups).
– Kava circles that display the ranks or power of participants in seating arrangements and speaking order (Evans 2001:34–35).
– Asymmetric obligations of giving/sharing and labor support from brother to sister, younger to older, wife to husband, and commoners to elites. Such sharing along asymmetrical or reciprocal lines is so predominant in many cases that attempts to

start small businesses generally fail due to the strong demands of kin and others
to share goods stocked in the stores (Stevens 1996:455, 468).
- Views of history dominated by events and quasi mythological accounts of
  corporate kinship groups or alliances (Howard 1993).

These traits constitute many of the distinctive and enduring characteristics of traditional Polynesian society and serve as the basis for defining it. However, on the
islands that have retained corporate land tenure and a basic traditional structure,
there are some variations. On larger islands like Tonga with more potential for cash
crops and better infrastructure connections to markets overseas, there has clearly
been some attrition of corporate land tenure, kinship systems, wealth exchanges, and
chiefly power. These developments have not yet progressed to the extent of trans-
forming or eliminating these traditions, although the situation today is very dynamic
and may soon change especially with increased amounts of outside aid, as in French
Polynesia. In Tonga, and even more so in the smaller, more remote islands, any cash
generated is used first and foremost for sponsoring feasts and wealth exchanges,
although funding the education of children is becoming an increasingly important
use of cash. Only limited amounts of cash are used to purchase the limited consumer
goods available (Evans 2001:25, 51–58, Grijp 2004:9).

On the larger traditional islands, the downsizing of corporate kinship groups has
generally been more pronounced than on some of the smaller more remote islands
like Futuna. Evans (2001:25) reports that the nuclear or extended family now constitutes the corporate kinship group on Tonga, although these families still retain
strong kin linkages. In contrast, on Futuna, the larger kin groups known as *kutuga*'s
(discussed below) are still quite strong. In all cases, the options and choices available to individuals continue to be strongly influenced by the individual's position in
kin groups and hierarchies (Stevens 1996:200). And, although somewhat diminished, traditional chiefs can retain many traditional roles and obtain power and
influence using traditional sociopolitical structuring techniques. Sometimes they
even retain exclusive claims to new political positions and power as in western
Samoa, or manage to remove any nation state control over their claimed fields of
authority (Lindstrom and White 1997:13–15). Similar retention of power by traditional elites using traditional strategies to obtain local political positions within
nation state frameworks have been recorded by Adams (1997:265, 275) and Crystal
(1974).

In addition to these broader considerations, the scanty early historical accounts
(summarized below) seem to indicate that the basic present-day feasting structure
has not fundamentally changed. The political and family structures also appear similar to those reported in the earliest records. Kirch (1994a) analyzed the earliest
detailed accounts of feasts on Futuna primarily using missionary accounts from
the 1830s. Most of the feasts recorded from that period appear to have persisted
with little change into the present (for more detailed documentation see Hayden and
Villeneuve 2002).

Given its small size, its remote location in relation to commodity markets, its
virtually nonexistent ability to produce cash products (with the minor exception of

copra), its constitutional exclusion of land tenure by non-Futunans, and the heavy reliance on subsistence agriculture for basic foods, Futuna certainly ranks among the most traditional of Polynesian islands and can be viewed as having retained a meaningful part of its traditional political framework. However, the recent infusion of massive amounts of French aid in the form of salaries, contracts, and aid programs together with the control of many of these funds by the Territorial legislature is certainly changing this situation, a topic to which we will return in final discussions. Nevertheless, our assessment is that many fundamental structural and cultural traits in Polynesia are so widespread and have such historical depth that they probably represent pre-contact values, basic social organization, and behavioral patterns. Thus we feel that there are good grounds for examining the more traditional aspects of Futunan society today in order to understand the internal dynamics of earlier sociopolitical organizations.

It is also worth mentioning that we walked into this research with a political model based on feasting and alliances. We viewed the military conquest theories for the emergence of chiefdoms as unrealistic since warfare seemed to be endemic among most or all ethnographic transegalitarian societies without generally resulting in more complex sociopolitical structures, a situation exemplified in New Guinea and Amazonia. Once again, a paradigm modification turned out to be necessary to accommodate overwhelming claims and data concerning the role that warfare played in creating Polynesian chiefdoms—an aspect contrary to our initial expectations. These are discussed below.

The Futunan Chiefdom

Futuna is a relatively small volcanic island, only 20 × 5 km. At first census, there were only 1,500 people divided into two chiefdoms with 7–10 villages in each polity (Figs. 5.1 and 5.2). However, archaeological and ethnohistoric data indicate that there may have been as many as 4,000 inhabitants at peak periods during the past (Frimigacci 1990, Rozier 1963:104). Today, with external support, 5,000 people live on the island and they are still politically divided into two competing chiefdoms with a total of 14 villages. The nearby island of Wallis is often associated with Futuna because of the strong similarities in their traditional culture and sociopolitical structures. There are certainly some differences as well, including the larger land area on Wallis, larger population, somewhat greater cash flows, and increased integration into the world economy. However, many of the feasting and family political traditions are similar and the available information on feasting there may provide additional insights into practices on Futuna.

Ethnographers, such as Goldman, Sahlins, Earle, and Howard use a number of different ways of categorizing chiefdoms. However, from our perspective the Futunan chiefdoms can be most usefully described as "simple constituent chiefdoms" in which regional integration exists but local village leaders maintain considerable autonomy, only ceding a portion of their authority to the regional

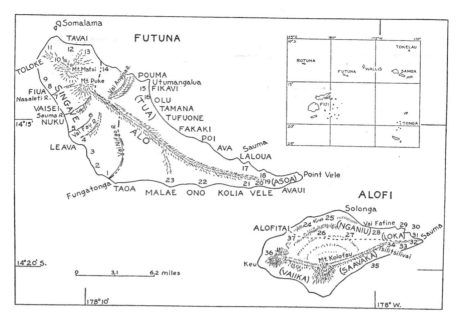

Fig. 5.1 A map of Futuna Island showing the current villages (Burrows 1936:6)

chief during periodic ceremonial or military occasions (Beck 2003:643, 656, Earle 1997:169). According to Beck's (2003:656) typology, these chiefdoms are based on persuasive political aggregation and are characterized by "endemic competition between local leaders to attract new followers" including raids and skirmishes intended to undermine the support base of rivals. This certainly seems to describe the contact situation on Futuna and the Marquesas, and even appears similar to the traditional societies on Tonga as reconstructed by Evans (2001:31–34), where internal shifts in title rank were due to changes in reproduction, war, political alliances, and political strength.

It is important to emphasize that pigs represent the consummate wealth item used for feasts in traditional Futunan society and Polynesian societies in general, while bark cloth and mats were highly valued wealth items produced by women (Gailey 1985). According to the Futunan data, pigs represent a household's major investment of surplus food and labor. Today, it generally takes about 2–3 years to raise a 600 kg pig at a cost of about 2–300 Polynesian Francs (US$ 1–1.50) per day, representing a total value of about 170,000 PFs (about US$ 2,000). In the more stratified and complex chiefdoms of the past such as Tahiti, elites ate much more pork than the commoners even though the lowest class of people did the breeding, rearing, fattening of pigs. Only those privileged enough to receive pork as a gift or tax, or powerful enough to require subordinates to raise pigs, ate pork on a regular basis. These highly valued foods were not generally available to women (Oliver 1974:

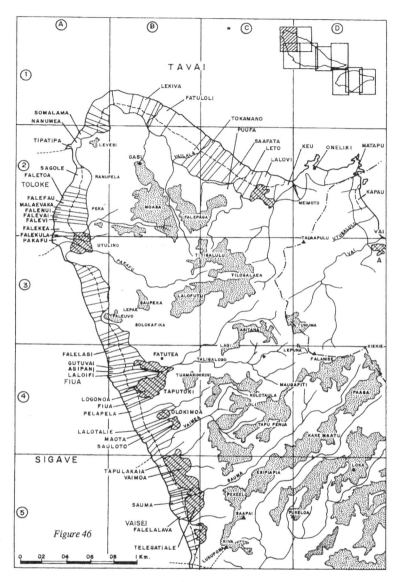

Fig. 5.2 Examples of kaiga corporate landholdings (the narrow strips extending from the coast inland) with communal swidden land (*unmarked*) in the interior of the island. Irrigated taro lands are indicated by *gridded areas* (Frimigacci 1990)

273–275). While the situation is more equitable on Futuna today, eating pork may have been a more exclusive privilege in the past.

The ultimate source of feasting-based power should be viewed as residing with the *kutuga* (corporate kindred) elders. In Futuna, it is the *kutuga* elders that wield the

elders are power wielders

most power and make the most critical decisions. They create alliances (factions), and the elders in the most powerful alliances largely determine who will be elected chief, who will be Territorial Representatives, and who will be given salaried positions or contracts. Futunans appear to assess the desirability of establishing alliances on the basis of the size, wealth, location, and motivation of the various *kutuga* kindreds. These characteristics are primarily gauged on the basis of the size and opulence of family feasts at key events such as first communions, marriages, funerals, and births. Prospective or currently allied elders from other *kutuga* are invited to these events. If there is a strong alliance relationship, the invited elder is expected to make a substantial gift contribution in support of the event, and will receive a substantial gift of food and prestige items to take back to his own *kaiga* (corporate household) or *kutuga* (corporate kindred) to distribute. The invited elder must also reciprocate with a similar invitation to his host whenever his kindred holds a major feast. As in transegalitarian and "traditional" Polynesian societies (Dening 1980:63, Evans 2001:34, 44, 50, Grijp 2004:189), this is the way that alliances are created, maintained, materialized, and made firm. Such practices require dependable levels of surplus production and explicit or implicit contractual agreements. Such tacitly agreed upon conditions have also been documented by Firth (1959:411–413, 416) and Goldman (1970:497) for wider Polynesia. These reciprocal exchanges constitute the major material and labor costs of creating non-egalitarian sociopolitical structures.

Futunan elders and their constituents obviously benefit from the system because it is they who hold title to the land (as descendants of the original conquerors) and ultimately decide all matters of importance. If a junior member of a family or *kutuga* (corporate kindred) requires help in marriage arrangements or in times of difficulty or in political contests, he or she is dependent on the kindred elder to underwrite and arrange those affairs. Thus support of one's kindred elder can provide real benefits to the general kindred membership, but there are many strings attached. Similar elder-kin power structures typify transegalitarian Southeast Asian communities. Today, as is also the case in Tonga (Evans 2001:142, Grijp 2002:28), elders still sit in prescribed seating orders at Futunan village meetings (*fono*) and at feasts, and they dominate the proceedings according to the standing of their families.

This system of allied corporate kindreds appears to be duplicated at a higher level in relationships between chiefs, with the paramount chief trying to hold together a coalition of allied village chiefs through a series of regularly renewed feasts, debts, and obligations. Perhaps in the past it was the inability of some village chiefs to meet their reciprocal obligations (due to incompetence, rival disruptive factions, poor luck, or other factors) that led to sociopolitical rupture within the paramount chief's alliance, and realignments of political/feasting allegiances to rival paramount chiefs. Such events may have happened frequently and often stimulated armed conflict between chiefdoms (Dening 1980:285, Goldman 1970:496, 519, Kirch 1991:125). In Futuna, elders are ranked according to the importance of their supporting corporate kindred group or *kutuga*. Traditionally, as in Tonga (Evans 2001:142) and the Marquesas Islands (Dening 1980:283) these ranks appear to have been subject to revision in order to correspond to material and demographic realities as well as success in warfare (discussed below).

There are scant references to political, social, or feasting characteristics by the earliest European visitors or residents on Futuna. The most useful information about early contact culture comes from the first missionaries who arrived in 1835, especially Père Chanel who was killed by a staunchly traditional chief. According to these early accounts, there were several island-wide feasts attended by *both* paramount chiefs together with representatives from all communities, and probably representatives from all major corporate kindred groups (*kutuga*) of the island. At least one of these *island-wide feasts* was held on the occasion of the first fruits harvest celebration—a ceremony generally used as a pretext for paying subsistence tribute to chiefs throughout Polynesia. The early missionaries recorded a series of *village feasts* attended by the paramount chief and other chiefs in the chiefdom alliance.

Village feasts were hosted and organized by individual village chiefs in consultation with their village administration and elders (Kirch 1994a:270). Such feasts were recorded when the first Europeans stopped at the island in 1616 (O'Reilly 1962:62). These types of feasts were still a major feature in the Futunan cultural landscape when Burrows conducted his ethnographic work (1936:100). In the past, these large feasts were said to be held in order to honor the gods (Smith 1892:46), while today each village has its patron saint in whose honor the feasts are held.

Prior to conversion, the gods were said to reside in the bodies of the chiefs (Rozier 1963:100–101). This claim of the elites helped provide them with material and political advantages by legitimizing their demands in ideological terms. Similar strategies are sometimes also used by aggrandizers in transegalitarian societies where special supernatural powers are claimed, particularly concerning garden magic or even involving powerful spirits residing in the chests of head men, as among the Yanomamo (Chagnon 1973). Similar ideological claims of supernatural ancestry also occur among the Natchez (e.g. Swanton 1911:101–102) and elsewhere.

The village feasts described in the earliest documents appear fundamentally similar to village feasts today (described below). A great deal of surplus was probably transferred to the chiefs at these events for their use and distribution, as is the case today. In other early accounts, some feasts were hosted by a pair of villages, perhaps constituting a district or the pooling of resources from smaller villages so as to compete with the amounts of food given away by larger villages. The same pattern of paired villages holding feasts persists today. Details of these early observations on ritual and feasting have been summarized by Kirch (1994a). The overriding impression is that the paramount chiefdom was an unstable confederation of villages with each village chief retaining a great deal of autonomy and able to switch allegiance according to political conditions as also documented in the Marquesas Islands (Dening 1980:71). Given the more limited resource base on Futuna, political fluidity was probably even more pronounced than has been documented for Tonga (Evans 2001: 31–34).

Benefits to Futunan Chiefs

As indicated earlier, there is some question as to whether chiefs and village elites benefit significantly from their positions due to the constant obligation to give resources away. However, there is substantial evidence that they (or more accurately, they, their supporting kindred, and other non-kin supporters) *do* benefit today, and appear to have benefited in the past. While it is the corporate kindred (the *kutuga*) rather than any individual that ultimately holds title to the land as well as owns administrative titles such as village chief or various "ministerial" positions, individuals within these corporate groups can vie to occupy the most powerful positions.

Once in power, what are the benefits that accrue to chiefs and their supporting *kutuga*? From historical sources, oral histories, and contemporary observations, the benefits can be listed as follows:

- Ownership and control over land;
- Labor contributions;
- Food contributions;
- Receipt of fines and penalties;
- Multiple wives and large families;
- Control over prestige goods;
- Wealth exchanges;
- Political power.

Many of the more material benefits are ultimately important in strategies to control labor and consolidate power. In this section, we provide more details about the above benefits on Futuna.

Ownership and Control Over Land

The most valued lands are the irrigated taro fields about which Kirch (1994b) has written so much. In fact, he argues that competition over irrigated taro fields accounts for most wars and is key to understanding the emergence of sociopolitical complexity in Polynesia. In 1936, Burrows (1936:97, 141) noted that the most tenacious lawsuits were over control of irrigated taro fields. Frimigacci (1990:131, 155) mapped out ownership of the largest taro garden complex on Futuna recording 70% of these lands as belonging to the families of the paramount chief and first minister, while the remaining parcels belonged to other noble families (Fig. 5.3). One consequence of this in the past was that elite families could produce large amounts of irrigated taro (a highly valued food used especially for feasting) as well as greater, more consistent surpluses that enabled them to raise more and larger pigs (Viala 1919:244), which would also enable them to host more and larger feasts. On Tonga, a similar situation seems to have obtained: those who had close relations with the chief obtained large land allotments (Stevens 1996:469).

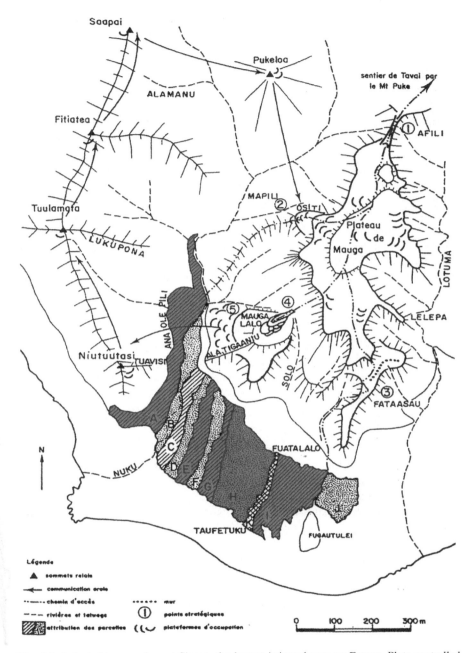

Fig. 5.3 Irrigated taro gardens at Sigave, the largest irrigated area on Futuna. Plots controlled by chiefly and ministerial corporate kindreds are *shaded*, amounting to over 70% of the area (Frimagacci 1990:131)

Labor Contributions

Labor contributions provided directly to the chiefs were widely reported in Polynesia (Firth 1959:296, Herskovits 1965:113, Oliver 1974:174, Stevens 1996:310, 388–389), even to the extent that when deprived of their *fatongia* labor, local Tongan chiefs complained that they could not get fish or agricultural products to live on. On Futuna, labor contributions were formerly supplied to chiefly families by all households to help in cultivating chiefly fields and in other productive endeavors. Control over resources and wealth was but one of the most effective means of achieving power, and chiefs sought power above all else (Goldman 1970:487). However, European style constitutions and legal systems eliminated the compulsory traditional work service to chiefs throughout Polynesia (Stevens 1996).

On Futuna, we were told by several people, including a former officeholder, that in the past chiefs had much more power and control over people. In the past, each *kaiga* (corporate household) had to provide 1–3 days of labor in the chief's fields per month and gave the chief manioc or coconuts to feed his pigs. We may surmise that such demands for labor may have been partly justified by claims that chiefs needed high levels of production to fulfill their duties of office, such as giving away food at feasts.

Food Contributions

Chiefs were given large amounts of food on a number of occasions, including first fruits feasts, village feasts, family feasts, calamity feasts, and while "touring" among constituent villages.

First Fruits

The most important of these occasions was the annual first fruits, or harvest, feast. These were, in essence, "tribute" feasts in which everyone contributed a great deal, everyone ate a great deal, and the chiefly elites kept a great deal. Kirch and Green (2001:226, 259) argue that the chiefly rights to a percentage of the first harvests, as well as chiefly holding of title to all land, is a general characteristic of ancestral Polynesian societies. On Futuna, first fruits feasts were among the first recorded by Europeans (Kirch 1994a:271, 283, Smith 1892:47). Melville (1846:171–184) appears to describe a similar early feast in the Marquesas Islands, and such feasts are well documented on Tahiti (Oliver 1974:259, 273–276).

In one of the few quantified accounts of what appears to have been a first fruits feast in Fiji in the early nineteenth century, 420 large pigs and 3,500 yams were divided as follows:

– 20 pigs and 500 yams were set aside for offerings at the tombs of past paramount chiefs (presumably appropriated by the families of the past paramounts);

– 100 pigs and 500 yams were given to the reigning paramount chief, and the same amount was given to the secular "king", the gods (priests), and the other ranking chiefs as a group (Douaire-Marsaudon 1998:117, 123).

A similar apportioning of feasting food occurred in Tahiti (Oliver 1974:260) and the Marquesas where commoners as a group received the equivalent of individual chiefs, or they received the last choice of food sometimes consisting of rotting portions (Goldman 1970:502, 508).

In the literature on Futuna, first fruits feasts generally appear to conform to the basic pattern described for Fiji, only on a smaller scale.

Certainly, each of the chiefly elites passed along a large portion of what they received to subordinate families in their kin groups or political domains; however, it is also apparent that chiefs favored some recipients over others and that the elite distributors controlled and may have kept a disproportionate amount for themselves (Douaire-Marsaudon 1998:100, also Oliver 1974:260, 1007). This was also the pattern that typified chiefdoms in some other locations such as the Natchez in North America (Gibson 1974:98, Swanton 1911:166). In some cases, the sheer size of food contributions indicates that chiefs received large amounts. For instance, one large Tongan feast in 1862 involved 150,000 large yams and 7,000 hogs, far more than could be consumed by the local populace (Stevens 1996:264–265, 416).

Village Feasts

Today, and probably in the past, each Futunan village has its separate feast day in the year so that the feasts rotate from one village to another over the course of the year and the rotation is repeated every year. As in the past, some villages are closely allied and sponsor feasts jointly perhaps in order to pool resources from smaller communities or *kutuga* and thus increase benefits. Chiefs from other villages and the paramount chief are invited and are obligated to attend barring incapacitating circumstances. The invited chiefs (on behalf of their villages) and other high-ranking guests are given lavish amounts of food. Village feasts are above all competitive displays of productive ability and success between villages that presumably serve as a major criterion for the creation of alliances and for negotiating power relationships between villages. Numerous lines of pigs, taro, yams, kava, mats, bark cloth, and other prestige items are laid out on the plaza in front of the main village feasting structure (*fale fono*–Figs. 5.4 and 5.5). The feast food and prestige item distribution (*katoaga*) occurs after the feasting, dancing, and ceremonies. On Wallis, the initial, public, distribution of these goods is carried out by the *faipule* (district chief).

On Futuna, each guest village chief typically receives one to two lines of pigs (about 6–8 large pigs) and gifts to be subsequently divided up among the households in his village. The recipient chief's aides transport the share given him back to his own village *fale fono* structure where the chief and representatives of all the village *kaiga's* corporate households gather for a second division of the *katoaga* gifts, which is a specialized task undertaken by one of the chief's assistants or someone that the chief has confidence in.

Fig. 5.4 A village feast at
Toloke with the pigs and gifts
to be given away (the
katoaga) displayed in front of
the *fale fono* (the village
ritual and feasting structure).
RFO TV

Fig. 5.5 An orator among
the pigs and gifts at the same
feast (RFO TV)

This distribution is supposed to be "equitable" for all *kaiga* corporate households
of the village but is not equal. There is a recognized hierarchical ranking of *kaiga*
that is reflected in the order and the amount of distribution. Those *kaiga* that are the
highest ranking and/or have given the most to support the feast and the system of
ranked kin groups, generally receive the most. The *village* chief should receive the
largest pig, and the other pigs are divided among the remaining *kaiga*. Thus the distribution of meat, food, and wealth constitute critical elements in demonstrating for
all to see (and we would suggest, in creating and maintaining) political structures.
Today, the *paramount* chief should receive two large pigs for his exclusive use and
for distribution to his most important family members or other supporters. While the
portion allotted to chiefs may have been reduced by European influences, the basic
patterns of distribution appear to have persisted.

In terms of organizing the production for feasting, it is important to realize that
the major roles are assumed by the village chiefs together with leading *kutuga*
(corporate kindred) elders—Kirch's "village council" (1975:78). These individuals
form a *fakatele* committee. This committee is responsible for arranging the logistics
of village feasts and ensuring that enough food and gifts will be supplied. While

considerable discussion about feast contributions occurs between the members of *kutuga's* prior to the formal planning for feasts, we were also told that the *fakatele* committee helped ensure specific targets or quotas were set for individual households to fill for feasts. One government official familiar with Futunan traditions told us that if a family did not supply their quota, fines and punishments were imposed.

Similar retributions and coercion are noted elsewhere in Polynesia such as in Tahiti, Tonga, Hawaii, and New Zealand (Firth 1959:400, Goldman 1970:496, 511, 519, 521–522, Kirch 1975:78, Oliver 1974:1010). While many of these societies exhibited much more centralized political control than the Futuna chiefdoms, the pattern appears to be a general one throughout Polynesia. On Futuna, this system seems also attested to by some of the earliest historical accounts (Burrows 1936:100, Kirch 1994a:270). Chiefs controlled enforcement cadres (see below) and used accounting systems to ensure that everyone met their quotas. Viala (1919:247) reported that "considerable quantities of provisions [were] brought either *as requisitioned by the chiefs* [or as] spontaneous gifts" (emphasis added). By way of comparison, it is interesting to note that non-contributors to feasts could be killed in Chumash chiefdoms (Noah 2005:47).

Other Feasts

In addition to first fruits tribute and village feasts, there are many other feasts sponsored by individual families or corporate kindreds that contributed food to chiefs. These were rarely recorded in early accounts, but given their persistent and pervasive Polynesian role in creating and maintaining corporate kinship groups and alliances, it is difficult to imagine that they were absent at any time in the past, or that they were significantly different from the family feasts recorded by Burrows and ourselves. These feasts include both intensely competitive, promotional events (especially first communion feasts–in the past these were circumcision feasts—marriage feasts, and funeral feasts) as well as primarily solidarity enhancing feasts (e.g., curing feasts, and birth feasts).

Today, at all promotional events, host families with pretensions of influence provide lavish gifts of food to those whose favor they wish to curry. They especially try to ensure that the village chiefs and paramount chiefs attend their family feasts, or at least receive significant amounts as gifts. Given the large number of these feasts that sometimes co-occur (especially for first communions), it is impossible for chiefs to accept all family feast invitations, although they certainly attend all village-level feasts barring exceptional circumstances.

To obtain some idea of the magnitude that these family feasts can attain, a single elite family on Futuna consumed or gave away 20 pigs to family, friends, and officials on the last day of their child's first communion in addition to many other pigs in the week leading up to this event. Funerals for minor Tongan chiefs involved 18 pigs, 4 cows, and a horse given away or consumed over 5 days by up to 350 people (Douaire-Marsaudon 1998:120). Among salaried families on Futuna, 60% or more of the income received can be spent on such feasting and gifts (similar to the 60% given as church donations or for education on Tonga—Evans 2001:124). In the case

of Futuna, the net result of these family feasts was that in 1 year, one village chief
received 47 large pigs and 30 small pigs from families celebrating first communions
alone.

Chiefs often receive some gifts from family feasts even if they do not attend
in person. A more detailed analysis of the number of pigs given away by households on a yearly basis, today, reveals that a small proportion of the households
in a village accounts for most of the pigs given to chiefs. Out of 13 households
in one village, only five provided feast contributions to the chief or other officials,
and these gifts amounted to only about 10 pigs in all for the year with one household providing four of these pigs. There are undoubtedly variations in the power
of chiefs between villages with changes occurring over time as well. However, our
household data do clearly illustrate the skewed contributions that some (presumably
politically ambitious) households make to high ranking individuals. Our household
data on the reported contributions to chiefs is also consistent with the generally more
modest household reports of the number of family feasts hosted per year among the
13 households interviewed. The average number of feasts hosted per year per household over a 5 year period was only 0.7 with a range of 0.2–1.5. Of these household
feasts, only 43% involved one or more large pigs (over 20 kg). Similarly, these same
households only reported providing an average of four pigs per year for their own
or others' feasts, again with large household variations. Half of the households provided only one pig per year, whereas two households provided about 15 pigs each
for various feasts. These results are similar to Adams (2004:74) data for Sumban
"protochiefdoms" (Figs. 5.6 and 5.7).

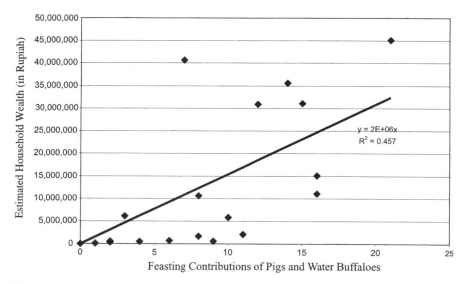

Fig. 5.6 A scattergram showing the relationship between household wealth and the total household contribution of pigs and water buffaloes for feasts over the last 10 years in West Sumba
(Adams 2004:74)

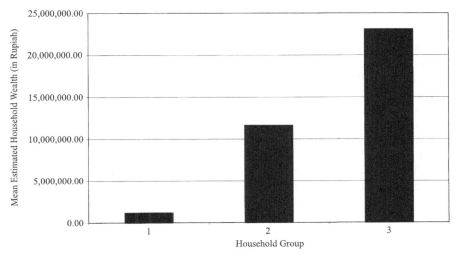

Fig. 5.7 A bar graph showing the average wealth of households contributing less than 5 pigs and water buffaloes to feasts over the last 10 years (Group 1), 5–12 pigs and water buffaloes (Group 2), and more than 12 pigs and water buffaloes (Group 3). Data are from the "protochiefdoms" of West Sumba (Adams 2004:74)

On nearby Wallis Island, with its greater economic development and cash flows, Douaire-Marsaudon (1998:99) reported that in 1998 each family gave 20 pigs to the chief, and three relatively small feasts (presumably smaller than village feasts) in 1988 involved the distribution of 14 tons of pork alone (Douaire-Marsaudon 1998:117). These cases may have been exceptional, perhaps pertaining only to a few highly ranked elite families. Such feast gifts represent significantly more than the amount we recorded on Futuna. It is difficult to determine where the discrepancies occur, although feast gifts on Wallis Island have become greatly inflated in recent years due to external cash inputs, especially among the families with access to cash resources. In one of the few quantified studies of actual food distributions in Polynesia, Betzig and Turke (1986:399) concluded that on Ifaluk "Food tends to flow to chiefly households more often than from them." As on Futuna, chiefs get food gifts from many family feasts even if they do not attend the feasts or contribute food to the feasts.

If the observations from Wallis, Futuna, and Ifaluk are representative, food and labor generally flowed up (and still flows up) the political hierarchies in an asymmetrical fashion with some families obviously contributing far more than others (Evans 2001:81, 91, Grijp 1993:226, Stevens 1996:173). Stevens (1996:13, 24) reports that Tongan family feasts cost about $1,500 each and are hosted by each family 3–7 times per year. If even a small portion of the food distribution from these feasts was given to the chief by each family, the total amount would rapidly become quite significant.

Thus chiefs today can receive very large amounts of meat, vegetable foods, and wealth from first fruit feasts, village feasts, and family feasts. Traditionally, chiefs may have been given larger proportions of all food produced as well as a portion of all fish caught, although total quantities of food involved were probably less than today (Douaire-Marsaudon 1998:123). Much of what the chiefs receive is redistributed to their general constituency, or is used for projects that benefit the community, e.g., contributions to feasts, building *fale fone*'s (feasting and meeting structures), churches, or roads. Much is also kept by chiefly families for their own use. We were also told that there is a preferential amount allocated so as to reflect existing political ranks which implies that such distributions were also used to solidify political power. Elsewhere in Polynesia, preferential distribution of feasting food appears to have been common (e.g., Betzig and Turke 1986, Herskovits 1965:417, Oliver 1974:261, 349, 1007). The traditional ideological construct that the chiefs were deities who owned all land and bestowed prosperity on their communities, thereby conferring on chiefs rights to receive a portion of all produce, was also widespread (Goldman 1970:485, 509).

Early accounts also record what we would term "calamity or propitiation feasts" organized by the paramount chiefs (Kirch 1994a:272, 275, Rozier 1963:117, Smith 1892:46). These included feasts held to request rain and stop storms. Ostensibly, calamity feasts were held to quell the wrath of one or more deities. Based on the fact that virtually all other major public feasts involved a contribution from all households to the chief, it seems likely that contributions were requisitioned from all households for this type of feast. However, unlike other public feasts, when considered in detail, there does not appear to be any social or political rationale for calamity feasts. One reason for holding such feasts that we can suggest from fieldwork in traditional Maya communities (where calamity/propitiation feasts were also held–Hayden and Gargett 1990) and other transegalitarian studies, is that calamities may have been utilized as pretexts by elites to gather additional surpluses and/or to marginalize weaker families by pressuring them to surrender assets and to go into debt at times when resources were scarce.

A final feast type that may have occurred on Futuna, although there is no certain record of it, are "touring feasts" in which chiefs acquired substantial amounts of food and gifts by visiting constituent villages. This was a common practice in Polynesia (e.g., Firth 1959:297) and may have also been a feature of traditional Futunan chiefdoms.

To summarize, the overall picture that emerges on Futuna and other Polynesian islands where families produce substantial surpluses for traditional gift exchanges (Evans 2001:77) is remarkably similar to the situation among chiefs on the Northwest Coast of North America, where one-fifth to one-half or more of all food produced was surrendered to chiefs for the stated purpose of redistribution in potlatch feasts. In reality, considerably less was redistributed than was received (Ruyle 1973:615). While some ethnographers imply or state that a chief's duty to give could render him destitute, it is clear that chiefs promoted others' duty to feed and support their chiefs so that they could hold the feasts, extend hospitality to other elites, undertake major community projects like temple and irrigation construction that benefited elites in the name of the communities, and make the redistributions required of their office (ibid; Oliver 1974:262, 314, 1002, 1010, Herskovits 1965:482, Firth 1959:133, 295–298, Goldman 1970:485). Perhaps it was primarily the administratively incompetent chiefs that were impoverished by the complex balancing of incoming resources, expenditures, needs to appear to be generous, political investments, feasting loans, acquisition of prestige items, and debts.

Fines and Penalties

A fourth benefit of being a chief that was recorded from informants involved the surrender of fines and penalties to the chiefs as well as figurative "spices" given to them when they served as judges. Throughout Polynesia, and on Futuna, chiefs imposed numerous taboos and laws on those under their rule, even if these decisions seemed arbitrary involving various species of birds, fruits, food preparations, touching various things, lighting fires, or performing various other activities (Dening 1980:51, 179, Rozier 1963:116, Viala 1919:229, 258). Such ploys are also apparent in many transegalitarian cultures where it is claimed that violations of community ritual traditions endanger the spiritual health of the community and especially the spiritual power of its leaders (e.g. Condominas 1977). One tangible consequence of such taboos is that they reinforce the control of aggrandizers over community behavior. Taboos also result in material benefits to those community leaders who receive the wealth, surpluses, or labor that are exacted from "wrongdoers" for transgressions.

On Futuna, chiefs are responsible for enforcing taboos and laws. Chiefs also receive fines for transgressions or disputes which, in the past, generally consisted of a month's labor or the surrender of a large pig (Panoff 1963:154, Viala 1919:229). Of additional interest are the differential degrees of guilt, extenuating circumstances, and variable fines that chiefs can impose upon transgressors who are affiliated with the elites versus those who have few connections. In the Marquesas, violations of taboos could result in death to the offenders (Dening 1980:248). In all these circumstances, as well as in the enforcement of feasting quotas, chiefs benefit considerably by controlling an enforcement cadre, or "police" force.

Oral history maintains that chiefs in the past ruled primarily through instilling fear of physical, economic, and social reprisals (Froment et al. n.d.) rather than through appealing to beliefs in the chiefs' supernatural powers alone or by appealing to respect for his social status or kinship rank. In the oral accounts, opposition to the chief could result in death. Enforcement institutions such as the *muru* of the Maori relying on physical force existed elsewhere in Polynesia prior to European colonization (Firth 1959:400), and as noted below, chiefs in a number of locations had the power to have people killed for insufficient gifts or other slights to their dignity (Goldman 1970:496, 511, 519, 521–522—compare also Ruyle 1973:616 for Northwest Coast enforcement cadres). Such behavior is not consistent with arguments that the chief's power stemmed from beliefs in his sacredness or from filling a role for the good of the community.

Multiple Wives

Chiefs and perhaps other wealthy, high-ranking men were generally the only ones to be polygynous in the community (Burrows 1936:67, Viala 1919:254). This indicates not only that they controlled considerably more resources and were more wealthy than other families, but that they probably needed more labor to productively exploit the resources that they owned. Multiple wives in general tend to characterize older wealthy men of high status in traditional societies (Frayser 1985:255, Levinson and Malone 1980:70), whether transegalitarian elites, chiefs, or early state royalty. In transegalitarian and simple chiefly societies, the acquisition of wives plays an important role not only in producing surpluses and wealth but also in creating wealth exchanges, extending alliances or political networks, and serving as status symbols. Today, under the aegis of Catholicism, polygyny no longer occurs on Futuna.

Control Over Prestige Goods

The exchange of prestige goods was also largely controlled by chiefs and at least in some areas of Polynesia, their monopoly was enforced by plundering foreign or unauthorized vessels (Ferdon 1981:226). Chiefly families were the only ones capable of underwriting the construction of the larger canoes used for inter-island trade (Dodd 1972:100–101, 138, Hayden 1983). In the nineteenth century, when European commerce began to impact the Pacific to a significant degree, the Futunan chiefs issued edicts to prohibit inter-island travel (Burrows 1936:87, Viala 1919:237). As with most long distance trade in prestige items, we suspect that inflated values were given to the prestige items acquired or manufactured by elites (compared to the actual procurement or manufacturing costs) thereby providing chiefs with considerable exchange advantages and profits. For instance, bark cloth made by or under the supervision of elite women is still used as prestige gifts in feasts, for ceremonial dress, and for wrapping bodies on Futuna. Godard (n.d.) reports that a 3 m^2 piece takes 6 months to produce, and we were told that lengths of 10 m are typically valued in terms of almost a thousand dollars. Goldman (1970:505–507) explicitly states that the prestige gifts of chiefs such as mats were more highly valued than the food that they received in exchange perhaps because chiefs controlled the supply (elite women basically controlled the production and distribution of these goods—Gailey 1985:6, Douaire-Marsaudon 1998:124). In other parts of the world, too, chiefs secured monopolies on ceremonial and prestige goods as well as using this control to create socioeconomic inequalities and complexity (Bishop 1987, Brunton 1975, Feinman 1991:247, Teit 1909:583, Tybjerg 1977).

Wealth Exchanges

Because chiefly elites only tend to marry into other elite families of similar wealth and political standing and only establish reciprocal feast and gift exchanges with other chiefly elites (Goldman 1970:505), they also reap the greatest benefits from feasting, marriage payments, and associated wealth exchanges. This is exemplified to a more extreme degree by the lavish gift exchanges documented in more stratified and complex chiefdoms such as Tahiti (Oliver 1974:446–452) and is mirrored by observations on Futuna (Burrows 1936).

Political Power

"By the selective distribution of food, goods, booty, women, and the like the chief rewards those who have rendered him service. Thus he builds up a core of officials, warriors, henchmen, retainers … it is through the shrewd and self-interested disbursement of taxes that the administrative machinery of the chiefdom … is built up" (Carneiro 1981:61).

In addition to the above material benefits, chiefs benefit from the exercise of great political power in the general defense of their own and their corporate family's interests, whether in litigation, in land disputes, or other domains. Today, there are other resources that have become available to the inhabitants of Futuna and Wallis. These take the form of salaried positions, funds for travel, or contracts provided by the French Territorial government as well as some commercial enterprises. As could be predicted by the political ecology view of elites benefiting from complex sociopolitical arrangements, the traditional chiefly political structures have been used by elites in order to gain economic advantages provided by the French administration, often to the detriment of more deserving and needy individuals.

Similar situations have evolved among Indonesian chiefdoms (Adams 1997, Crystal 1974) and on Tonga (Grijp 2004:187, Stevens 1996:185), although there now appears to be a more broadly based business community emerging there. On Futuna, only about 30% of Futunan families have salaried positions. We were told that all of these positions are held by elite family members who obtain their positions on the basis of political and family connections regardless of their competency or performance. Although some of these salaried employees carry out their duties in a responsible fashion, there are sometimes individuals who perform a minimum of actual productive labor. Such behavior is inconsistent with the notion that chiefs were given power to protect and promote communal well-being, but is consistent with the aggrandizer model of chiefdoms.

Informants on Futuna often said that "everything is politics" in Futunan society. Merit seems to have little place in the awarding of benefits. It should therefore come as little surprise that apparently all of the key political positions established by the French Territorial government are held by noble families—a situation that also seems to occur with traditional chiefdoms elsewhere (Adams 1997:265, 275, Crystal 1974). It is these "elected" officials on Futuna that control the purse strings for contracts and salaries. They are elected by dint of the support that they can muster and the success that they can demonstrate through feasts and the gifts that they are willing to distribute to supporters. Although today money is becoming a sign of success, men's importance is still largely assessed on the basis of the number of *large* pigs they can provide at feasts—an index of the extent and power of the individual's socioeconomic network. This is what impresses people most. Gifts of food and wealth are used in typical traditional chiefly types of strategies to retain political and economic support. Given the traditional power structure of the island and the important role that feasting plays in creating networks of mutual support between families (Hayden and Villeneuve 2002), it hardly seems surprising that these networks are effective in marshalling voting behavior of large factions of corporate families on the islands.

As we, and others, have noted, competition was always fierce in traditional Futunan society between families, between village chiefs or families vying for more desirable ranks within chiefly confederations, and between chiefdoms (Douaire-Marsaudon 1998:99, Sahlins 1983:77, Stevens 1996:264–265). Today, competition is rampant between elite families to control seats in the Territorial Council (the new locus of power and control over coveted cash resources). Candidates for territorial office publicly distribute 10,000 PF notes ($100 bills) to ceremonial dancers (who are generally from elite families) and provide enormous pigs for feasting events. Such overt competition or lavish displays of material success would make little sense from an ecological point of view if there were not substantial political or practical benefits to be gained.

Thus chiefs and elites do not seem to have used their offices simply for the good of the community. This is not to say that general community members did not also benefit (or at least they hoped to benefit) from supporting a successful chief (even though they had to work more and produce more just to obtain occasional favors and feast distributions). Chiefs were obligated to give back a certain proportion of goods and to provide certain services in order to retain supporters. However, it seems that self-interested opportunism is, and traditionally has been, a common theme in chiefdoms throughout Polynesia, if not everywhere. It is also recorded in more stratified chiefdoms like Tonga today (Stevens 1996:235–236). Despite the publicly proclaimed elite altruistic ideologies, these cases of opportunism display little concern or reciprocal obligations towards supporters.

Contrary to those who view leaders or elites as spiritually noble individuals who perform their roles for the betterment of their constituents, Goldman (1970:479, 497) and Firth (1959:133, 294, 298–299, 304, 398) state repeatedly that chiefs' wealth was used primarily for their aggrandizement and influence, that chiefs accrued the wealth of society in their own hands, that they accumulated considerable stores of wealth, that the possession of food was correlated with rank, that wealth was a major determinant of status and increased authority, that chiefs were like capitalists who accumulated wealth, and that elites profited materially from their positions, their exchanges, and their feasts. The exploitative nature of elites is also documented by Murphy (1980:204) for the Kpelle, by Nairn (1981) for the Kirghiz, by Ruyle (1973) for the Northwest Coast, and by Gibson (2000:259) for Irish chiefdoms.

Yet there were and are limits to how much most people were willing to do or produce for a chief, and on how much a chief could demand. Because of bilateral kinship relations, families could choose among a range of villages for residence and the chiefs that they would support (Evans 2001:40, Oliver 1974:767, 987). As a result, chiefs could be, and often were, deposed due to incompetence or overbearing demands and insufficient gifts to households under their jurisdiction

(Viala 1919:231). Thus elites had to provide a minimum level of redistributed feasting foods, land, defense, support for marriages, and similar advantages for the general populace or at least to heads of the corporate kindred groups.

One might consider the situation similar to contemporary land developers and businessmen who make the minimum necessary concessions to local residents or municipal councils in order to have a chance to reap substantial profits from the developments that they promote. They must also provide attractive products to customers. Such ventures also typically involve considerable risks. Like all businesses, a certain proportion of developers regularly succumb to bankruptcy. Unsuccessful chiefs, as well as big men in transegalitarian societies, not only might forfeit their prestige, status, and all that they owned, but they often forfeited their lives to competitors and rivals. The New Guinea big man, Ongka, recounted attempts on his life by his rivals (Nairn 1991), and there are many instances of Polynesian chiefs at all levels of complexity being sacrificed by victorious rivals as well as many accounts on Futuna of local and paramount chiefs being overthrown through intrigue or through war (Douaire-Marsaudon 1998:101, Viala 1919:231). As Earle (1997:140) notes, chiefs rarely died old; most died in conflicts (see also Kolb and Dixon 2002, Sahlins 1983:77, Stevens 1996:348).

We argue that this consistent extreme level of risk taking by elites (as well as the conflicts between them) would only make sense if there were very substantial benefits to be gained from occupying elite chiefly positions. Frequent dethronements and the acceptance of life-threatening risks are difficult to reconcile with the cognitive or functionalist views that were discussed at the outset regarding why chiefs take on these roles, but they are consistently associated with situations where individuals stand some chance to gain great wealth or power. If their subjects did believe that the chiefs had powerful mana and knowledge and that they harbored gods inside their bodies, how would anyone dare to dethrone a chief?

Warfare and Feasts in Chiefdom Dynamics

From a paleo-political ecology perspective, many community members may benefit in some ways from chiefly activities and indeed they must for chiefs to stay in power. However, supporters must also produce labor and surpluses to give to chiefs; and there must also be disproportionate benefits to particular (elite) families. These are critical to understanding the functioning of chiefdoms, otherwise there would be no incentives for chiefly families to take risks or engage in extra productive and organizational efforts. Before discussing this issue further, however, there is another key aspect of chiefdoms that needs to be addressed: the role of warfare.

With the many ecological and political models that purport to explain the origin of chiefdoms (described by Earle 1997), we had expected that there would be major production or distribution benefits (or other personal benefits) that underlay the origin of chiefdoms. We anticipated that economic and political factors such as the control of trade, irrigation, prime land, or other economic resources would emerge as making the most sense in terms of the basis for power consolidation.

While we expected competition in the economic sphere, it came as an unexpected surprise to find that warfare was so strongly—even adamantly—identified as the origin of the Futunan chiefdoms and a major determinant of claims to chiefly office (Frimigacci 1990:170–174). The chiefly rank of one of the *kutugas* on Futuna was established through the killing of an enemy paramount chief in 1838. The real merit and rank of this "newcomer" *kutuga* is still a matter of contention and rivalry (largely through feasting) between it and the more established *kutuga's* that also hold rights to paramount chiefly titles. Goldman (1970:486) makes a similar claim for the importance of warfare in the more complex chiefdoms in Tahiti and Hawaii. We had always assumed that warfare was more of a byproduct of chiefdom development, rather than a causal factor in its emergence. After all, intensive warfare also exists in transegalitarian societies such as those of New Guinea and Amazonia without resulting in chiefdoms. Yet, in investigating the ethnographic literature elsewhere in Polynesia, the same story was repeated over and over: chiefdoms were founded through war and conquest. Conquering groups, led by a war captain, established themselves as hereditary elites who owned all resources and demanded tribute from the disenfranchised local population, thus creating distinct classes and usually regional polities.

Farther afield, warfare was viewed as a critical factor in generating and maintaining the hierarchies in Irish chiefdoms and claimed to be a universal characteristic of chiefdoms (Gibson 2000:254, 258–259), while warfare was argued to be omnipresent in South American chiefdoms and tribes where a chief's greatness was measured in terms of the number of trophy heads he had obtained and the number of men he had eaten (Redmond 1994:44, 50). On a still broader scale, Carneiro (1970, 1981) claimed that chiefdoms universally originated from warfare; and Otterbein (1973:947) and Haas (2001) maintained that war was the origin of centralized political power, a point also emphasized by Little (1966:66). Roscoe (2002:158), too, identified warfare together with subsistence as the important determinants of sociopolitical complexity. Similarly, warfare was one of the central strategies that Earle (1999:105–131) identified as creating chiefly power, although in his view it was an unstable and difficult-to-control factor that was an insufficient base of power (a point also emphasized by Little 1966:66).

What are we to make of these claims? If war was so central, why did chiefdoms not arise in New Guinea or Amazonia? Redmond (1994:45) suggested that in tribes, warfare was motivated by revenge, whereas in chiefdoms it was motivated by a chief's desire to possess land and power. The critical difference according to Redmond would seem to be one of aggrandizer values, but this leaves open the question of why these should vary.

Carneiro's (1970, 1981) arguments about the role of population pressure in fomenting warfare do not seem to account for the emergence of chiefdoms or warfare since numerous researchers concluded in case after case that population pressure was insignificant in many transegalitarian and chiefdom societies (Brumfiel 1994:7, Clark and Blake 1994:19, Cowgill 1996, Earle 1997:122, Feinman 1991:248, Kang

2000, Kelly 2000:135, Knauft 1990:269, 281, Rousseau 1979, Stephens 1996: 197–199, 338, 469, 478–479). Several of these authors stressed that warfare did not emerge from scarcity, but rather was precipitated by the accumulation of surpluses and wealth that envious rivals coveted (Brumfiel 1994:7, Cowgill 1996, Kelly 2000:135). This latter position is entirely consistent with paleo-political ecology views of aggrandizers and their strategies and motivations. We would also agree with Earle that, by itself, warfare is an unstable and difficult-to-control basis for building power hierarchies because of the high costs of enforcement amidst a disenfranchised, resentful, and rebellious population.

We therefore suggest that the critical element in establishing a positive motivation for people to support conquest hierarchies is the hosting of feasts, the creation of debts through feasts, and the disbursement of prestige items. These features become necessary for the functioning of hierarchical societies. As Rambo (1991) has noted, the energy requirements of maintaining administrative structures increase geometrically as complexity increases (largely due to the food surpluses needed for feasts and support of craft or administrative personnel). Similarly, Gibson (2000:259) observed that chiefdoms were "expensive systems to maintain."

In Futuna and elsewhere, it is evident that while warfare may initially establish conquerors as chiefs and elites, it is the feasting and the gift giving of prestige foods and objects that provide the sociopolitical glue, the cohesion, the motivation that holds hierarchies together over the long term. As Kirch (1975:83) and Frimigacchi (1990:173) note, chiefdoms headed by paramount chiefs did not really function as economic units except during feasts, wars, and associated rituals. These were the chiefs' main responsibilities. Similarly, Rozier (1963:113) observed that Futunan chiefs only wore attire that distinguished them from others for feasts and wars indicating that these are the most important functions of chiefs. In his study of proto chiefdoms in Sumba (Indonesia), Adams (2007) also concludes that, today, feasts hold the political organizations of the island together, although traditionally warfare was also important. Even in hunting and gathering chiefdoms, the major role of chiefs is repeatedly described as organizing feasts, trade, and war (e.g., Noah 2005:46). These factors may constitute the essential core of all chiefdoms, although the form these take and the relative emphasis on individual components may have varied according to specific conditions as Earle (1997) has suggested in his staple versus wealth finance systems. It is, undoubtedly, this need for surpluses to underwrite feasts and prestige technologies that ultimately is responsible for Sahlins' (1958) observations that sociopolitical complexity in Polynesia is a direct function of island size and productivity.

War may have often provided the initial impetus that placed the title and rights to land in the hands of conquerors as described in the Polynesian and Melanesian literature (Forde 1963:182–183, 1938). This accords well with Gilman's (1981) view of extortionist aggrandizers creating the basis for social complexity. However, violence by itself often ultimately drives people away and leads to covert socioeconomic sabotaging of political hierarchies. For complex political structures to endure, positive motivation must also be provided. Thus, where there was not enough surplus to consolidate and integrate the subject populations (or at least key family heads) through feasting and prestige gifts, the hierarchies were bound to collapse over time.

To obtain some idea of the magnitude of surplus production necessary to maintain the simple chiefdom hierarchies on Futuna, our data indicate that the production of one surplus pig (plus considerable yams, taro, breadfruit, and fish) per feasting family per year appears to suffice for chiefs' needs (plus another three or more pigs needed for family feasts). These are average figures that do not reflect variability between households. Goldman (1970:505) makes the interesting comment that it was only the wealthy that could afford to engage in reciprocal feasting. This situation seems to be reflected in our household data from Futuna where only a few households provided most of the feasting contributions in a village. Thus only some households appear to be motivated and capable enough to actively promote the development of chiefly political structures. Most of these households are probably homes of aggrandizers or people that hope to benefit from supporting elites.

Threats of attack probably provided a strong synergistic motivation for people to produce surpluses so that they could hold feasts and thus maintain alliances for mutual defense. Enmities could flare up for many reasons, including feasting debts. Failure to honor expectations (or tacit contracts) resulted in sociopolitical rupture and hostility apparently at all levels of transegalitarian and chiefdom societies. Oliver (1974:232–233, 239, 349, 593) noted that in Tahiti, exchange agreements included penalties "that recognized the right of the aggrieved party to destroy some of the other's property in the event of nonperformance." In New Zealand, chiefs exacted "violent revenge" when they did not receive appropriate gifts (Goldman 1970:496). Elsewhere, as one New Guinea big man said, if his feasting rival failed to repay feasting gifts, he would slit his throat (Nairn 1991). On the Northwest Coast of North America, defaulting on debts could lead to seizing assets, death threats, village burning, or open warfare (Perodie 2001:200–201); and in the chiefdoms in California, failure to fulfill feast obligations could result in war (Noah 2005:46, 320, Wilson and Towne 1978:393).

The notion that conflict was used by chiefs as a strategy for holding the Futuna chiefdoms together is indicated by the persistence of two chiefdoms on Futuna and the high frequency of conflict between them. The first European residents recorded two major wars in just one year (1838). Given hostile relationships between chieftains, the participation of *both* paramount chiefs in the same island-wide ceremonies and feasts noted at first contact (and continuing today) appears puzzling. These chiefs do not appear to have been mortal enemies, but rather collaborators in some sense. It is also rather curious, even surprising, that over the 3,000 years of occupation on such a small island, neither chiefly polity was able to triumph militarily or politically over the other and establish complete control over the island. However, such an outcome would have resulted in peace. And a permanent state of peace may have largely eliminated the *raison d'être* for forming village alliances, feasting, and surplus production at least on relatively small islands where simple chiefdoms had poorly consolidated power structures. One can surmise that Futunan elites may have realized this and used Machiavellian manipulations to maintain a roughly equal balance of power and ensure recurring threats or incidences of armed conflict so as to secure their basis of power. Sillitoe (1978) documented such manipulation of conflict by big men in New Guinea, and Gibson (2000:259) observed that "instigating and perpetuating warfare . . . had the effect of demonstrating to the common populace the necessity of putting up with the aristocracy and their exactions."

Discussion

On the basis of experience with transegalitarian societies, the data from chiefdoms on Futuna, as well as observations from greater Polynesia and other chiefdoms, we side firmly with Earle (1997:12, 147) in his view that material leverage rather than cognitive leverage is the key to understanding the emergence of chiefdoms. However, we readily recognize that aggrandizive elites promoted ideologies and value systems that helped *justify* chiefly privileges—and probably even served as an auxiliary means to obtain compliance from those people who were prone to believing the ideologies advocated by elites. We also recognize that once established, belief systems can develop a certain "inertia" that will maintain them in the short run as long as there are no adverse consequences. However, without positive reinforcement, such belief systems eventually are eroded away by skeptics and other factions. To explain the origin of such systems, their spread, and their long-term persistence, we suggest that aggrandizers and aspiring chiefs developed alluring feasts, dances, rituals, and spectacles that had an innate appeal to those whom aggrandizers wanted to engage in their surplus generating schemes—just as business promoters today try to pander to popular tastes. Thus feasts became sumptuous affairs that embodied all the values and types of events that specific groups of people enjoyed the most, as well as featuring key aspects of ideology that aggrandizer organizers wanted to promote such as:

- the importance of ancestors (their abilities to bestow benefits and mete out retributions for unapproved behavior) and the holding of costly funeral feasts,
- marriages dependent on wealth payments,
- paying for injuries,
- ritual proscriptions,
- sicknesses or misfortunes stemming from social transgressions,
- powerful spirits that reside in the bodies of elites,
- the sacredness of chiefs' desires, and their actions being those of gods,
- the prosperity of the land stemming from the chief,
- crop failures or calamities caused by enemies of the community,
- mana and the danger of taboos,
- private ownership of resources and produce,
- the reciprocal and contractual nature of feasts and gift debts,
- derogatory terms for those who do not contribute to feasts (e.g. "moochers," "garbage men"),
- ascent of warriors to heaven.

While the manipulation of ideology in this way is extremely common (and specific ideological details vary), it is only one of a number of strategies that ambitious aggrandizers can use to achieve their goals. It is not an absolutely necessary component of hierarchical societies (contemporary society being an example with little reliance on religious ideological beliefs to maintain hierarchies), and the specific mix of strategies used by aggrandizers in the past probably depended on local conditions (especially population circumscription, control of trade, and the magnitude of capital investments in land), the effectiveness of other strategies, personalities, and historical events (Roscoe 2000:127–128). Where monopolistic control of resources was possible, the use of ideology-based strategies may have been less important than situations where tight control over resources was not possible.

However, on the basis of Hayden's work in the Maya Highlands, it appeared that even in the most "tradition-based" communities, about 10% of the households simply did not accept the dominant ideologies of the community. Izikowitz (1951:321) noted a similar situation among the Southeast Asian Lamet, and we found the same to be true in Futuna. Such proportions of nonconformists may represent a fairly general condition.

At the other extreme one might postulate that there could be 10–20% of any given population that was "gullible" or ready to believe whatever they were taught without question. We suggest that elite-promoted ideologies may have been effective as a means for influencing the portion of the population that was more easily influenced by charismatic aggrandizers and the ideologies they promoted. These ideologies were also undoubtedly good strategies for *justifying* elite power to a majority of the population and obtaining their acquiescence, at least as long as things went well. On the other hand elite ideologies were probably totally ineffective as a means of establishing power for another 10–20% of the population. It is this skeptical portion of the population (together with rival contenders and factions) that would have constantly worked to undermine elite ideological claims and spread doubt about elite traditions and elite claims to supernatural or ancestral powers. Without economic or practical leverages (such as the need for protection) chiefly ideologies would soon crumble under the attacks of skeptics especially if fueled by onerous extra efforts required for surplus production. Chiefs therefore must constantly work hard to instill their ideological visions.

Due to the fact that this body of promoted beliefs is constantly open to challenge and negotiation by skeptics and rivals who promote or defend their own self-interests, elites must regularly hold feasts and actively use other strategies to ensure continued acceptance of their versions of social, ideological, and political reality. Gestures to ancestors, respect for taboos, and many other components can be used in this process. However, the most effective strategies for achieving widespread acceptance, or at least acquiescence, of their value systems (including claims that chiefs harbored gods in their bodies and were responsible for community prosperity) involved material leverage including the manipulation of conflict and feasting as discussed by Dietler (2001) and Wiessner (2001).

Body Memories and Symbolic Capital

Recently, some theoretical discussions of transegalitarian societies and chiefdoms have argued for the importance of body memories (in the form of household features and structural divisions at Çatal Huyuk–Hodder and Cesford 2004) and "symbolic capital" (among historic East African chiefdoms—Bourdieu 1977, Hakansson 1998) or the transmission of ritual knowledge (Hollimon 2004:60, Potter 2000:297, 301) in the maintenance and presumably the creation of inequalities. These appear to be attempts to revive the earlier cognitivist models of inequality using a new vocabulary.

Symbolic capital is described as "social credit built by an individual or a group through the performance of an ostensibly public good that establishes indebtedness, which in turn supports positions of social power" (Hakansson 1998:265). In East African chiefdoms, this took the form of chiefly claims to control rain-making and land cooling rituals (viewed as essential for crops to grow) as the basis for chiefly power. On Futuna, the chiefs harbored the chief deity in their bodies and held rituals for relief from unfavorable weather. As in East African chiefdoms, they also took credit for the fertility of the land and all its produce. Such approaches situate the main source of chiefly power in the knowledge for, and performance of, rituals, (hence in an ideological basis) divested of economic or practical benefits for the roles of chiefs.

However, others such as Dietler and Herbich (2001:252–253) use "symbolic capital" in a fashion similar to our concepts of "promotion" or "advertising." In their case, it is a reputation for hosting lavish feasts that constitutes symbolic capital, and this reputation helps ensure that the host will attract the labor needed for work projects. The value of this symbolic capital, however, is based on providing practical benefits to the participants, without which the symbolic capital is relatively short-lived. As Hakansson himself insightfully observes, activities establishing "symbolic capital" are all costly, and there are substantial economic "requirements" for retaining both the political and spiritual leadership in the East African chiefdoms. Thus chiefs must be obtaining considerable economic benefits from some sources and might well justify their expenditures as necessary for community rituals and feasts, thereby justifying their demands on others' resources and labor to provide these "benefits" for the community. In fact, these African chiefdoms appear remarkably similar to the Futunan chiefdoms in a number of respects, and Hakansson's basic understanding on most fundamental issues is not very different from the one developed here.

The Spiritual Strategies of Aggrandizers

There may be a germ of truth in the notion that power stems from ritual knowledge and performance. A number of researchers have noted the absence of a direct link between political power and control over economic resources (Hakansson 1998).

Those in power often justify their power on the basis of claims of ownership of spiritual properties, generally including rituals, songs, paraphernalia, magical powers, spirit contacts, and knowledge. However, in these and other cases, ownership of such spiritual properties is strongly dependent on economic productivity, and ownership has to be validated by periodic expenditures for rituals and feasts. Essentially, it is those who can produce large surpluses and obtain prestige items who can acquire the paraphernalia, knowledge, songs, and rituals as well as host the feasts associated with the rituals that constitute the warrant for possessing spiritual powers. In turn, possession of spiritual power is presented as a warrant for controlling disproportionate amounts of resources in the community and for requisitioning labor and surpluses from other households. Thus the wealth of these households is used to maintain their claims on spiritual power. Such circular ideological constructs fit well with the more general cosmology that aggrandizers seem to promote almost universally: namely, that wealth is a sign of spiritual power, and spiritual power produces wealth.

Spiritual power is also generally viewed as a major criterion for assuming political positions. Aggrandizers therefore seek to monopolize the most potent spiritual powers for themselves through ritual organizations, secret societies, and elite ancestor cults (Hayden 2003). Similarly, aspiring elites in widely diverse geographical areas also promote the belief that they are responsible for the weather, soil fertility, animal and human fertility, prosperity, and the material happiness of their subjects. According to these ideological premises, it follows logically that their subjects owe elites a share of all produce and labor (for Polynesia, see Douaire-Marsaudon 1998:10, Goldman 1970:509). Responsibility for crop failures and other misfortunes is, of course, often off-loaded on the enemies of the community, those who break community taboos, or similar scapegoats. Such ideologies are difficult to explain in terms of the community good (contra Potter 2000:297, 301) but do make a great deal of sense in terms of elite strategies of control or justifications for exploitation. Other beliefs that make sense as elite control devices were that chiefs' desires were sacred, that their acts were actions of gods, and that warriors went to heaven (Rozier 1963:100–113).

What we suggest, then, is that this emphasis on spiritual authority and power is one of several strategies for acquiring power that has a number of advantages for aggrandizers in transegalitarian and chiefdom communities (Aldenderfer 1993, see also Chapter 4 by Aldenderfer this volume).

First, it provides a justification for controlling resources (through ownership or requisitions). Elites claim to protect the community and promote its prosperity through their supernatural knowledge and power. In return, the community owes elites goods and services to carry out these putative functions.

Second, it is also relatively easy to set up ritual systems in such a way that access to ritual knowledge can be hierarchically controlled (based in large part on material wealth).

Third, elites can argue that proper ritual performances for protection and prosperity require surpluses and costly paraphernalia. Therefore, not only cult members, but the community need to support the elites through material contributions for their own good. Secret societies such as the Kachina cult and elite ancestor cults are typical organizations that operate in this fashion (Johansen 2004, Hayden 2003: 142–147, 183–193, 165–166, 315–318). As Hollimon (2004:59) notes for the Chumash, the chief was the ceremonial leader, but the "major ceremonies were actually underwritten by the community at large." Chumash chiefs placed specialized shamans, singers, and dancers on a regular salary for these events thereby co-opting them for chiefly purposes.

Fourth, justifying power on spiritual grounds provides a means for deflecting accusations by others that elites control resources and exploit the labor of others. Such self-aggrandizing realities would likely be flashpoints of contention in weakly or non-stratified societies. Elite claims to power that were too blatant could easily be thwarted by clandestine depredations of elite resources, non-cooperation, accusations of sorcery, and other common tactics observed among the Maya and elsewhere (Blake and Clark 1999, Hayden 1996:53, Wiessner 1996). Transegalitarian aggrandizers typically camouflage their intentions, and chiefs seeking to serve their own interests undoubtedly do so as well. Claims to power based on the superior spiritual abilities of elites to promote and defend the interests of the community render elites relatively immune from attack as long as they do so convincingly. To justify exploiting others, it is far easier to hide behind claims of spiritual noblesse and community interests than one's own material greed.

Fifth, a spiritual strategy for claiming power has the additional advantage that supernatural knowledge cannot be stolen and can only be really challenged by specially gifted people, who, as some have noted, can often either be co-opted or killed (e.g., Hakansson 1998).

Thus, by using spiritual power as a subterfuge to justify and control excess resources and labor, to blunt possible accusations of self-aggrandizement, and as a commodity that cannot be stolen, aggrandizers could circumvent a number of problems in trying to promote their self-interests. Moreover, as previously noted, once established and generally accepted, such claims do have at least some short-term "inertia," or symbolic capital, in small communities that may carry some families through brief economic downturns.

It is reasonable to assume that it was aggrandizive individuals who invented this ideology of spiritual power and actively promoted it by dint of rhetoric, through feasts, and by providing gifts or favors to followers and the community in exchange for their aquiescence in accepting these values. Unfortunately, many ethnographers and archaeologists seem to have accepted such ideological claims unquestioningly at face value without understanding their deeper socioeconomic contexts or how they operate in the webs of aggrandizer strategies. The results have influenced claims that elites and chiefdoms develop due to ideological factors with little acknowledgement of who promoted those ideological changes, the economic leverage that underwrote the claims, the physical coercion sometimes used to instill fear and obtain compliance, how claims to spiritual power were used to justify economic privileges, or how these claims achieved widespread acceptance in communities—or, as is more likely, widespread acquiescence (see Rappaport 1999 on this important distinction).

Moreover, it is certainly possible that under conditions of rapidly changing demography and economic relationships (such as characterized the contact period between traditional and world economies), ritual roles may have been sometimes retained temporarily as the basis of political power (roles with symbolic capital) even where the economic and demographic bases for such positions had collapsed.

Funerals exhibit the same kinds of costs and advantages as claims to spiritual power, especially since the dead are generally portrayed as able to confer (and hence justify) material benefits on the living. The magnitude of benefits conferred by the dead is generally argued to be a function of how lavish the funeral is, and such funerals easily become used as measures of a household's or lineage's ability to produce surpluses and marshal labor, and viability for forming effective factional alliances (Hayden 2009).

Cognitive Versus Practical Consequences and Empirical Events

Some cognitive perspectives place great emphasis on certain parts or constellations of ideological belief systems as the basis for power. The political ecological perspective views such belief constellations as simply constituting one of several strategies both created and maintained by aggrandizers ultimately as a means to justify or promote their own self-interests, although such belief systems operate in a variety of ways. To what extent most people in traditional societies actually believed in the mana of the chief or any of the other associated concepts is an open question. In order to evaluate the relative merits of these theoretical models, we examined the effects on Futunan political organization of key changes in ideology and economics that occurred after European contact. Such changes provide a litmus test of contending explanations for chiefdom formation.

At the time of contact, the major ideological rationale for holding village feasts and providing economic support to chiefs was to honor the gods of the chiefs and, more precisely, to appease the anger of those gods (Rozier 1963:113–115, 118, Smith 1892). This was a common concept in Polynesian ideology prior to missionary influences. If religious ideology really was the basis for chiefly power then the political and social structure surrounding feasts and chiefly power should have collapsed with the adoption of the benevolent, loving god of Christianity who did not need to be appeased, who did not reside in chiefs' bodies, and who was employed to discredit the power of the old gods as well as the ritual knowledge of chiefs and thus the chiefly claims to power. However, nothing of the sort happened. Instead, the chiefly families continued to wield power; and village feasts continued to be as important as ever (although under the patronage of kindlier Christian saints). This is because feasts were integral structural elements in wielding and creating political power on Futuna. One can only conclude that the feasting and political system was maintained on Futuna because it provided important practical (political and socioeconomic) benefits for hosts and participants rather than being due to any deep-seated beliefs in traditional religious ideologies or the accumulation of "symbolic capital."

Other reasons have already been discussed for rejecting cognitive/symbolic and functionalist/communalistic models. These include: the documented benefits that chiefs obtain; the use of extortion, plundering, punishments, and physical force which chiefs often employed (Sahlins quoted in Stevens 1996:235–236); the attempts to create an exclusive elite monopoly on prestige item trade and on new resources such as salaried positions; the highly competitive and high risk nature of chiefly positions involving frequent dethronements and assassinations; and the self-proclaimed "need" for costly ritual, paraphernalia, and feasts used by chiefs.

Roscoe (2000) and Diehl (2000:19) suggest there was an ongoing dialectic between the self-interests of the chief (providing the underlying motivation for the strategies and beliefs that they promulgated) and the interests of supporters seeking advantages for the increased efforts and production that they were being asked to shoulder. The discrepancy between the elite rhetoric of helping their communities versus the actual exploitation of those under them is graphically portrayed in the documentary on "The Kirghiz of Afghanistan" (Nairn 1981), where the chief extols his altruism for his supporters while commoners complain bitterly about his exploitation. The chiefly version of their altruistic roles and the many benefits that they provide to their communities does not seem far removed from the kind of rhetoric that industrial land developers employ when they want to convince communities to permit development schemes (more jobs, more services, more prosperity). In a similar manner, white South African elites in the old republic were fond of portraying the apartheid system as conferring great advantages on the black population of South Africa. Like Stevens (1996:169), we suggest that earlier anthropologists who dealt almost exclusively with elites in Polynesian chiefdom societies were given similar arguments and accepted them at face value.

In contrast to the expectations of cognitive models about cultural changes that ought to occur consequent to revolutions in ideologies, the political ecology model used here, explains the popular support of such features as expensive feasting systems in practical sociopolitical terms that are not expected to change simply because of shifts in ideological justifications of practices—at least as long as the underlying economic and political structures persist fundamentally unaltered. Historically, this describes the case in Futuna.

On the other hand, major changes in feasting and chiefly sociopolitical systems should be expected to occur following fundamental changes in the nature of the economy and relations of productions. As noted earlier, in recent years, this is, in fact, what has transpired throughout Polynesia on islands suitable for producing world market goods.

Conclusions

Thus, from research on Futuna and Southeast Asia, cognitive, "symbolic capital," and communalistic or system-serving explanations for the emergence and maintenance of chiefdoms appear deficient. We certainly recognize the supporting role of ideologies in creating political power as well as the short-term power over some portions of communities that can be maintained by established ideologies. However, without continued material pressures to accept asymmetrical ideologies, they inevitably must be eroded by skeptics and competing ideological factions.

We also argue that claims to the effect that chiefs served their communities to their own material detriment are untenable and are inaccurate generalizations. It can be argued that while a small proportion of any population can usually be persuaded to sacrifice their own economic well-being for the larger community, it is unrealistic to base an enduring political institution on such individuals. It is doubtful that such individuals occur in small-scale societies with sufficient regularity, sufficient competence, or sufficient commitment so that political institutions can be sustained over the *longue durée*. As is the case in Sigave today, when practical benefits associated with chiefly titles are minimal or non-existent, it becomes increasingly difficult to find people to fill these and associated administrative roles requiring time and expenses. There is abundant literature to indicate that chiefs are no economic lemmings (e.g. Earle 1977, 1978, Rousseau 1979:241, Ruyle 1973: 615).

Nor do traditional chiefs appear to take up their positions primarily out of a sense of civic duty. On the basis of our Futunan research and the accounts available in the literature, it seems clear that chiefly families were the main beneficiaries of the chiefdom political organization and that it was the practical advantages that they hoped to obtain which provided the enduring basis of willing—actually eager—candidates with wealth ready to play the political game of chief to increase their fortunes and power even more despite the high risks and costs involved. We suggest that it was these aggrandizer types of individuals who constituted the driving forces behind the creation and maintenance of chiefdom organizations, even if once established occasional genuinely altruistic chiefs might be installed. Cognitive innovations and persuasions, or systems-serving needs certainly have roles to play in the strategies that aspiring elites used to achieve self-interested goals, but on their own do not seem able to account for the emergence of socioeconomic inequalities or chiefdoms.

Acknowledgments We would all like to thank the Tuiagaifo (King of Alo) and the Keletaona (King of Sigave) for their very hospitable reception and support. Their ministers and interpreters were invaluable aids in our study. Similarly, we are very grateful for the generous help given by M. Denis Deshayes (the French Delegué) and Susan Deshayes. Frédéric Dentand generously provided us with many insights and introductions to the traditional culture of Futuna, while Father Lafaele Tevaga discussed many aspects of contemporary feasts with us and very graciously allowed Villeneuve to use the mission facilities and provided her with food and a transport vehicle. We would also like to thank the many Futunan and French individuals who shared their knowledge of traditional and contemporary Futunan culture with us. The synthesis and interpretation of information that they supplied is, of course, our own and does not necessarily reflect their opinions. Funding for this project was provided by the Social Sciences and Humanities Research Council of Canada via a Standard Research Grant and the SSHRC Small Research Grant Program at Simon Fraser University.

References

Adams, K. 1997. Constructing and Contesting Chiefly Authority in Contemporary Tana Toraja, Indonesia. In White, G. and Lindstrom, L. (eds.), *Chiefs Today*, pp. 264–275. Stanford: Stanford University Press.

Adams, R. 2001. *The Ethnoarchaeology of Torajan Feasting*, Unpublished MA Thesis. Burnaby: Simon Fraser University.

Adams, R. 2004. An ethnoarchaeological study of feasting in Sulawesi, Indonesia. *Journal of Anthropological Archaeology* 23: 56–78.

Adams, R. 2005. Ethnoarchaeology in Indonesia: illuminating the ancient past of Çatalhöyük. *American Antiquity* 70: 181–188.

Adams, R. 2007. Maintaining Cohesion in House Societies of West Sumba, Indonesia. In Beck, R.A., Jr. (eds.), *The Durable House: House Society Models in Archaeology*, pp. 344–362, Center for Archaeological Investigations Occasional Paper No. 35. Carbondale: Center for Archaeological Investigations.

Anderson, L. 1994. *The Political Ecology of the Modern Peasant*. Baltimore: Johns Hopkins.

Arnold, J. 1996. The archaeology of complex hunter-gatherers. *Journal of Archaeological Method and Theory* 3: 77–126.

Barnard, A., and Spencer, J. 1996. *Encyclopedia of Social and Cultural Anthropology*. London: Routledge.

Beck, R. 2003. Consolidation and hierarchy: chiefdom variability in the Mississippian Southeast. *American Antiquity* 68: 641–661.

Betzig, L., and Turke, P. 1986. Food sharing on Ifaluk. *Current Anthropology* 27: 397–400.

Beynon, W. 2000. *Potlatch at Gitsegukla*. Anderson, M. and Halpin, M. (eds.). Vancouver: University of British Columbia.

Biehl, P., and Marciniak, A. 2000. The Construction of Hierarchy: Rethinking the Copper Age in Southeastern Europe. In Diehl, M. (ed.), *Hierarchies in Action: Cui Bono?* pp. 181–209. Carbondale: Center for Archaeological Investigations, Southern Illinois University.

Bishop, C. 1987. Coast-interior exchange: the origins of stratification in Northwestern North America. *Arctic Anthropology* 24: 72–83.

Blake, M., and Clark, J. 1999. The Emergence of Hereditary Inequality. In Blake, M. (ed.), *Pacific Latin America in Prehistory*, pp. 55–73. Pullman: Washington State University Press.

Bleige-Bird, R., and Smith, E. 2005. Signaling theory, strategic interaction, and symbolic capital. *Current Anthropology* 46: 221–249.

Boone, J. 2000. Status Signaling, Social Power, and Lineage Survival. In Diehl, M. (ed.), *Hierarchies in Action: Cui Bono?* pp. 84–112. Carbondale: Center for Archaeological Investigations, Southern Illinois University.

Bourdieu, P. 1977. *Outline of a Theory of Practice*. Cambridge: Cambridge University Press.

Brookes, S. 2004. Cultural Complexity in the Middle Archaic of Mississippi. In Gibson, J. and Carr, P. (eds.), *Signs of Power: The Rise of Cultural Complexity in the Southeast*, pp. 97–113. Tuscaloosa: University of Alabama Press.

Brookfield, H. 1972. Intensification and disintensificaiton in Pacific agriculture. *Pacific Viewpoint* 13(1): 30–48.

Brookfield, H.C. 1984. Intensification revisited. *Pacific Viewpoint* 25(1): 15–44.

Brumfiel, E. 1994. Factional Competition and Political Development in the New World: An Introduction. In Brumfiel, E. and Fox, J. (eds.), *Factional Competition and Political Development in the New World*, pp. 3–14. Cambridge: Cambridge University Press.

Brunton, R. 1975. Why do the trobriands have chiefs? *Man* 10: 544–558.

Burrows, E. 1936. *Ethnology of Futuna*, B.P. Bishop Museum Bulletin 138, Honolulu.

Campbell, B. 1983. *Human Ecology*. Chicago: Aldine.

Cancian, F. 1965. *Economics and Prestige in a Maya Community*. Stanford: Stanford University Press.

Carneiro, R. 1970. A theory of the origin of the state. *Science* 169: 733–738.

Carneiro. 1981. The Chiefdom as Precursor of the State. In Jones, G. and Kautz, R. (eds.), *The Transition to Statehood in the New World*, pp. 39–79. Cambridge: Cambridge University Press.

Carrasco, P. 1961. The civil-religious hierarchy in Mesoamerican communities. *American Anthropologist* 63: 483–497.

Cauvin, J. 2000. *The Birth of the Gods and the Origin of Agriculture.* Cambridge: Cambridge University Press.

Chagnon, N. (director). 1973. *Magical Death* (video recording). Pennsylvanian State University Audio-Visual Services, University Park.

Chazan, M. 2007. *World Prehistory and Archaeology.* Boston: Pearson Education.

Clark, J., and Blake, M. 1994. The Power of Prestige: Competitive Generosity and the Emergence of Rank Societies in lowland Mesoamerica. In Brumfiel, E. and Fox, J. (eds.), *Factional Competition and Political Development in the New World*, pp. 17–30. Cambridge: Cambridge University Press.

Clarke, M. 1998. *Feasting Among the Akha of Northern Thailand*, MA Thesis. Burnaby: Archaeology Department, Simon Fraser University.

Clarke, M. 2001. Akha Feasting: An Ethnoarchaeological Perspective. In Dietler, M. and Hayden, B. (eds.), *Feasts: Archaeological and Ethnographic Perspectives on Food, Politics, and Power*, pp. 144–167. Washington: Smithsonian Institution Press.

Condominas, G. 1977. *We Have Eaten the Forest.* New York: Hill and Wang.

Cowgill, G. 1996. Population, Human Nature, Knowing Actors, and Explaining the Onset of Complexity. In Meyer, D., Dawson, P., and Hanna, D. (eds.), *Debating Complexity*, pp. 16–22. Calgary: University of Calgary Archaeology Association.

Crystal, E. 1974. Cooking Pot Politics: A Toraja Village Study. *Indonesia* 18: 119–151.

Dening, G. (ed.). 1980. *Islands and Beaches: Discourse on a Silent Land, Marquesas 1774–1880.* Honolulu: University of Hawaii Press.

Dickson, D.B. 2006. Public transcripts expressed in theatres of cruelty. *Cambridge Archaeological Journal* 16: 123–144.

Diehl, M. 2000. Some Thoughts on the Study of Hierarchies. In Diehl, M. (ed.), *Hierarchies in Action: Cui Bono?* pp. 11–30. Carbondale: Center for Archaeological Investigations, Southern Illinois University.

Dietler, M. 2001. Theorizing the Feast. In Dietler, M. and Hayden, B. (eds.), *Feasts: Archaeological and Ethnographic Perspectives on Food, Politics, and Power*, pp. 65–114. Washington: Smithsonian Institution Press.

Dietler, M., and Herbich, I. 2001. Feasts and Labor Mobilization. In Dietler, M. and Hayden, B. (eds.), *Feasts: Archaeological and Ethnographic Perspectives on Food, Politics, and Power*, pp. 240–265. Washington: Smithsonian Institution Press.

Dodd, E. 1972. *Polynesian Seafaring.* New York: Dodd, Mead & Co.

Douaire-Marsaudon, F. 1998. *Les Premiers Fruits.* CNRS Editions/Editions de la Maison des Sciences de l'Homme, Paris.

Drennan, R. 1976. Religion and Social Evolution in Formative Mesoamerica. In Flannery, K. (ed.), *The Early Mesoamerican Village*, pp. 345–368. New York: Academic press.

Earle, T. 1977. A Reappraisal of Redistribution: Complex Hawaiian Chiefdoms. In Earle, T. and Ericson, J. (eds.), *Exchange Systems in Prehistory*, pp. 213–229. New York: Academic Press.

Earle, T. 1978. *Economic and Social Organization of a Complex Chiefdom: The Halelea District, Kauai, Hawaii.* Museum of Anthropology, University of Michigan Anthropology Papers, No. 63.

Earle, T. 1997. *How Chiefs Come to Power: The Political Economy in Prehistory.* Stanford: Stanford University Press.

Emerson, T., Hughes, R., Hynes, M., and Wisseman, S. 2003. The sourcing and interpretation of cahokia-style figurines in the Trans-Mississippi South and Southeast. *American Antiquity* 68: 287–313.

Emmons, G. 1991. *The Tlingit Indians*. Vancouver: Douglas and McIntyre.

Evans, M. 2001. *Persistence of the Gift: Tongan Tradition in Transnational Context*. Ottawa: Wilfrid Laurier University Press.

Excavations at La Venta, Extension Center for Media and Independent Learning, University of California. 1963 (16 mm film). UCECMIL, Berkeley.

Feil, D. 1987. *The Evolution of Highland Papua New Guinea Societies*. Cambridge: Cambridge University Press.

Feinman, G. 1991. Demography, Surplus, and Inequality: Early Political Formations in Highland Mesoamerica. In Earle, T. (ed.), *Chiefdoms: Power, Economy, and Ideology*, pp. 229–262. Cambridge: Cambridge University Press.

Ferdon, E. 1981. *Early Tahiti as the Explorers Saw It*. Tucson: University of Arizona Press.

Firth, R. 1959(1929). *Economics of the New Zealand Maori*. Wellington: R.E. Owen.

Forde, C.D. 1963. *Habitat, Economy, and Society*. New York: E.P. Dutton.

Forde, C.D. 1983. The role of a Fijian Chief. *American Sociological Review* 3: 542–550.

Foster, G. 1967. *Tzintzuntzan*. Boston: Little Brown.

Frayser, S. 1985. *Varieties of Sexual Experience*. New Haven: HRAF Press.

Frimigacci, D. 1990. *Aux Temps de la Terre Noire*. Paris: Peeters, Editions CNRS.

Froment, M.-M., Lextreyt, M., and Angleviel, F. n.d. Wallis et Futuna Entre Hier et Aujourd'hui. C.T.R.D.P: Noumea.

Gailey, C. 1985. The kindness of strangers: transformations of kinship in precapitalist class and state formation. *Culture* 5(2): 3–16.

Gell, A. 1993. *Wrapping in Images: Tattooing in Polynesia*. Oxford: Clarendon Press.

Gibson, B. 2000. Nearer My Chieftain to Thee. In Diehl, M. (ed.), *Hierarchies in Action: Cui Bono?* pp. 241–263. Carbondale: Center for Archaeological Investigation, Southern Illinois University.

Gibson, J. 1974. Poverty point: the first North American chiefdom. *Archaeology* 27(2): 97–105.

Gilman, A. 1981. The development of social stratification in Bronze Age Europe. *Current Anthropology* 22: 1–24.

Godard, P. n.d. *Wallis et Futuna. Carnets de Route du Pacifique*. Noumea: Editions Melanesia.

Goldman, I. 1970. *Ancient Polynesian Society*. Chicago: University of Chicago Press.

Grijp, P vander. 1993. *Islanders of the South*. Leiden: KITLV Press.

Grijp, Pv.ander. 2002. Selling is poverty, buying a shame. *Oceania* 73: 17–33.

Grijp, Paul van der. 2004. *Identity and Development: Tongan Culture, Agriculture, and the Perenniality of the Gift*. Leiden: KITLV Press.

Greenberg, J., and Park, T. 1994. Political ecology. *Journal of Political Ecology* 1: 1–12.

Hakansson, N.T. 1994. Grain, cattle, and power: social processes of intensive cultivation and exchange in precolonial Western Kenya. *Journal of Anthropological Research* 50: 249–276.

Hakansson, N.T. 1998. Rulers and rainmakers in precolonial South Pare, Tanzania. *Ethnology* 37: 263–268.

Haas, J. 2001. Warfare and the Evolution of Culture. In Price, T. and Feinman, G. (eds.), *Archaeology at the Millennium*, pp. 231—272. New York: Plenum Publishing.

Hayden, B. 2009. Funerals as Feasts. *Cambridge Archaeological Journal* 19:29–52.

Hayden, B. 2003. *Shamans, Sorcerers, and Saints: A Prehistory of Religion*. Washington: Smithsonian Books.

Hayden, B. 2001a. Fabulous Feasts: A Prolegomenon to the Importance of Feasting. In Dietler, M. and Hayden, B. (eds.), *Feasts: Archaeological and Ethnographic Perspectives on Food, Politics, and Power*, pp. 23–64. Washington: Smithsonian Institution Press.

Hayden, B. 2001b. Richman, Poorman, Beggarman, Chief: The Dynamics of Social Inequality. In Price, T. and Feinman, G. (eds.), *Archaeology at the Millennium*, pp. 231–272. Springer: New York.

Hayden, B. 1996. Thresholds of Power in Emergent Complex Societies. In Arnold, J. (ed.), *Emergent Complexity: The Evolution of Intermediate Societies*, pp. 50–58. Ann Arbor: International Monographs in Prehistory.

Hayden, B. 1983. Social characteristics of early austronesian colonizers. *Bulletin of the Indo-Pacific Prehistory Association.* 4: 123–134.

Hayden, B., and Cannon, A. 1984. The Structure of Material Systems: Ethnoarchaeology in the Maya Highlands, Paper No. 3. Washington: Society for American Archaeology.

Hayden, B., and Gargett, R. 1990. Big man, big heart? A Mesoamerican view of the emergence of complex society. *Ancient Mesoamerica* 1: 3–20.

Hayden, B., and Villeneuve, S. 2002. Preliminary Report on Futunan Feasting. In website: http://www2.sfu.ca/archaeology/dept/fac_bio/hayden/

Helms, J. 1994. Chiefdom Rivalries, Control, and External Contacts in Lower Central America. In Brumfiel, E. and Fox, J.(eds.), *Factional Competition and Political Development in the New World*, pp. 55–60. Cambridge University Press: Cambridge.

Helms, J. 1999. Political ideology in Complex Societies. In Bacus, E. and Lucero, L. (eds.), *Complex Polities in the Ancient Tropical World*, pp. 195–200, Archaeological Papers. Arlington: American Anthropological Association.

Herskovits, M. 1965. *Economic Anthropology.* New York: Norton.

Hodder, I. 2007. Çatalhöyük in the context of the Middle Eastern Neolithic. *Annual Review of Anthropology* 36: 105–120.

Hodder, I., and Cesford, C. 2004. Daily practice and social memory at Çatalhöyük. *American Antiquity* 69: 17–40.

Hollimon, S. 2004. The Role of Ritual Specialization in the Evolution of Prehistoric Chumash Complexity. In Arnold, J. (ed.), *Foundations of Chumash Complexity*, pp. 53–62. Los Angeles: Cotsen Institute of Archaeology, University of California.

Howard, A. 1993. History in Polynesia. *Bijdragen Totde Taal Land en Volkenkunde* 149: 646–660.

Izikowitz, K. 1951. *Lamet: Hill Peasants in French Indochina.* Goteborg: Uppsala.

Johansen, S. 2004. *Secret Societies in Ethnography and Archaeology,* M.A. Thesis. Burnaby: Archaeology Department, Simon Fraser University.

Johnson, G. 1982. Organizational Structure and Scalar Stress. In Renfrew, C., Rowland, M., and Segraves, B. (eds.), *Theory and Explanation in Archaeology*, pp. 389–421. New York: Academic Press.

Joyce, A., and Winter, M. 1996. Ideology, power, and urban society in pre-Hispanic Oaxaca. *Current Anthropology* 37: 33–45.

Kaberry, P. 1971. Political Organization Among the Northern Abelam. In Berndt, R. and Lawrence, P. (eds.), *Politics in New Guinea*, pp. 35–73. Nedlands: University of Western Australia Press.

Kang, B. 2000. A reconsideration of population pressure and warfare. *Current Anthropology* 41: 873–881.

Kelly, R. 2000. *Warless Societies and the Origin of War.* Ann Arbor: University of Michigan Press.

Kirch, P. 1975. *Cultural Adaptation and Ecology in Western Polynesia*, Ph.D. dissertation. New Haven: Yale University.

Kirch, P. 1991. Chiefship and Competitive Involution: The Marquesas Islands of Eastern Polynesia. In Earle, T. (ed.), *Chiefdoms: Power, Economy, and Ideology*, pp 119–145. Cambridge: Cambridge University Press.

Kirch, P. 1994a. The Pre-Christian ritual cycle of Futuna, Western Polynesia. *Journal of the Polynesian Society* 103(3): 255–298.

Kirch, P. 1994b. *The Wet and the Dry: Irrigation and Agricultural Intensification in Polynesia.* Chicago: University of Chicago Press.

Kirch, P., and Green, R. 2001. *Hawaiki, Ancestral Polynesia: An Essay in Historical Anthropology.* Cambridge: Cambridge University Press.

Kirkby, A. 1973. *The Use of Land and Water Resources in the Past and Present, Valley of Oaxaca, Mexico*, Memoir 5. Ann Arbor: Museum of Anthropology, University of Michigan.

Knauft, B. 1990. Melanesian warfare: a theoretical history. *Oceania* 60: 250–311.

Kolb, M., and Dixon, B. 2002. Landscapes of war: rules and conventions of conflict in Ancient Hawai'i (and Elsewhere). *American Antiquity* 67: 514–534.

Kottak, C. 1999. The new ecological anthropology. *American Anthropologist* 101: 23–35.

Kroeber, A.L. 1953. *Handbook of the Indians of California*. Berkeley: California Book Co.

Leach, E. 1954. *Political systems of highland Burma*. Boston: Beacon Press.

Levinson, D., and Malone., M. 1980. *Toward Explaining Human Culture*. New Haven: HRAF Press.

Lewis-Williams, D., and Pearce, D. 2005. *Inside the Neolithic Mind*. London: Thames and Hudson.

Lindstrom, L., and White, G. 1997. Introduction. In White, G. and Lindstrom, L. (eds.), *Chiefs Today*, pp. 1–19. Stanford: Stanford University Press.

Little, K. 1965. The political function of the Poro. *Africa* 35: 349–365.

Little, K. 1966. The political function of the Poro, Part II. *Africa* 36: 62–72.

Lockwood, V. 1993. *Tahitian Transformation*. Boulder: Lynne Rienner Pub.

Mauss, M. 1925. (republished 1967). *The Gift*. New York: Norton.

Melville, H. 1846. *Typee*, Republished (n.d.). New York: Dodd, Mead and Co.

Murphy, W. 1980. Secret knowledge as property and power in Kpelle Society. *Africa* 50: 193–207.

Myths and the Moundbuilders. 1995. *Public Broadcasting Associates (PBA)*, Image Media.

Nairn, C. (Producer). 1981. *Kirghiz of Afghanistan* (videorecording). Granada Television/Public Broadcasting Associates.

Nairn, C. (Producer). 1991. *Kawelka (Ongka's Big Moka)* (videorecording). Granada Television/Films Incorporated Video.

Nash, M. 1958. Political relations in Guatemala. *Social and Economic Studies* 7: 65–75.

Noah, A. 2005. *Household Economies: The Role of Animals in a Historic Period Chiefdom on the California Coast*. Ph.D. dissertation. Los Angeles: Anthropology Department, University of California.

Oliver, D. 1974. *Ancient Tahitian Society*. Honolulu: University of Hawaii Press.

O'Reilly, P. 1962. Le Maire et schouten a futuna. *Journal de la Société des Océanistes* 18: 57–80.

Otterbein, K. 1973. The Anthropology of War. In Honigmann, J. (ed.), *Handbook of Social and Cultural Anthropology*, pp. 923–958. New York: Rand McNally.

Panoff, M. 1963. Situation Présente de la Société Futunienne. *Journal de la Société des Océanistes* 18: 149–156.

Pauketat, T., and Emerson, T. (eds.). 1997. *Cahokia: Domination and Ideology in the Mississippian World*. Lincoln: University of Nebraska.

Peebles, C., and Kus, S. 1977. Some archaeological correlates of ranked societies. *American Antiquity* 42: 421–448.

Perloff, R. 2003. *The Dynamics of Persuasion*. Mahwah: Lawrence Erlbaum.

Perodie, J. 2001. Feasting for Prosperity: A Study of Southern Northwest Coast Feasting. In Dietler, M. and Hayden, B. (eds.), *Feasts: Archaeological and Ethnographic Perspectives on Food, Politics, and Power*, pp. 185–214. Washington: Smithsonian Institution Press.

Piazzi, A.Di., Frimigacci, D., and Keletoana, M. 1991. *Hommes au Four: Cuisine de Futuna*. Noumea: Editions d'Art Calédoniennes.

Potter, J. 2000. Ritual, Power, and Social Differentiation in Small-Scale Societies. In Diehl, M. (ed.), *Hierarchies in Action: Cui Bono?* pp. 295–316. Carbondale: Center for Archaeological Investigations, Southern Illinois University.

Price, B. 1972. The Burden of the Cargo. In Hammond, N. (ed.), *Mesoamerican Archaeology: New Approaches*, pp. 445–466. Austin: University of Texas Press.

Rambo, A.T. 1991. Energy and the Evolution of Culture: A Reassessment of White's Law. In Rambo, A. and Gillogby, K. (eds.), *Profiles in Cultural Evolution*, pp. 291–310. Ann Arbor: University of Michigan.

Rappaport, R. 1999. *Ritual and Religion in the Making of Humanity*. Cambridge: Cambridge University Press.

Reay, M. 1959. *The Kuma*. Melbourne: Melbourne University Press.

Redmond, E. 1994. External Warfare and the Internal Politics of Northern South American Tribes and Chiefdoms. In Brumfiel, E. and Fox, J. (eds.), *Factional Competition and Political Development in the New World*, pp. 44–54. Cambridge: Cambridge University Press.

Roscoe, P. 2000. Costs, Benefits, Typologies, and Power: The Evolution of Political Hierarchy. In Diehl, M. (ed.), *Hierarchies in Action: Cui Bono?* pp. 113–133. Carbondale: Center for Archaeological Investigations, Southern Illinois University.

Roscoe, P. 2002. The hunters and gatherers of New Guinea. *Current Anthropology* 43: 153–159.

Roscoe, P. n.d. *Great Men, Big Men, Prestige, and Power: New Guinea Leadership Revisited.* Ms. available from the author.

Rosman, A., and Rubel, P. 1971. *Feasting with Mine Enemy.* Prospect Heights: Waveland Press.

Ross, A. 1986. *The Pagan Celts.* London: Batsford.

Rousseau, J. 1979. Stratification and Chiefship: A Comparison of Kwakiutl and Kayan. In Turner, D. and Smith, G. (eds.), *Challenging Anthropology: A Critical Introduction to Social and Cultural Anthropology*, pp. 229–244. Toronto: McGraw-Hill.

Rousseau, J. 2001. Hereditary stratification in middle-range societies. *Journal, Royal Anthropological Institute (N.S.)* 7: 117–131.

Rozier, C. 1963. La Culture de Futuna: A L'Arrivée des Européens, D'après les Recits des Premiers Témoins. *Journal de la Société des Océanistes* 19: 85–118.

Ruyle, E. 1973. Slavery, surplus, and stratification on the Northwest Coast. *Current Anthropology* 14: 603–617.

Sahlins, M. 1983. Raw Women, Cooked Men, and Other "Great Things" of the Fiji Islands. In Brown, P. and Tuzin, D. (eds.), *The Ethnography of Cannibalism*, pp. 72–93. Washington: Society for Psychological Anthropology.

Sahlins, M. 1963. Poor man, rich man, big man, chief: political types in Melanesia and Polynesia. *Comparative Studies in Society and History* 5: 285–303.

Sahlins, M. 1958. *Social Stratification in Polynesia.* Seattle: University of Washington Press.

Saitta, D. 1999. Prestige, Agency, and Change in Middle-Range Societies. In Robb, J. (ed.), *Material Symbols: Culture and Economy in Prehistory*, pp. 135–149. Carbondale: Southern Illinois University Press.

Saitta, D., and Keene, A. 1990. Politics and Surplus Flow in Communal Societies. In Upham, S. (ed.), *The Evolution of Political Systems: Socio-Politics in Small-Scale Sedentary Societies*, pp. 203–224. Cambridge: Cambridge University Press.

Sillitoe, P. 1978. Big men and war in New Guinea. *Man* 13: 252–271.

Smith, S. 1892. Futuna, or Horne island and its people. *Journal of the Polynesian Society* 1: 33–52.

Stevens, C. 1996. *The Political Ecology of a Tongan Village*, Unpublished Ph.D. Dissertation. University of Arizona, Tucson.

Stott, P., and Sullivan, S. (eds.). 2001. *Political Ecology.* London: Edward Arnold.

Suttles, W. 1968. Coping with Abundance: Subsistence on the Northwest Coast. In Lee, R. and Devore, I. (eds.), *Man the Hunter*, pp. 56–68. Chicago: Aldine.

Swanton, J. 1911. Indian tribes of the lower Mississippi valley. *Bureau of American Ethnology, Bulletin* 43, Washington.

Teit, J. 1909. *The Shuswap.* New York: American Museum of Natural History.

Trenholm, S. 1989. *Persuasion and Social Influence.* Englewood Cliffs: Prentice Hall.

Tybjerg, T. 1977. Potlatch and trade among the Tlingit Indians of the American Northwest coast. *Temenos* 13: 189–204.

Van Dyke, R. 2004. Aesthetics, Legitimacy, and Construction of the Chacoan Subject. Paper presented at the Annual Meeting of the Society for American Archaeology, Montreal.

Vaughn, K. 2005. Crafts, and the materialization of chiefly power in Nasca. *Anthropology Papers, American Anthropological Association* 14: 113–130.

Vayda, A. 1969. *Environment and Cultural Behavior.* New York: Natural History Press.

Viala, M. 1919. Les Iles Wallis et Horn. *Sociétés Neuchâteloise de Géographie Bulletin* 28: 200–288.

Westbrook, R. 2003. *A History of Ancient Near Eastern Law.* Leiden: E.J. Brill.

Wiessner, P. 1996. Leveling the Hunter: Constraints on the Status Quest in Foraging Societies. In Wiessner, P. and Schiefenhovel, W. (eds.), *Food and the Status Quest*, pp. 171–191. Providence: Berghahn.

Wiessner, P. 2001. Of Feasting and Value. In Dietler, M. and Hayden, B. (eds.), *Feasts: Archaeological and Ethnographic Perspectives on Food, Politics, and Power*, pp. 115–143. Washington: Smithsonian Institution Press.

Wiessner, P. 2002. Vines of complexity. *Current Anthropology* 43: 233–369.

Wilson, N., and Towne, A. 1978. Nisenan. In Heizer, R. (ed.), *Handbook of North American Indians, Volume. 8, California*, pp. 387–398. Washington: Smithsonian Institution.

Winterhalder, B., and Smith, E. 1981. *Hunter-gatherer Foraging Strategies*. Chicago: University of Chicago Press.

Wolf, E. 1972. Ownership and political ecology. *Anthropological Quarterly* 45: 201–205.

Chapter 6
Traces of Inequality at the Origins of Agriculture in the Ancient Near East

T. Douglas Price and Ofer Bar-Yosef

The Beginnings of Inequality

Some thoughts and ideas concerning the close relationship between the origins of agriculture and the emergence of social inequality were previously expressed by one of us (Price 1995) in the volume *Foundations of Social Inequality*. Since then a wealth of evidence has accumulated in investigations of Neolithic sites in the Near East as reported by the other author (Bar-Yosef 2001a, 2002b). We thought it would be useful to put together an argument about the coterminous appearance of agriculture and hierarchy, focusing on the Near East. But before delving into the archaeological record, we need to discuss what criteria to look for in terms of the material concomitants of status differentiation in early farming communities. We do that in the following paragraphs in the context of a larger discussion of inequality.

Inequality is inherent in many species as documented in pecking orders, dominance behavior, and alpha males. Most primate groups exhibit distinctively hierarchical social organization (DeVore 1965, de Waal 1998, Perry 2006). What is intriguing is that most ethnographically known societies of hunter-gatherers exhibit evolved mechanisms for dampening dominance behavior in favor of the sharing of food and property, care of kin, and egalitarian relationships. Prestige was ephemeral and achieved; power and wealth were limited or non-existent, although several examples from the Upper Paleolithic suggest the presence of wealthier individuals (e.g. Hayden 2001). At some point in the past, however, the gloves came off and dominance behavior and hierarchy rose again. The question of interest in our discussion is whether, as a cause or consequence of the establishment of agricultural communities, inequality emerged in human prehistory? We therefore explore ideas about social inequality in general and then proceed to report some of the evidence for social change during the Early Neolithic of the Levant, a particular region within the Near East.

T.D. Price (✉)
Department of Anthropology, University of Wisconsin-Madison, Madison, WI, USA
e-mail: tdprice@wisc.edu

T.D. Price, G.M. Feinman (eds.), *Pathways to Power*, Fundamental
Issues in Archaeology, DOI 10.1007/978-1-4419-6300-0_6,
© Springer Science+Business Media, LLC 2010

Previously, we have individually discussed the emergence of institutionalized social inequality in the context of the transition to agriculture (Bar-Yosef 2000, Price 1995). We argued that these two phenomena are closely linked. Our basic premise is that the onset of status differentiation was associated with the beginnings of farming. The idea is not new, but rather restated and emphasized. This is in many ways a reiteration of the stimulating argument made by Bender (1978), elaborated by Matson (1985:245) when he noted, "the development of sedentism and status inequalities may both be necessary prerequisites for the development of agriculture." Hayden (1995) and a number of others have addressed this question on the rise of institutionalized inequality in human society.

Jeanne Arnold (1993) helpfully categorized various approaches to this question as either structural models, where change is spurred by system-wide problems which require managers, or agency approaches, focused on individuals bent on accumulating wealth, prestige, and/or power. The latter is the path that Hayden and others have chosen. Clark and Blake (1994), for example, argued that inequality emerged as an unintended consequence of individual action—aggrandizers pursuing self-interest and prestige. In their view, competition for prestige and temporary positions of authority lead inexorably to institutionalized social inequality.

Economists and sociologists have weighed in on the question of the emergence of status differentiation as well. Lenski's (1966) theory on the origins of social inequality invokes the role of economic surplus, derived from technological and environmental advantages, in creating demographic, productive, and political contexts that are responsible for the extent of inequality in material wealth. Lenski suggests that in societies with a reliable surplus, some households can accumulate larger shares as long as others can obtain the minimum needed to survive. He further argues that this surplus makes possible larger settlements, facilitates occupational specialization, and brings about the control of decision-making by a few. As Wiessner described this situation (2002:234), "Quantitative economic gains are applied to bring about alterations in the social order, which are then legitimized through ideology."

Haas (1993) examined Lenski's theory using data from 258 native North American societies coded for eight general variables (e.g., level of technology, environmental abundance, amount of economic surplus). He statistically measured the relationships among these variables and found that Lenski's theory was strongly supported. Haas argued that the North American data indicate that economic surplus plays a major role in the emergence of political and material inequality.

In addition to the ideas of numerous social scientists, limited ethnographic evidence is available on the subject of emerging inequality and the behavior of elites. Hayden and Gargett (1990) interviewed elders in contemporary, isolated, traditional Maya communities regarding the behavior of aggrandizers. Elite behavior was focused on self-interest, not the needs of the group. Elite individuals provided no help to their communities in times of stress.

In another recent study, already proclaimed a classic, Wiessner (2002) investigated the relationship between structure and agency recorded in the oral traditions of the Enga of highland New Guinea over the last several 100 years. Here, the introduction of the sweet potato and its potential for surplus production led to dramatic social changes. Wiessner reported that competition fostered by the productive sweet potato led to alliances and debts. These "chains of finance" evolved into the so-called Tee cycle, which in turn promoted long distance trade, beyond the borders of kinship reckoning (Wiessner 2002:240). Growing population in the Enga region led to warfare and peacemaking accompanied by gift giving and increased opportunities for competition and emerging elite.

The Archaeological Evidence

Theory and ethnography point us toward some of the potentially important variables in the rise of status differentiation, but ground truthing these projections is an archaeological task. The problem still remains, how do we identify emerging inequality? What is the material evidence for the onset of status differentiation? Social inequality is reflected in differential access to labor, resources, and information. Such differences should be visible archaeologically, particularly in the context of household and community organization. Commonly, the sources of information for such an inquiry are grave goods and body decorations, the variable dimensions of domestic architecture, and the presence of special built-up ceremonial centers. We describe a few examples from the Early Neolithic of the Near East, where the only substantial body of information on the transition to agriculture is available. We do not mean to imply that the presence of such evidence alone signifies social hierarchy, but it may help to build an argument for the emergence of status differentiation and institutionalized inequality.

We look at some of the evidence from the transition from hunting to farming in the ancient Near East, presented diachronically below from ca. 14500 through 8200 cal BP. Focus is on the Levant, with a glance north into eastern Anatolia, and on the time periods known as the Natufian (pre-Neolithic) and the Pre-Pottery Neolithic (PPN). The Natufian dates from ca.14500 to 11700/500 cal BP. The PPN is divided into two periods: A and B. PPNA is known from the first millennium of the Neolithic, ca. 11500–10500 cal BP and PPNB for the next 2000 years or so until ca. 8300 cal BP. The locations of archaeological sites mentioned in the text are shown in Fig. 6.1.

The Natufian Culture

Many years ago Dorothy Garrod, in her seminal 1957 paper on this period, suggested that there was some evidence for social inequality in the Natufian, ". . . there was only one decorated skeleton in the tomb . . . Finds in Mugharet el-Wad and at Erq el-Ahmar show that as a rule only one individual in each group burial was distinguished in this way. Presumably these were important people, heads of families, or clans. Of the two decorated skeletons in el-Wad whose sex could be determined both were men, but Erq el-Ahmar shows that women were not denied this privilege,

Fig. 6.1 Map of Near East with the locations of sites named in the text

at least to the extent of wearing a necklace" (Garrod 1957:223). Since Garrod's time, many individuals have pondered the question of status differentiation in the Natufian (e.g., Belfer-Cohen 1995, Boyd 2001, Byrd and Monahan 1995, Hayden 2001, Kuijt 1996, 2000, 2002, Kuijt and Goring-Morris 2002, Wright 1978).

Natufian graves have been uncovered in all excavated sites. In most places the graves were dug in abandoned pithouses, outside the domestic structures, or placed in specific locations within sites such as inside Hayonim, Hilazon, and El-Wad caves. Burials under house floors are definitely an exception (Belfer-Cohen 1995, Byrd and Monahan 1995). Graves are either shallow or deep and in rare cases were paved with stones (Hayonim Cave) or coated with lime plaster as at Eynan (Ain Mallaha). At Hayonim Cave, the location of the graves was marked by small cup-holes on one of the encircling stones, perhaps like tombstones.

The presence of adorned skeletons emphasizes the issue of social status, initially raised by Garrod. About 8% of Early Natufian skeletons had body decorations, composed of marine shells (mainly *Dentalia* sp.) and/or bone and animal teeth pendants. While these could have been the remains of garments, belts, head-gear, and the like, the decorations may also indicate a different status, position, or wealth within what seems to have been an egalitarian society. In a few graves bone tools, decorated bone objects, and figurines were placed as grave offerings.

Some aspects of the graves and their contents contain little information about inequality. There is nothing in the position of the corpses, for example, that would seem to reflect status more than the nature of changing mortuary practices. The number of inhumations varies from single to collective, although the latter are more common in the Early Natufian. Several cases of skull removals were observed in Late Natufian contexts, heralding a common treatment of particular adults in the Early Neolithic (Belfer-Cohen 1995). Secondary burials were either in special graves or mixed with primary burials. At several sites, there were relatively large areas uncovered with indications of spatial arrangement of the graves. On the terrace of el-Wad, for example, numerous individual graves were located (Garrod and Bate 1937). At Eynan, two concentrations of burials were identified (Perrot and Ladiray 1988).

Hayden (2004), following Henry (1989) and others (e.g. Bar-Yosef 2000, Belfer-Cohen 1991, Byrd 1994, Byrd and Monahan 1995, Flannery 1972, 2002), argues that ancestor worship, formal cemeteries, and secondary burials all point to the existence of corporate groups that controlled important resources. Some evidence for social units larger than the family is clearly present in the pre-Neolithic Near East.

Among the mundane brush huts erected over round stone foundations exposed at Natufian open air sites, there is one building at Eynan that stands out. This is a semi-circular house, 9 m in diameter, with a series of postholes indicating the presence of a roof (Valla 1988). Clusters of artifacts on the two superimposed floors included a group of pestles with a human cranium, tortoise shell, a group of 24 pebbles with three shaft straighteners, and a large amount of lithic artifacts and faunal remains near the two hearths. An additional smaller building at this site had a round bench covered with lime plaster, documenting the previously unknown use of pyrotechnology by the Natufians, and confirmed by the discovery of a lime kiln in Hayonim Cave (Bar-Yosef 2002a, Kingery et al. 1988). While alternative interpretations of this large house are possible, it seems that its special place within the community is undeniable. Was it where the elders of the group met? Was it a prototype for a ceremonial center later seen at Early Neolithic sites, currently compared in function to the "kiva" in the southwestern US pueblos (Stordeur 2000a, Stordeur and Abbès 2002)?

Other indications of labor-intensive works are provided by the manufacture of mortars, compared to grinding slabs. Manufacturing the common mortars, 20–40 cm deep with a diameter of 20–30 cm at the top, could have been an occasional domestic task, although the technique and time allocation for such activities has not been fully explored. Moreover, the three large "goblet shaped" basalt mortars that are known from the Natufian (one is ca. 60 cm high and ca. 40 wide at the top) appear to have served purposes other than daily, domestic pounding of foodstuff. Although the original contextual evidence is unfortunately lacking, it is possible that these large mortars could be attributed to food preparation for special events such as public feasting (Hayden 1997, Twiss 2008). The shaping of such large, symmetrical, well-smoothed mortars by pecking for many hours is hardly the business of a fully egalitarian society.

One of the unfortunate aspects of Natufian archaeology is the absence of direct evidence for storage facilities. Some indications for the presence of plastered pits at Eynan (Ain Mallaha) and for small, built-up storage installations in Hayonim Terrace have been reported, but the contents were not preserved (Perrot 1966, Valla 1991). More disturbing is the almost complete lack of plant remains from this period, in spite of the application of modern methods of flotation. Various recovery techniques have been employed by researchers since the late 1960s in Israel and Jordan where the majority of Natufian sites have been excavated. The extreme rarity of plant remains reflects conditions of preservation in both open-air and cave sites. Only the chance discovery of a waterlogged site such as Ohalo II (Nadel 1990), or a Natufian occupation layer buried directly beneath a Neolithic village rich in reworked ashes, such as in Jericho, may remedy the situation.

In sum, while the evidence remains limited, it can be argued that an incipient social hierarchy appeared within the Natufian, a society of complex hunter-gatherers that rapidly expanded during the favorable environmental conditions of the Bolling-Allerod climatic episode (ca. 14500–12800 cal BP) (Valla 2004). The following Younger Dryas period, known for colder and drier conditions in many parts of the northern hemisphere, had its biggest impact on the Natufian communities that survived at the margins of their distribution. Returning to more mobile foraging strategies was one solution taken up in the Negev-northern Sinai region witnessed as the Harifian (Goring-Morris 1991). The inhabitants of Hallan Çemi in eastern Turkey adopted a different solution; they became sedentary, thus maintaining control over their territorial resources (Rosenberg and Redding 2000, Savard et al. 2006).

Early Neolithic: The First Millennium (or the PPNA)

The Neolithic sequence of the Levant is still designated as the Pre-Pottery Neolithic A and B, a framework defined by Kenyon (1956) while digging at Jericho. The first part (PPNA) lasted from about 11700/500 until 10600/500 cal BP, and the second (PPNB) until ca. 8400/8200 cal BP. Here we review the evidence pertaining to social inequality uncovered in the few excavated and published PPNA sites during the first millennium of the Holocene.

Cultivation of several wild species, often referred to as "founder crops" (e.g. Bar-Yosef 1998, Harris 1998, Hillman 1996, Willcox 2005, Zohary and Hopf 2002), began with variable success during the PPNA (Colledge 2004, Nesbitt 2002, Weiss et al. 2006). The most prominent and abundant plants were einkorn and emmer wheat, barley, and possibly legumes. The complete process of domestication, to the point where whole fields produced non-shattering rachis for the cereals and seeds germinated annually, took some 800–1,000 years to be completed (Kislev 1997, Tanno and Willcox 2006). The fields were probably close around the settlements. The PPNA people also tended fruit trees such as figs, which may be the earliest domesticated plant (Kislev et al. 2006). These incipient cultivators continued to hunt, trap, fish, and gather a broad array of wild fruits, leaves, roots, and tubers. Farmers behaving as hunters are a known historical and ethnographic phenomenon (Kent 1989, 1992, Ingold 1987, Sponsel 1989). Such groups in the PPNA may have lived in largely kin-related villages. Villages were of different sizes, from 1.5 to 2.5 hectares. But settlements were definitely larger than in the previous Natufian period. Moreover, residential mobility was limited or nonexistent compared to the earlier Natufian. These PPNA villages were 10 times larger than Natufian hamlets, and the increase of population was likely an unconscious result of cultivation, resulting in permanent supplies of staple food and constructed storage facilities. In addition, cereals are among the most suitable weaning foods, increasing the chances of survival for newborns.

This reproductive success gave rise to settlements of 300–400 people, living together at the same location. The largest settlements accommodated a fully viable biological social unit. Computer simulations and ethnographic evidence demonstrate that a minimum number of individuals of all ages are needed for the reproductive survival of a group (Bar-Yosef and Belfer-Cohen 1989, Birdsell 1973, 1985, Wobst 1974). Given the similar ecological conditions, under stable climatic conditions territory size will reflect the relative number of individuals in the group. Territories may be marked by specific artifacts and material elements found in the villages and the presence of central ceremonial places where annual aggregations were held.

Given the size of these new sedentary communities and the number of co-resident individuals, one might expect new forms of organization to emerge. Personal property may have been important as substantial energy was invested in agricultural fields and in the maintenance of control over the land (e.g. Gibson 2007). Garbage accumulation, reworked ashes, fire cracked rooks, disposed mud bricks, lithic débitage, animal bones, and the repeated rebuilding of oval and rounded houses with flat roofs produced a rapid accumulation of layers and deposits from the Early Neolithic. However, most villages lasted no more than 200–400 years, based on the calibrated radiocarbon dates for various sites, and were then abandoned. Possible causes include epidemics, soil erosion, salinization, environmental deterioration due to known climatic fluctuations, or group conflicts.

The public buildings of this period stand out among the normal, domestic structures. A good example is the tower at Jericho, interpreted as a symbol for guarding the identity of the social unit, possibly with a small shrine on top (Bar-Yosef 1986, Naveh 2003, Ronen and Adler 2001). This monumental structure distinguishes Jericho from other PPNA sites in the southern Levant (Naveh 2003). Other architectural indications of communal activity are the "kiva-type" semi-subterranean structures, probably erected according to a social contract. Well-preserved examples were exposed in PPNA and early PPNB levels at Mureybet III and Jerf el-Ahmar

(Cauvin 2000, Stordeur 2000b, Goring-Morris and Belfer-Cohen 2002, Stordeur and Abbès 2002, Stordeur et al. 2000). These structures are considered as meeting places for the elders of the settlement, and possibly accommodated special storage facilities.

Among the burial evidence, there is a clear distinction between the skeletons of children that were left intact, and the adults whose graves were reopened and skulls removed to be kept in special places (Fig. 6.2). There is no evidence for body adornment or elaborate tombs for individuals, but one should keep in mind the very small number of PPNA sites excavated to date.

Fig. 6.2 Modeled skull from Kfar HaHoresh

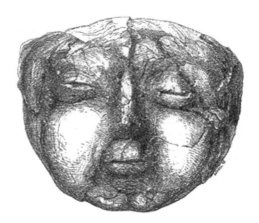

The archaeology of known PPNA sites documents the presence of storage facilities (e.g., Jericho, Dhra, Netiv Hagdud, Gilgal). Although the contents of these facilities are as yet unknown, they do provide another piece of architectural evidence that can potentially tell us about status differentiation. As Testart (1982:526) has argued, "Because of the part played by prestige, the custom of food giving takes on very different meaning among food-storing people. The transformation of foodstuffs into lasting goods stretches to an unprecedented extent the possibilities of exchange and gift and thus enhances the advantages of accumulating food." Certainly the shift from small Natufian hamlets without storage to the larger villages and household storage of the PPNA reflects a change in concepts of ownership and property (e.g. Byrd 1994, Flannery 2002, Kuijt and Findlayson 2009, Rollefson 1997). Food storage provides conditions for the emergence of status, but does not necessarily demonstrate the presence of such a phenomenon.

The evidence from site size in the PPNA of the Levant fits well in the context of Boyd and Richerson's (1988) convincing argument that stress on the conditions that allow reciprocal cooperation grows as group size increases. Comparison of food sharing intensity with community size using ethnographic data clearly suggests a negative relationship; sharing decreases as group size grows (Boyd and Richerson 1988). As Weissner (1997) has noted, the prevalence and strength of sanctions against the use of food for status distinction among most hunter-gatherers attests to the potential of this resource for creating, supporting, or challenging social differentiation.

The appearance of exotic, rare, and valued objects and materials likely is one of the primary indicators of status differentiation in past human societies, as a marker of difference in wealth and possession. What would be the purpose of these items? If people did not need these objects earlier in time, why did they need them at the beginning of the Neolithic? There are several kinds of exotic materials that appear for the first time in the PPNA. One of the best examples is the large quantity of Anatolian obsidian found at PPNA Jericho. Two neighboring and contemporary sites have very little obsidian—Netiv Hagdud with only a few pieces and Gilgal with none (Cauvin 2001, Garfinkel 1987). The quantity of exotic materials appears to mark the community of higher status individuals at Jericho. Other exotic materials, including marine shells (Bar-Yosef Mayer 2005), greenstones (all across the Levant), and chlorite (in the northern Levant), also show uneven distributions among PPNA sites.

As we shall see in the following paragraphs on the PPNB, the archaeology of the subsequent millennia suggests that the seeds of social inequality had already been sown in the Natufian and had sprouted during formative millennium of the PPNA.

Early Neolithic: The Next Two-and-Half Millennia (or the PPNB)

Archaeologists have generally assumed that status differentiation is reflected in architecture and settlement features, in contexts where certain patterned differences in house size, construction, and contents are observed. Monumental architecture also appears to be associated with more complex societies. Such construction may also reflect the presence of social inequality in some form, but the evidentiary connections are not well defined.

The only Early Neolithic village where a large area (some 5,000 m^2) has been excavated is Çayönü in eastern Turkey. The site map provides good evidence for the presence of both larger and smaller households, all of the same basic architectural plan, with a central open-air plaza (Ozdogan 1999). The indications for inequality come from differences in house size between the eastern and western halves of the site, and the construction of public plaza and the "Terazzo building" to the east. Comparison between the two halves of the village reveals that house size is larger and construction quality is better to the east around the plaza. The plaza houses have more elaborate architectural features in the form of porches and pavements. These eastern houses also contained more unusual and exotic artifacts than those to the west (Davis 1998).

Çayönü is possibly the best evidence for intra-village hierarchy and is not greatly different from what is known among other village or "household societies" in this period. While the evidence does not definitively confirm that the owners of the larger houses were also the members of an elite, a possible hint is provided by their location next to the local temple, the "Terazzo building." This structure consists of a rectangular, large room with a thick plaster floor (Fig. 6.3). Its similarity in plan to the temple at Navali Çori, which was much better preserved, should be noted.

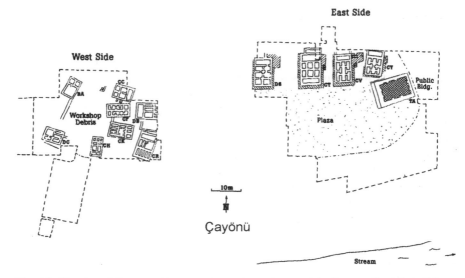

Fig. 6.3 Site plan of Çayönü with east and west sides, plaza, and the "terrazzo" public building

Unfortunately, the proximity of the "Terazzo" building to the surface meant that several millennia of erosion of late Holocene time reduced it to its "concrete-strong" floor.

A very similar pattern was noted by Lightfoot and Feinman (1982) in the Mogollon region of the American Southwest, where in the context of early agricultural societies, larger houses with somewhat more goods and/or wealth were found around a plaza and are argued to reflect status differentiation.

The evidence from the village of Çayönü in Turkey and from a number of partially excavated sites in the northern and southern Levant suggests the presence of particular territories that clearly point to an evolving complex social organization (Bar-Yosef and Bar-Yosef Mayer 2002). Elements that define the territories of what may have been ethno-linguistic groups include distinctive domestic house plans, technological differences in the flaking or polishing of heavy tools such as axes and adzes, variation in the form of projectile points, the presence of plastered skulls, stone masks, "white ware" vessels, stone bangles, and other distinctive diagnostic artifacts (Bogonofsky 2001, 2004, 2005). The primary focus of each territory is found at ceremonial centers that are often large sites, as well as special locations such as the storage facility for sacred paraphernalia in Nahal Hemar Cave in the Judean Desert (Bar-Yosef 2001b).

Several territories with common material culture attributes can be grouped as an interaction sphere. Given the state of current research, two interaction spheres can be identified in the Early Neolithic Near East (e.g., Asouti 2006, Aurenche and Kozlowski 1999, Koslowski and Aurenche 2005, Kuijt and Goring-Morris 2002). One, in the western wing of the Fertile Crescent and Anatolia, is recognized by the distribution of Big Arrowheads (to use the terminology suggested by Kozlowski); the other, in the eastern half of the Fertile Crescent, is characterized by the continuous use of microliths (Kozlowski and Aurenche 2005). Both of these spheres overlap in a zone of mutual interaction in Upper Mesopotamia and the northern Levant.

Evidence for what must have been organized and directed activities, not by a small, egalitarian group but rather by a society led by an elite (perhaps including shamans or priests), comes from the remarkable ceremonial center at Göbekli Tepe in Turkey. The quarrying and shaping of the numerous T-shaped pillars, and the carving in low relief of mammals, birds, and reptiles on the pillars, provides strong evidence for labor mobilization in these Early Neolithic societies. The transport of these pillars, weighing as much as one ton, up the hill on which the site sits and their erection inside large buildings in two complexes documents a major investment of energy and the role of organized labor in enhancing social values (Schmidt 2000). Later periods in Near Eastern history clearly indicate that such monumental buildings are the work of an organized labor force, as known from the cuneiform archives in Mesopotamia. Built from bricks, or based on stone foundations, the temples were constructed by communal efforts as tribute to the gods (e.g. Pollock 1999, Postgate 1992). Such evidence reminds us of the arguments of Aldenderfer (2005, in Chapter 4, this volume) regarding the importance of religion in the emergence of inequality.

The contents of the buildings at Göbekli Tepe are of prime importance as they reflect the same historical sacrificial practices in the ancient Near East in which male animals were preferred. Indeed, not surprisingly the ratio of bulls to cows at Göbekili Tepe is 5:1. At Gürcetepe IV, the village at the foot of the hill below the ceremonial center of Göbekili Tepe, the ratio is five cows to one bull (Peters et al. 1999).

The organized labor and the investment in high quality craftsmanship seen in the village temple and sculptures at the small site of Nevali Çori in eastern Turkey (Hauptman 1999) cannot be serendipitous, but rather conceived and directed. In a small community one might imagine the impact of a single family of higher social status among kin members. A huge, spectacular, ceremonial place like Göbekili Tepe, where domestic habitations either do not exist or are not yet exposed, cannot be the product of a small group with an important family, unless this was the family of the local chiefs. Moreover, the subsequent filling at a later date of the ceremonial buildings at both Göbekili Tepe and Çayönü with village garbage, may document an organized effort for religious purposes to sanctify these places (Özdogan and Özdogan 1998).

Burial and Mortuary Practice During the PPNB

Many archaeologists have emphasized the importance of burials and mortuary practices in the quest for information about social organization (e.g., Brown 1971, Hatch and Willey 1974, O'Shea 1984, Parker Pearson 1999, Saxe 1971, Tainter 1975, and many others). Peebles and Kus (1977) summarize some of the argument. They point out that it is not simply rich child or infant burials that indicate status differentiation. Peebles and Kus argue that a superordinate dimension of social personae will be visible in mortuary practices, beyond the normal differences associated with age and sex. In essence, symbols, grave dimensions or ornamentation, grave contents, and other variables that mark a particular category of individuals will crosscut the variation based on age and sex.

The burial evidence from the PPNB has been summarized in the literature (Kuijt and Goring-Morris 2002, 2005; Simmons et al. 2007). From this compilation we would like to recall the site of Çayönü where three of the four richest in-house burials were found in the plaza houses, the contents distinguished by large pieces of obsidian and many artifacts. In more general terms, the distribution of grave goods was distinctly unequal (Fig. 6.4). Only a small number of the buried individuals were provided with beads, tools, and/or obsidian.

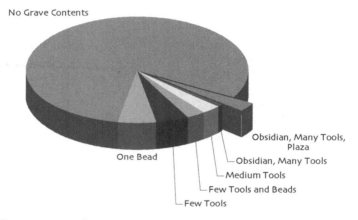

Fig. 6.4 Grave contents at Çayönü, Turkey

Eshed et al. (2009), Goring-Morris (2005), Kuijt (2008), and Kuijt and Goring-Morris (2002) describe the site of Kfar HaHoresh in the Lower Galilee of Israel, a regional ritual and funerary center from the Early Neolithic PPNB. The evidence from this site suggests the development of various institutions and rituals—such as communal construction, cult areas, and ceremonial installations. Goring-Morris argues that the distribution of material culture remains at Kfar HaHoresh, along with age and sex data, provides evidence of both ascribed and achieved status. The variety of graves—in terms of shape, location, fill, and context—within contemporary levels is a strong indication of status differentiation. Grave goods can be divided into two groups: those within the grave and those in the near vicinity of the grave. These two groups show a patterned distribution. The fact that some individuals from the same society were buried at the settlement sites, while others were interred separately at this funerary center suggests that differentiation is present. The villages generally appear to have a low number of burials relative to site size and expected population

Fig. 6.5 Kfar HaHoresh, proportion of males among burials compared to Ain Ghazal, Atlit Yam, and PPNB as a whole

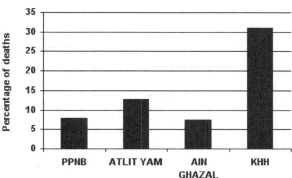

RELATIVE NUMBERS OF DEATHS

numbers. Moreover, there is a higher proportion of males, particularly young males, buried at Kfar HaHoresh than at nearby, contemporary settlement sites (Fig. 6.5). The diverse forms of burial treatment are applied equally to children at Kfar HaHoresh, a fact that Goring-Morris interprets as indicative of ascribed status in the population.

Another example comes from Tell Halula, an Early Neolithic site on the Middle Euphrates in Syria, which contains evidence for a series of occupations dated from 7900 to 5700 cal BC. Excavation of 15 houses from the PPNB revealed 107 sub-floor graves containing 127 individuals. Guerrero et al. (2008) report that these burials show distinctive differences in treatment and contents crosscutting age and sex distinctions, likely reflecting inequality.

Skulls of both male and female adolescents and adults with features modeled in plaster have been found at various sites in the Levant (Bonogofsky 2001a, b, 2005, Fletcher et al. 2009, Strouhal 1973). But not every buried individual at the site received this special treatment. Whether these skulls represent a "cult of ancestors" is perhaps less important than the observation that not all community members received the same treatment and attention. It can therefore be suggested that those skulls kept in domestic houses, sometimes on stands, represent the remains of members of the elite. In addition, the individuals modeled in a gelatinous material that resembled asphalt found at the Nahal Hemer Cave in the Judean Desert (Bar-Yosef and Alon 1988) probably had a special status that would help explain the other finds at the site, where a wide range of unusual paraphernalia (Nahal Hemar blades, wooden and plaster beads, stone masks, etc.) had been stored.

In view of the abundance of evidence, scholarly efforts to suggest that Neolithic societies employed changing mortuary practices in order to maintain the structure of an egalitarian society (e.g. Kuijt 1996) are hardly acceptable. However, no uniquely rich tombs have been discovered as yet. PPNB societies cannot be described as "chiefdoms" based on present evidence. However, ongoing fieldwork may change this situation in the foreseeable future.

House Contents During the PPNB

Haller et al. (2006), Smith (1987), and others have emphasized the significance of households for documenting differences in the kinds and amounts of foods and wealth present within a social group. Smith's excellent treatise (1987) is especially appropriate in a consideration of house contents. Smith uses ethnographic and historical data to document a strong positive relationship between household possessions and wealth. Wealth can include a variety of matter, energy, and information in the form of food, plants and animals and their products, clothing, equipment, labor, structures, and supplies. However, discussion of such differences should be based on a "Pompeii" situation, i.e. the presence of well-preserved house floors and contents—a condition that is hardly ever encountered in Neolithic excavations in the Near East. House contents are usually unknowable. In most cases either the floors had been cleaned or the houses had been filled in with trash when abandoned (at Jericho, Basta, Ain Ghazal, Bouqras, etc., e.g. see Akkermans et al. 1981). One of the rare exceptions is a building exposed at the site of Yiftahel in the lower Galilee in Israel, where a rich storage area above the floor was found containing numerous seeds from the broad bean plant (Garfinkel 1987).

Traded or exchanged items indicate a much wider zone of interaction in which sources and producers were located beyond the permeable boundaries of the PPNB Levantine-Anatolian societies (e.g. Aurenche and Kozlowski 1999). Among the better-known materials exchanged and "paid for " by the well to do (perhaps by tokens) are obsidian, chlorite bowls, asphalt, cinnabar, marine shells, and other materials (e.g. Aurenche and Kozlowski 1999, Bar-Yosef Mayer 2005, Rosenberg 1998). In addition, the discovery that naviform cores were made by specialized artisans reflects not only the emergence of craft specialists, but potentially also of nomadic craftsmen moving from one village to another, providing a precedent for the later metal workers.

Conclusions

We began this essay with the statement that *most* past societies of hunter-gatherers evolved mechanisms for reducing expressions or actions of dominance behavior in favor of food and property sharing, care of relatives, and egalitarian roles. Prestige, we assume, was ephemeral and achieved. Prior to the origins of agriculture, differential distribution of power and wealth appear to have been limited to a few groups we often call complex foragers, such as the Northwest Coast Indians. Other examples such as the early Jomon (Habu 2004), if not recorded ethnographically, are known from prehistory.

The success of early cultivation and the advantages afforded by the genetic mutations among plants and animals, allowed for rapid increase in human population (Bouquet-Appel and Bar-Yosef 2008, and papers therein). Cultivation also supported a stable economy with surplus that resulted in the formation of elite groups as predicted by Lenski (1966). One can imagine how successful individuals, under particularly favorable economic conditions, encouraged by stable climate, operationalized a natural temptation to dominate, to support their kin while at the same time accumulating wealth. Ideological changes emanating from these widespread and successful economic changes are predictable, as noted by Weissner (2002). The previously sporadic role of the Bull expanded to become a main component in the cosmology of northern Levantine Neolithic farmers, as described by Cauvin (2000, see also Hodder 2007). The concept was taken across Anatolia to Thessaly and Crete. However, the establishment of the new ideology seems to have been the result of, and not the motivation for, the agricultural revolution.

The marking of personal property, whether by individuals or extended families, is probably documented by the rare, flat, engraved pebbles and stamp seals in the PPNB. The engravings on these objects, as noted by Cauvin (2000), resemble pictographs used in early writing systems in the Near East. Similarly, tokens in PPNB contexts have been interpreted as components of a counting system (Schmandt-Besserat 1990).

Indeed, we have tried in these pages to point out the likelihood that status differentiation is documented in PPNB contexts when early farming societies had reached a full blown Neolithic economy with domesticated animals (sheep, goat, pig, and cattle) and plants, including cereals, legumes, flax, fig trees and more. We, therefore, cannot rule out the emergence of social inequality at this time. One cannot expect to find definitive evidence for status differentiation at the origins of cultivation, while hunting and gathering continued (i.e. during the PPNA). It is only after a millennium (or a bit more) of trial and error with various plants (Weiss et al. 2006) that we see the first signs for inequality clearly manifested during the Middle PPNB, and through the end of this period.

The elusive archaeological evidence for the roots of social inequality in the Natufian and the PPNA includes the differences in body decoration among Natufian skeletons, the communal building at Eynan (Ain Mallaha), the different treatments of children and adults in burials at PPNA village sites, and the first appearance of "kiva-type" buildings at Mureybet and Jerf el-Ahmar. The markers during the PPNB period (10500–8200 cal BP) are somewhat clearer; differences in quantities of obsidian among the villages, long distance transport of valued items (obsidian, shells, greenstone beads, chlorite, etc.), the presence of craft specialists (the production of blades from "naviform" cores), and in particular the indirect evidence for building large structures and public temples, such as Göbekli Tepe, that reflect organized labor, and perhaps control by a social elite. The presence of this sub-group is suggested by the plastered skulls that include both adults and children.

In spite of the variety of evidence from the Near East, a fully convincing argument for social inequality in the Neolithic remains is hard to convey. One of the major difficulties in identifying emergent social differentiation likely lies in the simple fact that it is emergent and difficult to recognize. We have looked for known indicators from the archaeology of later periods in the Near East, but perhaps other hallmarks escape our attention or we fail to interpret them correctly.

Detection of incipient inequality is also difficult because there are different paths to differentiation (e.g. Chapter 3 by Drennan et al. this volume, Feinman 1995,

Hayden 1995)—so the material expression of emergent inequality is not manifest in the same way at different places/times. In the same vein, emerging inequality is likely not a linear process. In other words, an individual or family may achieve wealth or power, only to be later put back in their place as conditions change or others gain advantage. Such cycling is reported in various archaeological (e.g., Anderson 1994, Marcus 1992) and ethnographically known cultures (Leach 1954).

Another problem in uncovering the origins of status differentiation lies in the fact that archaeological evidence for the origins of agriculture itself is minimal in most parts of the world. This absence suggests that perhaps this transition was rapid, punctuating equilibrium. It is simply astounding that there is so little information from the time of the initial transition to agriculture. Data on household and community size from the New World are almost non-existent with the exception of the Eastern United States. Information from China, Sub-Saharan Africa, and New Guinea is equally hard to come by. The best evidence we have can be found in the Near East. Outside of this region, it is almost impossible to find the answers necessary for understanding the relationship between farming and inequality because of the paucity of evidence. But of course that hasn't stopped us before.

Acknowledgments Thanks to Gary Feinman for his thoughtful comments and suggestions for this paper.

References

Akkermann, P.A., Fokkens, H., and Waterbolk, H.T. 1981. Stratigraphy, Architecture and Lay-Out of Bouqras. In Cauvin, J. and Sanlaville, P. (eds.), *Préhistoire du Levant Chronologie et Organisation de l'espace Depuis les Origines Jusqu'au Vie Millénaire*, pp. 485–501. Paris: CNRS.

Aldenderfer, M. 2005. Ritual, hierarchy, and change in foraging societies. *Journal of Anthropological Archaeology* 12: 1–40.

Anderson, D.G. 1994. *The Savannah River Chiefdoms*. Tuscaloosa: University of Alabama Press.

Arnold, J.E. 1993. Labor and the rise of complex hunter-gatherers. *Journal of Anthropological Archaeology* 12: 75–119.

Asouti, E. 2006. Beyond the pre-pottery Neolithic B interaction sphere. *Journal of World Prehistory* 20: 87–126.

Aurenche, O., and Kozlowski, S.K. 1999. *La naissance du néolithique au Proche Orient*. Paris: Editions Errance.

Bar-Yosef Mayer, D.E. 2005. The exploration of shells as beads in the palaeolithic and neolithic of the Levant. *Paléorient* 31: 176–185.

Bar-Yosef, O. 1986. The walls of Jericho: an alternative interpretation. *Current Anthropology* 27: 157–162.

Bar-Yosef, O. 1998. The Natufian culture in the Levant, threshold to the origins of agriculture. *Evolutionary Anthropology* 6: 150–177.

Bar-Yosef, O. 2000. The Context of Animal Domestication in Southwestern Asia. In Mashkour, M., Choyke, A.M., and Poplin, F. (eds.), *Archaeozoology of the Near East IV A: Proceedings of the 4th international symposium on the archaeozoology of southwestern Asia and adjacent areas*, pp. 184–194. Groningen: Centre for Archaeological Research and Consultancy; Groningen Institute for Archaeology; Rijksuniversiteit Groningen.

Bar-Yosef, O. 2001a. From Sedentary Foragers to Village Hierarchies: the Emergence of Social Institutions. In Runciman, G. (ed.), *The origin of Human Social Institutions*, pp. 1–38. London: The British Academy.

Bar-Yosef, O. 2001b. PPNB interaction sphere. *Cambridge Archaeology Journal* 11: 114–120.

Bar-Yosef, O. 2002a. The Natufian Culture and the Early Neolithic – Social and Economic Trends. In Bellwood, P. and Renfrew, C. (eds.), *Examining the Farming/Language Dispersal Hypothesis*, pp. 113–126. Cambridge: McDonald Institute Monographs.

Bar-Yosef, O. 2002b. Natufian: A Complex Society of Foragers. In Fitzhugh, B. and Habu, J. (eds.), *Beyond Foraging and Collecting: Evolutionary Change in Hunter-Gatherer Settlement Systems*, pp. 91–149. New-York: Kluwer Academic.

Bar-Yosef, O., and Alon, D. 1988. Excavations in the Nahal Hemar cave. *Antiqot* 18: 1–30.

Bar-Yosef, O., and Bar-Yosef Mayer, D.E. 2002. Early Neolithic Tribes in the Levant. In Parkinson, W.A. (ed.), *The Archaeology of Tribal Societies*, pp. 340–371. Ann Arbor: International Monographs in Prehistory.

Bar-Yosef, O., and Belfer-Cohen, A. 1989. The origins of sedentism and farming communities in the Levant. *Journal of World Prehistory* 3: 347–498.

Belfer-Cohen, A. 1991. The Natufian in the Levant. *Annual Review of Anthropology* 20: 167–186.

Belfer-Cohen, A. 1995. Rethinking Social Stratification in the Natufian Culture: The Evidence from Burials. In Campbell, S. and Green, A. (eds.), *The Archaeology of Death in the Ancient Near East*, pp. 9–16. Oxford: Oxbow Books (Monograph 51).

Bender, B. 1978. Gatherer-hunter to farmer: a social perspective. *World Archaeology* 10: 204–222.

Birdsell, J.B. 1973. A basic demographic unit. *Current Anthropology* 14: 337–350.

Birdsell, J.B. 1985. Biological Dimensions of Small, Human Founding Populations. In Finney, B.R. and Jones, E.M. (eds.), *Interstellar Migration and the Human Experience*, pp. 110–119. Berkeley: University of California Press.

Bogonofsky, M. (ed.) 2001. *The Bioarchaeology of the Human Head: Decapitation, Deformation, and Decoration*. Gainesville: University Press of Florida.

Bonogofsky, M. 2001a. Cranial sanding, not defleshing of two plastered skulls from Ain Ghazal. *Paléorient* 27: 141–146.

Bonogofsky, M. 2001b. *A new look at the ancestor cult in the Levant. Proceedings of the Near & Middle Eastern Civilizations Graduate Students Annual Symposia (1998–2000)*, pp. 141–151. Mississauga: Benben.

Bonogofsky, M. 2004. Including women and children: neolithic modeled skulls from Jordan, Israel, Syria and Turkey. *Near Eastern Archaeology* 67: 118–119.

Bonogofsky, M. 2005. A bioarchaeological study of plastered skulls from Anatolia: new discoveries and interpretation. *International Journal of Osteoarchaeology* 15: 124–135.

Boquet-Appel, J.-P., and Bar Yosef, O. (eds.). 2008. *Neolithic Demographic Transitions*. New York: Springer.

Boyd, B. 2001. The Natufian burials from el-Wad, Mount Carmel: beyond issues of social differentiation. *Journal of the Israeli Prehistoric Society* 31: 185–200.

Boyd, R., and Richerson, P.J. 1988. The evolution of reciprocity in sizeable groups. *Journal of Theoretical Biology* 132: 337–356.

Brown, J.A. (ed.). 1971. *Approaches to the Social Dimensions of Mortuary Practices*, Memoirs of the Society for American Archaeology 25.

Byrd, B.F. 1994. Public and private, domestic and corporate: the emergence of the southwest Asian village. *American Antiquity* 59: 639–666.

Byrd, B., and Monahan, C. 1995. Death, mortuary ritual, and Natufian social structure. *Journal of Anthropological Archaeology* 14: 251–287.

Cauvin, J. 2000. *The Birth of Gods and the Beginnings of Agriculture: The Revolution in Symbols in the Neolithic*. New York: Cambridge University Press.

Cauvin, J. 2001. Ideology before economy. *Cambridge Archaeology Journal* 11: 106–107.

Clark, J.E., and Blake, M. 1994. The Power of Prestige: Competitive Generosity and the Emergence of Rank Societies in Lowland America. In Brumfiel, E. and Fox, J. (eds.), *Factional*

Competition and Political Development in the New World, p. 1730. Cambridge: Cambridge University Press.

Colledge, S. 2004. Reappraisal of the Archaeobotanical Evidence for the Emergence and Dispersal of the "Founder Crops". In Peltenburg, E. and Wasse, A. (eds.), *Neolithic Revolution. New Perspectives on Southwest Asia in Light of Recent Discoveries in Cyprus*, pp. 49–60. Oxford: Oxbow books.

Davis, M.K. 1998. Social Differentiation at the Early Village of Çayönü, Turkey. In Arsebük, G., Mellink, M.J., and Schirmer, W. (eds.), *Light on Top of the Black Hill*, pp. 257–266. Istanbul: Ege Yayinlari.

DeVore, I. 1965. *Primate Behavior: Field Studies of Monkeys and Apes*. New York: Holt, Reinhart and Winston.

de Waal, F. 1998. *Chimpanzee Politics: Power and Sex Among Apes*. Baltimore: Johns Hopkins University Press.

Eshed, V., Hershkovitz, I., and Goring-Morris, A.N. 2009. A re-evaluation of burial customs in the pre-pottery Neolithic B in light of paleodemographic analysis of the human remains from Kfar Hahoresh, Israel. *Paléorient* 34: 91–103.

Feinman, G.M. 1995. The Emergence of Inequality: A Focus on Strategies and Processes. In Price, T.D. and Feinman, G.M. (eds.), *Foundations of Social Inequality*, pp. 255–279. New York: Plenum Press.

Flannery, K.V. 1972. The Origins of the Village as a Settlement Type in Mesoamerica and the Near East: A Comparative Study. In Ucko, P.J., Tringham, R., and Dimbleby, G.W. (eds.), *Man, Settlement and Urbanism*, pp. 23–53. London: Duckworth.

Flannery, K.V. 2002. The origins of the village revisited: from nuclear to extended households. *American Antiquity* 67: 417–433.

Fletcher, A., Pearson, J., and Ambers, J. 2009. The manipulation of social and physical identity in the pre-pottery Neolithic. *Cambridge Archaeological Journal* 18: 309–325.

Garfinkel, Y. 1987. Yiftahel: a Neolithic village from the seventh millennium BC in Lower Galilee, Israel. *Journal of Field Archaeology* 14: 199–212.

Garrod, D.A.E. 1957. The Natufian culture: the life and economy of a Mesolithic people in the Near East. *Proceedings of the British Academy* 43: 211–227.

Garrod, D.A.E., and Bate, D.M.A. 1937. *The Stone-Age of the Mount Carmel, I: Excavations at the Wadi Mughara*. Oxford: Oxford University Press.

Gibson, D.B. 2007. Chiefdoms and the emergence of private property in land. *Journal of Anthropological Archaeology* 8.

Goring-Morris, A.N. 1991. The Harifian of the Southern Levant. In Bar-Yosef, O. and Valla, F.R. (eds.), *The Natufian Culture in the Levant*, pp. 173–216. Ann Arbor: International Monographs in Prehistory.

Goring-Morris, A.N. 2005. Life, Death and the Emergence of Differential Status in the Near Eastern Neolithic: Evidence from Kfar HaHoresh, Lower Galilee, Israel. In Clarke, J. (ed.), *Archaeological Perspectives on the Transmission and Transformation of Culture in the Eastern Mediterranean*, pp. 89–105. Oxford: Council for British Research in the Levant and Oxbow Books.

Goring-Morris, A.N., and Belfer-Cohen, A. 2002. Symbolic Behavior from the Epipalaeolithic and Early Neolithic of the Near East: Preliminary Observations on Continuity and Change. In Gebel, H.G.K., Hermansen, B.D., and Jensen, C.H. (eds.), *Magic Practices and Ritual in the Near Eastern Neolithic*, pp. 67–79. Berlin: Ex Oriente.

Guerrero, E., Naji, S., and Bocquet-Appel, J.-P. 2008. The Signal of Neolithic Demographic Transition in the Levant. In Bocquet-Appel, J.-P. and Bar-Yosef, O. (eds.), *Neolithic Demographic Transitions*, pp. 57–80. New York: Springer.

Haas, A. 1993. Social inequality in aboriginal North America: a test of Lenski's Theory. *Social Forces* 72: 295–313.

Habu, J. 2004. *The Jomon of Japan*. Cambridge: Cambridge University Press.

Haller, M.J., Feinman, G.M., and Nicholas, L. 2006. Socioeconomic inequality and differential access to faunal resources at El Palmillo, Oaxaca, Mexico. *Ancient Mesoamerica* 17: 39–56.

Harris, D.R. 1998. The origins of agriculture in Southwest Asia. *The Review of Archaeology* 19: 5–11.

Hatch, J.W., and Willey, P. 1974. Stature and status in Dallas society. *Tennessee Archaeologist* 30: 107–131.

Hauptmann, H. 1999. The Urfa region. In Özdogan, M. and Basgelen, N. (eds.), *Neolithic in Turkey: The Cradle of Civilization. New Discoveries*, pp. 65–87. Istanbul: Arkeoloji ve Sanat Yayınları.

Hayden, B. 1995. Pathways to Power: Principles for Creating Socioeconomic Inequalities. In Price, T.D. and Feinman, G.M. (eds.), *Foundations of Social Inequality*, pp. 13–86. New York: Plenum.

Hayden, B. 1997. Feasting in Prehistoric and Traditional Societies. In Wiessner, P. and Schiefenhövel, W. (eds.), *Food and the Status Quest*, pp. 127–147. Providence: Berghahn Books.

Hayden, B. 2001. Richman, Poorman, Beggarman, Chief: The Dynamics of Social Inequality. In Feinman, G. and Price, T. (eds.), *Archaeology at the Millennium: A Sourcebook*, pp. 231–272. New York: Plenum Publishers.

Hayden, B. 2004. Sociopolitical Organization in the Natufian: A View from the Northwest. In Delage, C. (ed.), *The Last Hunter-Gatherer Societies in the Near East*, pp. 263–308. Oxford: BAR International Series.

Hayden, B., and Gargett, R. 1990. Big man, big heart? a Mesoamerican view of the emergence of complex society. *Ancient Mesoamerica* 1: 3–20.

Henry, D.O. 1989. *From Foraging to Agriculture. The Levant at the End of the Ice Age.* Philadelphia: University of Pennsylvania Press.

Hillman, G. 1996. Late Pleistocene Changes in Wild Plant-Foods Available to Hunter-Gatherers of the Northern Fertile Crescent: Possible Preludes to Cereal Cultivation. In Harris, D.R. (ed.), *The Origins and Spread of Agriculture and Pastoralism in Eurasia*, pp. 159–203. Washington: Smithsonian Institution Press.

Hodder, I. 2007. Çatalhöyük in the context of the middle eastern neolithic. *Annual Review of Anthropology* 36: 105–120.

Ingold, T. 1987. Territoriality and Tenure: The Appropriation of Space in Hunting and Gathering Societies. In *The Appropriation of Nature: Essays on Human Ecology and Social Relations*, pp. 130–164. Iowa City: University of Iowa Press.

Kent, S. (ed.). 1989. *Farmers as Hunters: The Implications of Sedentism.* Cambridge: Cambridge University Press.

Kent, S. 1992. The current forager controversy: real versus ideal views of hunter-gatherers. *Man, n.s.* 27(1): 45–70.

Kenyon, K. 1956. Excavations at Jericho, 1956. *Palestine Exploration Quarterly* 88: 67–82.

Kingery, W.D., Vandiver, P., and Prickett, P. 1988. The beginnings of pyrotechnology, Part II: Production and use of lime and gypsum plaster in the pre-pottery neolithic near east. *Journal of Field Archaeology* 15: 219–244.

Kislev, M. 1997. Early Agriculture and Palaeoecology of Netiv Hagud. In Bar-Yosef, O. and Gopher, A. (eds.), *An Early Neolithic Village in the Jordan Valley*, pp. 209–236. Cambridge: Peabody Museum of Archaeology and Ethnology.

Kislev, M.E., Hartmann, A., and Bar-Yosef, O. 2006. Early domesticated fig in the Jordan Valley. *Science* 312: 1372 – 1374.

Kozlowski, S.K., and Aurenche, O. (eds.). 2005. Territories, Boundaries and Cultures in the Neolithic Near East. Archaeopress – Maison de l'Orient et de la Méditennanée.

Kuijt, I. 1996. Negotiating equality through ritual: a consideration of the late Natufian and pre-pottery Neolithic A period mortuary practices. *Journal of Anthropological Archaeology* 15: 313–336.

Kuijt, I. (ed.). 2000. *Life in Neolithic Farming Communities: Social Organization, Identity, and Differentiation.* New York: Kluwer.

Kuijt, I. 2002. Reflections on Ritual and the Transmission of Authority in the Pre-Pottery Neolithic of the Southern Levant. In Gebel, H.G.K., Hermansen, B.D., and Jensen, C.H. (eds.), *Magic*

Practices and Ritual in the Near Eastern Neolithic, Studies in Early Near Eastern Production, Subsistence, and Environment, Vol. 8, pp. 81–90. Berlin: Ex Oriente.

Kuijt, I. 2008. The regeneration of life: neolithic structures of symbolic remembering and forgetting. *Current Anthropology* 49: 171–198.

Kuijt, I., and Goring-Morris, N.A. 2002. Foraging, farming, and social complexity in the prepottery neolithic of the Southern Levant: a review and synthesis. *Journal of World Prehistory* 16: 361–440.

Kuijt, I., and Bill, F. 2009. Evidence for food storage and predomestication granaries 11,000 years ago in the Jordan Valley. *PNAS* 106(27): 10966–10970.

Leach, E.R. 1954. *Political Systems of Highland Burma*. Cambridge: Harvard University Press.

Lenski, G. 1966. *Power and Privilege*. New York: McGraw-Hill.

Lightfoot, K.V., and Feinman, G.M. 1982. Social differentiation and leadership development in early pithouse villages in the mogollon region of the American Southwest. *American Antiquity* 47: 64–86.

Marcus, J. 1992. Dynamic cycles of Mesoamerican states. *National Geographic Research Explorations* 8: 392–411.

Matson, R.G. 1985. The Relationship Between Sedentism and Status Inequalities Among Hunter-Gatherers. In Thompson, M., Garcia, M.T., and Kense, F.J., *Status, Structure and Stratification: Current Archaeological Reconstructions*, pp. 245–252. Calgary: B.C. Press. Archaeol. Assoc., Univ. Calgary.

Nadel, D. 1990. Ohalo II—a preliminary report. *Mitekufat Haeven* 23: 48–59.

Naveh, D. 2003. PPNA Jericho: a socio-political perspective. *Cambridge Archaeological Journal* 13: 83–96.

Nesbitt, M. 2002. When and Where Did Domesticated Cereals First Occur in Southwest Asia? In Cappers, R.T.J., Bottema, S., *The Dawn of Farming in the Near East*, pp. 113–132. Berlin: Ex Oriente.

O'Shea, J.M. 1984. *Mortuary Variability: An Archaeological Investigation*. Orlando: Academic Press.

Özdogan, A. 1999. Çayönü. In Özdogan, M. and Basgelen, N. (eds.), *Neolithic in Turkey: Cradle of Civilization New Discoveries*, pp. 35–64. Istanbul: Arkeoloji ve Sanat Yayinlari.

Özdogan, M., and Özdogan, A. 1998. Buildings of Cult and the Cult of Buildings. In Arsebük, G., Mellink, M., and Schirmer, W. (eds.), *Light on Top of the Black Hill. Studies Presented to Halet Çambel*, pp. 581–601. Istanbul: Ege Yayinlari.

Parker Pearson, M. 1999. *The Archaeology of Death and Burial*. London: Sutton.

Peebles, C.S., and Kus, S. 1977. Some archaeological correlates of ranked societies. *American Antiquity* 42: 421–448.

Perrot, J. 1966. Le gisement natoufien de Mallaha (Eynan), Israel. *L'Anthropologie* 70: 437–484.

Perrot, J., and Ladiray, D. (1988). Les Sepultures. In Perrot, J. (ed.), *Les Hommes de Mallaha (Eynan) Israel*, Paris: Memoires et Travaux du Centre de Recherche Français du Jérusalem. Paris: Association Paléorient.

Perry, S.E. 2006. What cultural primatology can tell anthropologists about the evolution of culture. *Annual Review of Anthropology* 35: 171–190.

Peters, J., Helmer, D., von den Driesch, A., and Segui, M.S. 1999. Early animal husbandry in the Northern Levant. *Paléorient* 25: 27–47.

Pollock, S. 1999. *Ancient Mesopotamia*. Cambridge: Cambridge University Press.

Postgate, J.N. 1992. *Early Mesopotamia: Society and Economy at the Dawn of History*. London and New York: Routledge.

Price, T.D. 1995. Agricultural Origins and Social Inequality. In Price, T.D. and Feinman, G.M. (eds.), *Foundations of Social Inequality*, pp. 129–151. New York: Plenum Press.

Rollefson, G.O. 1997. Changes in Architecture and Social Organization at 'Ain Ghazal. In Gebel, H.G.K., Kafifi, Z., and Rollefson, G.O. (eds.), *The Prehistory of Jordan II, Perspectives from*

1997, Studies in Early Near Eastern Production, Subsistence and Environment, 4, pp. 287–307. Berlin: Ex Oriente.

Ronen, A., and Adler, D. 2001. The walls of Jericho were magical. *Archaeology, Ethnology and Anthropology of Eurasia* 2: 97–103.

Rosenberg, M. 1998. Cheating at musical chairs. Territoriality and sedentism in an evolutionary context. *Current Anthropology* 39: 653–684.

Rosenberg, M., and Redding, R.W. 2000. Hallan Çemi and Early Village Organization in Eastern Anatolia. In Kuijt, I., *Life in Neolithic Farming Communities: Social Organization, Identity, and Differentiation*, pp. 39–61. New York: Kluwer Acad./Plenum.

Savard, M., Nesbitt, M., and Jones, M.K. 2006. The role of wild grasses in subsistence and sedentism: new evidence from the northern Fertile Crescent. *World Archaeology* 38: 179–196.

Saxe, A.A. 1971. Social Dimensions of Mortuary Practices in Mesolithic Populations from Wade Halfa, Sudan. InBrown, J.A. (ed.), *Approaches to the Social Dimensions of Mortuary Practices*, pp. 39–56. Memoirs of the Society for American Archaeology 25.

Schmandt-Besserat, D. 1990. Symbols in the Prehistoric Middle East: Development Features Preceding Written Communication. In Enos, R.L., *Oral and Written Communication, Historical Approaches*, pp. 16–31. Menbury Park: Sage.

Schmidt, K. 2000. Göbekli Tepe, southeastern Turkey: a preliminary report on the 1995–95 excavations. *Paléorient* 26: 45–54.

Simmons, T., Goring-Morris, N., and Horwitz, L.K. 2007. What ceremony else? taphonomy and the ritual treatment of the dead in the pre-pottery Neolithic B Mortuary complex at Kfar HaHoresh, Israel. *BAR International Series* 1603: 100–126.

Smith, M. 1987. Household possessions and wealth in agrarian states: implications for archaeology. *Journal of Anthropological Archaeology* 6: 297–335.

Sponsel, L.E. 1989. Farming and Foraging: A Necessary Complementarityin Amazonia? In Kent, S. (ed.), *Farmers as Hunters: The Implications of Sedentism*, pp. 37–45. Cambridge: Cambridge University Press.

Stordeur, D. 2000a. Jerf el Ahmar: et l'émergence du Néolithique au Proche Orient. In Guilaine, J. (ed.), *Premiers paysans du monde: Naissances des agricultures*, pp. 31–60. Paris: Editions Errance.

Stordeur, D. 2000b. New discoveries in architecture and symbolism at Jerf el Ahmar (Syria), 1997–1999. *Neo-Lithics* 1/00: 1–4.

Stordeur, D., and Abbès, F. 2002. Du PPNA au PPNB: mise en lumière d'une phase de transition à Jerf el Ahmar (Syrie). *Bulletin de la Société préhistorique française* 99: 563–595.

Stordeur, D., Brenet, M., Der Aprahamian, G., and Roux, J.-C. 2000. Les Batiments communautaires de Jerf el Ahmar et Mureybet horizon PPNA (Syrie). *Paléorient* 26(1): 29–44.

Strouhal, E. 1973. Five plastered skulls from pre-pottery Neolithic B Jericho: anthropological study. *Paléorient* 1: 231–247.

Tainter, J.A. 1975. Social inference and mortuary practices: an experiment in numerical classification. *World Archaeology* 7: 1–15.

Tanno, K.-I., and Willcox, G. 2006. How fast was wild wheat domesticated? *Science* 311: 1886.

Testart, A. 1982. The significance of food storage among hunter-gatherers: residence patterns, population densities, and social. *Current Anthropology* 23: 523–537.

Twiss, K.C. 2008. Transformations in an early agricultural society: feasting in the southern levantine pre-pottery neolithic. *Journal of Anthropological Archaeology* 27: 418–442.

Valla, F.R. 1988. Aspects du sol de l'abri 131 de Mallaha (Eynan). *Paléorient* 14: 283–296.

Valla, F. 1991. Les Natoufiens de Mallaha et l'Espace. In Bar-Yosef, O. and Valla, F. (eds.), *The Natufian Culture in the Levant*, pp. 111–122. Ann Arbor: International Monographs in Prehistory.

Valla, F.R. 2004. Natufian Behavior in the Hula Basin: The Question of Territoriality. In Goren-Inbar, N. and Speth, J.D. (eds.), *Human Paleoecology in the Levantine Corridor*, pp. 207–220. Oxford: Oxbow Books.

Weiss, E., Mordechai, E., and Kislev, A.H. 2006. Autonomous cultivation before domestication. *Science* 312: 1608–1610.

Wiessner, P. 1997. Leveling the Hunter: Constraints on the Status Quest in Foraging Societies. In Wiessner, P. and Schiefenhövel, W. (eds.), *Food and the Status Quest*, pp. 171–191. Providence: Berghahn Books.

Wiessner, P. 2002. The vines of complexity. *Current Anthropology* 41: 233–269.

Willcox, G. 2005. The distribution, natural habitats and availability of wild cereals in relation to their domestication in the Near East: multiple events, multiple centres. *Vegetation History and Archaeobotany* 14: 534–541.

Wobst, H.M. 1974. Boundary conditions for paleolithic society. *American Antiquity* 39: 147–178.

Wright, G. 1978. Social Differentiation in the Early Natufian. In Redman, C. (ed.), *Social Archeology: Beyond Subsistence and Dating*, pp. 201–223. New York: Academic Press.

Zohary, D., and Hopf, M. 2002. *Domestication of Plants in the Old World*. Oxford: Clarendon Press.

Chapter 7
Decentralized Complexity: The Case of Bronze Age Northern Europe

Kristian Kristiansen

Introduction

The concept of complexity demands theoretical elaboration, especially in regard to decentralized social formations such as the Bronze Age chiefdoms of northern Europe (Artursson 2008, Goldhahn 2005, Gröhn 2004, Kristiansen 2007, Kristiansen and Larsson 2005, Ling 2007, Nordenborg Myhre 2004). I propose that analysis of their political economy will help us understand how complex power structures operate in a decentralized social and economic environment that lacks many of the attributes of more clear-cut stratified, or complex, societies. These more complex groups normally evolve in environments where high productivity in nodal areas can be controlled and monopolized, whereas decentralized complexity normally operates in environments where productive resources are widespread and difficult to control from a single center. Such economies are sometimes referred to as the Germanic mode of production (Gilman 1995), wealth finance (Earle 1997), or prestige goods systems (Kristiansen 1998b: Fig. 128). The differences between the two types of complexity, and their evolutionary trajectories have been recognized for many years (Renfrew 1974, Friedman and Rowlands 1977, Kristiansen 1998: Figs. 17 and 18, Hayden 1995 for a new evolutionary typology). In more recent works, their internal properties have been discussed and elaborated in concrete case studies (Earle 1997, Feinman 2001). Earle recently described networked strategies in chiefdoms in the following way:

> Networked strategies define relationships of people to people through kinship, trade partnerships, and alliances. In complex societies, network strategies create broad systems of ideological and material exchanges binding leaders, would-be leaders, and followers together in networks of mutual support and competition. These relationships are intensely personal and highly fluid, but they become materialized by the gifting of wealth objects. The form of networks is given physical reality and visibility with objects, and the control over the manufacture and distribution of these politically significant objects is critical to understanding the nature of the networks in societies without written contracts.

K. Kristiansen (✉)
University of Gothenburg, Gothenburg, Sweden
e-mail: kristian.kristiansen@archaeology.gu.se

T.D. Price, G.M. Feinman (eds.), *Pathways to Power*, Fundamental
Issues in Archaeology, DOI 10.1007/978-1-4419-6300-0_7,
© Springer Science+Business Media, LLC 2010

The Danish chiefdoms relied heavily on networked strategies, using systems of wealth finance to structure political hierarchies. (Earle 2002:17)

In the following I develop a theoretical and interpretative model to describe and explain the particular historical conditions that governed the operation of Bronze Age societies in northern Europe, as an example of decentralized complexity. I wish to make clear, however, that I employ a structural and functional definition of complexity, based on the nature and number of institutions and their internal organization in social reproduction. Complexity, in the wider sense of the word, undoubtedly characterized all societies since the arrival of modern humans in the Palaeolithic period, but not in a structural and evolutionary sense.

Ritual Landscapes and Social Institutions

The northern Bronze Age may be said to begin shortly after 2000 BC with the introduction and use of simple bronze tools, especially axes. At the same time, huge longhouses for large (chiefly) households emerged. With the more systematic adoption of metalworking bronze technology after 1750 BC (Vandkilde 1996), a diversified use of new tools, weapons, and ornaments made of bronze appeared, together with a new warrior elite. After 1500 BC these new institutions and technological skills were unified in the creation of a specific Nordic Bronze Age culture, characterized by the construction of thousands of large barrows (Fig. 7.1), a new Nordic material culture, and new more elaborate house architecture, based on the two-aisled construction. Barrows marked long lines of communication and interaction across the landscape (Fig. 7.2).

Fig. 7.1 A landscape of barrows (photo by Kristian Kristiansen)

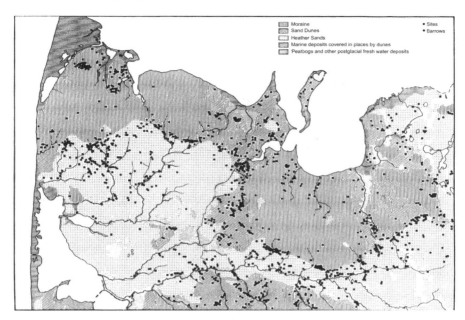

Fig. 7.2 Distribution of Bronze Age barrows in northwestern Jutland, in relation to landscape topography. This distribution documents the ideological role of barrows in a communication network that linked settlements together along the major routes (KK's own illustration)

In an article on spatial patterns of social organization in the Early Bronze Age (Johansen et al. 2004), the authors convincingly demonstrate the linear and contiguous nature of thousands of Bronze Age barrows in southern Jutland (Johansen et al. 2004: Fig. 2). The selected area of investigation covers 4,000 km² and contains 8,181 barrows, a majority from the Middle Bronze Age (1500–1150 BC). Through correspondence analysis of barrows and excavated settlements, they demonstrate that distances between them are regular and mostly less than 500 m. Thus barrow and settlements belong together and form small social units. The authors further demonstrate that, within the barrow networks, nodal points of high centrality exhibit an overrepresentation of male burial wealth in the form of gold and heavy solid-hilted swords, although the spatial distribution of wealth is generally ubiquitous within the networks (Johansen et al. 2004: Figs. 7.9, 7.10, 7.11, 7.12 and 7.13).

The discovery of the Bronze Age naturally began with hundreds of barrow excavations during the nineteenth and early twentieth centuries. The core of some of these barrows had been encapsulated by an iron pan artificially created by watering the mound fill. In some cases, this iron pan protected and preserved the oak coffin and its contents, including elaborate wooden objects and textiles (Figs. 7.3 and 7.4).

Fig. 7.3 Watercolor from the the nineteenth century excavation of the large Borum Eshøj barrow that contained three oak coffin burials, one of which is shown in Fig. 7.4 (from Jensen 1998:91)

Fig. 7.4 A Bronze Age burial from an oak coffin (from Jensen 1998:94)

The richness and abundance of the burial wealth in these barrows invited inter-pretations of the social organization of the mound builders, a phrase coined by Glob (1983). From the 1970s onward, quantitative methods were applied to demonstrate structured variation in burial wealth. The approach is exemplified by Randsborg (1974). His quantitative analysis of metal weights in the burials was used to argue for substantial and systematic wealth differences. I quantified wear patterns on bronzes to demonstrate spatial and temporal variation in circulation time and thus supplies and availability of metal (Kristiansen 1978). Later Thomas Larsson quan-tified wealth distributions in Sweden (Larsson 1986). These studies concluded that wealth was unevenly distributed and subject to regional and temporal variation that could be linked to the productive potential of the settlement system, along with demographic and ecological changes.

During the 1990s, qualitative studies of the social institutions of Bronze Age society appeared. It could be documented on empirical grounds that different sword types are meaningfully linked to different social roles and ultimately institutions (Kristiansen 2001 and 2004, Sørensen 1997). It has thus been possible to demon-strate that leadership was divided between a ritual leader with highly decorated full-hilted swords unsuited for practical use (Fig. 7.5) and a war leader with func-tional swords for practical use (Fig. 7.6). In this context, the ritual leader represented the highest authority. War leaders could have been linked to ritual leaders in a form of decentralized retinue that they would be mobilized in times of need (Fig. 7.7). This institutional structure is most clearly materialized in Montelius Period 2 of the Bronze Age and seen in hundreds of male burials (1500–1300 BC). After that time the rules of its material representation become less strict as burial rituals change.

Chronological chart for Nordic Bronze Age:

Period 1 1750–1500 BC Early Bronze Age
Period 2 1500–1300 BC Middle Bronze Age
Period 3 1300–1150 BC Middle Bronze Age
Period 4 1150–950 BC Late Bronze Age
Period 5 950–750 BC Late Bronze Age
Period 6 750–500 BC Late Bronze Age

It could also be demonstrated that long-distance travels were undertaken by war chiefs during the Bronze Age, both by land and sea, thereby maintaining political alliances and expanding the distribution of bronze (Kristiansen and Larsson 2005: Chapter 5, Ling 2005, 2007). The ritual chiefs, however, stayed home to maintain power. Women married out to maintain alliances between nearby polities; male war-riors might travel much longer distances along these networks of interlinked chiefly polities (Kristiansen and Larsson 2005: Fig. 107, Bergerbrandt 2007).

Among female burials it was possible to define a ritual priestess wearing a short corded skirt and employing the sun disc as the central ornament carried on the belly (Kristiansen and Larsson 2005: Figs. 135, 136 and 137). This group of belt plates has further been argued by Randsborg (2006: Chapter X) as containing complex astronomical knowledge. Another group of high-ranking women without sun discs

Fig. 7.5 Burial goods of a ritual chief characterized by a ceremonial dagger with spiral decoration and by the employment of star motives under drinking cups, referring to the sun cult (based on Boye 1896)

were using long skirts, elaborate hair styles, and were physically constricted in their movements, in opposition to the priestess dress. The institutional division into a high-ranking ritual and social group among men are thus paralleled in the female burials and hoards (for a most recent analysis see Bergerbrandt 2007).

It can further be demonstrated that the paired chiefly leaders mimic the major gods of the Bronze Age, known as the Divine Twins. Chieftainship in the Bronze Age was theocratic; ritual chiefs would therefore perform in the role of the Divine Twins in the re-enacting of central myths, as witnessed on rock art, ritual hoards and bronze figurines. In doing so they employed the material attributes of the Divine Twins: elaborately decorated ritual axes, lurs (blowing horns), helmets and shields, all of bronze and all displaying the most sophisticated technical skills. These were divine objects never associated with burials, but occasionally deposited in sacred

Fig. 7.6 Burial goods of a war chief characterized by an international warrior sword of the flange hilted type and no symbolic reference to the sun cult (based on Boye 1896)

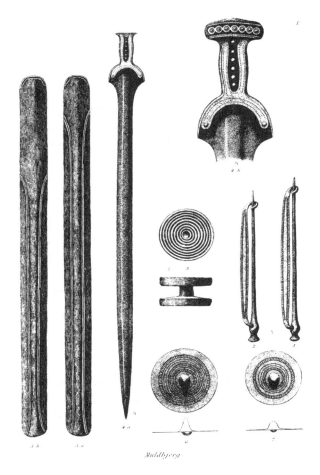

Muldbjerg

bogs, illustrated in rock art and decorated bronzes (Kaul 1998 and 2004, Kristiansen 2004). Figurines and models were employed as ritual sets, perhaps in the context of learning and in other now-lost ritual acts. Ritual chiefs were thus semi-divine and their authority must have been immense.

These institutions exhibit a longue-durée throughout the whole Bronze Age. Appearing in period 1, they are formalized from period 2 onwards with a standardized set of social and ritual paraphernalia, consisting of elaborate full-hilted swords, razors, and tweezers, while the ritual gear consists of ritual axes, lurs, and figurines. This recurring set of objects, defining the institution of ritual (twin) leaders, shows unbroken continuity until the end of Period 5, possibly persisting even into Period 6, during a span of almost 1000 years, or 33 generations. A generational perspective makes it easier to comprehend how tradition could be handed down through the

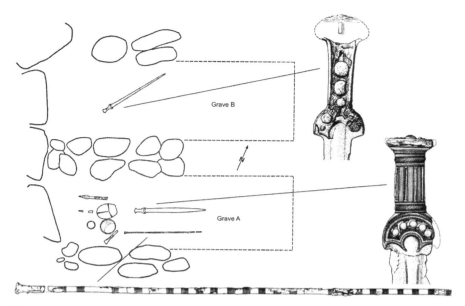

Grave B

Grave A

Fig. 7.7 Double burial of a ritual chief and a warrior chief (from Kristiansen and Larsson 2005: Fig. 122)

generations, which makes a much shorter genealogical period. It speaks of a highly persistent social and cosmological tradition, whose institutions were inherited as a rule from within the highest-ranking families, as they demanded the most exclusive social and religious qualifications (Kristiansen and Larsson 2005: Chapter 6).

Earle has further linked social and economic institutions to the institutionalized organization and use of the landscape (Earle 2001), which corresponded to a paradigmatic model of Bronze Age cosmology (Kristiansen 1998b, 2004). Thus social life in the Bronze Age was ritualized, and it took place in a similarly ritualized landscape. In this way, economy and ideology were unified in the reproduction of society.

Power Structures and Decentralized Complexity

Before approaching the question of power structures, it is necessary to discuss theoretical concepts linked to practice: what social processes operate in decentralized and yet complex societies and how can we transform them into theoretical tools of interpretation?

In his famous work: "Outline of a Theory of Practice," Pierre Bourdieu exemplifies the processes operating in establishing symbolic power (Bourdieu 1977: Chapter 4). He is concerned with the conversion of symbolic capital back into economic capital.

[handwritten annotation: Shift of economic into symbolic capital and vice versa]

"Thus we see that symbolic capital, which in the form of prestige and renown attached to a family and a name is readily convertible back into economic capital, is perhaps the most valuable form of accumulation in a society in which the severity of the climate (the major work-ploughing and harvesting—having to be done in a very short space of time) and the limited technical resources (harvesting is done with the sickle) demand collective labour" (Bourdieu 1977:179).

What are the mechanisms by which a local chief or renowned person can mobilize labor? In Bourdieu's words: "Thus this system contains only two ways (and they prove in the end to be just one way) of getting and keeping lasting hold over someone: gifts or debts, the overtly economic obligations of debt, or the 'moral,' 'affective' obligations created and maintained by exchange" (Bourdieu 1977:191). However, this mobilization needs to be socially or ritually sanctioned: "The endless reconversion of economic capital into symbolic capital, at the cost of a wastage of social energy which is the condition for the permanence of domination, cannot succeed without the complicity of the whole group .... As Mauss put it, the whole society pays itself in the false coin of its dream" (Bourdieu 1977:195). Finally: "To these forms of legitimate accumulation, through which the dominant groups or classes secure a capital of "credit" which seems to owe nothing to the logic of exploitation, must be added another form of accumulation of symbolic capital, the collection of luxury goods attesting to the taste and distinction of their owner" (Bourdieu 1977:197).

Figure 7.8 summarizes Bourdieu's argument into a dynamic theoretical model, which may explain how gift obligations are transformed over time into tribute and slavery.

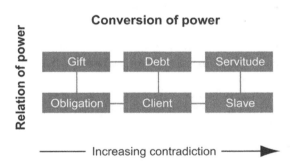

Fig. 7.8 Dynamic historical model of the potential transformation of gift obligations into tribute and slavery (from Kristiansen 2006)

We have now incorporated some of the basic social mechanisms through which chiefly institutions are maintained and eventually strengthened over time. Now we can proceed to combine the institutional and economic realities of the Early Bronze Age with the processes through which societies operated to build barrows and exchange metal and prestige goods (for an illuminating discussion, see Bennett 2004).

The recently excavated Skelhøj barrow in southern Jutland may serve as an example of how labour was mobilized at least in the case of the larger barrows (Holst et al. 2004, Holst and Rasmussen in press). Its construction was organized by dividing the ground plan into seven sections. Each section was then filled with grass turfs cut from field by a clan or family. Each section of the mound contains different types of grass turfs. Some were from fields that had never been stripped before, others were from previously stripped fields and therefore contained more subsoil. Thus the construction of the barrow reiterates the model of gift obligations and tributary relations between higher and lower status persons/families. These relationships are again part of a network of exchanges and obligations linked to metal and prestige goods. The fact that these could be accumulated at nodal points in the network documents the chiefs' abilities to extend the range of their trade partners and clients, allowing them to demand labor, war service, etc. in return. This observation follows Larsson's demonstration of the distinction between local centers of accumulation surrounded by larger areas of production. In his model their relationship is regulated through forms of tribute (Larsson 1986: Fig. 66). Thus, in Scania, concentrations of barrows would correspond to centers of accumulation and power competition, whereas surrounding areas with fewer barrows were areas of production. The centers were able to exploit these production areas in an unequal tributary relationship sanctioned by ritual and cosmological authority. These structures were institutionalized as they persisted over several 100 years (Olausson 1993, Strömberg 1982, Gröhn 2004). They represent the formalization of a cosmological order on the landscape that persisted throughout the Bronze Age (Kristiansen 1998b).

It is also clear, however, that while the institution of ritual chiefs represented the highest level of chiefly power, only enjoyed by a relatively small group among the upper chiefly clans, access to the warrior groups was more open, and membership could probably be recruited from a larger segment of the chiefly clans. We should envisage that barrows belonged only to members of chiefly clans, which amounted to ca. 15–20% of the population. These groups, however, were both numerous and highly diversified in terms of power and prestige, the lowest ranks being close to commoners, as indeed demonstrated by burial wealth and the huge differences in farm sizes.

In his classic book, *How Chiefs Come to Power*, Earle makes an interesting attempt to explain the relationship between power, wealth and production:

> I argue that control over the ideology of social ranking rested on control over the system of wealth finance. Wealth finance has a major advantage over staple finance. Its highly valued objects are easily transported over considerable distance and can be used to exert long-distance control over people (Earle 1997:73).

He then suggests that the pastoral economy of Early Bronze Age Thy in Denmark was used as mobile wealth, linking production of cattle to the production and distribution of prestige goods and control over people. "The primary advantage of cattle . . . would have been the ease with which they could have been managed and owned as currency in the political economy. An animal is a convenient unit of ownership and production. In herding chiefdoms, the preponderance of animals is owned by the local chief, who lends them out to individual households for their subsistence in return for support" (Earle 1997:100).

Here then we see the mechanism for exerting power in a decentralized, networking early Danish Bronze Age chiefdom.

What other career paths were open to ambitious, young male members of the chiefly clans? The most obvious way was to become a warrior, serve a prestigious chieftain and take part in raids to acquire fame. But warriors were part of a brotherhood of warriors stretching far outside the Nordic realm, as demonstrated by the distribution of flange hilted and octagonal hilted swords. Membership allowed warriors to travel long distances to take war service at famous chiefly houses. Having achieved fame they may return with this new symbolic capital. That capital could then be transferred in prestige and power, and perhaps access to compete for local chieftainship (Kristiansen 2004). In this way local chiefs would constantly have to compete to attract warriors to secure their own power base from being contested. The Early Bronze Age was thus a dynamic society characterized by a web of changing, competitive alliances, but regulated by the institution of ritual chiefs and war chiefs. These, and other institutions, lasted throughout the Bronze Age (Harrisson 2004), although they probably became increasingly powerful in a process that ultimately separated chiefs and commoners, and created a large group of enslaved commoners, according to the dynamic of Fig. 7.8. Towards the end of the Bronze Age, these processes had generated the conditions for the collapse of society when its lifeblood—metal supplies—declined and were finally cut completely.

In Fig. 7.9, I have summarized the evidence of Early Bronze Age social and economic organization, and its political economy (Earle 2002: Chapter 1), as a point of departure for future research and discussions. Chiefly clans served as the recruitment base for warriors/war chiefs and from among the highest ranked clans ritual rulers were appointed. Every local community would have had local chiefs and war leaders, but their power and status varied, as in Trobiand society (Burton 1975, Irwing 1983). Rank and power represented a continuum, although high-ranked clans would set themselves apart and could probably periodically mobilize alliances and support to create confederations of power covering larger areas. But as stated by

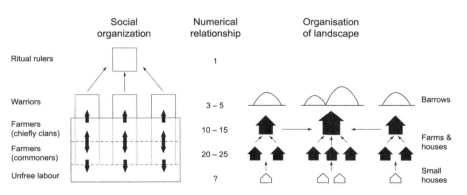

Fig. 7.9 Model of Bronze Age society, defined by the relationship between barrow, farms, and social organization (from Kristiansen 2006)

Earle: "The control of wealth exchange in the Danish case illustrates how difficult and unstable were network strategies and how problematic was finance based on wealth exchanges. The role of metal was apparently critical for the emergence of stratification in the EBA, but metals also proved problematic to control" (Earle 2002:313).

So far my attempt to quantify the relative numbers of rulers, warriors, farmers, and commoners is qualified guesswork. As to ritual leaders and warriors, the number of swords gives an indication, but the division between chiefly clans and commoners cannot yet be documented in the archaeological record. Slave labor is perhaps easier to demonstrate, as we have large chiefly farms that presuppose labor service whether voluntary or not. Very small farms could testify to both commoners and slave labor, but this is an area of research to be pursued in the future (Fig. 7.10).

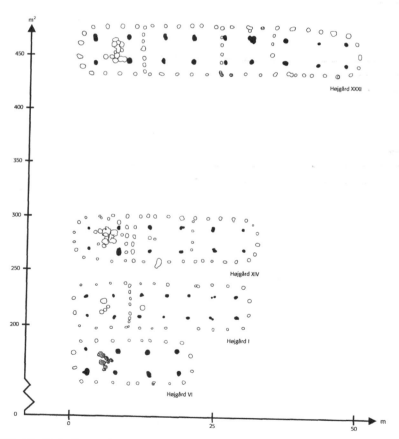

Fig. 7.10 The Early Bronze Age chiefly farm (reconstruction drawing by Bente Draiby)

Having now established a model of a decentralized Bronze Age society, I proceed to demonstrate how it operated from a long-term perspective.

Households and the Political Economy—a Temporal Outline

From Holland to northern Germany and Scandinavia, the historical and environmental processes of change were more or less similar in the Bronze Age. Through networks of exchange that originated in the third millennium BC (Single Grave culture and later Bell Beaker/Dagger culture), the Bronze Age societies of this vast region shared many traits of social and economic organization as well as burial rituals and cosmology. It is therefore meaningful to compare and discuss developments in household economies and cosmologies during the Bronze Age within this larger north European/Nordic region (Arnoldussen and Fokkens 2008, Assendorp 1997, Earle 2004). In the following paragraphs, I delimit the major temporal phases of changes in the political economy.

Beginning of Bronze Age

The Late Neolithic or Dagger period, starting ca. 2300 BC, marks the beginning of a Nordic/north European metal age as evidenced by the adaptation of metal models for flint dagger production and through a major intensification of exchange and farming, leading to a series of innovations from dress to burial ritual (Priego 2008, Vandkilde 1996, 2005). Late Neolithic expansion and the reorganization of late third millennium BC landscapes into more marginal forest such as in Småland and Värmland in Sweden is indicated by the building of stone cists and by pollen evidence for small-scale farming and grazing that opened up the forest (Heimann 2002, Lagerås 2000: Fig. 6, Lagerås and Regnell 1999). This settlement expansion mainly includes areas with closer proximity to central settlement areas, such as southern Småland. In Norway, the Late Neolithic or Dagger period represents the systematic introduction of farming proper and the opening of the landscape for grazing (Prescott 2005). Two-aisled houses/farmsteads were scattered across the landscape. Around 2000 BC large chiefly farmhouses for extended families are introduced from central Europe accompanying the first, more systematic use of metal (Artursson 2005, Nielsen 1999: Fig. 9, Lagerås and Strömberg 2005). During the Late Neolithic, the Nordic area was for the first time integrated into a common cultural and social form of society through the long-distance exchange of flint daggers and metal (Apel 2001, Lekberg 2004). To this was added a new social organization of leadership linked to large chiefly clan houses after 2000 BC with one or two smaller farms included in the household. It was from this basis that a Bronze Age economy extended through southern Scandinavia. We should envisage a political economy of settlement expansion and the rise of chiefly families that were able to extract tribute and labor from closer kin.

Middle Bronze Age Expansion and Re-organization of Landscape and Society

Massive clearance of the forest and the transformation of landscape into pastures and scattered fields took place from around 1750–1500 BC. A new organization of households, farm architecture, and landscape was introduced (Kristiansen 1998, Olausson 1999, Rasmussen 1999). Ownership of cattle was formalized, just as strict regulations of land use were introduced, seen in the Netherlands in the form of fences and other demarcations of land use (Arnoldussen and Fontijn 2005). This behavior represents the transformation of northern Europe into a more complex and ranked society characterized by physical boundaries to regulate the behavior of people and animals, from the interior divisions of houses to fences and field boundaries. The political economy saw the first division of labor between farms and communities that were linked together in a chiefly polity through exchange, tribute, and communal projects of barrow building, trade expeditions, raids, etc. This was a period of fierce competition between chiefly lineages, with some consolidation from Period 3 onwards (after 1300 BC). Chiefly families were now able to extract tribute, warriors, and labor from a wider network beyond the kin group. Slaves or dependent labor became a feature of chiefly households.

The Late Bronze Age from 1150 BC onwards represents yet another change in economy and society. Throughout Scandinavia larger farm houses were reduced in size from 200–400 to 100–150 m^2 and became more standardized. In other words— the smaller farmstead of the Early Bronze Age became dominant, while the large, local, chiefly farmsteads disappeared, or were replaced by more regional chiefly settlements, whose structure is still in need of systematic investigation. Small farms of 50–100 m^2 existed throughout the Bronze Age as part of larger farmsteads or hamlets (Fig. 7.11). This development represents a further transformation of society into a large group of commoners or peasants (the smaller family farm house), and a much smaller chiefly elite, sometimes buried in huge barrows with rich burial goods, such as Lusehøj near Voldtofte, and living in elaborate residences where they controlled the production and distribution of prestige goods and ritual gear (Thrane 1994, 2003b: Fig. 3). Chiefly leaders were now able to extract tribute from a larger chiefly polity and command labor and other services from this larger region. This pattern represents a level of complex chiefdoms or archaic decentralized states.

End of Bronze Age/Beginning of Iron Age

The fall of the Bronze Age chiefdoms was the result of a complex interplay of factors. That it was a period of dramatic change and internal unrest is demonstrated by the massive deposition of costly ritual gear, especially lurs, a majority of which were sacrificial during this period. We may note, however, that changes followed different trajectories in different parts of Scandinavia. In Jutland a major reorganization of the whole settlement structure took place. The Bronze Age farmsteads

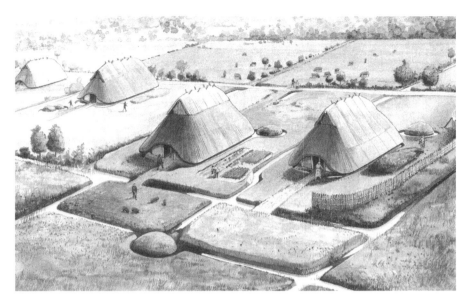

Fig. 7.11 The structure of Bronze Age chiefly hamlets, with one large chiefly farm and 2–3 smaller dependent farms (from Artursson 2009)

were abandoned and their households moved together in villages with an apparent egalitarian organization (Rindel 1999). Also cemeteries in the form of village urn-fields under low barrows exhibit the same absence of differentiation. In the rest of southern Scandinavia, Norway, and Sweden, there seems to be continuity in the settlement structure. Single farms of hamlets of farms continued to be the norm (Streiffert 2005).

The Pre-Roman Iron Age is characterized by a cultural and religious fragmentation of the former rather hegemonic Nordic Bronze Age culture into local and regional variation. This period witnessed a decline in international trade and in Nordic interaction that was only reopened again towards the end of the period in the first century BC, when a new episode of economic expansion began under the influence of Roman commercial and political strategies.

The Rise and Fall of Bronze Age Political Economies: A Long-Term Trajectory Towards Social Transformation

It can be demonstrated that the accumulation of short-term decisions by households create long-term unintended consequences beyond the predictive horizon of individual communities. By decisions made on a year-to-year basis, societies and households attempt to maintain their strategies and traditions. From one generation to the next such adjustments become visible in the archaeological record. At Legård in Thy, northwestern Jutland (Fig. 7.12), the first massive chiefly farm of

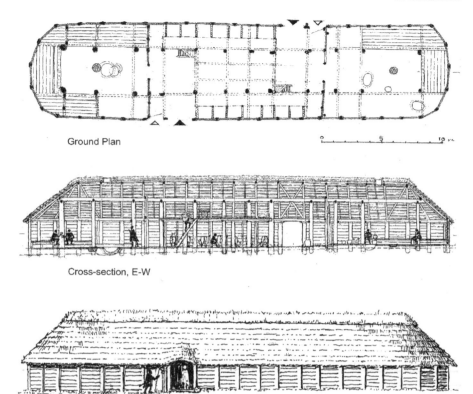

Ground Plan

Cross-section, E-W

Fig. 7.12 Reconstruction drawing of a Late Bronze Age hamlet from Holland (from Kooijmans et al. 2005. Drawing by Koen van der Velde)

period 2, around 1400 BC, was later replaced by one of exactly similar construction and size—except that timber for both wall posts and central posts were scaled down in size (Bech 2003: Fig. 9). This evidence testifies to the increasing shortage of building timber and mature forest, which over the next generations led to a downsizing of the houses. Thus we observe a direct line from decisions and adjustments made on a year-to-year basis to their impact upon long-term changes in the size of households. Compromises had to be made facing ecological overexploitation, yet the overall social and economic framework remained intact, as far as we can judge. Here a mixture of contradictory factors and forces were at work. Tradition in the form of ritual places, ancestor barrows, must have had a strong impact on decisions to stay rather than move when economic conditions worsened, as it happened in Thy. Here settlements even moved into economically non-viable habitats, but ones with good grass production, as at Bjerre. The worsening conditions can be seen in the use of smaller timber of bad quality for house construction and the use of bog turf for heating. The ecology had been overexploited and timber resources became scarce as grazing pressure increased (Bech and Mikkelsen 1999, Kristiansen 1998).

However, these conditions present in Thy already during the Early Bronze Age (Period 3) became widespread throughout Scandinavia in the course of the Late Bronze Age. Households and farms were reduced in size, individual farms and small hamlets of the Early Bronze Age became larger hamlets, and some settlement expansion took place. But generally speaking, the old inhabited areas of the Bronze Age remained unaltered until some fundamental thresholds were passed. Factors at work were a combination of population expansion and economic intensification that reached a first threshold by the end of Period 2 around 1300 BC in Thy, somewhat later in the rest of south Scandinavia (Thrane 2003b: Fig. 8). However, Period 3 already witnessed many local adjustments towards a more intensified economy, seen in the incorporation of new fertile land (Kristiansen 1978:11, Poulsen 1993). Many primary barrows were still erected in new locations, suggesting continued competition for resources and power. By the early to middle Period 3, during the thirteenth century BC, supplies of metal from central Europe came to a temporary halt due to revolutionary social and religious changes (e.g. the Urnfield expansion during Ha A1). Consequently, over the next one or two generations chiefly swords throughout northern Europe were kept in circulation until their hilts were worn through and the clay core laid bare. This exceptional disruption, which could have meant the end of the Bronze Age, was terminated by the arrival of new supplies of metal towards the end of Period 3 (Ha A2). The old worn out swords were finally put into the graves as tradition prescribed—for the last time on such a massive scale. From that point in time, barrow building ceased, having taken its toll of good grazing land. As the average was three hectares per barrow, and an estimated 50,000 barrows were constructed during the period 1500–1150 BC; a minimum of 150,000 hectares of grazing land was devastated during this period. At the same time, metal was ritually economized as urn burials became the norm, and ritual hoarding took precedence (Fig. 7.13). We should of course not underestimate the religious implications of these changes, but on the whole the rituals that were introduced by the beginning of the Late Bronze Age were part of a social and economic consolidation of the ruling elite that included the conservation of economic resources.

A series of adjustments took place throughout the Late Bronze Age to intensify the economy—from the introduction of the composite and for more efficient plowing to new, more resistant crops. Manuring was practised to some extent, just as the more tolerant and wool-producing sheep became the dominant animal in many regions. The reduction of farm size was also a part of these adjustments, as more and smaller households replaced the earlier larger farmsteads. The social changes accompanying these changes in physical properties are illuminated at Appalle in Sweden (Ullen 1994). The house became increasingly the domain of a single, multigenerational family with their animals. Chiefly households seem to have become bigger and fewer during this period, whereas the ordinary farming family household becomes the norm. Using the evidence from southwestern Funen, Denmark, this change has been interpreted as a development of more hierarchical forms of rulership, where regional chiefs were in control of a much larger territory than during the Early Bronze Age (Thrane 2003b). A new type of local and regional ritual meeting

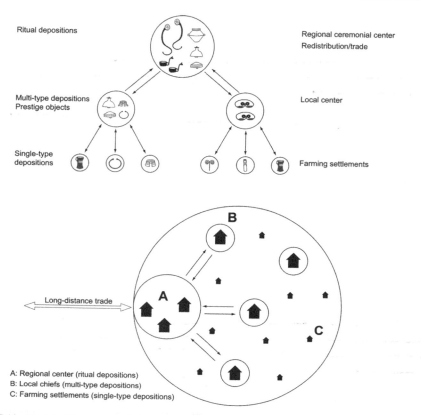

Ritual depositions

Regional ceremonial center
Redistribution/trade

Multi-type depositions
Prestige objects

Local center

Single-type
depositions

Farming settlements

Long-distance trade

A: Regional center (ritual depositions)
B: Local chiefs (multi-type depositions)
C: Farming settlements (single-type depositions)

Fig. 7.13 Model of the structured deposition of metalwork in hoards during the Late Bronze Age, corresponding to the settlement structure (from Kristiansen 2006)

place defined by rows or groups of cooking pits, sometimes several hundred, emerge (Gustafson et al. 2005).

Increasing population pressure in old settlement areas and a degradation of the environment should, from a rational economic perspective, have caused a major colonization to release the pressure during this period. However, this did not happen on a large scale, but to a limited degree, as seen in the evidence from Småland. In western Jutland and Thy some regeneration of forests suggest local migrations to more fertile regions. In most of southern Scandinavia, more farmsteads were constructed in the previously inhabited areas. The reason can only be the cosmological force of tradition and power inherent in the old settlement areas. A landscape of memory and genealogical power had been constructed through several centuries; heavy economic investments in land had also been made. To compensate for the increased internal competition caused by more people and households, farms and households became smaller. More farmers became dependent on the chiefly households, according to the model of Fig. 7.13. Dependent peasants or commoners were now in the majority, compared to the Early Bronze Age, when chiefly lineages were still numerous throughout local communities. Indeed the economic degradation and intensification of the Late Bronze Age would have served as an ideal catalyst for the processes towards dependency for larger groups of farmers exemplified in the model. Old chiefly lineages are still honored by barrow construction for urn burials. But in some regions, such as Scania, urn cemeteries were emerging, suggesting a new ritual status for larger groups dislocated from the old barrow. Thus religious change to cremation and urn burials in Scandinavia were integrated into the existing social framework and helped introduce necessary changes in ritual practice that would conserve the ecology and lower the consumption of metal in burials.

What we see is an economic and social adjustment of Bronze Age households over the long term, perhaps in combination with increased regional settlement hierarchy summarized in (Fig. 7.14). During the Early Bronze Age households were generally bigger and richer. Differences in scale were gradual, although small dependent households did exist in the Early Bronze Age. During the Late Bronze Age, households are generally reduced in size, to conform to single-family units, probably under the protection of a chiefly household. This paved the way for the

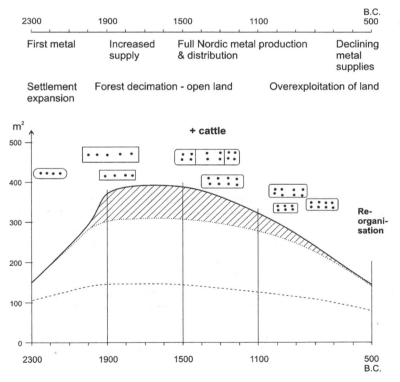

Fig. 7.14 Long-term model of the rise and decline of the Bronze Age farm, compared to changes in metal supplies and ecology (from Kristiansen 2006)

reorganization taking place at the beginning of the Iron Age, when suddenly all hamlets were abandoned, and in some regions, such as Jutland, everyone moved together into small villages. This pattern represented a significant break with a 1000-year-old settlement pattern, with a corresponding cosmology carved out in the landscape and its infrastructure. It must have demanded negotiations and decisions that deliberately broke with traditions and created a new ideology for coming together under a new social and economic order as it was accompanied by the introduction of regulated field systems. Was it a rebellion of many ordinary farmers against an outdated chiefly culture, economically undermined and lacking legitimacy? Or was it the result of the chiefly elites' capacity to reinvent them under a new banner of collective village life? We don't know, but there is little sign of chiefly elites in the settlement evidence. I am rather inclined towards the first alternative—a widespread revolution linked to a new social ideology of collective farmers. This pattern is further reflected in the introduction of collective cemeteries that are much larger than those existing during the Late Bronze Age. In other regions in Scandinavia the break in settlement structure was not so drastic, and some Bronze Age traditions were continued. It corresponds to a pattern of regional and local diversification during the earlier Pre-Roman Iron Age, as the intensive interaction of the Bronze Age fell apart (Jensen 1994).

After Transformation—Dark Age or Creative Democratization? The Beginning of a New Evolutionary Cycle

The changes in northern Europe took place at a time when similar revolutionary changes undermined and erased the royal Hallstatt courts in central Europe, paving the way for the first Celtic migrations (Kristiansen 1998: Chapter 6.3). And in Greece, tyrants were overthrown and democracy introduced for the free farmers and citizens. It was thus a turbulent period in Europe where new social and religious ideas spread and in some regions found conditions ready for change. In Denmark, however, it was the result of a nearly 1000-year-long period of a rather stable social formation, whose trajectory had finally come to its historical end, both in terms of environmental and social constraints. Thus it is the accumulating historical forces of the long term that pave the road for social transformations, but it is the collective social forces of individuals that create change by inventing or adopting a new more democratic social order in conjunction with new technological and economic practices. It was only when the potential for change and adjustments within the social and cosmological formation of Bronze Age society had been exhausted that it was possible—and perhaps necessary—to break with that tradition. It therefore became a fundamental change—the creation of a new social order that over the next 1000 years would run through the same cycle of economic growth, expanding households, and final decline with the eventual reorganization into the medieval village.

While at first glance the Bronze Age/Iron Age transformation may appear to be a cultural and economic decline, characterized by the collapse of international trade in metal, this change introduced a number of social and economic innovations that became decisive for further economic growth during the Iron Age. This matches Chew's observations from his study of Dark Ages (Chew 2006: Chapter 6). The easy, local access to iron empowered local communities, socially and economically, while the new democratic social and religious order enabled a new settlement expansion into the heavy soils of south Scandinavia that had largely been avoided by the herding economy of the Bronze Age. New field systems introduced more efficient land use, while the scythe enabled a systematic use of low-lying lands for hay production. These new economic practices gradually established the ecological and economic foundations of Iron Age societies, and when they were finally linked to the expanding Celtic and Roman economy around 150 BC it triggered new development towards increased local and regional hierarchies, the introduction of large chiefly farms in local communities, and the formation of international trade and exchange of Roman luxury goods, in many ways comparable to the introduction of a Bronze Age technology 1500 years earlier. In this respect the Bronze Age long-term cycle of growth and decline exhibits a number of evolutionary regularities that should be further explored by comparative studies in other regions.

References

Apel, J. 2001. *Daggers, Knowledge & Power*. The Social Aspects of Flint-Dagger Technology in Scandinavia 2350–1500 BC. Coast to Coast Books No. 3. Uppsala.

Arnoldussen, S. and Fokkens, H. (eds.). 2008. *Bronze Age Settlements in the Low Countries*. Oxford: Oxbow Books.

Arnoldussen, S., and Fontijn, D. 2005. Towards familiar landscapes? On the nature and origin of middle bronze age landscapes in the Netherlands. *Proceedings of the Prehistoric Society* 72: 289–317.

Artursson, M. 2005. Byggnadstradition, bebyggelse och samhällsstruktur I Sydskksandinavien under senneolitikum och alder bronsålder. Goldhahn, I.J. (red.), *Mellan sten och järn*. Del I & II. Rapport från det 9:e nordiska bronsålderssymposiet, Göteborg 2003-10-09/12: 13–39. Gotarc Serie C. Arkeologiska Skrifter No 59. Göteborg.

Artursson, M. 2008. *Bebyggelse och samhällsstruktur*. Södra och mellersta Skandinavien under senneolithikum och bronsålder 2300-500 f. Kr. Gotarc Series B. Gothenburg.

Assendorp, J.J. (ed.). 1997. *Forschungen zur bronzezeitlichen Besiedlungen Mittel- und Nordeuropas*. Internationales Symposium vom 9.11. Mai 1996 in Hitzacker. Internationale Archäologie 38, Espelkamp.

Bech, J.-H. 2003. The Thy Archaeological Project – Results and Reflections from a Multinational Archaeological Project. In Thrane, H. (ed.), *Diachronic Settlement Studies in the Metal Ages*, pp. 45–60.

Bech, J.-H., and Mikkelsen, M. 1999. Landscapes, Settlement and Subsistence in Bronze Age Thy, NW Denmark. In Fabech, C. and Ringtved, J. (eds.), *Settlement and Landscape*. Proceedings of a conference in Århus, Denmark May 4–7, 1998: 69–78. Århus: Jutland Archaeological Society.

Bennett, J. 2004. Iconographies of Value: Words, People and Things in the Late Bronze Age Aegean. In Barrett, J. and Halstead, P. (eds.), *The Emergence of Civilisation Revisited*, pp. 90–106, Sheffield Studies in Aegean Archaeology. Oxford: Oxbow Books.

Bergerbrandt, S. 2007. *Bronze Age Identities: Costume, Conflict and Contact in Northern Europé 1600–1300BC*. Stockholm: Stockholm Studies in Archaeology no 43.

Bourdieu, P. 1977. *Outline of a Theory of Practice*. Cambridge: Cambridge University Press.

Boye, V. 1896. *Found af Egekister fra Bronzealderen i Danmark*. Høst og Søns Forlag. København.

Burton, R. 1975. Why do the Trobriands have chiefs?. *Man* 10: 544–558.

Chew, S. 2006. *The Recurring Dark Ages*. Ecological Stress, Climate Changes, and System Transformation. Lanham: Alta Mira Press.

Earle, T. 1997. *How Chiefs Come to Power*. The Political Economy in Prehistory. Stanford: Stanford University Press.

Earle, T. 2001. Institutionalization in Chiefdoms. Why Landscapes Are Built. In Haas, J. (ed.), *From Leaders to Rulers*, pp. 105–124. New York: Kluwer Academic/Plenum Publishers.

Earle, T. 2002. *Bronze Age Economics*. Westview: The Beginnings of Political Economies.

Earle, T. 2004. Culture Matters: Why Symbolic Objects Change. In Demarrais, E., Gosden, C., and Renfrew, C. (eds.), *Rethinking Materiality, the Engagement of Mind with the Material World*, pp. 153–160. Cambridge: McDonald Institute Monographs.

Feinman, G.M. 2001. Mesoamerican Political Complexity. The Corporate-Network Dimension. In Haas, J. (ed.), *From Leaders to Rulers*, pp. 151–176. New York: Kluwer Academic/Plenum Publishers.

Friedman, J., and Rowlands, M. 1977. Notes towards an epigenetic model of the evolution of 'civilization'. In Friedman, J. and Rowlands, M. (eds.), *The Evolution of Social Systems*: 201–227, 6 London: Duckworth.

Gilman, A. 1995. Prehistoric European Chiefdoms: Rethinking "Germanic" Societies. In Price, T.D. and Feinman, G.M. (eds.), *Foundations of Social Inequality*, pp. 235–254. New York and London: Plenum Press.

Glob, P.V. 1983. *The Mound People*. London: Paladin.

Goldhahn. (ed.). 2005. *Mellan sten och järn*. Del I & II. Rapport från det 9:e nordiska bronsålderssymposiet, Göteborg 2003-10-09/12. Gotarc Serie C. Arkeologiska Skrifter No 59. Göteborg.

Gröhn, A. 2004. *Positioning the Bronze Age in Social Theory and Research Context*. Acta Archaeologica Lundensia Series 8° No 47. Lund: Almqvist & Wiksell.

Gustafson, L., Heibreen, T., and Martens, J.; (red.). 2005. *De gåtefulle kokegroper*. Varia 58. Fornminnesektionen, Oslo: Kulturhistorisk Museum.

Harrisson, R. 2004. *Symbols and Warriors*. Images of the European Bronze Age. Bristol: Western Academic& Specialist Press Limited.

Hayden, B. 1995. Pathways to Power: Principles for Creating Socioeconomic Inequalities. In Price, T.D. and Feinman, G.M. (eds.), *Foundations of Social Inequality*, pp. 15–86. New York and London: Plenum Press.

Heimann, C. 2002. Neolitisering i Västvärmland. Boplatser, näringsfång och landskap. In situ 2001–2002: 27–55.

Holst, M., Kähler, R., and Breuning-Madsen, H. 2004. Skelhøj. Et bygningsværk fra den ældre bronzealder. *Nationalmuseets Arbejdsmark*: 11–25, København.

Holst, M.K., and Rasmussen, M. In press. Combined efforts. The cooperation and coordination of barrow-building in the Bronze Age. In Jessen, M.D., Johannsen, N.N., and Jensen, H.J. (eds.), *Excavating the Mind: Cross-Sections Through Culture, Cognition And Materiality*. Aarhus: Aarhus University Press.

Irwin, G.J. 1983. Chieftainship, Kula and Trade in Massim Prehistory. In Leach, J.W. and Leach, E. (eds.), *The Kula. New Perspectives on Massim Exchange*, pp. 32–72. Cambridge: Cambridge University Press.

Jensen, J. 1994. The Turning Point. In Kristiansen, K. and Jensen, J. (eds.), *Europé in the First Millennium B.C*, pp. 111–124. Sheffield, Archaeological Monographs 6.

Jensen, J. 1998. *Manden i kisten*. Gyldendal, Copenhagen.

Johansen, K.L., Laursen, S.T., and Holst, M.K. 2004. Spatial patterns of social organization in the early bronze age of South Scandinavia. *Journal of Anthropological Archaeology* 23: 33–55.

Kaul, F. 1998. *Ships on Bronzes. A Study in Bronze Age Religion and Iconography.* Publications from the National Museum Studies in Archaeology and History Vols. 3.1 and 3.2, Copenhagen.

Kaul, F. 2004. *Bronzealderens religion.* Studier af den nordiske bronzealders ikonografi. Det Kongelige Nordiske Oldskriftsselskab. København.

Kooijmans, L.P.L., van den Broecke, P.W., Fokkens, H., van Gijn, A.L. (eds.), 2005. The Prehistory of the Netherlands. Amsterdam.

Kristiansen, K. 1978. The Consumption of Wealth in Bronze Age Denmark. A Study in the Dynamics of Economic Processes in Tribal Societies. In Kristiansen, K. and Paludan-Müller, C. (eds.), *New Directions in Scandinavian Archaeology*, pp. 158–190. Copenhagen: The National Museum of Denmark.

Kristiansen, K. 1998a. The Construction of a Bronze Age Landscape. Cosmology, Economy and Social Organisation in Thy, Northwest Jutland. In Hänsel, B. (ed.), *Mensch und Umwelt in der Bronzezeit Eropas*, pp. 281–293. Kiel: Oetkers-Voges Verlag.

Kristiansen, K. 1998b. *Europe before History.* Cambridge: Cambridge University Press.

Kristiansen, K. 2001. Rulers and Warriors: Symbolic Transmission and Social Transformation in Bronze Age Europe. In Haas, J. (ed.), *From Leaders to Rulers*, pp. 85–104. New York: Kluwer Academic/Plenum Publishers.

Kristiansen, K. 2004. Institutions and Material Culture. Towards an Intercontextual Archaeology. In Demarrais, E., Gosden, C., and Renfrew, C. (eds.), *Rethinking Materiality, the engagement of mind with the material world*, pp. 179–193. Cambridge: McDonald Institute Monographs.

Kristiansen, K. 2006. Cosmology, economy and long-term change in the Bronze Age of Northern Europe. In Sjögren, K.G. (ed.), *Ecology and Economy in Stone- and Bronze Age Scania*, Riksantikvarämbetet. Skånska spor – arkeologi langs Västkustbanan, pp. 149–171.

Kristiansen, K. 2007. The Rules of the Game. Decentralised Complexity and Power Structures. I. In Kohring, S. and Wynne-Jones, S. (red.), *Socialising Complexity. Structure, Interaction and Power in Archaeological Discourse.* Oxford.

Kristiansen, K., and Larsson, T. 2005. *The Rise of Bronze Age Society.* Travels, Transmissions and Transformations. Cambridge: Cambridge University Press.

Lagerås, P. 2000. Gravgåvor från växtriket. Pollenanalytiska belägg från en senneolitisk hällkista I Hamneda. I P. Lagerås (red.): *Arkeologi och paleoekologi I sydvästra Småland.* Tio artiklar från Hamnedaprojektet. Riksantikvarämbetet. Avdelningen för arkeologiska undersökningar, Skrifter nr. 34.

Lagerås, P., and Regnell, M. 1999. Agrar förändring under sydsvensk bronsålder. En diskussion om skenbare samband och ulösta gåtor. I M. Olausson (red.): *Spiralens öga – tjugo artiklar omkring aktuell bronsåldersforskning. Riksantikvarämbetet, Avdelningen för arkeologiska undersökningar, Skrifter* 25: 263–276.

Lagerås, P., and Strömberg, B. (ed.). 2005. *Bronsåldersbygd 2300–500 f.Kr.* Skånska spor-arkeologi langs Västkustbanan. Riksantikvarämbetet.

Larsson, T.B. 1986. *The Bronze Age Metalwork of Southern Sweden.* Aspects of Social and Spatial Organization 1800–500BC. Archaeology and Environment 6. University of Umeå, Umeå.

Lekberg, P. 2004. Lives of Axes – Landscapes of Men. On Hammer Axes, Landscapes and Society of the Late Neolithic in Eastern Central Sweden. In Knutsson, H. (ed.), *Coast to Coast – Arrival.* Results and Reflections. Proceedings from the Final Coast to Coast Conference 1–5 October in Falköping, Sweden, pp. 259–295. Uppsala.

Ling, J. 2005. The Fluidity of Rock Art. In Goldhahn, J. (ed.), *Mellan sten och järn.* Del I & II. Rapport från det 9:e nordiska bronsålderssymposiet, Göteborg 2003-10-09/12: 437–460. Gotarc Serie C. Arkeologiska Skrifter No 59. Göteborg.

Ling, J. 2007. *Elevated Rock art. Towards a Maritime Understanding of Rock Art in Northern Bohuslän, Sweden.* Gothenburg: Gotarc Series B, No 49.

Nielsen, P.O. 1999. Limensgård and Grødbygård. Settlements with House Remains from the Early, Middle and Late Neolithic on Bornholm. In Fabech, C. and Ringtved, J. (eds.), *Settlement and Landscape.* Proceedings of a conference in Århus, Denmark May 4–7, 1998: 149–166. Århus: Jutland Archaeological Society.

Nordenborg Myhre, L. 2004. *Trialectic Archaeology*. Monuments and space in Southwest Norway 1700–500 BC. AmS-Skrifter 18. Stavanger.

Olausson, D. 1993. The Bronze Age Barrow as a Symbol. In Larsson, L.(ed.), *Bronsålderns gravhögar*. pp. 91–115 Lund: Rapport fra et Symposium.

Olausson, M. 1999. Herding and stalling in Bronze Age Sweden. In Fabech, C. and Ringtved, J. (eds.), *Settlement and Landscape*. Proceedings of a conference in Århus, Denmark May 4–7, 1998: 319–328. Århus: Jutland Archaeological Society.

Poulsen, J. 1993. Nyt om ældre bronzealders gravhøje i Danmark. In Larsson, L. (ed.), *Bronsålderns gravhögar*: 59–68. University of Lund, Inst. Of Archaeology, Report Series No. 48. Lund.

Prescott, C. 2005. Settlement and economy in the late neolithic and bronze age of southern Norway: some points and premises. *AmS-Varia* 43: 123–134, Stavanger.

Prieto-Martinez, P. 2008. Bell Beaker Communities in Thy: The First Bronze Age Society in Denmark. Norwegain Archaelogical Review, Vol. 42(2).

Randsborg. 1974. Social stratification in early bronze age Denmark: a study in the regulation of cultural systems. *Praehistorische Zeitschrift* 49.

Randsborg, K. 2006. Opening the Oak-coffins. New dates – New Perspectives. In Randsborg, K. and Christensen, K. (eds.), Bronze Age Oak-coffin Graves. *Acta Archaeologica*, Vol. 77. Copenhagen: Blackwell Munksgaard.

Rasmussen, M. 1999. Livestock Without Bones. The Long-House as Contributor to the Interpretation of Livestock Management in the Southern Scandinavian Early Bronze Age. In Fabech, C. and Ringtved, J. (eds.), *Settlement and Landscape*. Proceedings of a conference in Århus, Denmark May 4–7, 1998: 281–290. Århus: Jutland Archaeological Society.

Renfrew, C. 1974. Beyond a Subsistence Economy: The Evolution of Social Organisation in Prehistoric Europe. In Moore, C. (ed.), *Reconstructing Complex Societies*. An Archaeological Colloquium. Supplement to the Bulletin of the American Schools of Oriental Research No. 20.

Rindel, P.O. 1999. Development of the village community 500BC-100AD in west Jutland, Denmark. In Fabech, C. and Ringtved, J. (eds.), *Settlement and Landscape*. Proceedings of a conference in Århus, Denmark May 4–7, 1998: 79–99. Århus: Jutland Archaeological Society.

Streiffert, J. 2005. Boningshusets rumsbildningar. Tolkningar av de halländska boningshusens rumsliga funktioner under yngre bronsålder och alder järnålder. I. J. Streiffert, *Gårdsstrukturer I Halland under bronsålder och alder järnålder*, pp. 13–157. Riksantikvarämbetets arkeologiska undersökningar Skrifter 66/ Gotarc Series B, No. 39.

Strömberg, B. 1982. *Ingelsstorp. Zur Siedlungsentwicklung eines südschwedisches Dorfes*. Acta Arch. Lundensia, Ser. 4,14. Bonn, Lund.

Sørensen, M.L.S. 1997. Reading dress: the construction of social categories and identities in Bronze Age Europé. *Journal of European Archaeology* 5/1: 93–114.

Thrane, H. 1994. Centres of Wealth in Northern Europé. In Kristiansen, K. and Jensen, J. (eds.), *Europé in the First Millennium B.C*: 95–110. Sheffield: Archaeological Monographs 6.

Thrane, H. 2003. Diachronic Settlement Studies in the South Scandinavian Lowland Zone – the Danish Persepctive. In Thrane, H. (ed.), *Diachronic Settlement Studies in the Metal Ages*. Report on the ESF workshop Moesgård, Denmark, 14–18 October 2000. Aarhus.: Jutland Archaeological Society/Aarhus University Press. pp. 13–27.

Ullen, I. 1994. The power of case studies. Interpretation of a late bronze age settlement in central Sweden. *Journal of European Archaeology* 2.2: 249–262.

Vandkilde, H. 1996. *From Stone to Bronze*. The Metalwork of the Late Neolithic and Earliest Bronze Age in Denmark. Århus: Jutland Archaeological Society Publications XXXII.

Vandkilde, H. 2005. A Review of the Early Late Neolithic Period in Denmark: Practice, Identity and Connectivity. On website: www.jungsteinzeitSITE.de

Chapter 8
Bitter Arrows and Generous Gifts: What Was a 'King' in the European Iron Age?

Tina L. Thurston

Introduction

What is power? How does it work? Is power in politically complex societies always constituted in the same, repeated ways, with variation only in the contextual details? This chapter examines the European Iron Age, a protohistoric archaeological context that may help answer these questions. When archaeologists think of power, they usually think of leaders or rulers, yet in no society is power held exclusively by elites. In some cultures, elite power is highly constrained and balanced by the power of ordinary people. For many prehistoric sequences, it is difficult to find archaeological proxies for the power of a non-elite majority, but in some protohistoric cases this kind of power is archaeologically visible and lends itself to study: Iron Age Europe is one of these and may help shed light on our understanding of other sequences as well.

For nearly two decades, vigorous debates over the nature of the European Iron Age have persisted, largely outside the awareness of most archaeologists. Since the period is fairly recent, encompassing "Celts," "Britons," and "Germanic" peoples to which many individuals still strongly relate, this debate has had some significant and widespread repercussions. The issues under scrutiny have been varied yet principally boil down to disagreements over the concepts used to describe and explain social, political, and economic organization and change—more directly, power, and how it operates.

This chapter does not attempt to address the entire debate, which is extensively reviewed elsewhere (Collis 1997, James 1999, Thurston 2009). Instead, it addresses one aspect of Iron Age society that warrants renewed examination: the development of political organization and the nature of political power. After discussion of the debate's theoretical underpinnings, I review evidence beginning with the most recent part of the time-transgressive European Iron Age (Fig. 8.1): the Scandinavian Iron

T.L. Thurston (✉)
Department of Anthropology, The University at Buffalo, State University of New York, Buffalo, NY, USA
e-mail: tt27@buffalo.edu

T.D. Price, G.M. Feinman (eds.), *Pathways to Power*, Fundamental Issues in Archaeology, DOI 10.1007/978-1-4419-6300-0_8,
© Springer Science+Business Media, LLC 2010

Fig. 8.1 Simplified
chronology for Iron Age
Europe

Southern Europe	Central Europe	Northern Europe
Hallstatt / Villanovan 1020-780 BC	Hallstat 800 - 450 BC	Pre-Roman Iron Age 500 - 1 BC
Roman 780 BC - AD 410	La Tene 400 -150 BC	Roman Iron Age AD 1 - 400
Late Antiquity AD 410 - 500	Roman Conquest 150 BC - AD 410	Germanic Iron Age / Migration Period AD 400 - 800
Early Medieval AD 500 - 1000	Late Antiquity AD 410 - 500	Viking Age AD 800 - 1075
	Early Medieval AD 500 - 1000	Early Medieval AD 1075 - 1300

Iron Age Europe - Simplified Chronology

Age, including the Viking Age, which lasted from about 500 BC to about AD 1075.
Discussion then moves backward chronologically into the British and Continental
Iron Ages, and finally, the Italian Pre-Roman Iron Age, seeking to understand the
development of political institutions and their change and persistence through time.

The Twentieth Century Roots of Power Theories in the Social Sciences

In global perspective, some societies are indisputably on the "egalitarian" end of
the political spectrum, while others display evidence of centralized political hierarchies. Within twentieth century archaeology, *in absentia* of a recognized political
format between these two extremes, cultures that have lain in the middle along what
is now understood as an organizational continuum created significant confusion.
This dichotomous conceptualization of political power, characterized by Price and
Feinman (1995b) as squeezing alternative social and political structures into rigid
and narrow models that did not really fit, was long embedded in general archaeology. A flurry of case studies has explored such mischaracterizations and alternative
interpretations in many world regions over the last decade, but many archaeologists
continue to implicitly theorize political development with older models borrowed
from other disciplines. Without an explicit orientation toward the study of how
power "works," ideas about political organization are often introduced simply by
repeating the rationalizations of earlier approaches, read, re-read, and internalized
over many decades, perpetuating a narrow understanding of the ways in which
political power can be constituted and expressed.
    Before presenting the Iron Age as a case study, a brief look at the ways that social
scientists have recently defined power itself will be helpful. While there is a deep
stratigraphy of modern-era thought on power stretching back at least to philosophers

such as Machiavelli, it is largely the ideas of theorists working after the Second World War that underlie concepts recognizable in many twentieth century archaeological theories on power. After the defeat of fascist leaders in 1945, many social scientists became fascinated with the power of what they termed "ruling elites" (Dahl 1961, 1969, Hunter 1953, Lasswell et al. 1952, Mayhew 1973, Medding 1982, Mills 1959, Moore 1979, Prewitt and Stone 1973)—how they get, legitimize, maintain, and lose power. It is clear why post-war theorists were interested in such topics—figures like Hitler and Mussolini had only recently persuaded, coerced, or forced the majority of their people, both elites and non-elites, into supporting rapacious expansionism and notorious acts of ethnocide and genocide. A continuous interest in exploring the subject of power and governance was maintained during the remainder of the twentieth century, which saw Cambodia, Rwanda, and Bosnia-Herzegovina embroiled in similar troubles, and each year saw dozens of other less-publicized episodes of corruption, violence, and inhumanity.

Any historian or archaeologist can attest that the use of power to benefit a few while oppressing the majority is nothing new; what was new in 1945 were the still youthful disciplines of sociology, political science, and anthropology, all seeking through different avenues the origins and meaning of such events. In a social-scientific attempt to explain the causes and effects of ruling elite power, mid-century theorists aimed to describe the "mechanisms" of power, identify measurable indicators, and predict the types of relationships that might be found within such sequences. While one robust theory of rulership and legitimation already existed in the form of theoretical Marxism, the post-war West rejected the idea of "class" as the determinant of all social phenomena and thus found the concept of "elites" preferable—elites had many ways to dominate, not merely by owning the means of production. This permitted a public discourse (Balbus 1971) at a time when "Marxist theory" was equated with Communism, and the House Un-American Committee was active.

Since the mid-twentieth century, power relations between elites and non-elites have alternately been described as having several forms: "power with" (McFarland 2004), "power to" (Stone 1989), and "power over" (Dahl 1957, Weber 1946). While archaeologists are familiar with several discussions of the difference between "power to" and "power over" (Bender 1990, Miller and Tilley 1984, Saitta 1994, Saitta and Keene 1990) and how one can shift to the other, many know less about the long and deep history these authors drew on in using them. Some abbreviated discussions of this history have seen print (Miller and Tilley 1984:5) yet attributed divergent views on power incorrectly, perhaps since their goal was to dismiss them rather than elaborate on them—a goal with which I agree. The aim of this discussion differs; I focus on demonstrating how some of these early ideas entered into the corpus of twentieth century archaeological frameworks.

Too many authors to mention have written about power, elites, and government, but some have had substantial influence on archaeology. Mosca (1939), an Italian political scientist who "invented" the post-Marxian study of elites, became influential in the United States through his postmortem translations (1972), and Pareto, an Italian sociologist, had written about elites in the early twentieth century, translated from the Italian in the 1960s and also impacting Anglophone social sciences (Pareto 1923, 1966). Weber (e.g. 1946) was the first to discuss something akin to "power over" and his influence is also seen in later ideas. "Power over" as a specific conceptual idiom was defined early on by Dahl (1957:203) as the ability to get others to do things they wouldn't otherwise do, an idea that Miller and Tilley attributed to Lukes, who was in fact delivering a critique of Dahl's definition.

"Power over" was initially equated with the power of a ruling elite (Bottomore 1966) to make decisions: one can track power by observing, "... who participates, who gains and who loses from alternative outcomes, and also who prevails in decision making" (Polsby 1963:4). "The political elite comprises the power holders of a body politic. The power holders include the leadership and the social formations from which the leaders typically come and to which accountability is maintained" (Lasswell 1961:66). Also referred to as a "power elite," they were said to be "in positions to make decisions having major consequences. ... [T]hey are in command of the major hierarchies and organizations of modern society" (Mills 1959:3–4). This type of power was conceptualized in terms of direct conflict, substantiated by empirical observation of what people say and do. As long as the decision maker wins by initiating policies or actions or vetoing those of others, they are said to have power (Dahl 1957:66).

Before long, "power over" was incorporated into a burgeoning "ruling elite theory" and the phrase "ruling elite" (Medding 1982, Moore 1979, Prewitt and Stone 1973) soon spread from academia into the idioms of popular debate during the Vietnam era (Jeffreys-Jones 1999), with the government using the term to describe the Soviets, the North Vietnamese, and as many academics became vocal critics of the war, the radical left began using it to characterize the American government.

Yet this view of what constituted "elite power-over" was very soon to be labeled a naive and one-dimensional view by the sociological and political science community that spawned it (Lukes 1974). The theory only takes into account simple behaviors, and then only where there is observable conflict between what different actors hope to achieve. Almost within the same breath that its authors created the idea, others were already deconstructing it:

> A paradox is attached to the concept "political elite." Few theoretical constructs can boast its obvious and powerful intuitive appeal. It is by now a commonplace to view societies as characterized by an asymmetric distribution of political power. Still, the concept's apparent ability to "carve at a joint of nature" has run into peculiar difficulties. Attempts to locate its empirical referents and, thereby, to specify the occupants of the "data container" political elite have led to a morass of conflicting definitions. Recent attempts to use the concept in powerful explanatory theories have been infrequent and unsuccessful. (Zuckerman 1977:324–325).

To this one-dimensional conceptualization of power, theorists soon added new ideas. One of them was the self-proclaimed "two-dimensional" theory involving the "mobilization of bias" (Bachrach and Baratz 1970:43)—that is, the protection of self-interest by those who have "power over" others. In order to assure that their interests were protected, these theorists believed that ruling elites would frequently shift their alliances—loyalty to none—if it would advance their causes. The creation of power relations is always situated within a

> set of predominant values, beliefs, rituals, and institutional procedures ('rules of the game') that operate systematically and consistently to the benefit of certain persons and groups at the expense of others. Those who benefit are placed in a preferred position to defend and promote their vested interests. More often than not, the 'status quo defenders' are a minority or elite group within the population in question (Bachrach and Baratz 1970:43).

It was the ruling elite theory popular in the 1960s and 1970s that archaeologists used to construct a perspective that soon became popular: "ruling elites" appear to be recognizable in many archaeological contexts, and their relative power to force their decisions upon others was believed to be testable through various measures of centralization, control, and the ability to coerce. A more nuanced sociological "ruling elite theory" soon superseded this, in which "interrelations of...four sources of social power: ideological, economic, military, and political are overlapping networks of social interaction, not dimensions, levels, or factors of a single social totality...They are also organizations, institutional means of attaining human goals" (Mann 1986:2). This also made its way into archaeology, but much later, in initial critiques of traditional concepts of power (Blanton et al. 1996).

Another importation into archaeology at the same moment was the concept of the "decision-making hierarchy" (Frisbie 1974, Hage and Aiken 1967, Hermansen 1970, Keren and Levhari 1979, Martin 1971, Simon 1944), which saw vast publication in other fields and also seemed to resonate with "new" or "processual" archaeologists' ability to map the places where elite decision makers might dwell and flow-chart the direction of authority and hierarchical chains of command.

The work of some leading archaeological theorists of the era cites or refers to these extradisciplinary sources on "decision-making hierarchies," "power," "ruling elites," and the "administrative hierarchies" of ruling elites: for just a few examples from different decades, Johnson (1982, 1983) cites Blau (1968) and Mayhew and Levinger (1976), Miller and Tilley (1984) cite Benton (1981), Lasswell and Kaplan (1950), Lukes (1974), Weber (1968), and Yoffee (1991) cites Bottomore (1966), Mann (1986), Mills (1959), Pareto (1966) and discusses Weber. These concepts soon became incorporated into archaeological theories of political economy, peer polity interaction, and many others (Brumfiel and Earle 1987, Costin 1990, 1991, 1998, 2001, Costin and Earle 1989, D'Altroy and Earle 1985, Earle 1987, 1997, 2004; Renfrew and Shennan 1982). Fifty to thirty years later, we still see the long-term impact of these ideas, for example in Lekson's view of the American Southwest, where a Chaco "ruling elite" perpetuated themselves at any cost by moving their power base to a region in which they could dominate control of all valuable resources (Lekson 1999). I point out this example specifically because within contemporary understanding of the Ancestral Pueblo, this seems likely to be a case of "squeezing" as described by Price and Feinman (1995b). Yet in other contexts, these ideas persist ubiquitously and without much question. The typology of "power" in this model "embraces coercion, influence, authority, force and manipulation" (Lukes 1974).

It is a well-known aphorism that archaeologists readily borrow from other disciplines, representing a strength through the injection of new ideas but also a weakness. Traditionally, the borrowing is selective and usually delayed: middle-range theory was pilfered in the 1970s from sociological thinking of the 1940s and 1950s (Raab and Goodyear 1984). The concept of landscape was adopted in the late 1980s and 1990s from the cultural geography of the 1960s and 1970s (Ashmore and Knapp 1999). In sociology, the rejection of sociopolitical "prime movers" and their replacement with multicausal theories began with Weber (Weber 1978 [1921], Kalberg 1994) but did not fully impact archaeology until the 1980s. Often, our borrowed "innovations" come from the initial postulations of new ideas in other social sciences; only rarely is there consistent follow-up of later self-critiques and paradigm shifts in the disciplines that generated them, and thus significant theoretical revisions to ideas appropriated long ago have yet to be widely contemplated. One important modification involves the concepts of power, hierarchy, centralization, and political development, and critically, the linkages between them:

> The short-term perspective of many of the most prestigious sociological theories of our time finds its expression in law-like abstractions from selected aspects of contemporary "advanced" societies, presented with the claim to be applicable to societies of all ages and regions...theories woven around concepts such as "social system" are an example. They reduce the long-term processes of structured and directional changes, to which the concept of development applies and of which processes of industrialisation, bureaucratisation, scientification, urbanisation, or state- and nation-building processes are examples, to an unchanging state as its permanent condition, while these changes themselves are perceived...as an unstructured flow, as 'history' (Elias 1972).

Elias, who founded "process sociology," framed human experience as comprising networks of interdependent people related through shifting asymmetrical power balances. Several decades ago now, he noted problems inherent in the concept of "process" when the endpoint is viewed as a permanent condition, as well as the implicit idea that the "course of history" is unstructured rather then representing the outcome of accord, negotiation, or conflict between many groups, classes, factions, and individuals, combined with the occasional natural or humanly induced *force majeure*. Instead, many archaeologists adopting the ideas of Dahl, Polsby, Bachrach, and others long conceptualized the development of political power across time and space in only one way: driven by newly authoritative elites asserting their growing abilities to centralize, enforce, and control, to co-opt or coerce the labor or products of others and compel them into new organizational modes, either through economic monopoly, military strength, spiritual threats or rewards, awe-inspiring displays of status and prestige, or some combination of these factors. This condition would then persist, unchanging or increasing, until some external force, usually in the form of conquest or environmental disaster, toppled it.

Models of archaeological states proposed in the 1970s also stressed the idea that increasing hierarchy is always and necessarily concomitant with increasing centralization (e.g. Flannery 1972, Trigger 1972, 1974, Webster 1975), an idea that became embedded in many twentieth century views of state origins (i.e. Haas 2001, Knapp

1993, Roscoe 1993), along with related ideas that "rulers" habitually lived in "centers," and that of necessity they expressed their power by demonstrating it at every possible opportunity. Today, we understand this as linked to a mid-twentieth century social milieu in the culturally, politically, and economically dominant nations of the "powerful" Western world—a context within which many theoretical archaeologists of the era were educated. The climate of the 1960s and 1970s has been described as one that fomented an obsession with control and central authority, with the top-down power of political elite masterminds, creating archaeologists who were ready to adopt sociological theories of power aimed at their own era, who were "more interested in social ranking than in social equality, and. . . ready to deny social equality on the grounds that political authority was centralized" (Osborne 2007:143). This seems an odd notion for citizens of Western democracies, supposedly living under systems of checks and balances, with power divided between centralized and decentralized institutions. Yet it was virtually impossible for anyone at the time to consider past societies as capable of forming and maintaining structures parallel to our own "democratic" heterarchies (Cowgill 1997:152). For the same reasons, few were willing to hypothesize that such political structures could have comprised valued social principles that past people might have been ideologically invested in— even while debates over "modern" communism versus capitalism, heavily loaded not only with economic and political overtones but with essentialized, idealized social values, were being argued around the world.

In sum, for much of the later twentieth century, the primary archaeological frameworks for understanding the creation, management, and use of power were aimed at understanding only the ways in which elites wrested power away from others and exercised authority, usually through the mechanisms proposed by ruling elite theory, environmental/ecological theories, various permutations of structural Marxism and interaction theories like peer polity, core-periphery, and prestige goods economics, all dependent on the concept of rising elites, rising complexity, the importance of elite-to-elite interactions and the ever-increasing centralization of elite authority over non-elites, who had no power at all.

One of many examples is found in the ecological adaptationist models, where centralization was seen as key to spreading and minimizing risk through redistribution schemes that supposedly yielded benefits, not only for newly empowered rulers but for all by conquering environmental challenges or coordinating the many interwoven, productive parts of the state or chiefly system (Flannery 1972, Sanders and Price 1968). Structural approaches also saw centralization as key, not for managing nature but for managing rival elites by manipulating the system to exclude them from power (Brumfiel 1983, Renfrew 1986, Schortman 1989). Large, state-constructed public works, vast "managed" agricultural systems, industrial-strength state workshops, state-supported religious precincts, palatial structures, and ideological monuments supposedly provided clear evidence of elites materializing or symbolizing their centralized power. Models using combinations of these variously economic, ideological, and social factors were indeed an improvement over earlier prime movers and were hailed as examples of multicausal explanation.

When it came to political organization, cultures that defied some or all aspects of these models—best-known examples being the Anasazi, Harappans, and Teotihuacanos—were long labeled puzzling "anomalies" that appeared politically complex yet displayed little evidence for one or more of the typically expected "indicators": aggrandizement of individual rulers, centralized institutions, and deeply or markedly stratified social classes. They were interpreted in two ways. Some authors claimed that despite their appearance as chiefly or state societies, rulers did not exist, since the expected suite of kingly or chiefly elaborations were not found (Graves et al. 1982, Pasztory 1997, Possehl 1998). Others took the opposite tack, stating that despite the lack of evidence these cultures were "without doubt" centralized and that we had just not yet stumbled over the evidence for it— since their complexity could not be created or sustained without management by a top-down decision-making hierarchy, crowned by an emperor, king, or paramount chief. The more cautious simply postulated that rulers with centralized authority *must* have existed, while more creative authors extrapolated centralized, micro-managing elite hierarchies from any sort of standardized object, measurement, or pattern (Charlton 1969, Fairservis 1977, Jacobson 1979, Kurtz 1987, LeBlanc 1999, Lekson 1999, Millon et al. 1965, Shaffer 1982, Upham and Plog 1986, Wheeler 1968, Wilcox 1993, 1999).

Many strange interpretations followed from the inability to conceptualize other forms of organization. Despite their relatively accessibility, Indus and Anasazi ritual and civic structures, for example, were characterized as socially "exclusive" (Possehl 1990:272, Powers 1984). Despite the fairly flat social hierarchy seen in burial contexts or grave offerings, exaggeration of finds theorized a class of powerful centralized rulers (Possehl 1990:272, Mathien 2001:113). The most elaborate of the modest offerings probably correlate with members of socially and politically powerful lineages (Mathien 2001:116) but do not represent conspicuous consumption meant to inspire awe at inordinate levels of wealth. At the other end of the spectrum, excavators at Grasshopper initially concluded that lack of mortuary or other elaboration indicated that there were no leaders within the society (Graves et al. 1982).

At Teotihuacan, while enormous architecture and substantial wealth is present, the absence of publicly visible royal tombs, palaces (other than richer, larger apartment compounds), stelae, or murals elaborating the identities of individual rulers led to many hypotheses: rule by an oligarchic republic (Millon 1976); perhaps committees of priests from the site's many temples. Pasztory (1992), an influential art historian, suggested a "utopian" society more like a modern democracy, an idea garnering both critique and consideration. The persistence of questions about the city's form of rule is a symptom of how difficult it is to grapple with the idea that rulership at a site with structures like the Pyramids of the Sun and Moon could be expressed differently than by Egyptian pharaohs or Shang emperors. The appearance of infrastructures without trappings of domination, absence of aggrandized elites, and lack of well-documented and celebrated centralizing rulers seemed to dumbfound researchers and certainly intrigued the public. As noted by Feinman et al. (2000:450), archaeologists "failed to recognize the potential for hierarchy and equality to coexist simultaneously in all human societies."

To this list could have been added Iron Age Europeans, had their cultures been entirely prehistoric. But the evidence for "anomalous behavior" such as urbanization without centralization, the circumscribed nature of rulers' powers, the often-negligible levels of elite aggrandizement, and the horizontal nature of social organization were ignored by the researchers considered most expert for many reasons—notably the availability of a poorly interpreted ethnohistoric record. Oddly, the ethnohistoric record makes frequent reference to these unexpected forms of organization, often precisely because they were noteworthy to the authors, who were largely Roman, but archaeologists long read them selectively. Others, under the influence of some leading proponents of the New Archaeology, pointedly ignored "history" which was considered irrelevant to "process." The certainty surrounding the application of the centralized hierarchy model and its apparent logic and ele- gance caused them to overlook both empirical and textual indications of Iron Age sociopolitical organization.

Within the disciplines that had spawned the original ideas on power, further refinement of the "power-over" concept was soon forthcoming, as well as wholly divergent conceptualization of the way power works. Of "power over" Lukes asked in 1974:

> Is it not the supreme exercise of power to get another or others to have the desires you want them to have—that is, to secure their compliance by controlling their thoughts and desires?... The most effective and insidious use of power is to prevent such conflict from arising in the first place (Lukes 1974:23).

A ruling elite may artificially create a desire among ordinary people to accept or emulate their values and worldviews, viewing them as natural, correct, just, and worthy—even if these values go against the direct self-interest of the non-elite. This is a variant of the Marxist concept of false consciousness—that oppressed people often buy into the oppressing status quo wholeheartedly because the ruling elite has created a worldview in which it must be accepted. This worldview can be so attractive that those outside the system are willing, even asking, to be part of it— the power called hegemony. Lukes added that such "thought control" need not stem from brainwashing but "takes many less total and more mundane forms, through the control of information...[and]...the processes of socialisation."

Alternative Perspectives on Power

Beginning in the 1990s, many previously confidant social scientists began to feel a collective shock at the collapse of "modernity"—the cultural and intellectual move- ments, and the social, economic, and political "world order" as it existed, according to some, from the Early Modern era until recently. During that time, Western expec- tations of social and cultural norms were relatively fixed, as were the boundaries of nations and states, religious and economic geography, and the like. Eventually many Westerners—both intellectuals and non-intellectuals—have come to acknowledge that the impact of the forces of globalization, interdependence, corporate economic domination, new kinds of powerful, diasporic political and military structures, have been so great that most of what once was "the way things have always been and always will be" is no longer so—at least that is how many (though not all) social theorists see the current era. Since the era of "post-modernity" is just beginning, we have little idea of where it is going, making our time in particular one of both anxiety and denial. One might expect that archaeologists, who study sweeping epochal transitions as a routine, would have intuitively anticipated post-modernity, but as it was self-referential it was difficult to grapple with. Many eventually came to see that some archaeological notions about the past were unwittingly or unconsciously rooted in the ideas and expectations of modernity. While some such perspectives have fallen apart across all academic disciplines as a reflection of wider processes, this paradigm shift has also been a great engine for theory—once the implications of post-modernity had been contemplated, alternative models could finally be theorized and offered.

Within other social sciences, post-modernity became a topic of concern by the late twentieth century (Giddens 1990) and led to the development of new ideas about power. In the 1970s, Lukes, with what he then called his "radical" and "three-dimensional" addition of hegemony and false consciousness, was still mired in the power as "power-over" idea, which today we would say only deals with power as domination. While "power over" is ubiquitous, there are other types. The "power to" concept, imported from sociology (Benton 1981), is connected to the ideas of agency, practice, and structure that were just then filtering into archaeology. Discussions of "power to" were published by a small but well-known group of archaeologists (Bender 1990, Miller and Tilley 1984, Saitta 1994) in their quest to explain not only the entrenched power of states but also the origins of that power. They emphasized that in non-hierarchical societies power is not always coercive—it may start out as "bestowed"—given willingly to elders, respected individuals, or those with supernatural gifts. These authors posited that such "power to" accomplish tasks, evaluate choices, and suggest actions, only turns into coercion when redefined and reconstituted through time. Voluntary support, offered in loyalty or trust, can turn into obligation as each generation comes to hold the rules it was born into as the norm. After a while, through the process of structuration as conceived by the increasingly popular sociologist Giddens (1984), archaeologists could hypothesize that what would have seemed inconceivable to earlier generations might seem ordinary to their heirs. "Power to" can become "power over" in only a short amount of time.

In the 1980s the Comaroffs, ethnographers working in apartheid South Africa, and Scott, a political theorist working with cross-cultural cases of peasantry also defined another type of power: that of resistance (Comaroff and Comaroff 1986)—the subverting or undermining of traditional forms of dominative power by ordinary people. A number of archaeologists in the 1980s and 1990s cited Foucault on this aspect of power, although rarely noting how his views changed during his career. Beginning with the idea that power was an omnipresent and oppressive method of control (Foucault and Sheridan 1979), a type of instrument, he later admitted it was relational and could not exist without certain freedoms among those who are subject to it and their ability to resist and challenge (Foucault 1982). Arendts on

consensus

the other hand saw power wholly as the product of consensus: people must agree to place power in the hands of people or institutions; she dismisses the idea of a purely autocratic and authoritarian use of power (1970:44), using ideas she deemed traceable to Iron Age Greece and Rome:

> Power is never the property of an individual; it belongs to a group and remains in existence only so long as the group keeps together. When we say of somebody that he is 'in power' we actually refer to his being empowered by a certain number of people to act in their name. The moment the group from which the power originated to begin with (*potestas in populo*, without a people or group there is no power), disappears, 'his power' also vanishes.

In a sense then, Foucault (at the end of his life) and Arendts each stressed ideas of both power to and power over, in that they acknowledged the role of subjectivity and agency—that is, self-awareness and directed action. They diverged in that Foucault saw power as normatively (although not always) repressive, while Arendts saw it as "communicative," normatively (although not always) positive.

Yet more recently others have discussed that neither of these views accounts for the ability of people acting together to overcome individuals or institutions wielding power in ways perceived to be wrong, unjust or harmful (Kriesi 1995). Even those who focused entirely on "power over" conceded that "Elitism...is neither foreordained nor omnipresent: as opponents of the war in Viet Nam can readily attest, the mobilisation of bias can and frequently does benefit a clear majority" (Bachrach and Baratz 1970). Allen (2002:143) states that Arendt's "attempt to exclude strategic action from the domain of the political altogether paints too rosy a picture of our political life" but also that "it is impossible, using a strictly Foucaultian understanding of power, to explain and analyze the power that binds together social movements—the explosive and invigorating power of the people that is let loose in revolutionary movements." Allen calls this kind of power "solidarity"—others have called it "power with."

power with

The concept of "power with" has been defined (Townsend 1999:31) as "the capacity to achieve with others what one could not achieve alone...too often dismissed as an impractical socialist ideal in this competitive world." The immensely popular writings of James Scott have familiarized archaeologists with the idea that there are two types of false consciousness: a "thick version" in which victims actually believe in the status quo and a "thin version" in which they do not believe in it, but see themselves as powerless to change things, and thus are resigned to compliance (Scott 1985, 1989, 1990). Yet Scott underscores "power with" in such circumstances: how the powerless can in fact contest authority, individually and collectively, in subtle and more apparent ways. Also popularized were the ideas of political theorist Gramsci, whose writings from inter-war era were not translated until the 1970s and only then "rediscovered" by social scientists. Gramsci defined the modern use of the hegemony concept (1971) and believed that both ideologies and resistance could be initiated within subaltern communities: territories or groups outside of hierarchic or hegemonic power structures, with little or no recognized power.

More indirect leveraging of power has also been documented, for example, in the creation of "agendas" or the building up of feelings among the public that certain issues or questions are of primary importance, even if not really the case. When an

public agendas

individual, or a group, defines such issues, they can in effect change the conversation by redefining what is important—making the status quo irrelevant and pointing the way to some new set of ideas that captures the public imagination. Once accomplished, leaders attached to former ideas can be dismissed (Rochefort and Cobb 1993). "In this light, social conflict becomes a process of successive, competitive problem definitions by opposing sides angling for advantage and issue expansion." (Rochefort and Cobb 1993:57). This has been called "non-decision-making" power.

The changes abroad in the social sciences beginning in the 1980s led to new archaeological paradigms a decade later, which initially met with some resistance. In terms of those pertinent to the Iron Age in Europe, the origin and development of decentralized states became a topic of interest in archaeological research from that time forward (e. g. Adams 1992, Barber and Joyce 2006, Blanton 1998, Blanton et al. 1996, Carmean and Sabloff 1996, Feinman 2001, Feinman et al. 2000, Fox et al. 1996, Hammond 1991, Manahan 2004, McAndrews et al. 1997, Peregrine 2001, Swenson 2006, White 1995, and many others). Even so, others (e.g. Chase and Chase 1996) continue to argue against such models, even characterizing centralization as an "achievement"—and that to argue against it comprises "denigration" of the subject society (Chase and Chase 1996:803). This typifies the confusion between political hierarchy and political centralization. A society can be markedly hierarchic yet still relatively decentralized. Although the intent of such statements in their context vis à vis earlier, racist claims of a "simple Maya" is thoroughly understandable (Fraser 1986), the contemporary question of whether centralization itself represents an "achievement" is left to the reader.

Making the distinction between power based on hierarchy and power based on centralization, which may or may not be conflated and can change through time, became easier through the heterarchy concept, introduced into archaeology by Carole Crumley (Crumley 1994a, b, Crumley and Marquardt 1990). Heterarchy describes an alternative to a vertical, pyramid-like arrangement of power, proposing a form of organization in which there is a horizontal spreading of power across different but equal social institutions, each of which is internally hierarchic, but where none has precedence over others. A complementary framework is dual-processual theory (Blanton et al. 1996), often called "corporate-network" theory, another alternative approach to political organizing principles, incorporating many of the more astute observations about political power made during the 1970s and 1980s, but which had never been connected to each other through an attempt at a unifying theory.

Corporate-network theory advocates first that hierarchy and centralization can be uncoupled, and second, that in states developing from cultures with strongly horizontal political structures and corresponding political ideologies, increasing political power is not always marked by ostentatious acts or displays of legitimation. In corporate societies, labor, food production, social groups, and even rulership may be controlled through "broad, integrative ritual and ideological means" (Feinman et al. 2000:453) and extreme differentiation between leaders and followers is suppressed or disguised. As characterized by Bender (1990), there is still a strong emphasis on "power to" in such societies, while "power over" can be achieved, but only by subtle methods. Rulers in such societies often appear more constrained than they actually are; ordinary people in such societies often feel they have more power than they really do.

In the "network" mode, power is predicated upon a network of elites and their contacts; elite controlled long-distance trade, a prestige-goods economy, status and class-laden burials, and elite-attached craft specialization. Ordinary people are excluded from many activities and roles; they have less power, and often feel as if they have little at all, and thus rarely challenge authority openly. Into this mode fit many of the cultures from which archaeological data were used to create traditional conceptualizations of centralized political power.

These strategies signify two ends of a continuum; most societies fall toward one or the other and are likely to change over time. The movement from one end of the continuum toward the other occurs as political power, ideology, military strength, economic control, and other factors are negotiated in different ways by various groupings within society—factions, classes, kin-groups, and those harder to distinguish, rooted in gender, age, and ethnicity. Corporate states function for long periods in a highly decentralized manner, even while opposing forces within society may be advocating for either a preservation or deconstruction of such traditions, pulling their political organization back and forth on a path along which power is marked in different ways at different times. Finding and analyzing the evidence for such sequences lies with each individual archaeologist's program of research.

Some authors have used corporate-network theory more as a descriptor than a way of interpreting past sequences—something Blanton et al. (1996) hoped would not become the case. As an attempt to move beyond description, some archaeologists have used various permutations of Giddens' (1984) and Pred's (1984, 1986) structuration theory (Barrett 1994, Ferguson 1996, Gardner 2002), Hägerstrand's (1982, 1985) time-space geography (e.g. Giles 2007, Halls and Miller 1996, Johannesen 2004, Mizoguchi 2002, Staaf 2000, Thurston 1999, Whitridge 2004), and some new methods for tracking such shifting social structures have been proposed recently (Beck et al. 2007), such as the application of Sewell's (2005) concept of the "transformational event," a reworking of structuration theory with more emphasis on linkages between materiality and power—thus pertinent to archaeology. All of these explorations have added to our ability to understand past social trajectories of change, including concepts about getting and wielding power.

In this light, several authors on the Teotihuacan state note that Maya records refer to leaders at Teotihuacan, and a fairly deep social hierarchy is apparent, making it doubtful that there were no rulers there; rather, they simply did not celebrate their own status by covering structures, stelae, ceramics, or other media with their own image or references to their own deeds—at least not in obvious ways. The state may have originated in a more network mode, then shifted over time to a more corporate one, where "acts rather than actors; offices rather than office-holders" (Cowgill 1997:137) were most important. Linda Manzanilla, based on the site's many iconographic and architectural traditions, has suggested that four co-rulers, with heterarchic authority over different institutions, ruled the state (Lloyd 2005); some, citing other data, have suggested two (Barbour personal communication 2007).

The heterarchy concept has successfully been used to reinterpret some so-called "mysterious" groups (Mills 2002, 2004, Feinman 2001) but has also been used to understand cultures formerly interpreted as centralized hierarchies. Some now appear to comprise somewhat different structures than previously assumed, while others that eventually became hierarchic appear to have had phases during which they may have passed from one format into another: Mississippian, Mayan, Mesopotamian, Aegean, Asian, and several Andean states for example (Blanton et al. 1996, Carmean and Sabloff 1996, Feinman et al. 2000, Manahan 2004, McAndrews et al. 1997, Parkinson and Galaty 2007, Peregrine 2001, Porter 2002, Swenson 2006, White 1995).

For Europe, the narrow theorization of political development within Iron Age societies was long entrenched as preeminent scholars repeatedly were solicited to publish or anthologize major overviews on Iron Age society (i.e. Cunliffe 1979, 1994, 1997, 2004, Collis 1977, 1984a, 1997). A large number of Iron Age specialists, at least in terms of acknowledgement or citation, appear unaware of the origins of familiar ideas about elites, power, and hierarchy, or that they have been supplanted by much more interesting and complex ideas over the last 30 years. While law-like generalities of state formation labeled "prime movers" *were* abandoned in the 1980s, other ideas—about the processes surrounding rulership, politics, and power—conceal significant paradoxes but continue to remain embedded in much current scholarship. Beginning in the late 1980s, a small number of archaeologists began publishing work informed by the wide historical array of thought on power. The neo-Marxist re-assessment of "primitive democracy" among Iron Age cultures described by Marx as the "Germanic mode of production" (Gilman 1995, Hunt and Gilman 1998) was among the first calls to reconsider what had long been postulated for Iron Age sociopolitical structure. Today, evidence mounts that rulers rarely redistribute anything unless they are forced to do so by the power of their constituencies (e.g. Fisher 2000). Similarly researchers increasingly question the idea that there must be elite planning and management of any and all complex systems, some of which have demonstrably been created by ordinary people (Erickson 1993, Frederick 2007, Hauser-Schäublin 2003, Lansing and Kremer 1993). Iron Age polities are well described by the concept of the "corporate state" with a heterarchic structure. It is these new perspectives that are reviewed in the remainder of this chapter.

Power, Heterarchy, and Decentralization in Iron Age Europe

To examine how the above history of thought has affected the archaeology of Iron Age Europe, and why, I review not only recent work but also traditional frameworks. Today, many archaeologists would argue that centralization would have been a pipe dream for elites in Iron Age Europe, and political power itself was hardly an entitlement for any individual. Power was spread through many facets of society, and the power of those we typically imagine as rulers, the warrior elite, lay at a nexus between camaraderie and incentive, self-abasement and aggrandizement, and much like the indirect expressions of power described by Gramsci, Lukes, Benton, and Townsend, couched in highly ideological frameworks of brotherhood, *devotio*, and fate. It was a dangerous space within which to live, with death in battle the result of a successful balancing act, and death at the hands of one's own kin or followers for those who strayed outside its narrowly defined bounds. Numerous Iron Age social aggregates (Fig. 8.2), as outlined below, not only suppressed elite power, but also attempted to display marked status differences with many leveling mechanisms, between elites of similar renown, and between high status and petty elites. Even the distance between rulers and ordinary people was blurred. Political decision making and judicial processes were large-scale public affairs, expansive in nature: "power to" and "power with" stood in opposition to excesses of any "power over."

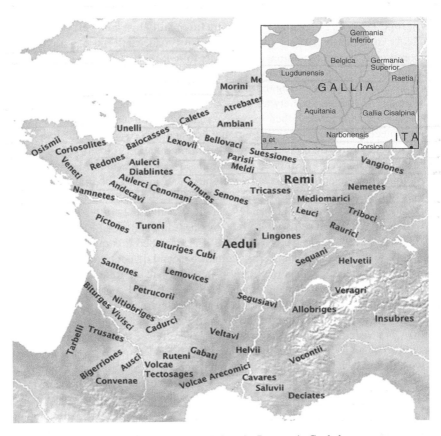

Fig. 8.2 Pre-Roman indigenous groups recorded by the Romans in Gaul alone

The Northern Iron Age

Although this discussion eventually leads back to the very beginnings of the Iron Age in Europe, we start with its latest expression in Scandinavia, beginning around 500 BC and including the so-called Viking Age, from AD 800 to AD 1075. Until the later twentieth century, Anglophone interpretations of Germanic and Nordic groups stressed their "non-state" nature (Cohen 1977, Wells 1984) and described them as "emigrating people" or "invaders." In American textbooks, they continued to be described, in contrast to the Greeks and Romans, as "warlike tribes" (Fagan 1989:87) or "violent tribes who lived without the benefit of cities, writing, money, or bureaucracies" (Wenke 1980:454–455). While American students learned multi-causal explanations for southwest Asian and Mesoamerican states through political economy and interaction theories, they were taught that the main conduit for understanding Iron Age Europe was the study of "axes and adzes, battle axes, daggers, swords, spearheads, shields, and an enormous range of brooches, pins and other ornaments" (Fagan 1989:477) due to seemingly endless publication on comparative material culture (e.g. Graham-Campbell 1973, 1975, 1981, 1985, 2001, Hall 1973, Jope 1962, 1971, Warner 1973), a tradition still alive and well. This changed markedly in the early 1980s, when evidence of broader and more complex political configurations led Scandinavian scholars to rectify the perception of Germanic and Nordic groups as tribal, chaotic, and politically unorganized. This revision was undertaken by those embracing the elite centralized hierarchy model, since it was the only model of complex society accepted at the time. For the most part, the powers of rulers were exaggerated, their exclusive rights to be buried with gold neckbands, gaming pieces, and horse gear overemphasized and described as indicative of deep social stratification, when they were similar to Indus and Puebloan "riches"—status indicators, but markedly restrained in comparison with those interred at Ur and Giza.

Mapping and hypothesizing the development of an elite, centralized hierarchy continued as the main paradigm for the next two decades and is still reflected in the work of many Scandinavian archaeologists (Roesdahl 1982, 1999, 1998, Ethelberg and Hansen 2000, Fabech 1999a, b, Graham-Campbell et al. 1994, Helgesson 2003, Näsman 2000). Randsborg (1980, 1981) straddled this question early on by implicitly acknowledging both centralizing forces and de-centralization in different publications, which, if one explicitly examines late Germanic political structures, is true. Fabech (1994) and others (Hedeager 1997, Larsson 2007, Lundqvist et al. 1993, Söderberg 2003) implicitly discuss heterarchy when they note significant episodes of centralization, or the co-option of religious authority by warlords, as "new" to Scandinavian organization, but generally see this as an inevitable process toward state formation without any explicit consideration of corporate systems as well defined and indigenously venerated modes of institutional organization. Magnusson Staaf (2003:317) states that in regard to early Iron Age towns like Uppåkra, although there is no local or regional evidence of any elite class, one *must* have existed, since a complex settlement system could not develop without central elite planning. In the next sentence, he states that "There might have been cultural codes for signaling status that are difficult to discern in the archaeological record" yet never approaches the topic of either the implications of corporately "disguised" power or the contemporary critique of the idea that elites are necessary for every organized activity. As Cowgill stated of American archaeologists in the 1970s and their occasional misinterpretation of their own data, they "know this but do not *realize* it" (Cowgill 1975:509). This problem was long endemic to the study of Iron Age Europe.

In the last decade, interpretations that include discussions of decentralized power in Scandinavia have begun to appear from archaeologists, historians, and even sociologists (e.g. Andersson 2003, Andrén 2000, Bagge 1999, 2005, Ertman 1997, Gustafsson 2006, Jørgensen 2000, and many more in the Scandinavian languages). The argument that Iron Age Scandinavia was politically decentralized should not be confused with the argument that they had complex or state-level societies. Decentralized power within a politically complex and stratified society is often seen in heterarchic organization. This was the case in the Nordic region, where the political power of the warlord and warband was balanced by the power of the assembly, or *ting/thing*, at both local and national levels, where free males met to vote for or against local leaders' plans, find justice through the oral law codes, and occasionally vote for or against a new king. The third strand of power was religious—religious specialists existed in the Early Iron Age; chieftains later overtook responsibility for many religious rituals, while other forms of religion formed a parallel system, included healing, seeking, and protecting through several forms of shamanism. Despite this spate of publication, the normative centralized hierarchy model, pervasive in the traditional literature, continues to have a substantial impact. In a recent article (Kurrild-Klitgaard and Tinggaard Svendsen 2003), a Danish political scientist and an economist perform analyses of Viking and early medieval political economy, using citations only of well-worn Anglophone work (Jones 1984 [1968], Logan 1983, Roesdahl 1997 [1991], Sawyer 1982), to argue that the Danish "Vikings" had a centralized government as early as the ninth century AD.

What Was a King in the So-Called Viking Age?

The title of this chapter is drawn from the traditions of Scandinavia, a region where the Iron Age lasted much longer than other parts of Europe, and a continuous practice, albeit a clearly changing one, was preserved. No indigenously written ethnohistories derive from the Pre-Roman Gauls or Britons; all later chronicles were produced by Roman conquerors, or by Romanized provincial descendants—former or reformed "barbarians." The never Romanized, only recently Christianized (ca. AD 1000–1100), Scandinavians did record their own traditions, either during or just after these changes. Much like Mesoamericans in the sixteenth century, they often wrote that their recently abandoned beliefs and the deities of their ancestors were preposterous, yet these traditions were still deeply embedded in Nordic identity, and authors were enough attached to them to record their lore for posterity as faithfully as they could (Heinrichs 1994). In terms of social customs and political forms, they continued to hold firmly to their older traditions: ancient laws of precedent, the right of voting in the assembly, the right to reject overbearing leaders—even as their kings occasionally attempted to increase the scope of their power and made a slow course toward pushing their system from the corporate to the network mode. While they must be read critically, they provide important insights into Iron Age politics:

> Men shed many tears when they bore the generous king to the grave; that was a heavy burden to those whom he had given gold.

Generosity here is described by Oddr Kikinaskald, a court poet of the Late Viking Age, after witnessing the death of Magnus the Good of Norway in AD 1047. He and others characterize the powerful as gift givers, largesse distributors, hosts par excellence to their own warband and their peers. In our own cultural context, we might view such statements with cynicism: a king's followers motivated by pure self-interest, bemoaning the loss of easy handouts. This is at odds with the poet's intent—distributions of treasure were not "bribes" split among a ruler's entourage of warriors and councilors. They were an integral part of a ruler's proof that he sincerely adhered to a system in which class or status differences were artificially and purposefully flattened and suppressed (Hedeager 2000). The *Knytlinga Saga* describes what was deemed admirable in Knut the Great, who ruled Denmark and England from AD 1018 to 1035. Probably written between 1241 and 1260 by Ólafr Thórðarson, nephew of the Icelandic historian Snorri Sturluson, it characterizes Knut as an ideal ruler of his era:

> There was never a king in Scandinavia more generous than Knut, for it is said in all truth that he went far beyond other kings... (Pálsson and Edwards 1986:41).

Beowulf, a more famous text, involves both mythic characters and some probable historic figures. Composed around AD 800, committed to writing around AD 1000 in England by the Anglo-Saxon descendants of Scandinavian settlers, its tells a story set in Denmark between AD 450 and 600. A major debate continues over whether the poem is the product of Christianized Anglo-Saxons or the original pre-Christian Anglos and Saxons who first colonized Britain, with a majority leaning toward authenticity, especially since the identification of the Danish Iron Age site of Lejre as a probable model for Heorot, the royal hall of the poem. For our purposes, the point is moot—Anglo-Saxons of both periods conceptualized kingship in similar (though not identical) ways, with rulers subject to election by public acclamation, ritual generosity, peripatetic royal courts, and highly decentralized and distributed forms of power. In the story, Hrothgar, a wise old king, explains to young Beowulf some fundamental aspects of Iron Age rulership:

> God...grants [a ruler] every pleasure in his home, and a well-garrisoned stronghold to defend, while making wide regions of the earth subject to him as well, till in his conceit the man can see no end to it...The world does as he wants of it, and to him misfortune is a stranger. But within him arrogance grows and festers. Conscience falls asleep...Then the man is off his guard and is pierced right to the heart by a bitter arrow against which he does not know how to defend himself: what he has had for so long does not seem to him enough. Greedily he covets and no longer gives away collars of gold, as honor ordains...he pays no attention to the workings of destiny (Wright 1957:67–68).

The "bitter arrow" refers not to a weapon but to the insidious invasion of a ruler's nature by qualities abhorrent to Iron Age people: outward displays of arrogance, pride, and acquisitiveness, described as both a failure in leadership and a betrayal of a sacred trust—concepts at odds with many more familiar traditions of royal rule, in which rulers underscore their right or even obligation to command and display wealth or prestige at levels far higher than ordinary people and much higher than even their own client elites, as well as demonstrate authoritarian power.

Creation of social distance, through the flaunting of possessions controlled by rarity, cost, or sumptuary laws, delineates the strict boundaries between rulers and others. Such conduct by an Iron Age European ruler usually resulted in his own death; proper social conduct involved sanctioned braggadocio, wide advertisement of military prowess, but treatment of followers as brothers-in-arms, who followed him because he inspired admiration, was lucky in war and obtaining riches, and generously shared them. In his fictional speech, which essentializes royal failings and virtues, Hrothgar concludes by saying to Beowulf:

> In the end, this is what generally happens. His mortal body (which is doomed to die) perishes, and someone else who is untroubled by his miserly qualms succeeds to the throne and carelessly shares out the man's long-hoarded treasures (Wright 1957:68).

This would make things right again, restore order and proper lordship. The "miserly" ruler is a figure of ridicule.

The flattened, or foreshortened, nature of the differences between leaders and followers in the Iron Age is generally visible archaeologically. With few exceptions, cemeteries of the Scandinavian Iron Age (Hedeager 1992, Ilkjær 2002, Sjternquist 1955, Watt 2003) show that even at its most dramatic expression, grave goods differentiating classes of elites were not extraordinary: one group bears neckbands and armbands of gold, the next of silver, others of bronze, all in similar burial contexts, yet clearly reflective of hierarchic ordering, including the types of weapons and personal effects they carried. Chiefs or petty kings lived in large halls, bigger and more elaborate versions of the ordinary longhouse, not unlike the differentiated apartment compounds of Teotihuacan. The richest estates yet excavated indicate a high-ranking elite kept 80 cattle in a byre to supply himself and a garrison, while a lower-ranking man kept 20 and an ordinary farmer 10 or 12 cows (Hvass 1980, 1983, 1989, Jørgensen and Skov 1980, Nielsen 1980, Stoumann 1980). These are significant, visible class- and/or wealth-based differences, yet not exponential ones. Even during phases in which kingship was fully and firmly expressed, royal burials, such as those at Gamla Uppsala, Jelling, Oseberg, and elsewhere, consist of large earthen mounds, 5–10 m high, with beautiful objects, rich fabrics, carved wood, personal adornments, and symbols of leisure such as gaming, feasting and drinking equipment, but in comparison with rulers in other traditions with similar or lesser resources, relatively modest. The Knytlinga saga (Pálsson and Edwards 1986) specifically describes how in the eleventh century Knut the Holy enraged the Danes by traveling the country in lavish style far exceeding that of earlier kings. Thus, while some aspects of "network" political elites were emergent, others were not.

Could Viking Age elites conceptualize a society in which rulers possessed and displayed wealth and power at extraordinary levels? Of course they could—many warriors, including royal offspring (kings-to-be) were well traveled and frequent visitors to the Mediterranean world and beyond, some serving as guards to the Emperors at Constantinople, as earlier Iron Age men had gone to fight for the Greeks and Romans. They viewed and experienced the super-stratification and staggering displays of wealth found in Byzantium and the Islamic Caliphates. If one rephrases the question to ask, could they achieve similar lifestyles in their own lands, the answer is "not yet."

The gap was not wide between the material trappings of eliteness from leader to follower, and the authority of rulership was highly circumscribed, but the *power gap* between Iron Age warlords and the petty elite of the war band was more significant. Rulers had rights to conscript farmer–citizens to fight for them, to send specific numbers of manned warships for the royal navies, and they could levy taxes; they could also use their gravitas to influence matters outside their jurisdiction. On the other hand, as the region emerged into historic times and we have records of Viking Age and early medieval relations between the rulers and their constituencies, we find that their reach was not unlimited, and even where they were conceded power it was suppressed within a formalized social code that was followed aggressively.

Denmark was perhaps the most dangerous of the Scandinavian countries in which to be a king, with the largest recorded number of royal assassinations, going back at least to the killing of Godfred in the ninth century, for aspiring to autocratic power during his struggles with the Carolingians. A cluster of Danish regicides in the eleventh and twelfth centuries is no coincidence. Often simply termed "civil war," they are far more complex: they were in a long tradition within Iron Age social relations, and all were in the context of calls to restore earlier norms. They corresponded with draconian attempts by kings to suppress earlier forms of rule, in which ordinary people had much more power, and leadership was heterarchically spread across several institutions. Strategies toward stronger and wider powers included execution of those publicly protesting royal actions and demanding the restoration of "ancient rights and laws," a type of protest that had previously been a rightful expression (Thurston 2007b), massive reorganization of settlement landscapes, only visible in the archaeological record, in order to facilitate taxation (Porsmose 1981, Ridderspore 1988, Tesch 1991, Thurston 1999, 2001, 2006, 2007a), increased demands for taxes and military service from each administrative district, execution and exile of numerous well-respected local chieftains, not only recorded textually but seen archaeologically in the abrupt abandonment of many chiefly centers all at once around AD 1000, simultaneous with the founding or elaboration of royal towns and fortresses, and tax penalties for any infractions (Thurston 2007b).

Despite the acquisition of these powers by the turn of the first millennium, kings were still subject to public protest in the assembly, the refusal of supposedly conquered provinces to submit to central authority, uprisings, tax rebellions and the like. Knut the Holy, even though his father had endorsed him as heir, had to plead his case before the assembly of all Denmark but was still passed over in deference to tradition, and his older brother was made king before he got his turn (Pálsson and Edwards 1986). Once a king, a man might levy taxes, command wealth, and own 1,000 farms, each with 80 cattle, but he was careful not to flaunt his resources. If a leader overstepped correct behavior—failed to be generous, behaved haughtily, worst of all styled himself a king in our commonly understood sense—he was as good as dead at the hands of his own people. This is the upshot of the bitter arrow: the perceived widening of the gap between himself and his constituency, leading to sanctioned or even mandated assassination.

For Denmark alone one can refer to the aforementioned Godfred, then to Knut the Holy, who eventually became king but was killed by a farmer army in 1086, led by nobles that included his kin, as punishment for the flaunting of his wealth, unprecedented taxation, unpopular new legislation favoring royal rights, and the hitherto unheard of executions of those who questioned him in the assembly. King Niels was assassinated 1134 by commoners dissatisfied with his family's usurpation of local elites—supposedly, when warned not to walk the streets with only a body-guard, he asked, "should I fear tinkers and tailors?" Apparently, the answer was yes. According to ethnohistoric texts, Erik Emune was assassinated in 1137 by a local wealthy farmer, Plow the Black, whose father had been put to death by the king "for no worse offence than speaking out against him at a certain assembly" according to Knytlinga Saga (Pálsson and Edwards 1986:143). Some rulers managed to escape assassination by bargaining with their subjects and nobles and giving in to their demands, such as Valdemar the Great who dealt with uprisings in the late twelfth century by conceding to public ultimatums, but not enough to stop quickly ensuing rebellions.

Public outrage at royal abuses, which in more centralized and truly hierarchic societies would merely be seen as expected royal behavior, led to uprisings and attempts at overthrow in other parts of Scandinavia as well. Protests and conflicts, all with claims to restore "ancient rights and laws" from Iron Age legal codes are found in Sweden until the sixteenth century (Andrén 2000, Cederholm 2007, Skre 2001), where kings tried to centralize beginning around AD 1000, an attempt marred by the non-compliance of stubbornly decentralized areas. Especially, problematic was suppressing long-established traditions among the small kingdoms the larger state had subsumed (Sigurðsson 2006), where royal authority was stymied by local lords' and farmers' tendency to feign ignorance or forgetfulness of taxes and laws, procrastinate in paying, hide assets when the taxman came, all "weapons of the weak" as conceptualized by political theorist Scott (1985, 1989). All eventually led to uprising and rebellion. In Norway, royal figures attempted to overthrow the Iron Age social code in the late ninth century, similarly attempting to impose central-izing controls on formerly decentralized institutions, and a new and heavy taxation system. These early centralizing kings made some headway against tradition by con-verting to Christianity and thus finding reason to eject "pagan" elites (Bagge 2005). This was met by protest, which was met by outlawry and, to a greater extent than in early Denmark and Sweden, the increased power of the king during that era. This did not last; by the later Middle Ages the nobles were in revolt against the king once more (Bagge 2005).

Norwegian centralizing attempts also led to the colonization of Iceland by angry lower-level elites and common people who established what is now called the Icelandic Free State (Byock 1988), where eleventh century chroniclers said there was "no king but the law" (Tschan 1959). The sequence began with establishment of a purposeful system of decentralized power, combined with rule by law and an assembly, where elite self-aggrandizement was controlled by the specification that a leader's clients could, as in earlier times, abandon his service for one of his better-liked peers. This was an ideological reiteration of the Iron Age code but was not identical to "ancient" ways—it was an invention of its own time. Although eventually abandoned, this code functioned well for many centuries (Runolfsson Solvason 1992, 1993). Thus Scandinavia as a whole saw attempts at both the consolidation of power and the protest of its increase.

Ethnographies of Power from the Continental Iron Age

The preceding textual examples come from indigenously written records, some "historical," others literary. They are a product of the latest and last phase of the Iron Age in Europe, the mid- to late first millennium AD, or directly thereafter, and as all ethnohistories, they reflect certain social and political agendas and particularistic intentions unique to the time and place they were written, as well as the periods which they purport to describe. Fortunately, careful philology combined with archaeology can untangle some of these problems and indicate what information can cautiously be supported as approximating authenticity.

The texts dealing with the earlier Iron Age date from the Roman era, from the later Republican period up through the first century AD. Despite their usefulness as windows on an ancient world, we are in some ways unlucky that such texts exist. They shed light on what would otherwise be inscrutable evidence, but stem from sources outside the cultures they describe. They can also be biased, purposefully or unintentionally (Dunham 1995), and even when not innately biased they can be misread or misinterpreted by historians and archaeologists alike, who tend to take from them what they wish to find. Primarily Roman authors wrote about Britain, Germania, Iberia, and Gaul during conquest, or shortly after, or of their interactions with unconquered peoples (Fig. 8.3). Roman authors also wrote about Rome's own earlier Iron Age history, with sometimes questionable accuracy but largely earnest intent, something that has been inexplicably ignored by prehistoric archaeologists who eagerly read Tacitus and Caesar for information on barbarians.

Despite these drawbacks and their past misuse, these texts have undergone a great deal of scrutiny, and currently there is a general consensus about which authors are mostly accurate or knowledgeable and which merely repeated public opinion. There was a long tradition of "ethnography" among the Greeks and later the Romans, that is, the research and writing of texts explicitly meant to describe the lifeways of distant or unfamiliar peoples. While "fabulous" details sometimes found their way into such writings, most classical authors made efforts to research and record

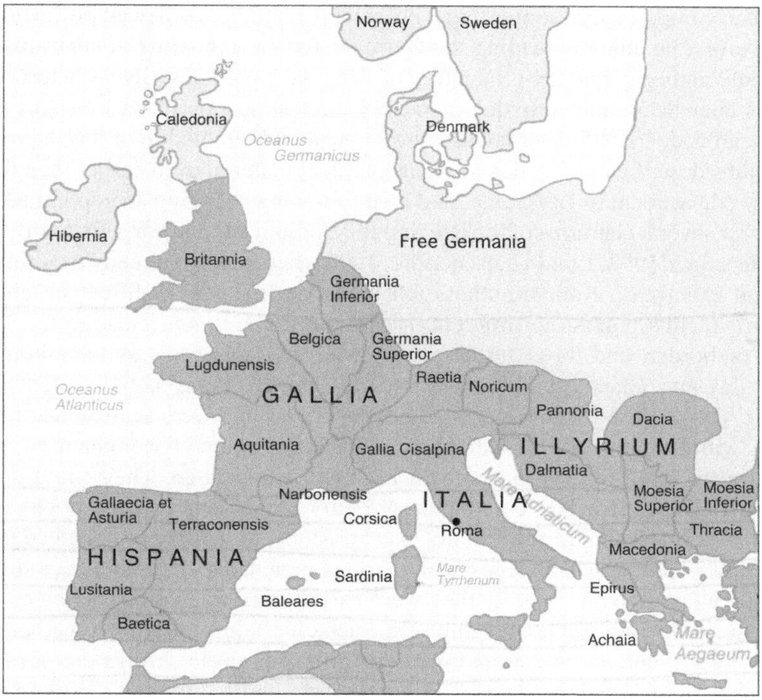

Fig. 8.3   Roman and non-Roman Europe in the Late Iron Age and Roman eras

accurate details, and archaeologists have found much of the materiality they describe to be accurate (Hedeager 1992, Watt 2003, Wells 1999, 2001).

Even authors with first-hand knowledge must be read carefully (Büchsenschütz and Ralston 1988, Wilkes 2007). Julius Caesar, who conquered Gaul and attempted to conquer Britain, may have been vindicating his over-expenditures and promoting his own heroic cult of personality when writing his *Commentaries on the Conquest of Gaul*. While he may have attempted to truthfully describe Gallic culture, he often imposed Roman concepts on them as well (Dunham 1998). One occasionally reads that Tacitus used "second hand information" and therefore is not wholly trustworthy; this is untrue. Tacitus, a consul, provincial governor, and historian was himself Gallic. His father-in-law Agricola, with whom he was extraordinarily close, had been a general in and then governor of Britain, and his own father had been procurator (chief financial administrator) for Gallia Belgica, a Germanic province. He was friends with Pliny the Elder, who wrote his own eyewitness ethnography of the Germans, now lost. All of this gave him substantial authority to write the ethnography *Germania* (Church and Brodribb 1877) in AD 98 as well as similar accounts of Britain and Gaul. Tacitus clearly also used the Germans as a foil for his criticism of Roman life and morals, underscoring his perception of positive Germanic qualities while denigrating comparable Roman behaviors. Furthermore, he was a Republican in the early imperial era, supporting a political format that eschewed powerful kings or emperors; he enjoyed lauding the Germans for their mistrust of centralized and autocratic authority and their valuation of what we would describe as heterarchy.

Was later Scandinavia unique or merely the last bastion of an Iron Age corporate social code? The Scandinavians have done an admirable job of linking material conditions described by Tacitus to archaeological material even earlier than the first century AD account of *Germania*, and then following changing sociopolitical structures over several centuries of the late first millennium BC and early first millennium AD (Hedeager 1992, Lund Hansen 1987, 1990) that we have already examined.

What exactly do Roman authors tell us about Iron Age political structures in Europe? Tacitus points out differences between the *Germani* close to the Roman *limes*, or border, and those further away, whom he describes as inhabiting huge peninsulas and islands, a reference to Scandinavia that is not disputed by any scholar. Those close to the border had adopted coins and were accustomed to interactions with Rome, while those further away had undergone fewer changes. Among all *Germani*, the power of leaders was highly circumscribed. They could not pass on their rank to offspring; correct lineage only gained entry into a pool of eligible elites, perhaps akin in spirit, if not exact practice, to tanistry as practiced in early medieval and probably Iron Age Ireland. Young men had to apprentice to older men, and if they failed to have ability they were barred from rulership. There was a warrior class, collecting tribute, waging war. Each chieftain supported a warband with food, housing, entertainment, and precious gifts such as neckrings and armbands. Chieftains were in theory equal with each other; being more clever, more gifted, more successful gave one authority to influence less talented peers but not the right to enforce an agenda. If a leader was too peaceful, unlucky, or inept, the small group of professional warriors who lived off his largesse had a socially sanctioned right to leave his service for that of a preferred warlord.

Yet there were other power structures. Rule was not solely in the hands of the warrior class. Ordinary people provided tribute voluntarily, at least in theory, and could, if they didn't care for a leader, procrastinate or draw out this support to make him uncomfortable—the same thing is reported for the Gauls by Julius Caesar in *De Bello Gallico*. An assembly that met at regular, predetermined intervals had the right to approve or vote down the plans of chieftains. When the men of the assembly "muttered and grumbled" according to Tacitus, the plan was dead. There were local, regional, and "national" assemblies in Gaul and Germania, a custom that continued into Late Iron Age and Viking Age Scandinavia.

For Gaul, Caesar describes men of the elite class who created power for themselves by amassing property and money, giving largesse to many, supporting a personal bodyguard, fomenting political intrigues and intermarrying with ruling families—politicians rather than warlords. During his conquests, Caesar often was greeted by groups of "ambassadors" who spoke for the *oppida,* or indigenous towns, possibly comprising such men.

Tacitus says that among Germanic groups, a separate priestly class acted not only as intercessors with the supernatural but as judges at disputes in the assembly, also presiding over the assembly's organization, and lawspeakers had lawcodes committed to memory for these occasions, specifically so that the law could not be corrupted by any party. The Gaul's religious specialists had power to spiritually sanction misdeeds but also oversaw the election of a magistrate or *Vergobretus* at the assembly, who was elected annually for a single year, with administrative and legal powers over a defined "people" and territory. Election could not be secret, and the law forbade two men from one family to be elected while both were alive.

Among both Germans and Gauls, during times of outside threat, a well-regarded chief was chosen as a paramount to coordinate war activities, but no matter how badly threatened society became, the chief elected as coordinator could only command for as long as a conflict lasted. It is also clear that rulers occasionally attempted to undermine the code in bids for increased authority. When they achieved this authority, their constituencies usually protested it, and often they did not hold it for very long. If a leader tried to remain in power, he could be removed with a socially sanctioned assassination. There are several textual examples of such assassinations that were endemic among the Gauls as well as the Germanic peoples, showing that a similar ethic was traditional in each region, and as among the later Nordic groups they were similarly performed by the ruler's own followers or even family, as with honor killings. These are recorded in several instances—remarkable for what is an extremely patchy historic record.

Julius Caesar (*De Bello Gallico,* MacDevitt 2005) discusses Orgetorix (I:II–IV), an elite of the first century BC who "aspired to kingship" by conspiring with other elites to seize power. When his intentions were discovered, he was brought before judges to receive the sentence of death this crime carried. In a classic balanced opposition, he summoned all his followers to oppose his execution, while the magistrates summoned theirs, and Orgetorix died in the confrontation. The leader Celtillus (*De Bello Gallico* VII:IV, MacDevitt 2005) had held the paramount chieftainship of all Gaul and had been put to death by his fellow citizens because he aimed at retaining sovereign power over too long of a term. His son, Vercingetorix, led the Gauls in a war against the Roman conquerors in 52 BC. After some errors in judgment, he was forced to come before a large assembly, a council of all Gaul held in the *oppida* of Bibracte, and "communicate his plans of conducting the war," or else relinquish command to his critics, and Caesar (*De Bello Gallico* VII:LXIII, MacDevitt 2005) reported that "the decision is left to the votes of the mass: all to a man approve of Vercingetorix as their general."

In Germany a few decades later, Tacitus reported on Arminius (*Annals,* Goodyear 1981), the chieftain of the Germanic Cherusci, who having been a petty elite within the Roman system, understood their intent to incorporate German territories into the empire. He launched an effort to unite several Germanic groups against Rome and in the fall of AD 9, in the so-called Battle of the Teutoburg Forest—which probably took place near the Wiehengebirge hills (Wells 2003)—his alliance ambushed and annihilated three Roman legions, about 20,000 troops. After this victory, Arminius was expected to immediately relinquish his overlordship under the Germanic code. Because the Roman threat was clear, he tried to create a permanent alliance, and led a number of other victories over Rome, but after constant challenges and critiques from his peers, in AD 19 he was assassinated by his own kin and people, who accused him of trying to make himself a king.

Much of this chapter has so far dealt with resituating the warlord/warband structure within a larger context, and hence often male forms of power. It would be unfortunate if in deconstructing one type of bias, others were to be introduced. Although it is largely outside the scope of this focused discussion, there is considerable evidence across Iron Age Europe for female rulers, religious leaders, and civic and political participation by ordinary women. Although atypical, female leadership figures appear with some regularity from the earliest Iron Age to the late Nordic phases. In terms of rulership, in the textually documented periods, women were acceptable, and often exceptional, rulers when male lines of succession were exhausted or annihilated and capable elite women of appropriate lineages were willing and available. Every British schoolchild knows of the Iceni ruler, Boudica, who led an uprising of several East Anglian peoples against the occupying Roman forces (Hingley and Unwin 2005), and the army that she led in a war chariot, estimated at over 100,000 fighters, contained both male and female soldiers according to the Roman governor Gaius Suetonius Paulinus who fought against her (*Tacitus Agricola 16*, Church and Brodribb 1877; *Cassius Dio Historiae Romanae LXII:2*, Carey 1924, Hingley and Unwin 2005). Tacitus further clarified "...for Britons make no distinction of sex in their leaders" (*Tacitus Annals*, Braund 1996:71). Tacitus also described a female ruler allied with Rome, Cartimandua of the Brigantes. In the neighboring region inhabited by the Parisi, two women's ditched-enclosure chariot burials have been excavated since 1980 (Dent 1985, Hill 2001), along with male burials of the same type, dating back to about 300 BC, the La Tène period; they cannot simply be assigned as merely "marking elite status" when the historic record discusses such vehicles being used by women leaders in pitched battles. Female leaders are suggested archaeologically on the Continent in the La Tène period (Arnold 1991, 1996, Knüsel 2002) and described ethnohistorically in Ireland (Slavin 2005), and in Scandinavia both ethnohistorically (Arwill-Nordbladh 2003, Monsen 1932:36) and archaeologically, such as with the early Viking Age Oseberg burial, the only such rich "royal" burial containing women, perhaps a ruler or a ritual specialist (Holck 2006, Nordström 2006) or both.

Disputed Interpretations of Iron Age Europe

All archaeologists are necessarily mistrustful of historic documents, which can "lie" about many things, yet they also bear evaluation through archaeological testing. Despite these references to decentralized rule and the maintenance of an ideologically flattened hierarchy, most archaeologists of the mid-twentieth century, strongly influenced by the prevailing social science discourse on power, ruling elites, and hierarchy, simply attached themselves to the term "king." The term is occasionally but not always used by some—and not other—ancient authors. Also, the fact that there were, in some areas, "centers" in the form of *oppida* (towns) and

hillforts (high elevation enclosures) while in others there were not, was important from this perspective. Kings + "centers" = centralization and elite hierarchy.
Absence of kings + no centers = chaotic, acephalous alliances of tribes or warrior
bands (Lönnroth 1963, 1977, Wells 1984, Wilson 1981). Thus, for the Gauls and
Britons, centralized hierarchies were assumed, while for the Germans, various ter-
minologies of "lesser complexity" were usually described. This is problematic for
three reasons, the most obvious and oft noted being that classical authors may have
applied their own word, "king," in ways that were not really applicable. On the other
hand, the term "king" may in fact be acceptable but our understanding of kingship
at fault. Substantial powers associated with rulership are not expressed similarly
in all societies. Among historic states where kingship has limited power, the term
is appropriate, with caveats on what the contextually situated powers of that office
were. Modern democracies are purposely designed to be both corporate and heterarchic; we would hardly be tempted to call a prime minister, president, or other chief
executive a "chieftain" because of this.

Finally, despite the real fact that Germanic and Celtic social systems are described by multiple sources as nearly identical in their ethos, they were read selectively by archaeologists who extracted from them only what they expected to find.
The failure to re-examine the interpretations may be assigned to the certainty with
which scholars felt they "knew" or understood the Iron Age so well and so famil-
iarly, that there was little else to discover beyond what they had already accepted
(Hill 1989, Ralston 1992, 1997). All Iron Age societies have evidence of elite cultures with internal hierarchy, most of which grew somewhat more articulated over
time yet rarely lost all of their corporate trappings. The problems lie in the expectations imposed on this group and their relationships to other groups within society.

A number of archaeologists (e.g. Hill 1989, 1993, 1995a, James 1998, 1999) have
pointed out that many still accept a supposedly textually derived "pyramid shaped"
Iron Age social structure (Fig. 8.4), ruled by warlords, shepherded by druids or
priests of Odin and the like, celebrated by artisans, skalds, or bards, fed by farmers, and served by slaves, a notion that Iron Age authority Simon James has said he
at first reiterated (James 1993), yet later began to question in his own treatment of
"Celts" in Iron Age Europe (James 1998, 1999, 2000). This is mirrored in a forced
model of settlement hierarchy—with central places often conflated from several distinct types of sites, supposedly serving as locales inhabited by authoritarian rulers,
from which orders emanated in an outward direction, and some degree of services
were provided to a populace, incorporating many mid-twentieth century concepts
discussed earlier.

It should be noted that it was not through theories or untested ideas that interpretive errors at many sites were realized. It was through careful and unbiased
examinations of the actual data collected and published by their excavators, who
eventually acknowledged that the re-interpretations are better supported than their
initial conclusions, plus the addition of new data. From a hypothetico-deductive perspective, it might be said that between 1970 and 1990 or so, a particular model of
Iron Age Europe's sociopolitical structure was tested. It appeared to fit the data
in 1970, yet over time, more and more data accumulated, old data were more

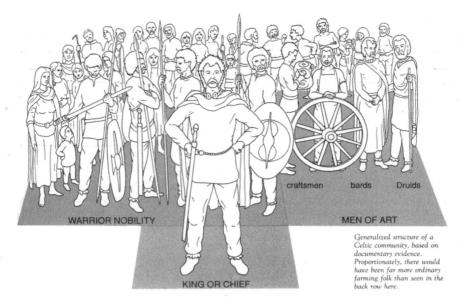

Generalized structure of a Celtic community, based on documentary evidence. Proportionately, there would have been far more ordinary farming folk than seen in the back row here.

Fig. 8.4 The often-assumed sociopolitical pyramid of Celtic society, as drawn, presented, and critiqued by Simon James (1993:53)

objectively examined in light of new findings, and eventually, the model and the data no longer fit each other. This is an ordinary and unexceptional progression of scientific or social scientific inquiry. However, reinterpretation was largely coincident with the beginning of the so-called post-processual critique, in the UK, Europe, and eventually the Americas and beyond, and thus it emerged as a debate within this framework. Since new interpretations incorporated ideas that would never have been considered within the framework of classic processualism, this is somewhat justified, although much of it could also simply be classified as a quite ordinary paradigm shift based on an accumulation of new evidence.

old model no longer fit w. accumulation of new info from techno. development

Reinterpreting Sociopolitical Development in Iron Age Europe

Many aspects of Continental and Insular Iron Age culture are currently being reconsidered, although examples discussed in this chapter are limited to just a few aspects having to do with political development, authority, and rulership: *oppida*, or town-like settlements found in Britain, France, Spain, Portugal, Germany, Belgium, Hungary, Poland, and Slovakia, that often have been described as the aristocratic "seats" or "administrative centers" of powerful centralizing rulers with attached populations, and hillforts, typically high-elevation enclosures, often viewed as a resident central elite's defended military garrison. This is further complicated by the fact that some oppida are walled, high-elevation sites, while others are not, and that many other types of non-urban hilltop sites with a variety of characteristics were all lumped together and called hillforts. Only recently has anyone suggested that these places may have had many different functions.

Hillforts may be the most extensively re-evaluated site type of the Iron Age. These geographically prominent, enclosed sites often (but not always) contain the remains of small non-residential structures, pits filled with animal bones, and pits with small amounts of grain. They are not, like oppida, ever characterized by a town-like infilling of houses. A description typical from the 1970s until recently states that "one characteristic of developed hillforts is that the community, under some form of coercive power, invested part of its surplus in the provision and maintenance of defensive works" (Cunliffe 1976:138). Also theorized as centers in redistributive chiefdoms (Cunliffe 1984a, Gent and Dean 1986), they were seen as places "with political legitimacy and a center of regional authority"—the military strongholds of rulers (Cunliffe 1983, 1984b). Originally conceptualized in the New Archaeology era, this model appears in even recent editions of authoritative works on the period (Cunliffe 1997, 2005). While calling on us to dispose of "the worst excess of the old New Archaeology" (Cunliffe 1995:1060) the same ideas continue to be repeated even as authors acknowledge critique and reinterpretations (e.g. Cunliffe 2005:390).

What were hillforts? Central places of warrior-elite authority or centers of something else? Archaeological data in support of the aristocratic seat model are difficult to find, and the texts that the model is supposedly derived from also provide very little support. Reinterpretations have come partly from a new generation but also from those who published more traditional views in the 1970s (Collis 1976, 1984b, Haselgrove 1976, 1982, Hill and Cumberpatch 1995). Collis argues that simple differences in terminology make huge differences in our assumptions and how they become calcified (Collis 1994, 1997b): rubbish pit vs. pit containing animal bones defensive fortification vs. socially imposed boundary or warrior grave vs. burial with weapons. Since this perspective has been introduced, entirely new types of sites and features have been recognized, as well as the probability that the spatial organization and placement of features within ordinary farming settlements and individual houses have cosmological significance (Bradley 2003, 2005, Fulford 2001, Oswald 1997).

The landscapes around British hillforts are filled with highly visible features from pre-Iron Age societies, clearly important to the builders. Some were religious, others more mundane. They may provide not only insight into what occurred at the sites but who built them and why. In some regions, pre-hillfort times saw the construction of large-scale earthen boundaries and other monumental intensification features for agriculture—certainly with communal labor. Such agricultural efforts might possibly have caused a

> changing in [the] ways different communities interacted with one another, which may have resulted in the establishment of new senses of community identity. The potential for co-operation as well as conflict and competition that arose as a result probably helped to establish the conditions that made the construction of the early hillforts possible (Wigley 2002b:4–5, 2002c).

This suggests that early hillforts could have been built by ordinary people for community use rather than, as previously hypothesized, through elite command during an episode of major cultural change.

The non-military, non-administrative nature of many such places is supported by several studies using magnetometry, which indicate that early Iron Age hillfort walls often correspond directly to linear ditch features built on hilltops in the Late Bronze Age, generally accepted as being religious or ritual in nature and not in any way defensive (Bowden et al. 2005). Iron Age builders could have made their later additions more easily by destroying these ritual features, cutting or transecting them with "ramparts," but instead chose to parallel and incorporate them, apparently still finding significance in them (Bowden et al. 2005). Even later, when massive enclosure walls with impressive gates were built, these features originally were only constructed on the east-facing sides—toward the sunrise—with insignificant efforts in other directions. Wall configurations were only extended during the last part of the Iron Age, enlarging the enclosures, perhaps when the meaning of the ideas represented by early linear features was forgotten (Bowden et al. 2005), or as redoubts during a few decades in the first century BC when indigenous Britons were fighting invading Romans.

There is also no evidence in Britain that elites lived in them. Before remote sensing clarified the construction sequences, this was usually explained with the idea that the sites acquired a sacred function later, rather than earlier, and that resident paramount chiefs may have moved away from them to elite estates, forming a disembedded hierarchy away from centers (Cunliffe 1976:140). Even recent papers have contradictorily emphasized that while their "small number and their spacing in the region" indicates they *must* be chieftain's administrative hubs, "the lack of high status artifacts suggests that status was probably demonstrated by other means such as having larger herds of cattle or sheep or more wives" (Hutt et al. 2006)—an assumption based on negative evidence and unfounded suppositions about gender and marriage.

Other evidence suggests that hillforts began as central places, but for different types of community activities. At Oldbury, Danebury, and others, the presence of hundreds of pits containing animal remains are found, as well as small pits where grain was deposited. In older models, with the assumption that hillforts were chiefly garrisons, the small pits were interpreted as rubbish produced by soldiers who buried the remains of meals. This was seen primarily as an indicator of the herding economy, linking hillfort locales with water availability. Pits with grain were interpreted as storage pit for "seed corn" controlled by elites (Cunliffe 1976, 1984, 1997:196, Wilson 1992).

In recent years this has been questioned, due to the ubiquity of these small pits at investigated sites, which, however, could contain only a fraction of what should have been consumed or planted over many centuries of use. Many researchers (Fitzpatrick 1997, Grant 1984, 1989, Hill 1995b, 1996, McOmish 1996, Poole 1995, Smith 2001, Wilson 1999) now hypothesize that these deposits represented offerings within the newly understood ritual meaning of the hilltop sites, perhaps the result of repeated visits over a long time. Unusual and repeated combinations of animals called

offerings in pits

structured depositions—dog and horse, or unusual animals, such as ravens—have been cited as evidence for a ritual function, as none were Iron Age food animals. While some pits contain cattle bones, most of these appear elsewhere, especially in the ditches, as huge accumulations of butchered and processed bone, deposited en masse, indicating feasting or public meals (McOmish 1996). Grain deposits are too small to represent either storage or seed corn and often are accompanied by ceramics or carved chalk figures and shapes. These are now almost universally interpreted as ritual deposits for fertility or to appease chthonic deities (van der Veen and Jones 2006, Williams 2003), and even long-time advocates of "pits as refuse" have acknowledged their probable ritual origins (Cunliffe 1995, 2005, Wilson 1999).

In Britain, many newly investigated small, low-elevation enclosures, in areas both with hillforts and those lacking them altogether, contain features and structures nearly identical with those at large, prominent, high-elevation sites like Danebury. This blurs the supposed function of such enclosures and suggests some kind of continuum of sites with similar foci but different contexts (Wigley 2002a). Further work is needed to determine if all hillforts were intended for ceremonial or community uses, if some were indeed military, or if their purpose changed through time.

Spain's Celtiberian Pre-Roman hilltop enclosures are also being reconsidered, since traditionally, many types of high-elevation sites have been categorically lumped together. Among them are *castros,* small groups of houses enclosed by walls, in which no class or status differences can be detected architecturally or in mortuary treatment, and which are often simply labeled "peasant villages." Some are hilltop *turres* or towers, and even densely populated high-elevation *oppida* towns are sometimes classified in the same way. In one case, despite claims that "no cases of houses built outside the defensive walls" have ever been documented at a hillfort (Burillo Mozota 2005:432), "the internal organization was quite different from the Celtiberian urban model" (Lorrio and Ruiz Zapatero 2004, Ruiz Zapatero and Álvarez-Sanchís 2002), since religious statuary and altars are apparent within while the habitations lie outside the walls (Lorrio and Ruiz Zapatero 2004, Ruiz Zapatero and Álvarez-Sanchís 1999). Dissimilar and diverse, some are perhaps military and defensive, others, ritual sites that created a focal point for disparate interacting communities (Fernández-Posse and Sánchez-Palencia Ramos 1998, Parcero Oubiña 2003, Parcero Oubiña and Fernández 2004).

The towns are also controversial. For Britain and Continental Europe, many (Collis 1995a, 1995b, Hamilton and Manley 2001, Harding 2001, 2004, 2006, Haselgrove 1995, Köhler 1995, Ralston 1992, Woolf 1993, Zapatero and Alvarez-Sanchís 1995) have seriously called into question whether *oppida*, like hillforts, form a "class" of settlement at all. Previously, they were interpreted as fairly uniform regional urban administrative hubs of centralized political hierarchies (Collis 1984b, Cunliffe 1976, 1983), located defensively in high places with walls. They were typically also seen as centers of craft production and economic activity controlled by elites (Alvarez-Sanchís 2005, Bott et al. 1994, Wells 1993). Today it is clear that they were not uniform, either in form or function—some are decidedly less urban than once thought (Haselgrove 1995), or occupied very briefly, or they developed for different reasons, were used for different purposes, and fluoresced at different times. They differ not only from region to region but also within any given area.

Oppida in Spain were long conceptualized as the seats of Celtiberian "aristocrats" who had centralized, authoritarian power over a countryside they "owned," populated by obedient and tightly constrained peasants (Burillo Mozota 2005), a perception that certainly is constructed from medieval models and then imposed anachronistically upon the past—a highly critiqued practice. Upon examination, residential structures inside Iberian *oppida* have little evidence to infer any social hierarchy, especially in early periods (Almagro-Gorbea 1995:175). Mortuary data exhibit minimal or no social differentiation, without status markers of unusual power or proxies of political authority (Burillo Mozota 1993:226).

Garcia Moreno argues that Roman authors, as with Gaul and Germany, described a warlord-warband structure in the third century BC that is "Celtic" in nature, meaning that there were reciprocal relations between leader and follower, with artificially flattened social differentiation, even drawing parallels between groups in Iberia and those coming from Denmark in the second century BC: the Cimbri and Teutones who waged war against the Romans at that time (Garcia Moreno 2006:378). Classical authors also indicate that the Celtiberian sociopolitical ethos reflects a heterarchic organization: even in the latest parts of the Iron Age, when the status of warrior-elites was most fully expressed, *oppida* (and smaller settlements) were organized through the institutions of a public assembly, councils of elders and/or nobles, and an elaborate ritual sector (Lorrio and Ruiz Zapatero 2004:210). For Spain, there is also textual evidence that the social structures of these urban sites included the practice of *hospitium*, or ritual acceptance of strangers into a community (González-Ruibal 2006, Sanchez-Moreno 2001), similar to Germanic "guest-rights"; clientship, in which those of higher standing engaged in relationships of mutual obligations with those socially beneath them, and *devotio*, a concept already mentioned in terms of Scandinavia: the idea that sacred bonds between warlord and warrior necessitated that the soldier would die on the lord's behalf (Salinas 2001). In Scandinavia, this also meant that the warlord agreed to die with his men; whether Iberian *devotio* differed is not clear.

Mortuary elaboration indicates that between 500 BC and 200 BC (Lorrio 1997, Lorrio and Ruiz Zapatero 2004), the warrior class developed internal stratification, but recent work has identified the existence of several elite social categories in addition to "warrior" within some oppida, displaying difference according to class, gender, and perhaps occupation (Zapatero and Alvarez-Sanchis 1995). Thus, while in the later Iron Age fighting men may have formed an important conduit of power with a set of privileges and priorities, they do not appear to have had absolute power as envisioned in earlier models. This is not inconsistent with evidence from Scandinavia, Gaul, and Britain. The classical, and thus fairly late, description of these heterarchic institutions and corporate concepts of obligation between leaders and followers point to a very different, decentralized political scenario, even in a society with internal social class differentiation.

While Anglophone authors have commented on the now uncertain roles of both insular and continental *oppida* and hillforts (e.g. Woolf 1993), central Europe has seen little published on this. While it is acknowledged that occupation and "fortifications" were present from the Neolithic and Bronze Age on such hilltops, they are uniformly described as defensive in nature, without reference to possible shifting functions through time. Long-term, changing, developing trajectories are often presented as if the endpoint was an eternal state. A number of prominent high-elevation, walled sites in this region such as Mont Beuvray, Heuneburg, Manching, and others were also long described as "princely seats" through implicit use of the centralized hierarchy model. Within these town-like walled sites are the remains of structures and productive activities but not much resembling palaces or elite residences. Cumberpatch (1995) argues that data from central and eastern European *oppida* indicate that economic activities do not represent any real change from pre-*oppida* times, in either the scale or organization of crafts production, debunking the idea of purposeful elite concentration of such activities for reasons of "control." Similarly, evidence from the Netherlands (van den Broeke 1995) also contradicts assertions of a centralized elite-controlled salt trade, since the actual scale and organization of production and distribution is small and decentralized. While there is also little or no evidence that elites lived in *oppida*, much points to their occupation of rural estates (Brunaux and Méniel 1997, Büchsenschütz 1995, Büchsenschütz and Richard 1996, Crumley 1995, Menez 1997). Recent work in France (Brunaux and Méniel 1997, Menez 1997) has shown that single farms located out in the countryside were sometimes Pre-Roman elite residences, possibly of a religious nature, that in some cases continued as elite villas under the Gallo-Roman system.

On a broader level, the role or use of *oppida* as an important axis along which Celts were defined in relation to Germans, once a given, is also no longer clear: Wells (2001) notes that when Caesar encountered people east of the Rhine, whom he called Germani, he described them as lacking *oppida* and as more rural and pastoral in nature and less politically and socially complex than the Gauls. But in doing so, Caesar may have given distinctions to people who were in fact largely undifferentiated, as he also (*De Bello Gallico* IV:XIX, McDevitt 2005) states that he burned the *oppida* of the Suebians, a powerful Germanic group whose territory lay close to Gaul. Wells (2001:100–101) is not the only scholar to propose that it was Roman disruption in the west that brought about a domino-like collapse of possible eastern *oppida*, the abandonment of most cereal farming, and the appearance of a less complex political formation. Romans, who encountered the further Germani only after the collapse of their centers, may have misinterpreted what they observed.

Decentralized power in the central European Iron Age is also seen in expressions of elite mortuary ritual in the landscape around these sites, illuminating changing social ideologies, such as the contrast between that Hallstatt Iron Age and the later La Tène Iron Age. A network-style Bronze Age ideology was initially maintained by the transition-spanning Hallstatt culture, characterized by tumulus cemeteries, where each mound contains a single, notably wealthy elite burial, while in the later La Tène period these rich and marked trappings were replaced by a more egalitarian material culture, typical of Late Iron Age elite. La Tène mounds feature a central primary burial, but without the extravagant wealth, and closely surrounded by a large group of male and female individuals in secondary burials. This could reflect a shift from an individual-focused network to a more corporate-group-focused mode. Elite burials are, unless created during times of siege (Arnold 2002), always situated at significant distances outside of towns, for example at the Heuneburg *oppida,* a half kilometer away, with what may have been the elite residence burned and buried beneath the burial mound.

Also developing in the La Tène period were *Viereckschanzen*: rectangular ritual enclosures (Murray 1996) where offerings were made and feasting activities took place in the Late Iron Age, as at British hillforts. *Viereckschanzen* were increasing in use as monumental individual burial mounds were disappearing (Arnold 2002:132). Arnold (2002:133) discusses this fading of early, richly furnished single burial mounds as a change in the manipulation of the dead by the living, away from the purpose of aggrandizing the living. Arnold (2002) notes that both types of structures represent accumulations of social capital of some kind—she believes political, while Knüsel (2002) argues that some burials, like Vix, represent a religious leader within a heterarchy. The debate over the meaning of such evidence is echoed in the conflicting interpretations of non-monumental burials: the ubiquity of weapons found in La Tène cemeteries have prompted many archaeologists to believe in a warrior elite, perhaps even a warrior caste (Nash 1984), while Collis (1994:33) states the opposite, that the presence of weapons in a large percentage of the graves shows that weapons were spread more equitably through a much more egalitarian society and were probably possessed by ordinary farmers who served as fighters in wartime, in addition to some full-time, high-status warriors (Collis 1994:33).

Such data cross gender lines as does evidence for political leaders. Irish texts usually assigned an "Iron Age" origin display linguistic categories not only for woman-doctor and woman-bard but also woman-warrior (Bitel 1998:37). Some have interpreted the references to such women, and those in other European epics and sagas, simply as invented foils against which "good women" could be compared, but that is no longer universally believed. Adomnán was a seventh century Irish abbot whose several preserved texts date from between AD 690 and 700. In a land that only began to be slowly Christianized in the mid-fifth century, where indigenous practices of many kinds persisted, he claimed to have liberated women from the "pagan" tradition of "their husbands flogging them on to battle," "babes on one arm, provisions and pikes on the other" (Bitel 1998:84, Meyer 1905:2). In early Anglo-Saxon contexts, a number of non-elite female weapon graves have been identified through DNA analysis (Russell 2005). Some simply call these examples of male artifacts re-purposed as female symbols (Williams 2007) while others see them as indicating, as with elite female chariot graves, undifferentiated defense of the community as per the Roman records, or even pointing to alternative genders.

Corporate organization does not necessarily indicate an actual disappearance of elites with significant powers but represents the possibility that they purposefully disguise their power by embracing populism. Artificial (contrived) flattening (de-hierarchization) of authority has often been a means for elites to avoid overthrow or rejection and hold on to power when society moves toward new ideologies in which leaders are no longer allowed the same privileges, and ritual and civic gatherings become community rather than elite-focused events. Elites of the preceding Bronze Age, whose traditions were carried forward into the early Hallstatt Iron Age, are usually interpreted as more autocratic and authoritarian. In the transition to the later Iron Age, all such markers evaporated. In historic and contemporary societies where public opinion turns against them, elites frequently accede to a corporate mode of power as part of a strategy to preserve their power. As noted by Lukes (1974), the de-emphasis on aggrandizement is a different kind of manipulation, but still a manipulation. Rochefort and Cobb (1993) point out that when agendas defined as important evaporate, so does the power of elites, who must redefine themselves or wind up irrelevant, disempowered, or dead.

There are no archaeologists who question whether an Iron Age warrior elite existed. They did. Nor does anyone dispute that they had power. What must be questioned is the type of authority they held in their respective societies and who else held power. A second branch clearly constituted religious specialists, such as druids, whom the Romans identified as the source of British military resistance, the servants of Germanic deities like Odin, Thor, and Frey who presided over legal, political, and religious events, but Celticists have also argued for a separate shamanic tradition among the Celts (Aldhouse-Green 2001, Aldhouse-Green and Aldhouse-Green 2005, Green 1998), and Scandinavian finds of high-status women's graves with metal staffs, narcotic plants, and unusual symbolic items (Price 2004) support saga descriptions of the female shamanic tradition of *seidr* (Borovsky 1999, McKinnell 2000, Quinn 1998, Wanner 2007); there are also archaeological and textual indicators of male and transgendered shamans (Blain and Wallis 2000, Grambo 1989, Price 2004, Solli 1997).

The third facet of heterarchic power were ordinary people, "the masses" described by Caesar, as determined by each society, although we are not sure who was permitted to vote in the assembly—property owners, people of a certain class? Free men? Men and women? In the later Scandinavian Iron Age, women, especially older women past child bearing, spoke authoritatively in the civic assembly, such as Aud the Deep-Minded, who appears in many Icelandic records and was certainly a real woman: one of the early ninth century settlers whose father was the Norwegian ruler of the Viking Hebrides colony. It is uncertain if similar eligibility was found in earlier insular or continental contexts as the texts are silent, but as women, according to Tacitus, appear to have sometimes soldiered in British armies, they might possibly have had a vote in the assembly—or not. In any case, there is no reason to presume that even late in the Iron Age any single institution was automatically accorded central authority over others, although they may well have been seeking it.

Pre-Roman Italy

Finally, we turn to Pre-Roman Italy, a context not usually considered by those interested in Celts, Britons, and Germans. While many classicists might regard the ethnohistoric, philological, and archaeological information about the Italian polities of the seventh and sixth centuries BC to be meager, to those dealing with the

Early Iron Age elsewhere in Europe, these data seem substantial, even given the caveat that some important texts were written by later Roman authors and must not be taken literally in every detail. Long before the Roman Republic or Empire was ever imagined, these Iron Age polities were organized into several alliance-based political leagues, one in Campania, one in the Po Valley, and one in Etruria—the Etruscan League or *dodecapoli*—the last believed to have consisted of 12 "peoples." Since their organization may or may not have been anything like earlier or contemporary Greek "city-states," it is safer to de-couple them from this loaded term and simply say they were organized around towns, that may (or may not) have worked in cooperation to repel the early Romans who sought to conquer them.

Each town in the *dodecapoli* was autonomous but sometimes acted under the hegemony of one peer ruler who was elected as a paramount, chosen each year at an assembly of the twelve peoples that met annually at the *Fanum Voltumnae* (Cornell 1978:171), a civic-ceremonial gathering that was pointedly outside of any of their towns, on neutral, often hilltop or hillside grounds reserved for ritual and symbolic activities. Livy reported that it was at this gathering that the annually elected paramount ruler was chosen, and the phrase *zilath mexl rasnal* occurs in several Etruscan inscriptions and signifies the elected "president" of the league of twelve. Exactly what this person's powers were are uncertain, but he was elected and served only a short term. The *Fanum Voltumnae* and other similar rites are often referred to as "festivals," a term misleading to the uninitiated. They were not fairs or celebrations but serious events marked by ritual and political feasts and sacrifices.

Politically, the Etruscan league long puzzled many Romanists, although recent work has broken new ground. Some have argued that it controlled a "federal" army for mutual aid, while others point out that recorded requests for help by member cities were usually turned down and that "there is clear evidence that relations between the Etruscan cities were characterized by instability and political enmity throughout the historical period, a fact which has led many scholars to suppose that the league was a purely religious association" (Cornell 1978:170). This exact situation of course describes the well-accepted understanding of the Germanic "tribes" and the kingdoms or chiefdoms of the Gauls, Britons, and Germans, described by Tacitus, Julius Caesar, and others, as sometimes allied, sometimes at war, in fluid and ever-changing confederations.

Later, a Latin League was established, a confederation of peoples in the vicinity of Rome, purportedly for similar reasons—a mutual protection pact and defense against hostile adjoining communities. Alba Longa, an important town, initially led the league. Again, an annual religious and civic-ceremonial occasion, the *Feriae Latinae*, at which courts of law were also called, was held outside the city on the "Alban Mount," a hill where temples and shrines were located. Donahue (2003:430) notes that the Latins had a

> tendency to equate eating with political status...seen in the *Feriae Latinae*, a moveable feast in honor of Jupiter Latiaris...Representatives from the forty-seven member cities took part in the festival and sacrifices. Each member city received one bull, which was to be sacrificed in common. Additionally, each city brought different graded portions of food to

the common feast while receiving differential portions of meat from the sacrificial bull. Furthermore, the more powerful cities received larger portions of meat than lesser members. A city that had shrunk to political insignificance could be denied a portion altogether. Clearly, the *Feriae Latinae* featured both inclusion and hierarchical ordering, as it celebrated the political unity of the Latin League but also, through the careful controlling of food, the differences in rank among its members. (Donahue 2003:430).

Fentress and Guidi (1999:466) note that during this time in Latium, a wealthy warrior class was in evidence, identified through their graves and mortuary treatment, along with a separate priestly class, evident in extra-urban "sanctuaries...important, here, as evidence for the appearance of priests along with kings or aristocrats" indicating that there were different types of elites—a priestly group and a noble group at least—that held sway in non-intersecting geographic space, a heterarchic sharing of power across different kinds of elite institutions noted also by Cornell (2000:221–223). Fentress and Gouidi also note (1999:465) that despite the appearance of these classes, in the seventh and sixth centuries, there is a "general problem of the [lack of] self-representation of elites in the archaic Early States" that baffles many archaeologists working here. While this wouldn't surprise anyone working at Harappa or Teotihuacan, Fentress and Gouidi are among the few scholars who hypothesize that

> It is possible that the social strategy of these elites was, in the earlier phase of the proto-urban centres, a careful ideological masking of social differences. In a later phase, during the period in which it had consolidated its power, the adoption of an heroic ideology and its open display was the best way for the elite to represent itself, emphasizing strong political control and, especially, distance from the rest of the population (1999:465).

This evolved over the next few centuries, until in sixth and fifth centuries BC more elaborate, although not palatial, elite residences appeared, and while most competitive display was funneled not into personal aggrandizement but into sanctuary construction aimed at group legitimation, more self-promotion is apparent than in earlier times.

Thus a tradition of mutual protection alliances, which were mutable and changing, among a group of states or proto-states that were supposed to be peers, who also agreed upon a temporary paramount ruler, was the norm in Pre-Roman Italy. These peers met annually at extra-urban hilltop sites for activities that included religious rites, legal rulings, and presumably alliance-cementing ceremonialism and feasting. There was also an apparent concern with the suppression of the visible aspects of elite power, until such time as this aspect of the Iron Age social code could be challenged and overturned.

It is also true that these Italian polities may or may not have selectively adopted formulations of political power from the Greeks and Phoenicians with whom they had contact. This is an interesting topic, but it is not important to the issues investigated here; in line with what is known about how contact and even colonization impacts both indigenous and intruder societies at this time and in this context, theoretically and in light of new evidence, it is selective, uneven borrowing, usually of expedient material culture rather than deeply ingrained institutions (Burgers 2005, De Angelis 2003, Dietler 1996, 1997b, 1999, Fitzjohn 2007, Hall 2004, Kolb and

Speakman 2005, Leighton 2005). If we compare political organizations across all of Iron Age Europe, the similarities between the Italian and transalpine groups support the idea that the Italians retained many pre-contact elements. Many Europeans had direct contact with Greek and Phoenician peoples in the Iron Age, while others had indirect, negligible, or no interaction. Contact of any type is unlikely to have been responsible for political organization in Norway, yet the overarching political structures of the far north and Italy are demonstrably similar.

The Latin League eventually included the Romans, who dominated and then dissolved it in favor of kingship. In ethnohistoric tradition, the first four kings of the Roman region were "weak," while the last three, the Tarquins, who were Etruscans and thus foreigners, were autocratic, centralizing figures. Around 509 BC the Romans drove them out and replaced a hated monarchy with a republic—the toppling of a rulership tradition that originated under the earlier Iron Age social code, yet whose central figures had fallen victim to the "bitter arrow" and assumed creeping king-like powers. In Roman tradition, their betrayal of the Iron Age ideal of rulership was resented not only by sub-elites but by commoners as well. As were many others described in later European chronicles, these rulers were deposed or killed, replaced with something more ideologically akin to the ideal. This may be paralleled by the apparent casting down of Hallstatt elites and their replacement by later Iron Age elite (Avery 1986) of the more restrained and subtle corporate mode.

The purposeful promulgation of a "weak" ruler by people who had become outraged over the excesses of kings has been pointed out by generations of scholars. Over a century ago, Shumway noted that upon the overthrow of the Tarquin kings by Iron Age Latins, "The new constitution distributes the functions of the king. Its main changes (not all *immediately* introduced) are to make the central executive office weak, elective, held but a year, and shared by two Consuls. The judicial magistrate becomes the Praetor. The religious supremacy is bestowed on the *Pontifex* and, subject to him, the *Rex Sacrificulus*. The function of making up the roll of the Senate, citizens, and their property, was given to the *Censor*. Whatever functions the *comitia centuriata* may have had, it now was the legislative body" (Shumway 1902:102).

While Iron Age traditions persisted, the intended leveling mechanisms behind these arrangements were largely circumvented by the Roman conquest of Italy and the creation of the Republic, abrogating the autonomy of all other sovereign peoples in the region. Yet the Republic itself refers to these traditions by including elected offices, a balance between various powers in society, and a sense that elites should be public servants—another disguising of the fact that the former peers were now subjects. Another long-debated Roman structural component was that of the *gens*, which was a lineage or clan-like descent group whose leaders competed among themselves for power and prestige and also contended with the office of Dictator over the state's self-appointed powers, played out historically in later Roman times through senatorial infighting and battles with the state. In the Republican era, a "dictator" was a temporarily elected figure, who only served a term that lasted as long as any particular crisis, exactly like other Iron Age European groups. The office was then to be relinquished. This continued heterarchic structure and the masking of centralizing tendencies makes the Roman Republic a good example of a corporate state.

This system was in turn overthrown by an imperial venture, first by Julius Caesar, who declared himself "dictator for life" and was promptly killed by his own peers for being too "king-like." It was not until Gaius Octavius became Augustus Caesar that this pervasive Iron Age tradition was finally extinguished—almost. The Roman people still reserved the right to cast unacceptable leaders down the bloody Gemonian stairs into the Tiber. There were numerous occasions when elites below the emperor removed him with subtle or emphatically clear methods. While these acts may have been motivated by personal aspirations of would-be rulers, they were nearly always labeled, publicly, in terms of ending abuses of power and restoring a right order of rule. The Roman imperial sequence thus represents the endpoint of an extraordinar- ily long and drawn-out transition from corporate to network political structure—one of the longest, comparable to the extended transition seen in Scandinavia, which can be followed from around AD 1–1000, as rulers struggled (extremely carefully) against the corporate social code and non-rulers sought to maintain it (Thurston 2001, 2006, 2007a).

The social code and political format among the Pre-Roman Iron Age Italians (and those of the Republican period as well) is, upon close examination, remarkably like that of the groups they eventually "discovered" in central and northwestern Europe. For many decades, Romanist archaeologists noted this similar social code, described parts of it, and recently have theorized it as a political strategy, yet the inordinate focus on Imperial Rome has led to general lack of acknowledgment that the Italians, Gauls, Britons, Germans, and Nordic groups broadly shared many Iron Age tradi- tions, different in each region, changing at different rates and on different temporal scales but ideologically similar, certainly related through either a common origin, interaction, or both. Kristiansen (1998a, b, Kristiansen and Larsson 2006) has suggested that this pattern arose from an angry overthrow of autocracy and absolutism in the Late Bronze Age and earliest Iron Age, when peoples across Europe were in close communication, followed by the widespread establishment of rulership rooted in a "never again" mentality.

For understanding the record of the Gauls, Britons, and others, the initial, naive concepts developed by mid-twentieth century scholars to abstractly model and describe "power" do not seem helpful. Traditions of the far-removed medieval era or any ethnopoetic, literary ideals are closer but may also be misleading. A much closer and more cogent model—the Italians with their *Fanum Voltumnae* and the *Feriae Latinae*—could improve our conceptualization of clearly important places such as hillforts, *oppida*, extra-urban elite compounds, and other disputed types of places. Are there similarities between Italy and central and northern Europe, in that Iron Age civic-ceremonial rituals that took place at clearly demarcated, neutral, extra-urban, often hilltop locations, where annually, representatives of allied polities congregated and performed a series of related religious, political, legal, and social events? These included offerings and sacrifices that incorporated the symbolic use of animals, and rituals meant to invoke or represent the shifting power among the allied peoples, others to cement mutual protection agreements, some to propitiate the gods, capped by the selection of a paramount ruler or "high king." There is no record of how the animal bones from Italian politically and religiously symbolic sacrifices and subsequent feasts were discarded, but one might imagine they were disposed of in a deferential way; if they are ever found, perhaps they will parallel finds at Danebury and other Iron Age sites in Europe north of the Alps. We need not expect that the traditions of groups from Scandinavia to Britain to Italy reflected every aspect of each other's practices, but if an analog is to be found, this one is more direct than the medieval or modern eras.

Similarities between the Pre-Roman Italians and their counterparts to the west and north at least suggest that they shared a similar system. Europe is relatively small with many lines of communication along which ideas and shared traditions flowed. The Romans underwent a historically contingent process in which negotiation, power, and force were all used to move Roman organization away from the corporate end of the spectrum and toward the network side—a rough ride, since many powerful leaders of different types recognized and opposed such a shift. To simplify this history a great deal, because of the chaos that followed Julius Caesar's assassination, his great-nephew and adopted heir Octavian was able to parlay his own skill and Caesar's legacy into the establishment of a centralized imperial state, although many vestigial elements of the corporate state remained.

Thus, when the Romans ventured outside of Italy only to find barbarians whose "democracy" many of them so admired, they were really meeting themselves, a few generations removed. Because of the differences in their historically situated trajectories, the Romans had changed a great deal, while the peoples to the north had not experienced so much alteration of their political systems. In the rest of Europe, other rulers hadn't yet managed to pull off similar shifts, not because the tendency was not there but because their histories were different.

One older perspective on the meeting between Romans and other Europeans is the now highly critiqued concept of "Romanization"—an antiquated perspective from the nineteenth century that among Classicists has been questioned for decades (Storey 1999, Woolf 1997). This is the belief that all things Roman were desired and emulated by "barbarian" people who welcomed Roman culture into every aspect of their lives as a great improvement over their own estate. An undivided focus of scholars on the admittedly fascinating subject of Rome effectively kept this paradigm alive for a long time.

Classicists were not the only parties promoting the now-abandoned Romanization concept. For example, Cunliffe (1997:231) states that the Gallic, British, and Germanic tradition of rule by the assembly and the rejection of leaders who seized power inappropriately was an imitation of the Roman Republic, only recently "learned" from the invaders. This is inexplicable: if we used textual bases alone, Tacitus explicitly identifies the assembly as a tradition among "tribes" just coming into contact with Rome and those with little or no contact, and Caesar, in his discussion of Vercingetorix's election to paramount leader by the assembly at Bibracte, refers to it as a native institution. Furthermore, the archaeological and linguistic evidence for the Germanic social code, which includes the assembly institution, can be seen operating in the far northern parts of Scandinavia at an early date, when contact with Rome was negligible (Hedeager 1992)—certainly with an impact, but not one that included reshaping the entire society in emulation of Rome. Even as late as the Viking Age, the indigenous *ting* or assembly, and the weak powers of Scandinavian rulers, was described by Frankish, English, and German missionaries. Wickham (1992:240) notes that "It may be that the conscious desire to keep political leaders weak has parallels elsewhere in Europe; both the continental Saxons before the Frankish conquest, as described in the *vita Lebuini*, and the late tenth-century Slav confederation of the Liutizi seem to have developed structures that kept individuals from accumulating too much power. . ."

In another unusual reading of Caesar, Cunliffe states that in the above cases of Oregtorix and Celtillus, the actions of the elected judges in trying to prevent rulers from seizing kingly power was proof that the Gauls had *a long tradition of kings*, only recently replaced by "elected officials"—these groups being more "socially evolved" through contact with Rome. He asserts that "The incident is informative in that it shows that among certain tribes government by elected magistrates had replaced kingship" (1997:232) and then goes on to say that the "new system" had just gotten underway and was still fragile, as an explanation of why the rules against kingship were so strong, again asserting that these changes were inspired by the Roman example and that, elsewhere in Gaul, kings "still" were the norm. Akin perhaps to the "powerful Harappan kings" inferred only through finds of standardized weights, such conditions are not described by Caesar or any Roman author, and found nowhere in the archaeological record as we understand it today.

Caesar reserves the term "king" for only a couple of the many figures in his accounts of the Gallic wars, such as Ariovistus, a Germanic leader who invaded Gaulish lands and exercised detested autocratic powers that caused the afflicted Gauls to plead for Caesar's help by stating how unusual and uncustomary such power was among them (*De Bello Gallico* I:XXXI). Later, when Ariovistus argued with Caesar about these powers, he says it was the Romans who styled him "king" and now they had to live with it. Caesar later describes another, Commius, who he himself created king (dbg II:XXI). The purposeful manipulation of Iron Age corporate rulers by designating them as "kings" in order to foment tension among barbarians is a well-known Roman strategy discussed by both historians and archaeologists (García Quintela 2005:551–552), and the Romans, who knew perfectly well that the transalpine European social code necessitated the removal of such power hoarders, frequently went to the extent of suggesting to indigenous people that it was wise to eliminate the over-ambitious leaders, e.g.:

> Viriatus, who led a Lusitanian coalition, was killed in an act of treachery by his own people at the instigation of the Romans, and the coalition of the *Helvetii*, as well as the coalitions led by Cassivellaunus in Britain, and by Vercingetorix in Gaul, equally fell before Caesar. Yet the Romans themselves knew how to promote these chieftains when they fell in line with their plans. This was the case with Deyotarus in Galaica and Cogidumnus in Britain, who, in the garb of the Roman institutional figure of the *rex amicus*, had great local and internal power, providing they accepted the policies established by their Roman masters (García Quintela 2005:552).

It is well understood that while scholars make references to

> ...kings in the Celtic world, these had little to do with the social, institutional, and political image of European monarchs from the mediaeval period to the present day, or even with the models offered by Hellenistic royalty or the Roman emperors... They were characterised by the contrast they presented between their limited effective power and the strength of the ideology at their disposal. Their capacity for command was derived from their efficiency as redistributors of resources that were often obtained by force, as above all they were warrior chiefs crowned for their successes. Thus, it is not surprising to see the presence of numerous kings, each of them ruling over a very small territory (García Quintela 2005:518).

It has been long noted by numerous scholars that Roman terms applied to indigenous people in Europe cannot be accepted *verbatim* (Dunham 1998), nor is the uncritical use of Roman assessments by modern scholars good practice when we know that the Romans often used various terms for rulers, possibly indiscriminately. Some have noted that "Britain was ruled by a number of independent leaders, called alternatively 'kings,' 'princes,' 'chiefs,' 'judges' (reges, tyranni, principes, duces patriae, judices)" (Morris 1957:3). Yet it may not be so simple. It may be that these were careless Roman errors, or it may be quite correct—that such differing terms were an attempt to differentiate the many types of authority figures, with somewhat different powers, that existed across Europe—some judicial, some political, and some sacred in nature.

The Romans were not always so obtuse that they did not recognize both difference and similarity, and not surprisingly, also equated their *gens* with the ethnic groups observed among the Gauls and Germans, e.g. Helvetii, Cherusci, Aedui, and hundreds more, usually labeled "tribes" in English translation. Within themselves, leadership of these groups were the focus of prestige and contests of power, and competition between them was a matter of honor—not unlike in Rome, where similar groups had eventually resulted in the Roman naming convention of *tria nomina*, or three names: *praenomen* (given name), *nomen gentilicium* (after the *gens*), and *cognomen* (lineage within the *gens*), and leading families within these structures came to dominate the senate.

In conclusion, did more authoritarian rulers precede what I characterize as later Iron Age corporate elites? Yes, across many parts of Iron Age Europe, a group of Late Bronze Age and sometimes Early Iron Age elites controlled important aspects of society, reflected in "highly visible, self-referential mortuary landscapes [that] reinforce the impression of extremely formalized ritual practices controlled by them" (Arnold 2002:132). Did such systems undergo significant reordering, in varying ways, during the transition from the Bronze Age into the Iron Age? Clearly; in Italy perhaps twice, as an initially corporate system of earlier times had to be restored after a period of kingship by the establishment of the Roman Republic, supposedly around 509 BC. In central Europe this may have occurred later, perhaps witnessed in the burning of Hallstatt period hillforts in the sixth century BC and their final abandonment, e.g. at the Heuneburg and Mount Lassois in the mid-fifth century, a period of violent upheaval in evidence even at small chiefly compounds (Jope 1997). While later re-occupied, a substantive break in the use and meaning of such sites in Britain occurred around the same time (Avery 1986). In Scandinavia, ordinary people saw much continuity in the transition to the Iron Age; significant and archaeologically visible is the overturning of earlier elite social, political, and religious organization around 500 BC, followed by several centuries in which any upper sociopolitical class was virtually invisible. Out of this a new kind of elite eventually emerged, less aggrandizing, less centralized, and embedded in a heterarchic system. In all cases, these transitions, gradual or punctuated, occurred long before the Roman Republic made contact with transalpine or northern Europe.

Sources and Consequences of Contention

So, we have new data pointing to new interpretations. What's the big deal? Such critiques often assign blame to individual archaeologists who staked their careers on earlier ideas, such as "Pleistocene overkill" or "vacant ceremonial centers," but this is not always the case; rather, the causes for the apparent inertia embody the complex links between the Iron Age, modern struggles to understand both regional and European identities, and the connections that non-archaeologists have with their past.

Hints of these issues emerge upon examination of the counter-critiques, especially the use of medieval models, not only because they are ill-supported by the evidence (Hill 1989, Poole 1995) but because of their assumptions that the long Roman interlude in most of Europe had no impact, and that society would simply have "reverted" to ancient ways (Hill 1989), producing a long continuum without breaks. Few would argue that Mesoamericans would have returned to fifteenth century Maya, Tarascan, or Aztec-like ways after Spain lost control of the region in 1821, or try to model late prehistory on post-colonial society. Furthermore, the Late Iron Age, which is the subject of Roman texts, is often reconstructed as identical to the Early Iron Age, yet the data discussed above indicate that while there were some long-term continuities, society was changing in numerous ways.

Some suggest that the desire to use a medieval model for the Iron Age lies in a corresponding desire to create a familiar, non-threatening Iron Age that can be reconstructed at experimental farms for the pleasure of school children and tourists (James 1998). Hill states that not only the public but archaeologists themselves may be guilty of seeking personal genealogy in archaeology—ancestors who are rational and understandable—like us (Hill 1989). Hill has lamented this fact: using theoretically informed archaeology, we have a contemporary understanding of the prehistoric European Neolithic and Bronze Ages with which to explore monumentality, elaborate excarnation rites, rituals of seasonality, gender, and age related to a distinct cosmological order. On the other hand—fast forward just a couple of centuries, add a few ethnohistoric bits and pieces, and the descendants of the same people have been replaced by your local suburban neighbors dressed in suitable primitive attire (Fig. 8.5).

Fig. 8.5 Rendition of a "Celt" for popular consumption at the "award-winning educational website" http://celts.mrdonn.org/

If those who see analogs of the medieval in Iron Age data have come under fire, so have those who attempt to match archaeological finds across Europe with the culture described in the Romano-Gallic record and insular ethnopoetics such as the Ulster Cycle (Hill 1989, James 1998). Some aspects of these textual records can provide clues to help interpret empirical materiality, or as hypotheticals against which to test the data. The Scandinavians have excelled in this area, neither trusting or discarding sagas and ethnohistories, but with historians, linguists, and archaeologists working closely together, carefully sieving all evidence for an approximation of reality (Andersson 2003, Andrén 1989, Brink 2002a, b, Brzandt et al. 2002, Winkler 2006). Elsewhere in Europe, archaeologists have been accused of simply assuming their own regional texts, recorded by Celtic-speaking Christians of a later era, are accurate, using them uncritically as a model for the La Tène Iron Age, assuming that groups mentioned by the Romans are identifiable through stylistic traits found earlier in parts of Europe (James 1999).

Some take this further back, and claim Celticity for the "warrior-elite" culture of the Hallstatt period, also based on Roman and Greek descriptions of the social and political organization of the *Keltoi*. In opposition, others point out that material culture termed the "Celtic" style, archaeologically, is in fact dissimilar over large regions (James 1998, Parzinger 1995), that motifs associated with La Tène Celts are shared by Germanic groups of the same era, which have never been considered "Celtic" (Hulthén 1991). Dietler (1997a, b), in his summary of Mediterranean France, noted that this region, like many others, is recognizably neither "Hallstatt" nor "La Tène" during these respective eras and calls for a reexamination of material culture in light of new ideas on ethnicity. Many have now proposed that there are differences between people who share a group of related languages, people who share material culture, and people who self-identify as an ethnic group with an acknowledged shared history, origin, and traditions. Others have argued that ethnicity should be left aside, but a "Celtic" system of sociopolitical structure can be studied (Pittock 1999), indicating unities across large regions. The debate between critics and champions of pan-European Celticity has sometimes been bitter. One group suggests the other is biased by their own romantic relationship with a heroic past; in return they are accused of disclaiming a past "Celtic" unity due to their own modern resistance to the European Union or English colonialism in Ireland. Such suggestions have embroiled many archaeologists in a so-called Celtic debate (Bradley 2003, 2005, Champion 1987, Chapman 1993, Collis 1997, Hill 1989, 1993 1995, b, 1996, 1997, 1999, James 1998, 1999, Megaw 2005, Megaw and Megaw 1994, 1995a, b, Merriman 1987).

Retheorizing the Iron Age: Some Thoughts for the Future

Elias, in his 1972 article, complained about the manner in which sociologists were prone to model the past on the present, despite clear evidence of both subtle and radical shifts over time. This practice, found by some in the fragile idea of Celticity, is also clear in the opposite tendency of reading extreme differences between Gaul, German, Briton, or Iberian, purely based on historical regionality (Wells 1995, 1998). While the debate over the contentious topics of ethnicity and language will continue, few have looked at Iron Age Europe in a multiscalar, nested manner, in which polities lie in within territories, territories are nested within sub-regions, within regions, and macro-regions, that together constitute a continent-wide scale of phenomena, all differentiated by local histories but connected through their shared history of interaction or common origins and their organization into local and regional alliances, trading relationships, and belief systems. Woolf (1997) is among the few that have noted that "unity and diversity" characterize the Pre-Roman Iron Age, where broadly shared elements contrast with regional distinctiveness.

In this light, perhaps the most convincing evidence is not of a pan-European ethnicity but a shared ideology, a thing that is not tied to ethnicity and can easily transcend other socially defined and constituted categories. Ideologies, especially of the sociopolitical types discussed here, can link peoples who share some broadly similar threads but who differ in self-concept, language, and culture. Overarching similarities in political ideologies are also not necessarily identical in their local expression. Like the several forms of modern socialism or democracy, they can vary in detail and implementation from region to region. The possibility that *this* is what linked Iron Age Europeans, rather than ethnicity, is perhaps clarified through data from Italy, a productive case study of decentralized political organization.

Retheorizing exactly how Iron Age life was organized leads back to reconceptualizing "power." So far we have discussed different concepts of rulership, and power constituted as a shared responsibility or privilege. The significant agency of ordinary people that seems apparent in the ethnohistoric material has been noted, as well as those powers implicit in the leveling mechanisms imposed on rulers, which can be seen textually and archaeologically. What further can be said? Some have begun to theorize the non-elite as economically and politically autonomous within the context of a heterarchic political structure. The household was of course noted by Marx as the Germanic unit of production, an idea reiterated by neo-Marxists (Gilman 1995). One current interpretation involves the "house society" proposed by Lévi-Strauss (1987), which has been recently reinvigorated within anthropology and archaeology (Gillespie 2000, Joyce 2000). This idea has been used to reinterpret the independent household in Europe, embedded in a farm, as the unit of production and the main "building block" of Iron Age society (Blanco et al. 2003, González-Ruibal 2006:157, Hill 1995:51, Hingley 1995:187). As independent, freestanding units, these households, made up of related and unrelated people, may have been largely unregulated by elites and their concerns, which were focused on warfare, hunting, some types of ritual and trade, and other activities. Sastre (2002) conceptualized a segmentary agrarian Iron Age society, in which households manipulated social structures and practices in order to benefit themselves—completely leaving out the idea of social class, eliteness, and other traditional explanations for the origins, maintenance and elaboration of "power over." Remembering the sometime signifi-cant power of ordinary people, conceptualizing both social equality *and* inequality, and understanding that they both operate simultaneously in most societies will be an important focus of future work.

References

Adams, R.M. 1992. Ideologies: Unity and Diversity. In Demarest, A. and Conrad, G. (eds.), *Ideology and Precolumbian Civilization*, pp. 205–221. Seattle: University of Washington Press.

Aldhouse-Green, M. 2001. Cosmovision and metaphor: monsters and shamans in gallo-british cult expression. *European Journal of Archaeology* 4(2):203–232.

Aldhouse-Green, M.A., and Aldhouse-Green, S.A. 2005. *The Quest for the Shaman: Shape-Shifters, Sorcerers and Spirit Healers in Ancient Europe*. London: Thames & Hudson.

Allen, A. 2002. Power, subjectivity, and agency: Between arendt and foucault. *International Journal of Philosophical Studies* 10(2):131–149.

Almagro-Gorbea, M. 1995. From Hill Forts to Oppida in 'Celtic' Iberia. In Cunliffe, B. and Keay, S. (eds.), *Social Complexity and the Development of Towns in Iberia: From the Copper Age to the Second Century AD*, pp. 175–207. Oxford: Oxford University Press.

Álvarez-Sanchís, J.R. 2005. Oppida and celtic society in western Spain. *e-Keltoi* 6:255–285.

Andersson, H. 2003. The early town system and attempts at urbanization. Reflections provoked by a symposium volume. *Norwegian Archaeological Review* 36(1):81–84.

Andrén, A. 1989. State and towns in the middle ages. *Theory and Society* 18(5):585–609.

Andrén, A. 2000. Against war! Regional identity across a national border in late medieval and early modern Scandinavia. *International Journal of Historical Archaeology* 4(4):315–334.

Arendt, H. 1970. *On Violence*. San Diego: Harcourt Brace.

Armit, I. 1997. Architecture and the Household: A Response to Sharples and Parker Pearson. In Gwilt, A. and Haselgrove, C. (eds.), *Reconstructing Iron Age Societies*, pp. 266–269. Oxford: Oxbow Monographs.

Arnold, B. 1991. The Deposed Princess of Vix: The Need for an Engendered European Prehistory. In Walde, D. and Willows, N.D. (eds.), *The Archaeology of Gender: Proceedings of the 22nd Annual Chacmool Conference*, pp. 366–374. Calgary: University of Calgary.

Arnold, B. 1996. "Honorary males" Or women of substance? Gender, status and power in Iron Age Europe. *Journal of European Archaeology* 3(2):153–168.

Arnold, B. 2002. A landscape of ancestors: the space and place of death in Iron Age west-central Europe. *Archeological Papers of the American Anthropological Association* 11(1): 129–143.

Arwill-Nordbladh, E. 2003. A Reigning Queen or the Wife of a King – only? Gender Politics in the Scandinavian Viking Age. In Nelson, S.M. (eds.), *Ancient Queens: Archaeological Explorations*, pp. 19–40. Walnut Creek: Altamira.

Ashmore, W., and Knapp, A.B. 1999. *Archaeologies of Landscape: Contemporary Perspectives*. Massachusetts: Blackwell Publishers.

Avery, M. 1986. 'Stoning and fire' at hillfort entrances of southern Britain. *World Archaeology* 18(2):216–230.

Bachrach, P., and Baratz, M.S. 1970. *Power and Poverty: Theory and Practice*. New York: Oxford University Press.

Bagge, S. 1999. The structure of the political factions in the internal struggles of the Scandinavian countries during the High Middle Ages. *Scandinavian Journal of History* 24(3):299–320.

Bagge, S. 2005. Christianization and state formation in early Medieval Norway. *Scandinavian Journal of History* 30(2):107–134.

Balbus, I. 1971. Ruling elite theory vs. Marxist class analysis. *Monthly Review* 23(1):36–46.

Barber, S.B., and Joyce, A.A. 2006. When Is a House a Palace? Elite Residences in The Valley of Oaxaca. In Christie, J.J. and Sarro, P.J. (eds.), *Palaces and Power in the Americas. From Peru to the Northwest Coast*. Austin: University of Texas Press.

Barrett, J.C. 1994. *Fragments from Antiquity: An Archaeology of Social Life in Britain, 2900–1200 BC*. Oxford: Blackwell.

Beck, R.A.J., Bolender, D.J., Brown, J.A., and Earle, T.K. 2007. Eventful Archaeology: the place of space in structural transformation. *Current Anthropology* 48(6):833–860.

Bender, B. 1990. The Dynamics of Nonhierarchical Societies. In Upham, S. (ed.), *The Evolution of Political Systems. Sociopolitics in Small-Scale Sedentary Societies*, pp. 247–263. Cambridge: Cambridge University Press.

Benton, T. 1981. 'Objective' interests and the sociology of power. *Sociology* 15(2):161–184.

Bitel, L.M. 1998. *And of Women: Tales of Sex and Gender from Early Ireland*. Ithaca: Cornell University Press.

Blain, J., and Wallis, R.J. 2000. The 'ergi' seidman: Contestations of gender, shamanism and sexuality in northern religion past and present. *Journal of Contemporary Religion* 15:395–411.

Blanco, R., Mañana, P., and Ayán, X. 2003. Archaeology of Architecture: Theory, Methodology and Analysis from Landscape Archaeology. In Blanco, R. and Mañana, P. (eds.), *Archaeotecture: Archaeology of Architecture*, British Archaeological Reports, pp. 17–39. Oxford: International Series.

Blanton, R. 1998. Beyond Centralization. In Feinman, G.M. and Marcus, J. (eds.), *Archaic States*, pp. 135–172. Santa Fe: SAR Press. UNCORRECTED PROOF

Blanton, R., Feinman, G., Kowalewski, S., and Peregrine, P. 1996. A dual-processual theory for the evolution of Mesoamerican civilization. *Current Anthropology* 37(1):1–14.

Blau, P.M. 1968. The hierarchy of authority in organizations. *American Journal of Sociology* 73(4):453.

Borovsky, Z. 1999. Never in public: women and performance in Old Norse literature. *The Journal of American Folklore* 112(443):6–39.

Bott, R.D., Grosse, G., Wagner, F.E., Wagner, U., Gebhard, R., and Riederer, J. 1994. The oppidum of Manching: A center of Celtic culture in early Europe. *Naturwissenschaften* 81(12): 560–562.

Bottomore, T.B. 1966. *Elites and Society*. Harmonsworth: Penguin.

Bowden, M., Payne, A., and Winton, H. 2005. Oldbury Castle, Wiltshire: Reinterpreting a Great Iron Age Hill Fort. In Wilmott, T. (ed.), *Research News: Newsletter of the English Heritage Research Department*, pp. 6–9. Portsmouth: English Heritage.

Bradley, R. 2003. A life less ordinary: The ritualization of the domestic sphere in later prehistoric Europe. *Cambridge Archaeological Journal* 13(1):5–23.

Bradley, R. 2005. *Ritual and Domestic Life in Prehistoric Europe*. London: Routledge.

Braund, D. 1996. *Ruling Roman Britain: Kings, Queens, Governors and Emperors from Julius Caesar to Agricola*. London: Routledge.

Brink, S. 2002a. Slavery in Scandinavia, as Reflected in Names, Runes and Sagas. In Iversen, T. (eds.), *New Perspectives on Slavery*. Trondheim: Trondheim University Press.

Brink, S. 2002b. Nordic Language History and Archaeology. In Bandle, O. (ed.), *The Nordic Languages*. Berlin & New York: de Gruyter.

Brumfiel, E.M. 1983. Aztec state making: Ecology, structure, and the origin of the state. *American Anthropologist* 85(2):261–284.

Brumfiel, Elizabeth M., and Timothy K. Earle 1987a Specialization, Exchange, and Complex Societies: An Introduction. In Specialization, Exchange, and Complex Societies. E. M. Brumfiel and T. K. Earle, eds. Pp. 1–9. Cambridge: Cambridge University Press.

Brunaux, J.-L., and Méniel, P. 1997. *La residence aristocratique de montmartin (oise) du iii e au ii e s*. Av. J.-C. Maison des Sciences de l'Homme

Brzandt, K., Müller Wille, M., and Radtke, C. (eds.). 2002. *Haithabu und die frühe stadtentwicklung im nördlichen Europa (Hedeby and early town development in northern Europe)*. Neumünster: Wachholz Verlag.

Büchsenschütz, O. 1995. The Significance of Major Settlements in European Iron Age Society. In Arnold, B. and Gibson, D.B. (eds.), *Celtic Chiefdom, Celtic State*, pp. 53–63. Cambridge: Cambridge University Press.

Büchsenschütz, O., and Ralston, I.B.M. 1988. En realisant la buerre des Gaules. *Aquitania Supplement* 1:383–387.

Büchsenschütz, O. and Richard, H. (eds.). 1996. *Bibracte: L'environnement du Mont Beuvray*, Centre Archéologique Européen du Mont Beuvray, Glux-en-Glenne.

Burgers, G.J. 2005. Western Greeks in Their Regional Setting: Rethinking Early Greek-Indigenous Encounters in Southern Italy. In Tsetskhladze, G.R. (ed.), *Ancient West & East*, pp. 252–282. Leiden and Boston: Brill.

Burillo Mozota, F. 1993. Aproximación a la arqueología de los Celtíberos. In Almagro-Gorbea, M. and Ruiz Zapatero, G.R. (eds.), *Los Celtas: Hispania y Europa*, pp. 223–253. Madrid: Actas.

Burillo Mozota, F. 2005. Celtiberians: problems and debates. *e-Keltoi* 6:411–480.

Byock, J.L. 1988. *Medieval Iceland: Society, Sagas, and Power*. Berkeley: University of California Press.

Carey, E. 1924. *Cassius Dio, Historiae Romanae*. Cambridge: Harvard University Press.

Carmean, K., and Sabloff, J.A. 1996. Political decentralization in the Puuc region, Yucatán, Mexico. *Journal of Anthropological Research* 52(3):317–330.

Cederholm, M. 2007. *De värjde sin rätt: senmedeltida bondemotstånd i Skåne och Småland* (They Defended Their Rights: Late Medieval Peasant Resistence in Scania and Småland) Studia historica Lundensia No. 14. Lund : Historiska institutionen, Lunds Universitet.

Champion, T.C. 1987. The European Iron Age: assessing the state of the art. *Scottish Archaeological Review* 4:98–108.

Chapman, M.K. 1993. *The Celts: The Construction of a Myth*. London: Macmillan.

Charlton, T.H. 1969. Sociocultural implications of house types in the Teotihuacán valley, Mexico. *The Journal of the Society of Architectural Historians* 28(4):284–290.

Chase, A.F., and Chase, D.Z. 1996. More than kin and king: Centralized political organization among the late classic Maya. *Current Anthropology* 37(5):803–810.

Church, A.J., and Brodribb, W.J. 1877. *Tacitus, the Agricola and Germania*. London: Macmillan.

Cohen, S. 1977. The Earliest Scandinavian Towns. In Herlihy, D., Lopez, R.S., Miskimin, H.A. and Udovitch, A.L. (eds.), *The Medieval City*. New Haven: Yale University Press.

Collis, J. 1976. Town and Market in Iron Age Europe. In Cunliffe, B.W. and Rowley, T. (eds.), *Oppida: The Beginning of Urbanization in Barbarian Europe*, pp. 3–24. Oxford: BAR Supplementary Series.

Collis, J. 1977. *The Iron Age in Britain*. Sheffield: Department of Prehistory & Archaeology, University of Sheffield.

Collis, J. 1984a.*The European Iron Age*. New York: Schocken Books.

Collis, J. 1984b. *Oppida: Earliest Towns North of the Alps* Sheffield: University of Sheffield.

Collis, J. 1994. Reconstructing Iron Age Society. In Kristiansen, K. and Jensen, J. (eds.), *Europe in the First Millennium BC*, Sheffield Archaeological Monographs, pp. 31–39. Sheffield: J. R. Collis Publications.

Collis, J. 1995a. The First Towns. In Green, M. A. (ed.), *The Celtic World*, pp. 159–175. London & New York: Routledge.

Collis, J. 1995b. States Without Centers? The Middle La Tene Period in Temperate Europe. In Arnold, B. and Gibson, D.B. (eds.), *Celtic Chiefdom, Celtic state*, pp. 75–80. Cambridge: Cambridge University Press.

Collis, J. 1996. Celts and Politics. In Graves-Brown, P., Jones, S. and Gamble, C. (eds.), *Cultural Identity and Archaeology: The Construction of European Communities*, pp. 167–178. London:

Collis, J. 1997a Celtic myths. *Antiquity* 71(271):195–201.

Collis, J. 1997b. Dynamic, Descriptive and Dead-End Models: Views of an Ageing Revolutionary. In Gwilt, A. and Haselgrove, C. (eds.), *Reconstructing Iron Age Societies*, pp. 297–302. Oxford: Oxbow Monograph.

Comaroff, J., and Comaroff, J. 1986. Christianity and colonialism in South Africa. *American Ethnologist* 13(1):1–22.

Cornell, T. J. 1978. Principes of Tarquinia *The Journal of Roman Studies* 68: 167–173.

Cornell, T.J. 2000. City-States in Latium. In Hansen, M.H. (eds.), *A Comparative Study of Thirty City-State Cultures. An Investigation Conducted by the Copenhagen Polis Centre*, pp. 209–228. Copenhagen: The Royal Danish Academy of Sciences and Letters.

Costin, C. L. 1991 Specialization: Issues in Defining, Documenting, and Explaining the Organization of Production. In *Archaeological Method and Theory*, Volume 3, ed. by M. Schiffer, pp.1–56. Tucson: University of Arizona Press.

Costin, C. L. 1998 Concepts of Property and Access to Non-agricultural Resources in the Inka Empire. In *Property in the Economy*, edited by B. Hunt and A. Gilman, pp. 119–138. Monographs in Economic Anthropology No. 14. Lanham, MD: University Press of America.

Costin, C. L. 2001 Production and Exchange of Ceramics. In Empire and Domestic Economy by T. D' Altroy, C. Hastorf and Associates, pp. 203–242. New York: Kluwer Academic/Plenum Publishers.

Costin, C. L. and Earle, T. K. 1989. Status Distinction and Legitimation of Power as Reflected in Changing Patterns of Consumption in Late Prehispanic Peru *American Antiquity* 54 (4): 691–714.

Cowgill, G.L. 1975. On causes and consequences of ancient and modern population changes. *American Anthropologist* 77:505–525.

Cowgill, G.L. 1997. State and society at Teotihuacan, Mexico. *Annual Review of Anthropology* 26:129–161.

Crumley, C., and Marquardt, W.H. 1990. Landscape: A Unifying Concept in Regional Analysis. In Allen, K., Green, S., and Zubrow, E. (eds.), *Interpreting Space: Gis and Archaeology*, pp. 73–79. London: Taylor and Francis.

Crumley, C.L. 1994a. Historical Ecology: A Multidimensional Ecological Orientation. In Crumley, C. (ed.), *Historical Ecology: Cultural Knowledge and Changing Landscapes*, pp. 1–16. Santa Fe: School of American Research Press.

Crumley, C.L. 1994b. The Ecology of Conquest: Contrasting Agropastoral and Agricultural Societies' Adaptation to Climatic Change. In Crumley, C. (ed.), *Historical Ecology: Cultural Knowledge and Changing Landscapes*, pp. 183–201. Santa Fe: School of American Research Press.

Crumley, C.L. 1995. Building an Historical Ecology of Gaulish Polities. In Arnold, B. and Gibson, D.B. (eds.), *Celtic Chiefdom, Celtic State*, pp. 26–33. Cambridge: Cambridge University Press.

Cumberpatch, C.G. 1995. Production and Society in the Later Iron Age of Bohemia and Moravia. In Hill, J.D. and Cumberpatch, C.G. (eds.), *Different Iron Ages: Studies on the Iron Age in Temperate Europe*, pp. 67–94. Oxford: BAR International Series.

Cunliffe, B. 1976. The Origins of Urbanization in Britain. In Cunliffe, B.W. and Rowley, T. (eds.), *Oppida: The Beginning of Urbanization in Barbarian Europe*, pp. 135–162. Oxford: BAR Supplementary Series.

Cunliffe, B. 1979. *The Celtic World*. New York: McGraw-Hill.

Cunliffe, B. 1983. *Danebury: Anatomy of an Iron Age Hillfort*. London: Batsford.

Cunliffe, B. 1984a *Danebury: An Iron Age Hillfort in Hampshire.* CBA Research Report No. 52, 2 vols, Council for British Archaeology, London.

Cunliffe, B. 1984b. Iron Age Wessex: Continuity and Change. In Cunliffe, B. and Miles, D. (eds.), *Aspects of the Iron Age in Central Southern Britain,* pp. 12–45. Oxford: University of Oxford Committee for Archaeology.

Cunliffe, B. 1994. *The Oxford Illustrated Prehistory of Europe.* Oxford: Oxford University Press.

Cunliffe, B. 1995. Review: Europe in the First Millennium BC. *Antiquity* 69(266):1060–1061.

Cunliffe, B.W. 2004. *Iron Age Britain.* London: BT Batsford Ltd.

Cunliffe, B.W. 2005. *Iron Age Communities in Britain: An Account of England, Scotland and Wales from the Seventh Century BC Until the Roman Conquest.* London: Routledge.

Dahl, R.A. 1957. The concept of power. *Behavioral Science* 2:201–215.

Dahl, R.A. 1961. *Who Governs? Democracy and Power in an American City.* New Haven: Yale University Press.

Dahl, R.A. 1969. A critique of the ruling elite model. *Political Power: A Reader in Theory and Research* 463:69.

D'Altroy, T. N. and Earle, T. K. 1985. Staple Finance, Wealth Finance, and Storage in the Inka Political Economy *Current Anthropology* 26(2):187–206

De Angelis, F. 2003. Equations of culture: the meeting of natives and Greeks in Sicily (ca. 750-450 BC). *Ancient West & East* 2(1):19–50.

Dent, J. 1985. Three cart burials from Wetwang, Yorkshire. *Antiquity* 59(226):85–92.

Dietler, M. 1996. Feasts and Commensal Politics in the Political Economy: Food, Power, and Status in Prehistoric Europe. In Wiessner, P. and Schiefenhovel,W. (eds.), *Food and the Status Quest: An Interdisciplinary Perspective,* pp. 87–125. Oxford: Berghahn Books.

Dietler, M. 1997b. The Iron Age in Mediterranean France: Colonial encounters, entanglements, and transformations. *Journal of World Prehistory* 11(3):269–358.

Dietler, M. 1999. Rituals of Commensality and the Politics of State Formation in the "Princely" Societies of Early Iron Age Europe. In Ruby, P. (ed.), *Les princes de la protohistoire et l'émergence de l'état,* pp. 135–152. Cahiers du Centre Jean Bérard. Naples: Institut Français de Naples 17 – Collection de l'École Française de Rome 252.

Donahue, J.F. 2003. Toward a typology of Roman public feasting. *American Journal of Philology* 124:423–441.

Dunham, S. 1995. Caesar's Perception of Gallic Social Structures. In Arnold, B. and Gibson, D.B. (eds.), *Celtic Chiefdom, Celtic State.* Cambridge: Cambridge University Press.

Fagan, B. M. 1989. *People of the Earth* Glenview, Ill: Scott, Foresman,.

Earle, T. K. 1987. Chiefdoms in Archaeological and Ethnohistorical Perspective *Annual Review of Anthropology* 16:279–308.

Earle, T.K. 1996. Specialization and the Production of Wealth: Hawaiian Chiefdoms and the Inka Empire. In Preucel, R.W. and Hodder, I. (eds.), *Contemporary Archaeology in Theory.* Oxford: Blackwell.

Earle T. K. 1997. *How chiefs come to power.* Stanford: Stanford University Press.

Earle T. K. 2004. Culture Matters in the Neolithic Transition and Emergence of Hierarchy in Thy, Denmark. *American Anthropologist* 106:111–125

Elias, N. 1972. *Processes of State Formation and Nation Building* Transactions of the 7th World Congress of Sociology, 1970, ISA, Sofia, pp. 274–284.

Erickson, C.L. 1993. The Social Organization of Prehispanic Raised Field Agriculture in the Lake Titicaca Basin. In Scarborough, V. and Isaac, B. (eds.), *Economic Aspects of Water Management in the New World,* pp. 367–424. Greenwich: JAI Press.

Ertman, T. 1997. *Birth of the Leviathan: Building States and Regimes in Medieval and Early Modern Europe.* Cambridge: Cambridge University Press.

Ethelberg, P., and Hansen, U.L. 2000. *Skovgårde: Ein bestattungsplatz mit reichen frauengräbern des 3. Jhs. N. Chr. Auf Seeland,* Copenhagen: Det Kongelige Nordiske Oldskriftselskab.

Fabech, C. 1994. Reading Society from the Cultural Landscape. South Scandinavia Between Sacral and Political Power. In Nielsen, P.O., Randsborg, K. and Thrane, H. (eds.), *The Archaeology of Gudme and Lundeborg,* pp. 169–183. Copenhagen: Universitetsforlag i København.

Fabech, C. 1999a. Centrality in Sites and Landscapes. In Fabech, C. and Ringtved, J. (eds.), *Settlement and Landscape*, pp. 455–473. Aarhus: Jutland Archaeological Society.

Fabech, C. 1999b. Organising the landscape: a matter of production, power, and religion. *Anglo-Saxon Studies in Archaeology and History* 10:37–47.

Fairservis, W.A.J. 1977. Excavations at the Harappan site of Allahdino: the graffiti; a model in the decipherment of the Harappan script. *Pap. Allahdino Exped* 3.

Feinman, G.M. 2001. Mesoamerican Political Complexity: The Corporate-Network Dimension. In Haas, J. (eds.), *From Leaders to Rulers*. New York: Kluwer Academic/Plenum Publishers.

Feinman, G.M., Lightfoot, K.G., and Upham, S. 2000. Political hierarchies and organizational strategies in the Puebloan southwest. *American Antiquity* 65(3):449–470.

Fentress, E., and Guidi, A. 1999. Myth, memory and archaeology as historical sources. *Antiquity* 73:463–467.

Ferguson, T.J. 1996. *Historic Zuni Architecture and Society: An Archaeological Application of Space Syntax*. Tucson: University of Arizona Press.

Fernández-Posse, M.D., and Sánchez-Palencia Ramos, F.J. 1998. Las comunidades campesinas en la cultura Castrexa. *Trabajos de Prehistoria* 55(2):127–150.

Fisher, W.H. 2000. *Rainforest Exchanges: Industry and Community on an Amazonian Frontier*. Washington and London: Smithsonian Institution Press.

Fitzjohn, M. 2007. Equality in the Colonies: Concepts of Equality in Sicily During the Eighth to Six Centuries BC. *World Archaeology* 39(2):215–228.

Fitzpatrick, A.P. 1997. Everyday Life in Iron Age Wessex. In Gwilt, A. and Haselgrove, C. (eds.), *Reconstructing Iron Age Societies*, pp. 73–86. Oxford: Oxbow Monographs.

Flannery, K.V. 1972. The cultural evolution of civilizations. *Annual Review of Ecology and Systematics* 3:399–426.

Foucault, M. 1982. The subject and power. *Critical Inquiry* 8(4):777–795.

Foucault, M., and Sheridan, A. 1979. *Discipline and Punish*. New York: Vintage Books.

Fox, J.W., Cook, G.W., Chase, A.F., and Chase, D.Z. 1996. Questions of political and economic integration: Segmentary versus centralized states among the ancient Maya. *Current Anthropology* 37(5):795–801.

Fraser, V. 1986. A new look at the Maya. *The Burlington Magazine* 128(1004):826–827.

Frederick, C. 2007. Chinampa Cultivation in the Basin of Mexico: Observations on the Evolution of Form and Function. In Thurston, T.L. and Fisher, C.T. (eds.), *Seeking a Richer Harvest. The Archaeology of Subsistence Intensification, Innovation and Change*, pp. 107–124. New York: Springer.

Frisbie, P. 1974. Measuring the degree of bureaucratization at the societal level. *Social Forces* 53:563.

Fulford, M. 2001. Links with the past: pervasive 'ritual' behaviour in Roman Britain. *Britannia* 32:199–218.

García Moreno, L.A. 2006. Celtic place- and personal-names in Spain and the socio-political structure and evolution of the Celtiberians. *e-Keltoi* 6:375–388.

García Quintela, M.V. 2005. Celtic elements in northwestern Spain in pre-Roman times. *e-Keltoi* 6:497–569.

Gardner, A. 2002. Social identity and the duality of structure in late Roman-period Britain. *Journal of Social Archaeology* 2(3):323.

Gent, H. and Dean, C. (1986). Catchment analysis and settlement hierarchy: a case study from Pre-Roman Britain. Grant, E. (ed.), *Central Places, Archaeology and History*, pp. 27–36. Sheffield: The University of Sheffield.

Giddens, A. 1984. *The Constitution of Society: Outline of the Theory of Structuration*. Cambridge: Polity Press.

Giddens, A. 1990. *The Consequences of Modernity*. Cambridge: Polity Press.

Giles, K. 2007. Seeing and believing: Visuality and space in pre-modern England. *World Archaeology* 39(1):105–121.

Gillespie, S.D. 2000. Rethinking ancient Maya social organization: replacing lineage with house. *American Anthropologist* 102(3):467–484.

Gilman, A. 1995. Prehistoric European Chiefdoms: Rethinking Germanic Societies. *Foundations of Social Inequality* Price, T. D. and Feinman, G. M. (Eds.). New York: Springer, pp. 235–254

Gonzalez-Ruibal, A. 2006. House societies vs. kinship-based societies: an archaeological case from Iron Age Europe. *Journal of Anthropological Archaeology* 25(1):144–173.

Goodyear, J.R.D. 1981. *The Annals of Tacitus, Books 1–2*. Cambridge: Cambridge University Press.

Graham-Campbell, J. 1973. The Lough Ravel, Co. Antrim, Brooch and Others of Ninth-century Date' *Ulster Journal of Archaeology* 36/37:52–57.

Graham-Campbell, J. 1975. Bossed penannular brooches: a review of recent research *Medieval Archaeology* 19:33–47.

Graham-Campbell, J. 1981. The Viking-Age Silver Hoards of the Isle of Man. In Fell, C., Foote, P., and Graham-Campbell, J. (eds.), *The Viking Age in the Isle of Man*, pp. 53–80. London: Viking Society for Northern Research.

Graham-Campbell, J. 1985. A lost Pictish treasure (and two Viking-age gold arm-rings) from the Broch of Burgar, Orkney. *Proceedings of the Society of Antiquaries of Scotland* 115:241–261.

Graham-Campbell, J. 2001. *The Viking World*. London: Frances Lincoln.

Graham-Campbell, J., Batey, C. E., Clarke, C., Page, R. I., Price, N. S. (eds) 1994 1994. *Cultural Atlas of the Viking World,* Facts on File, New York.

Grambo, R. 1989. Unmanliness and Seiðr: Problems Concerning the Change of Sex. In Hoppál, M. and von Sadovszky, O. (eds.), *Shamanism Past and Present,* ISTOR Books, Hungarian Academy of Sciences, pp. 103–113. Budapest: Ethnographic Institute.

Gramsci, A. 1971. The Intellectuals. In Nowell Smith, G. (ed.), *Selections from the Prison Notebooks*, pp. 3–23. New York: International Publishers.

Grant, A. 1984. Survival or Sacrifice? A Critical Appraisal of Animal Burials in Britain in the Iron Age. In Grigson, C. and Clutton-Brock, J. (eds.), *Animals and Archaeology*, pp. 221–227. Oxford: British Archaeological Reports International Series.

Grant, A. 1989. Animals and rituals in early Britain: The visible and the invisible. *L'Animal dans les pratiques religieuses: les manifestations matérielles. Anthropozoologica* 3:Numéro Special 79–86.

Graves, M.W., Longacre, W.A., and Holbrook, S.J. 1982. Aggregation and abandonment at Grasshopper Pueblo. *Journal of Field Archaeology* 9:193–206.

Green, M. 1998. Crossing the boundaries: Triple horns and emblematic transference. *European Journal of Archaeology* 1(2):219–240.

Gustafsson, H. 2006. A state that failed? *Scandinavian Journal of History* 31(3):205–220.

Haas, J. 2001. Cultural Evolution and Political Centralization. In Haas, J. (eds.), *From Leaders to Rulers*, pp. 3–18. New York: Kluwer Academic/Plenum Publishers.

Hage, J., and Aiken, M. 1967. Relationship of centralization to other structural properties. *Administrative Science Quarterly* 12(1):72–92.

Hägerstrand, T. 1982. Diorama, path and project. *Tijdschrift voor Economische en Sociale Geografie* 73:323–339.

Hägerstrand, T. 1985. Time-Geography: Focus on the Corporeality of Man, Society and Environment. In Aida S. (ed.), *The Science and Praxis of Complexity*, pp. 193–216. Tokyo: The United Nations University.

Hall, J. 2004. How "Greek" Were the Early Western Greeks? In Lomas, K. (ed.), *Greek Identity in the Western Mediterranean. Papers in Honour of Brian Shefton*, pp. 35–54. Leiden and Boston: Brill.

Hall, R. 1973. A hoard of Viking silver bracelets from Cushalogurt, Co. Mayo. *Journal of the Royal Society of Antiquaries of Ireland* 103:78–85.

Halls, P., and Miller, A. 1996. *Of Todes and Worms: An Experiment in Bringing Time to Arcinfo.* Proceedings of ESRI Annual User's Conference, Palm Springs

Hamilton, S., and Manley, J. 2001. Hillforts, monumentality and place: A chronological and topographic review of first millennium BC hillforts of South-east England. *European Journal of Archaeology* 4(1):7.

Hammond, N. 1991. Inside the Black Box: Defining Maya Polity. In T.P. Culbert (ed.), *Classic Maya Political History: Hieroglyphic and Archaeological Evidence*, pp. 253–284. Cambridge: Cambridge University Press.

Harding, D.W. 2001. Later prehistory in South-east Scotland: A critical review. *Oxford Journal of Archaeology* 20(4):355–376.

Harding, D.W. 2004. *The Iron Age in Northern Britain: Celts and Romans, Natives and Invaders*. London: Routledge.

Harding, D.W. 2006. Redefining the Northern British Iron Age. *Oxford Journal of Archaeology* 25(1):61–82.

Haselgrove, C. 1976. External Trade as a Stimulus to Urbanization. In Cunliffe, B.W. and Rowley, T. (eds.), *Oppida: The Beginning of Urbanization in Barbarian Europe*, pp. 25–50. Oxford: BAR Supplementary Series.

Haselgrove, C. 1982. Wealth, Prestige and Power: The Dynamics of Late Iron Age Political Centralisation in South-East England. In Renfrew, C. and Shennan, S. (eds.), *Ranking, Resource, and Exchange*, pp. 79–88. Cambridge: Cambridge University Press.

Haselgrove, C. 1995. Late Iron Age Society in Britain and Northwest Europe: Structural Transformation or Superficial Change? In Arnold, B. and Gibson, D.B. (eds.), *New Directions in Archaeology*, pp. 81–87. Cambridge: Cambridge University Press.

Hauser-Schäublin, B. 2003. The precolonial Balinese state reconsidered. A critical evaluation of theory construction on the relationship between irrigation, the state, and ritual. *Current Anthropology* 44(2):153–181.

Hedeager, L. 1992. *Iron Age Societies. From Tribe to State in Northern Europe, 500 BC to AD 700*. Oxford: Blackwell.

Hedeager, L. 1997. Odins offer. Skygger af en shamanistisk tradition i Nordisk folkevandringstid. *Tor* 29:265–278.

Hedeager, L. 2000. From Warrior to Trade Economy. In Fitzhugh, W.H. and Ward, E.I. (eds.), *Vikings: The North Atlantic Saga*, pp. 84–85. Washington: Smithsonian Institution.

Heinrichs, A. 1994. The search for identity: A problem after the conversion. *Alvíssmál* 3:43–62.

Helgesson, B. 2003. Central places and regions in Scania during the Iron Age: Some examples. *Centrality – regionality. The social structure of Southern Sweden during the Iron Age*. Acta Archaeologica Lundensia Series in 8, Lund:323–335.

Hermansen, T. 1970. Regionalisation of national planning–some methodological issues. *Environment and Planning* 2:429–442.

Hill, J.D. 1989. Re-thinking the Iron Age. *Scottish Archaeological Review* 6:16–24.

Hill, J.D. 1993. Can we recognise a different European past? A contrastive archaeology of later prehistoric settlements in Southern England. *Journal of European Archaeology* 1:57–75.

Hill, J.D. 1995a. How Should We Understand Iron Age Societies and Hillforts? A Contextual Study from Southern Britain. In Hill, J.D. and Cumberpatch, C.G. (eds), *Different Iron Ages: Studies on the Iron Age in Temperate Europe*, pp. 45–66. Oxford: BAR.

Hill, J.D. 1995b. *Ritual and Rubbish in the Iron Age of Wessex*. Oxford: British Archaeological Reports British Series.

Hill, J.D. 1996. The Identification of Ritual Deposits of Animals. A General Perspective from 'Special Animal Deposits' from the Southern English Iron Age. In Anderson, S. (ed.), *Ritual Treatment of Human and Animal Remains*, pp. 17–32. Oxford: Oxbow books.

Hill, J.D. 2001. A new cart/chariot burial from Wetwang, East Yorkshire. *Past* 38:2.

Hill, J.D. and Cumberpatch, C.G. (ed). 1995. *Different Iron Ages: Studies on the Iron Age in Temperate Europe*. Oxford: Tempus Reparatum.

Hingley, R. 1995. The Iron Age in Atlantic Scotland: Searching for the Meaning of the Substantial House. In Hill, J.D. and Cumberpatch, C.G. (eds.), *Different Iron Ages: Studies on the Iron Age in Temperate Europe*, pp. 185–194. Oxford: BAR International Series.

Hingley, R., and Unwin, C. 2005. *Boudica: Iron Age Warrior Queen*. London: Hambleton and London.

Holck, P. 2006. The Oseberg ship burial, Norway: New thoughts on the skeletons from the grave mound. *European Journal of Archaeology* 9(2–3):185–210.

Hulthén, B. 1991. Notes on Scandinavian finds of anthropomorphic heads and masks from the pre-Roman and Roman Iron Age. *Acta Archaeologica Lundensia* Series in 8(20): 169–176.

Hunt, R., and Gilman, A. 1998. *Property in Economic Context*. Lanham: University Press of America.

Hunter, F. 1953. *Community Power Structure: A Study Of Decision Makers*. Chapel Hill: University of North Carolina Press.

Hutt, A., Goodenough, P., and Pyne, V. 2006. *Reinterpreting Iron Age hillforts in and around Berkshire*. Cardiff: Cardiff School of History & Archaeology.

Hvass, S. 1980. Vorbasse: The Viking-age settlement at Vorbasse, Central Jutland. *Acta Archaeologica* 50:137–172.

Hvass, S. 1983. Vorbasse: The development of a settlement through the first millenium AD. *Journal of Danish Archaeology* 2:127–136.

Hvass, S. 1989. Rural Settlements in Denmark in the First Millennium AD. In Randsborg, K. (eds.), *The Birth of Europe: Archaeology and Social Development in the First Millennium AD*, pp. 91–99. Rome: Analecta Romana Instituti Danici.

Ilkjær, J. 2002. *Illerup Ådal. Archaeology as a Magic Mirror*. Aarhus: Moesgard.

Jacobson, J. 1979. Recent developments in South Asian prehistory and protohistory. *Annual Review of Anthropology* 8:467–502.

James, S. 1993. *The World of the Celts*. London: Thames & Hudson.

James, S. 1998. Celts, politics and motivation in archaeology. *Antiquity* 72(275):200–210.

James, S. 1999. *The Atlantic Celts: Ancient People or Modern Invention?* London, Madison: British Museum Press, University of Wisconsin Press.

James, S. 2000. A reply to Amy Hale. *Folklore* 111:307–313.

Jeffreys-Jones, R. 1999. *Peace Now!: American Society and the Ending of the Vietnam War*. New Haven: Yale University Press.

Johannesen, J.M. 2004. Operational Ethnicity. Serial Practice and Materiality. In Fahlander, F. and Oestigaard, T. (eds.), *Material Culture and Other Things. Post-disciplinary Studies in the 21st Century*. Gothenburg: University of Gothenburg.

Johnson, G.A. 1982. Organizational Structure and Scalar Stress. In Renfrew, A. C., Rowlands, M. J. and Segraves, B.A. (eds.), *Theory and Explanation in Archaeology, the Southhampton Conference*. pp. 389–421. New York: Academic Press.

Jones, G. 1984. *A History of the Vikings*. Oxford: Oxford University Press.

Jope, E.M. 1962. Iron Age brooches in Ireland: A summary'. *Ulster Journal of Archaeology* 24–25: 25–38, 1961–1962.

Jope, E.M. 1971. The Witham shield. *The British Museum Quarterly* 35:61–69.

Jope, E.M. 1997. Bersu's Goldberg iv: A petty chief's establishment of the 6–5th centuries BC. *Oxford Journal of Archaeology* 16(2):227–241.

Joyce, R.A. 2000. Heirlooms and Houses: Materiality and Social Memory. In Joyce, R.A. and Gillespie, S.D. (eds.), *Beyond Kinship. Social and Material Reproduction in House Societies*, pp. 189–212. Philadelphia: University of Pennsylvania Press.

Jørgensen, L. 2000. Political Organization and Social Life. In Fitzhugh, W.H. and Ward, E.I. (eds.), *Vikings: The North Atlantic Saga*, pp. 72–85. Washington: Smithsonian Institution.

Jørgensen, L., and Skov, T. 1980. Trabjerg: A Viking age settlement in northwest Jutland. *Acta Archaeologica* 50 (Viking Age Settlements in Western and Central Jutland).

Kalberg, S. 1994. *Max Weber's Comparative-Historical Sociology*. Cambridge: Cambridge University Press.

Keren, M., and Levhari, D. 1979. The optimum span of control in a pure hierarchy. *Management Science* 25(11):1162–1172.

Knapp, A.B. 1993. Social complexity: incipience, emergence, and development on prehistoric Cyprus. *Bulletin of the American Schools of Oriental Research* 292:85–106.

Knüsel, C.J. 2002. More Circe than Cassandra: the Princess of Vix in ritualized social context. *European Journal of Archaeology* 5(3):275–308.

Köhler, M. 1995. Understanding the Oscillating Nature of Hillfort Settlement in Hallstatt Thuringia. In, Hill, J.D. and Cumberpatch, G. (eds.), *Different Iron Ages: Studies on the Iron Age in Temperate Europe*, pp. 195–212. Oxford: Tempus Reparatum 602.

Kolb, M.J., and Speakman, R.J. 2005. Elymian regional interaction in Iron Age Western Sicily: a preliminary neutron activation study of incised/impressed tableware's. *Journal of Archaeological Science* 32(5): 795–804.

Kriesi, H. 1995. The political opportunity structure of new social movements: its impact on their mobilization. In Jenkins, J. C. and Klandermans, B. (eds.) *The Politics of Social Protest*, pp. 167–198. Minneapolis: U. of Minnesota Press; London: UCL Press.

Kristiansen, K. 1998a. *Europe Before History*. Cambridge: Cambridge University Press.

Kristiansen, K. 1998b. Chiefdoms, States and Systems of Social Evolution. Social Transformations in Archaeology: Global and Local Perspectives. In Earle, T.K. (ed.) *Chiefdoms: Power, Economy, and Ideology*, pp. 16–43. Cambridge: Cambridge University Press.

Kristiansen, K. and Larsson, T. B. 2006. *The Rise of Bronze Age Society: Travels, Transmissions, and Transformations*. Cambridge: Cambridge University Press.

Kurrild-Klitgaard, P., and Tinggaard Svendsen, G. 2003. Rational bandits: plunder, public goods, and the Vikings. *Public Choice* 117(3):255–272.

Kurtz, D.V. 1987. The economics of urbanization and state formation at Teotihuacan. *Current Anthropology* 28(3):329–353.

Lansing, J.S., and Kremer, J.N. 1993. Emergent properties of Balinese water temple networks: Coadaptation on a rugged fitness landscape. *American Anthropologist* 95:97–114.

Larsson, L. 2007. The Iron Age ritual building at Uppåkra, Southern Sweden. *Antiquity* 81(Pt 311):11–25.

Lasswell, H.D. 1961. Agenda for the Study of Political Elites. In Marvick, D. (ed.), *Political Decision-Makers*. Glencoe: The Free Press.

Lasswell, H.D., and Kaplan, A. 1950. *Power and Society: A Framework for Political Inquiry*. London: Yale University Press.

Lasswell, H.D., Lerner, D., and Rothwell, C.E. 1952. *The Comparative Study of Elites: An Introduction and Bibliography*. Stanford: Stanford University Press.

LeBlanc, S.A. 1999. *Prehistoric Warfare in the American Southwest*. Salt Lake: University of Utah Press.

Leighton, R. 2005. Later prehistoric settlement patterns in Sicily: Old paradigms and new surveys. *European Journal of Archaeology* 8(3):261.

Lekson, S.H. 1999. *The Chaco Meridian: Centers of Political Power in the Ancient Southwest*. Walnut Creek: Altamira Press.

Lévi-Strauss, C. 1987. *Anthropology and myth: Lectures 1951–1982*. Oxford: Blackwell.

Lloyd, M. 2005. Getting physical inside a pyramid. *Chronicle of Higher Education* 51(24):A14.

Logan, F.D. 1983. *The Vikings in History*. London: Unwin Hyman.

Lönnroth, E. 1963. The Baltic Countries *The Cambridge Economic History of Europe III. Economic Organization and Policies in the Middle Ages*, pp. 361–396. Cambridge: Cambridge University Press.

Lönnroth, E. 1977. *Scandinavians: Selected Historical Essays*. Göteborg: Eckerstein.

Lorrio, A.J. 1997. *Los Celtíberos*, Complutum Extra 7. Alicante: Universidad de Alicante.

Lorrio, A.J., and Ruiz Zapatero, G. 2004. The Celts in Iberia: An overview. *e-Keltoi* 6:168–254.

Lukes, S.S. 1974. *Power: A Radical View*. London: Macmillan Press, Ltd.

Lund Hansen, U. 1987. *Romischer Import im Norden*. Copenhagen: Det Kongelige Nordiske Oldskriftselskab.

Lund Hansen, U. 1990. Langdistancehandel i Romersk Jernalder—fra gaveudveksling til aftale-handel. *Hikuin* 16:63–88.

Lundqvist, A.L., Rosengren, E., and Callmer, J. 1993. En fyndplats med guldgubbar vid Slöinge, Halland. *Fornvännen* 88(2):65–70.

MacDevitt,W.A. 2005. *Caesar's Commentaries: On the Gallic War and on the Civil War*. El Paso: Norte Press.

Magnusson Staaf, B. 2003. Places in Our Minds. In Larsson, L. and Hårdh, B. (eds.), *Centrality - Regionality: The Social Structure of Southern Sweden During the Iron Age*, pp. 311–321. Stockholm: Almqvist & Wiksell.

Manahan, T.K. 2004. The way things fall apart. Social organization and the classic Maya collapse of Copan. *Ancient Mesoamerica* 15:107–125.

Mann, M. 1986. *The Sources of Social Power: A History of Power from the Beginning to A.D. 1760.* New York: Cambridge University Press.

Martin, R. 1971. The concept of power: A critical defence. *The British Journal of Sociology* 22(3):240–256.

Mathien, F.J. 2001. The organization of turquoise production and consumption by the prehistoric Chacoans. *American Antiquity* 66(1):103–118.

Mayhew, B.H. 1973. System size and ruling elites. *American Sociological Review* 38(4):468–475.

Mayhew, B.H., and Levinger, R.L. 1976. On the emergence of oligarchy in human interaction. *American Journal of Sociology* 81(5):1017.

McAndrews, T.L., Albarracin-Jordan, J., and Bermann, M. 1997. Regional settlement patterns in the Tiwanaku valley of Bolivia. *Journal of Field Archaeology* 24(1):67–83.

McFarland, A.S. 2004. *Neopluralism: The Evolution of Political Process Theory.* Lawrence: University Press of Kansas.

McKinnell, J. 2000. Encounters with Völur. In Barnes, G. and Ross, M.C. (eds.), *Old Norse myths, literature and society: Proceedings of the 11th International Saga Conference*, pp. 239–251. Sydney, Australia: University of Sydney, Centre for Medieval Studies.

McOmish, D. 1996. Chisenbury: Ritual and rubbish at the Bronze Age-Iron Age transition. *Antiquity* 70:68–76.

Medding, P.Y. 1982. Ruling elite models: A critique and an alternative. *Political Studies* 30: 393–412.

Megaw, J.V.S. 2005. The European Iron Age with—and without—Celts: A bibliographical essay. *European Journal of Archaeology* 8(1):65–74.

Megaw, J.V.S., and Megaw, M.R. 1995a. Paper tigers, tilting at windmills and the Celtic Cheshire cats: A reply to Tim Taylor. *Scottish Archaeological Review* 9/10:248–252.

Megaw, J.V.S., and Megaw, M.R. 1995b. The Prehistoric Celts: Identity and Contextuality. In Kuna M., Venclová N. (eds.), *Whither Archaeology? Papers in Honour of Evzen Neustupny*, pp. 230–245. Praha: Institute of Archaeology.

Megaw, J.V.S., and Megaw, M.R. 1996. Ancient Celts and modern ethnicity. *Antiquity* 70:175–181.

Megaw, J.V.S., and Megaw, M.R. 1997. Do the ancient Celts still live? An essay on identity and contextuality. *Studio Celtica* 31:107–123.

Megaw, M.R., and Megaw, J.V.S. 1994. Through a window on the European Iron Age darkly: Fifty years of reading early Celtic art. *World Archaeology* 25(3):287–303.

Megaw, M.R., and Megaw, J.V.S. 1999. Celtic Connections Past and Present: Celtic Ethnicity, Ancient and Modern. In Black, R. et al. (eds.), *Celtic connections: Proceedings of the 10th International Congress of Celtic Studies*, pp. 19–81. East Linton: Tuckwell Press.

Menez, Y. 1997. *Une ferme de l'Armorique Gauloise: Le boisanne a Plouer-sur-Rance (Cotes d'Armor).* Paris: Maison des Sciences de l'Homme.

Merriman, N. 1987. Value and Motivation in Prehistory: The Evidence for 'Celtic' Spirit. In Hodder, I. (eds.), *The Archaeology of Contextual Meanings*, pp. 111–116. Cambridge: Cambridge University Press.

Meyer, K. 1905. *Cáin Adamnáin: A Old Irish treatise on the Law of Adamnan.* Oxford: Oxford University Press.

Miller, D., and Tilley, C. 1984. Ideology, Power and Prehistory: An Introduction. In Miller, D. and Tilley, C. (eds.), *Ideology, Power and Prehistory*, pp. 1–16. Cambridge: Cambridge University Press.

Millon, R. 1976. Social Relations in Ancient Teotihuacan. In Wolf, E.R. (eds.), *The Valley of Mexico*, pp. 205–248. Albuquerque: University of New Mexico Press.

Millon, R., Drewitt, B., and Bennyhoff, J.A. 1965. The Pyramid of the Sun at Teotihuacan: 1959 investigations. *Transactions of the American Philosophical Society* 55:1–93.

Mills, B.J. 2002. Recent research on Chaco: Changing views on economy, ritual, and society. *Journal of Archaeological Research* 10(1):65–117.

Mills, B.J. 2004. The establishment and defeat of hierarchy: Inalienable possessions and the history of collective prestige structures in the Pueblo Southwest. *American Anthropologist* 106(2): 238–251.

Mills, C.W. 1959. *The Power Elite*. Oxford: Oxford University Press.

Mizoguchi, K. 2002. *An Archaeological History of Japan: 30,000 BC to AD 700*. Philadelphia: University of Pennsylvania Press.

Monsen, E. (ed. and trans.). 1932. *Heimskringla or the Lives of the Norse Kings, by Snorre Sturlason*. Cambridge: W. Heffer.

Moore, G. 1979. The structure of a national elite network. *American Sociological Review* 44(5):673–692.

Morris, J. 1957. Celtic saints: A note. *Past and Present* 11:2–16.

Mosca, G. 1939. The Ruling Class (elementi di scienza politica). In Livingston, A. (eds.). New York: McGraw-Hill.

Mosca, G. 1972. *A Short History of Political Philosophy*. New York: Crowell.

Murray, M.L. 1996. Viereckschanzen and feasting: Socio-political ritual in Iron Age Central Europe. *Journal of European Archaeology* 3(2):125–152.

Nash, D. 1984. The Basis of Contact Between Britain and Gaul in the Late Pre-Roman Iron Age. In Macready, S. and Thompson, E. (eds.), *Cross-Channel Trade Between Gaul and Britain in the Pre-Roman Iron Age*, pp. 92–107. London: Society of Antiquaries.

Näsman, U. 2000. Raids, migrations and kingdoms – the Danish case. *Acta Archaeologica* 71: 1–7.

Nielsen, L.-C. 1980. Omgård: A settlement from the Late Viking period in Western Jutland. *Acta Archaeologica* 50, (Viking Age Settlements in Western and Central Jutland):173–208.

Nordstrom, N. 2006. From Queen to Sorcerer. In Andren, A., Jennbert, K. and Raudvere, C. (eds.), *Old Norse Religion in Long Term Perspective*, pp. 399–404. Lund: Nordic Academic Press.

Osborne, R. 2007. Is archaeology equal to equality? *World Archaeology* 29(2):143–150.

Oswald, A. 1997. A Doorway on the Past: Practical and Mystic Concerns in the Orientation of Roundhouse Doorways. In Gwilt, A. and Haselgrove, C. (eds.), *Reconstructing Iron Age Societies*, pp. 87–95. Oxford: Oxbow.

Pálsson, H., and Edwards, P. 1986. *Knytlinga Saga*. Odense: Odense University Press.

Parcero Oubiña, C. 2003. Looking forward in anger: Social and political transformations in the Iron Age of the North-Western Iberian peninsula. *European Journal of Archaeology* 6(3):267–299.

Parcero Oubiña, C., and Fernández, I.C. 2004. Iron Age archaeology of the Northwest Iberian peninsula. *e-Keltoi* 6, (The Celts in the Iberian Peninsula):1–72.

Pareto, V. 1923. *Trattato di sociologia generale*. Firenze: Barbera.

Pareto, V. 1966. *Sociological Writings*. London: Pall Malt.

Parkinson, W.A., and Galaty, M.L. 2007. Secondary states in perspective: An integrated approach to state formation in the prehistoric Aegean. *American Anthropologist* 109(1):113–129.

Parzinger, H. 1995. The Beginning of La Tène Culture in Central Europe. In Hill, J.D., Cumberpatch, C.G. (eds.), *Different Iron Ages: Studies on the Iron Age in Temperate Europe*. Oxford: Tempus Reparatum.

Pasztory, E. 1992. Abstraction and the Rise of a Utopian State at Teotihuacan. In Berlo, J.C. (ed.), *Art, Ideology, and the City of Teotihuacan*, pp. 281–320. Washington: Dumbarton Oaks.

Pasztory, E. 1997. *Teotihuacan: An Experiment in Living*. Norman: University of Oklahoma Press.

Peregrine, P.N. 2001. Matrilocality, corporate strategy, and the organization of production in the Chacoan world. *American Antiquity* 66(1):36–46.

Pittock, M.G.H. 1999. *Celtic Identity and the British Image*. Manchester: Manchester University Press.

Polsby, N.W. 1963. *Community Power and Political Theory*. New Haven: Yale University Press.

Poole, C. 1995. Study 12: Pits and Propitiation. In Cunliffe, B. (ed.), *Danebury: An Iron Age Hillfort in Hampshire*, pp. 249–275. London: Council for British Archaeology.

Porsmose, E. 1981. *Den regulerede landsby. Studier over bebygglesudviklingen på Fyn i tiden fra ca 1000 til ca 1700 e. Kr. Fødsel* Odense University Studies in History and Social Sciences 72, vols. 1–2.

Porter, A. 2002. Death and the contest for social order in the Euphrates river valley. *Near Eastern Archaeology* 65(3):156–173.

Possehl, G.L. 1990. Revolution in the urban revolution: The emergence of Indus urbanization. *Annual Review of Anthropology* 19:261–282.

Possehl, G.L. 1998. Sociocultural Complexity Without the State: The Indus Civilization. In Feinman, G.M. and Marcus, J. (eds.), *Archaic States*, pp. 261–291. Santa Fe: School of American Research Press.

Powers, R.P. 1984. Outliers and Roads in the Chaco System. In Noble, D.G. (eds.), *New Light on Chaco Canyon*, pp. 45–58. Santa Fe: School of American Research Press.

Pred, A. 1984. Place as historically contingent process: Structuration and the time geography of becoming places. *Annals of the Association of American Geographers* 74(2):279–297.

Pred, A. 1986. *Place, Practice and Structure*. New York: Barnes & Noble.

Prewitt, K., and Stone, A. 1973. *The ruling elites: Elite Theory, Power, and American Democracy*. London: HarperCollins Publishers.

Price, N. 2004. The archaeology of Seiðr: circumpolar traditions in Viking pre-Christian religion. *Brathair* 4(2):109–126.

Price, T.D. and Feinman, G.M. (eds). 1995a. *Foundations of Social Inequality*. New York: Plenum Press.

Price, T.D., and Feinman, G.M. 1995b. Pathways to Power: Principles for Creating Socioeconomic Inequalities. In Price, T.D. and Feinman, G.M. (eds.), *Foundations of Social Inequality*, pp. 1 3–14. New York: Plenum Press.

Quinn, J. 1998. "Ok verðr henni ljóð á munni"— eddic prophecy in the Fornaldarsögur. *Alvíssmál* 8:29–50.

Raab, L.M., and Goodyear, A.C. 1984. Middle-range theory in archaeology: A critical review of origins and applications. *American Antiquity* 49(2):255–268.

Ralston, I.B.M. 1992. *Les enceintes fortifiées du Limousin: Les habitants protohistoriques de France non Méditerranéenne*. Paris: Maison des Sciences de l'Homme.

Ralston, I.B.M. 1997. Untitled review. *Journal of Field Archaeology* 24(4):501–505.

Randsborg, K. 1980. *The Viking Age in Denmark: The Formation of a State*. London: Duckworth.

Randsborg, K. 1981. Burial, Succession and Early State Formation in Denmark. In Chapman, R., Kinnes, I. and Randsborg, K. (eds.), *The Archaeology of Death*, pp. 105–121. Cambridge: Cambridge University Press.

Renfrew, C. 1986. Introduction: Peer Polity Interaction and Socio-Political Change. In Renfrew C. and Cherry J. (eds.), *Peer Polity Interaction and Socio-Political Change*, pp. 1–18. Cambridge: Cambridge University Press.

Renfrew, C., and Shennan, S. 1982. *Ranking, Resource and Exchange*. New York: Cambridge University Press.

Ridderspore, M. 1988. Settlement site—village site: Analysis if the toft-structure in some Medieval villages and its relation to Late Iron Age settlements. A preliminary report and some tentative ideas based on Scanian examples. *Geografisk Annaler* 70B(1):75–85.

Rochefort, D.A., and Cobb, R.W. 1993. Problem definition, agenda access, and policy choice. *Policy Studies Journal* 1(21):56–71.

Roesdahl, E. 1982. *Viking Age Denmark*. London: Colonnade.

Roesdahl, E. 1997. *The Vikings*. New York: Penguin Books.

Roesdahl, E. 1998. *The Vikings* London: Penguin Books

Roesdahl, E. 1999. The Vikings, revised edition, New York: Penguin Books.

Roscoe, P.B. 1993. Practice and political centralization. *Current Anthropology* 34:111–140.

Ruiz Zapatero, G., and Álvarez-Sanchís, J.R. 1999. Ulaca: La "Pompeya" Vettona. *Revista de Arqueología* 216:36–47.

Ruiz Zapatero, G., and Álvarez-Sanchís, J.R. 2002. Etnicidad y arqueología: Tras la identidad de los Vettones. *Spal* 11:253–275.

Ruiz Zapatero, G.R., and Alvarez-Sanchis, J.R. 1995. Las Cogotas: Oppida and the Roots of Urbanism in the Spanish Meseta. In Cunliffe, B. and Keay, S. (eds.), *Social Complexity and the Development of Towns in Iberia: From the Copper Age to the Second Century AD*, pp. 209–235. Oxford: Proceedings of the British Academy/Oxford University Press.

Runolfsson Solvason, B.T. 1992. Ordered anarchy: Evolution of the decentralized legal order in the Icelandic Commonwealth. *Icelandic Economic Papers* 17.

Runolfsson Solvason, B.T. 1993. Institutional evolution in the Icelandic commonwealth. *Constitutional Political Economy* 4(1):97–125.

Russell, C. 2005. The Anglo-Saxon influence on Romano-Britain: Research past and present. *Durham Anthropology Journal* 13(1):1–7.

Saitta, D. 1994. Agency, class, and archaeological interpretation. *Journal of Anthropological Archaeology* 13(3):201–227.

Saitta, D.J., and Keene, A.S. 1990. Politics and Surplus Flow in Prehistoric Communal Societies. In Upham, S. (ed.), *The Evolution of Political Systems. Sociopolitics in Small-Scale Sedentary Societies*, pp. 203–224. Cambridge: Cambridge University Press.

Salinas, M. 2001. Fides, hospitium y clientela en Hispania. In Villar, F. and Fernández Álvarez, M.P., (eds.), *Religión, lengua y cultura prerromanas de Hispania Ediciones*, pp. 241–255. Salamanca: Universidad de Salamanca.

Sanchez-Moreno, E. 2001. Cross-cultural links in ancient Iberia: Scoio-economic anatomy of hospitality. *Oxford Journal of Archaeology* 20(4):391–414.

Sanders, W.T., and Price, B. 1968. *Mesoamerica: The Evolution of a Civilization*. New York: Random House.

Sastre, I. 2002. Forms of social inequality in the Castro culture of North-west Iberia. *European Journal of Archaeology* 5(2):213–248.

Sawyer, P. 1982. *Kings and Vikings*. London: Methuen.

Schortman, E.M. 1989. Interregional interaction in prehistory: The need for a new perspective. *American Antiquity* 54(1):52–65.

Scott, J.C. 1985. *Weapons of the Weak: Everyday Forms of Peasant Resistance*. New Haven: Yale University Press.

Scott, J.C. 1989. Everyday Forms of Resistance. In Colburn, F.D. (eds.), *Everyday Forms of Peasant Resistance*, pp. 3–33. Armonck: M. E. Sharpe, Inc.

Scott, J.C. 1990. *Domination and the Arts of Resistance: Hidden Transcripts*. New Haven: Yale University Press.

Sewell, W.H. 2005. *Logics of History: Social Theory and Social Transformation*. Chicago: University of Chicago Press.

Shaffer, J.G. 1982. Harappan Commerce: An Alternative Perspective. In Pastner, S.L. and Flam, L. (eds.), *Pakistan: Recent Socio-Cultural and Archaeological Perspectives*, pp. 166–210. Ithaca: Cornell University.

Shumway, E.S. 1902. Some view-points of Roman law prior to the twelve tables. *The American Law Register* 50(2):97–104.

Sigurðsson, J.V. 2006. Tendencies in the Historiography on the Medieval Nordic States (to 1350). In Isaacs, A.K. and Hálfdanarson, G. (eds.), *Public Power in Europe Studies in Historical Transformations, Edizioni Plus*, pp. 1–15. Pisa: Pisa University.

Simon, H.A. 1944. Decision-making and administrative organization. *Public Administration Review* 4:16–30.

Skre, D. 2001. The social context of settlement in Norway in the first millennium AD. *Norwegian Archaeological Review* 34(1):1–12.

Slavin, M. 2005. *The Ancient Books of Ireland*. Belfast: McGill-Queen's University Press.

Smith, A. 2001. *The Differential Use of Constructed Sacred Space in Southern Britain, from the Late Iron Age to the 4th Century AD*. Oxford: Archaeopress.

Söderberg, B. 2003. Integrating power: Some aspects of a magnate's farm and presumed central place in Järrestad, South-east Scania. *Acta Archaeologica Lundensia* Series in 8(40): 283–310.

Solli, B. 1997. Odin the queer. Om det skeive i norrøn mytologi. *Universitetets Oldsaksamling Årbok* 98:7–42.

Staaf, B.M. 2000. Hannah Arendt and Torsten Hägerstrand. Converging Tendencies in Contemporary Archaeological Thought? In Holtorf, C. and Karlsson, H. (eds.), *Philosophy and Archaeological Practice. Perspectives for the 21st Century*, pp. 135–153. Göteborg: Bricoleur Press.

Stjernquist, B. 1955. *Simris: On Cultural Connections of Scania in the Roman Iron Age*, Lund: W.K. Gleerups.

Stone, C.N. 1989. *Regime Politics: Governing Atlanta, 1946–1988*. Lawrence: University Press of Kansas.

Storey, G.R. 1999. Archaeology and Roman society: Integrating textual and archaeological data. *Journal of Archaeological Research* 7(3):203–248.

Stoumann, I. 1980. Sædding: A Viking Age village near Esbjerg. *Acta Archaeologica* 50, (Viking Age Settlements in Western and Central Jutland):95–118.

Swenson, E.R. 2006. Competitive Feasting, Religious Pluralism and Decentralized Power in the Late Moche Period. In Isbell, W.H. and Silverman, H. (eds.), *Andean Archaeology III, North and South*, pp. 112–142. New York: Springer.

Tesch, S. 1991. A Central Settlement Region on the Coastal Plain in the Early Iron Age, the Late Iron Age, and the Early Middle Ages. From Habitation Site to Village Site in the Köpinge Area. In Berglund, B. (ed.), *The Cultural Landscape During 6000 years in Southern Sweden: The Ystad Project*, pp. 132–140. Copenhagen: Munksgaard International.

Thurston, T.L. 1999. The knowable, the doable and the undiscussed: Tradition, submission, and the 'becoming' of rural landscapes in Denmark's Iron Age. *Antiquity* 73(281):661–671.

Thurston, T.L. 2001. *Landscapes of Power, Landscapes of Conflict: State Formation in the Danish Iron Age*. New York: Kluwer Academic/Plenum Publishing.

Thurston, T.L. 2006. The Barren and the Fertile: Central and Local Intensification Strategies Across Variable Landscapes. In Marcus, J. and Stanish, C. (eds.), *Agricultural Strategies*, pp. 131–161. Los Angeles: Cotsen Institute of Archaeology Press.

Thurston, T.L. 2007a. Infields, Outfields, and Broken Lands: Agricultural Intensification and the Ordering of Space in Iron Age Denmark. In Thurston, T.L. and Fisher, C.T. (eds.), *Seeking a Richer Harvest: The Archaeology of Subsistence Intensification, Innovation and Change*, pp. 155–191. New York: Springer.

Thurston, T.L. 2007b. Rituals of rebellion: Cultural narratives and metadiscourse of violent conflict in Iron Age and Medieval Denmark. *Journal of Conflict Archaeology* 3(1):267–293.

Thurston, T.L. 2009. Unity and diversity in the European Iron Age: Out of the mists, some clarity? *Journal of Archaeological Research* 17(4):7–84.

Townsend, J.G. 1999. Empowerment Matters: Understanding Power. In Townsend, J.G. (ed.), *Women and Power; Fighting Patriarchies and Poverty*, pp. 19–45. New York: Zed.

Trigger, B.G. 1974. The archaeology of government. *World Archaeology* 6(1):95–106

Trigger, B.G. 1972. Determinants of Urban Growth in Pre-industrial Societies. In Ucko, P.J., Tringham, R., and Dimbleby, G.W. (eds.) *Man, Settlement and Urbanism*, pp. 575–599. London: Duckworth.

Tschan, F. 1959. *The History of the Archbishops of Hamburg-Bremen*. New York: Columbia University Press.

Upham, S., and Plog, F. 1986. The interpretation of prehistoric political complexity in the Central and Northern Southwest: Toward a mending of the models. *Journal of Field Archaeology* 13(2):223–238.

van den Broeke, P. 1995. Iron Age Sea Salt Trade in the Lower Rhine Area. In Hill, J.D. and Cumberpatch, C.G. (eds.), *Different Iron Ages: Studies on the Iron Age in Temperate Europe*, pp. 149–162. Oxford: BAR International Series.

van der Veen, M., and Jones, G. 2006. A re-analysis of agricultural production and consumption: Implications for understanding the British Iron Age. *Vegetation History and Archaeobotany* 15(3):1–12.

Wanner, K.J. 2007. God on the margins: Dislocation and transience in the myths of Óðinn. *History of Religions* 46:316–350.

Warner, R. 1973. The re-provenancing of two important pennanular brooches of the Viking period. *Ulster Journal of Archaeology* 36:58–70.

Watt, M. 2003. Weapon Graves and Regional Groupings of Weapons Types and Burial Customs in Denmark 100 BC – 400 AD. In Jørgensen, L., Storgaard, B. and Gebauer Thomsen, L. (eds.), *The Spoils of Victory. The North in the Shadow of the Roman Empire*, pp. 180–193. Copenhagen: National Museum of Denmark.

Weber, M. 1946. Class, Status, Party. In Gerthe, H.H. and Mills, C.W. (eds.), *Max Weber: Essays in Sociology*. New York: Oxford University Press.

Weber, M. 1968. *Economy and Society*. New York: Bedminster Press.

Weber, M. (ed). 1978 [1921]. *Economy and Society: An Outline of Interpretive Sociology*, 2 vols. Berkeley: University of California Press.

Webster, D. 1975. Warfare and the evolution of the state: A reconsideration. *American Antiquity* 40(4):464–470.

Wells, P.S. 1984. *Farms, Villages, and Cities. Commerce and Urban Origins in Late Prehistoric Europe*. Ithaca: Cornell University Press.

Wells, P.S. 1993. *Settlement, Economy, and Cultural Change at the End of the European Iron Age: Excavations at Kelheim in Bavaria, 1987–1991*. Ann Arbor: International Monographs in Prehistory.

Wells, P.S. 1995. Identities, material culture, and change: 'Celts' and 'Germans' in Late Iron Age Europe. *Journal of European Archaeology* 3(2):169–185.

Wells, P.S. 1998. Identity and material culture in the later prehistory of Central Europe. *Journal of AQ129 Archaeological Research* 6(3):239–298.

Wells, P.S. 1999. *The Barbarians Speak: How the Conquered Peoples Shaped Roman Europe*. Princeton: Princeton University Press.

Wells, P.S. 2001. *Beyond Celts, Germans and Scythians: Archaeology and Identity in Iron Age Europe*. London: Duckworth.

Wells, P.S. 2003. *The Battle that Stopped Rome: Emperor Augustus, Arminius, and the Slaughter of the Legions in the Teutoberg Forest*. New York: W. W. Norton.

Wenke, R. J. (1980). *Patterns in Prehistory: Mankind's First Three Million Years*, Oxford: Oxford University Press.

Wheeler, M. 1968. *The Indus Civilization*. Cambridge: Cambridge University Press.

White, J.C. 1995. Incorporating heterarchy into theory on socio-political development: The case from Southeast Asia. *Heterarchy and the Analysis of Complex Societies. Archeological Papers of the American Anthropological Association* 6(1):101–123.

Whitridge, P. 2004. Landscapes, houses, bodies, things: "place" and the archaeology of Inuit imaginaries. *Journal of Archaeological Method and Theory* 11(2):213–250.

Wickham, C. 1992. Problems of comparing rural societies in Early Medieval Western Europe. *Transactions of the Royal Historical Society* 2:221–246.

Wigley, A. 2002a *Building Monuments, Constructing Communities: Landscapes of the first millennium BC in the central Welsh Marches*. University of Sheffield. Unpublished PhD thesis.

Wigley, A. 2002b *Fugitive pieces: towards a new understanding of the later second and first millennia BC in Shropshire* Paper commissioned by the West Midlands Regional Research Framework for Archaeology, University of Birmingham, Institute of Archaeology and Antiquity.

Wigley A. 2002c. *Touching the void: Iron Age landscapes and settlement in the West Midlands*. Paper commissioned for the West Midlands Regional Research Framework for Archaeology, University of Birmingham, Institute of Archaeology and Antiquity.

Wilcox, D.R. 1993. The Evolution of the Chacoan Polity. In Malville, J.M. and Matlock, G. (eds.), *The Chimney Rock Archaeological Symposium General Technical Report no. Rm-227*, pp. 76–90. Fort Collins: U.S.D.A. Forest Service.

Wilcox, D.R. 1999. A Peregrine View of Macroregional Systems in the North American Southwest, AD. 750–1250. In Neitzel, J.E. (eds), *Great Towns and Regional Polities in the American Southwest and Southeast*, pp. 115–141. Albuquerque: University of New Mexico Press.

Wilkes, J. (2007). Sailing to the Britannic Isles: Some Mediterranean Perspectives on the Remote Northwest from the Sixth Century BC to the Seventh Century AD. Gosden, C., Hamerow, H., de Jersey, P. and Lock, G. R. (eds.), *Communities and Connections: Essays in Honour of Barry Cunliffe*, pp. 3–14. Oxford: Oxford University Press.

Williams, H.M.R. 2007. The emotive force of Early Medieval mortuary practices. *Archaeological Review from Cambridge* 22(1):107–123.

Williams, M. 2003. Growing metaphors. The agricultural cycle as metaphor in the later prehistoric period of Britain and North-western Europe. *Journal of Social Archaeology* 3(2):223–255.

Wilson, B. 1992. Considerations for the identification of ritual deposits of animal bones in Iron Age pits. *International Journal of Osteoarchaeology* 2(4):341–349.

Wilson, B. 1999. Displayed or concealed? Cross cultural evidence for symbolic and ritual activity depositing Iron Age animal bones. *Oxford Journal of Archaeology* 18(3):297–305.

Wilson, D. 1981. The Vikings Strike. In Roesdahl, E. (eds.), *The Vikings in England*, pp. 15–18. London: Anglo-Danish Viking Project.

Winkler, A.-C. 2006. *Vallby—en övergiven Medeltida by på Visingsö* Uppsala: Uppsala University.

Woolf, G. 1993. Rethinking the oppida. *Oxford Journal of Archaeology* 12(2):223–234.

Woolf, G. 1997. Beyond Romans and natives. *World Archaeology* 28(3):339–350.

Wright, D. 1957. *Beowulf: A Prose Translation*. New York: Penguin Books.

Yoffee, N. 1991. Maya Elite Interaction: Through a Glass, Sideways. In Culbert, T.P. (eds.), *Classic Maya Political History: Hieroglyphic and Archaeological Evidence*, pp. 285–310. Cambridge: Cambridge University Press.

Zuckerman, A. 1977. The concept "Political elite": Lessons from mosca and pareto. *The Journal of Politics* 39(2):324–344.

Chapter 9
A Dual-Processual Perspective on the Power and Inequality in the Contemporary United States: Framing Political Economy for the Present and the Past

Gary M. Feinman

> *"I took an oath, and I take that oath to the President very seriously," former White House aide Sara Taylor told the Senate Judiciary Committee. Taylor's testimony prompted a clarification from Senator Patrick Leahy: "No the oath says that you take an oath to uphold and protect the Constitution of the United States."*

For *Foundations of Social Inequality* (Price and Feinman eds. 1995), I prepared a chapter (Feinman 1995) that laid out two ends of a continuous range of pathways to power and inequality—corporate and exclusionary/network. The arguments in that paper built on a discussion regarding these different modes or sources (corporate/exclusionary) of political-economic power, referred to as dual-processual theory (Blanton et al. 1996). To characterize the exclusionary strategy, political actors endeavor to consolidate and monopolize sources of power. Rule is autocratic, ostentatiously displayed, and negotiated largely through a network of personal and/or familial ties. The economic foundations of power tend to have their roots in the spoils of war, long-distance exchanges, or other forms of easily concentrated wealth. For the corporate strategy, in contrast, power is shared and divested in different groups or social segments. The distribution of wealth is somewhat more evenly distributed, while the trappings of personal power are relatively understated. Economic underpinnings are rooted in basic production or manufacturing. The corporate and exclusionary modes or strategies are envisioned as two ends of a continuum of organizational strategies that can be seen in societies that vary widely in both spatial scale and hierarchical complexity (sensu Service 1971).

Here, I expand the applicability of the analytical approach inherent in the dual-processual model beyond the deep past through a broad-brush historical analysis

G.M. Feinman (✉)
Department of Anthropology, The Field Museum, Chicago, IL 60605, USA
e-mail: gfeinman@fieldmuseum.org

T.D. Price, G.M. Feinman (eds.), *Pathways to Power*, Fundamental
Issues in Archaeology, DOI 10.1007/978-1-4419-6300-0_9,
© Springer Science+Business Media, LLC 2010

that focuses on the political and economic scene in the contemporary United States. This effort is made in order to place the core features of the dual-processual model in a broader temporal and conceptual context that ultimately aims to shed light on structures and strategies of inequality and power in both the past and the present (see Harvey 1990; Jones 2004 for parallel aims). At the same time, the focus on the present permits the engagement of a richer empirical record, more suitable to address key questions and concerns.

More specifically, two questions regularly have been raised regarding the contrasts drawn between the corporate and exclusionary modes and the historical utility of these concepts. One question (e.g., Ashmore 1996:47) involves whether this variation in the different ways that power is manifest is not more aptly viewed as characteristic of distinct cultural traditions. In other words, if this were the case, temporal shifts from more corporate to more exclusionary sources and manifestations of power (or the reverse) would not be expected over time within a specific cultural or societal context; rather, certain modes (and their practice) would be inexorably linked with certain cultural traditions. A second issue involves the kinds of decisions or factors that would spur such shifts in the sources of power (and how it was wielded and implemented) over time within a specific cultural/geographic setting (e.g., Ashmore 1996:47–48; Brumfiel 1996:48). The remainder of this discussion addresses these theoretical concerns through a focus on an empirical setting that is both data-rich and familiar to most of us, the recent history of the United States.

The principal aims of this analysis are to illustrate that shifts along the corporate/network continuum indeed can occur within a specific cultural setting and that these changes can take place within relatively short increments of time (certainly from an archaeological perspective). At the same time, I briefly explore some of the possible factors that may be driving these shifts. Finally, although my expertise is not in contemporary American history, I modestly hope that this analysis might make a small contribution to current analyses and our understanding of the present both by putting these recent changes in a broader comparative context and by analytically linking changes in the political and economic realms. The focus of the dual-processual perspective is by definition political and economic in character, and yet so many of the written sources that I drew from here, as ample as they are, tended (much like our everyday newspaper sections) to compartmentalize examinations of economy from analyses of politics. However, before turning to the empirical case, it is necessary to review dual-processual theory and to elaborate why the two questions to be discussed are important in the context of long-standing anthropological/archaeological approaches to long-term culture change. By addressing these questions, I endeavor to elaborate the role an approach, like dual-processual theory, can have for building a broadened conceptual/theoretical frame that more fully accounts for the various paths through which inequality was institutionalized and the various ways that it has been manifested over time.

Theoretical Background

For at least half a century (Sahlins and Service eds. 1960; Steward 1949), anthropological archaeologists who have taken a comparative approach to understanding societal variation have focused on two major axes of explanation—hierarchical complexity and culturally specific traditions—to account for diversity and change. In the original formulation, these axes were referred to as general and specific evolution (Sahlins and Service eds. 1960), although a more current and modified perspective (Flannery 1983) defines the latter as divergent evolution. A related approach (Sanders and Price 1968) refers to these principal interpretive frames as grades (the stepped variability associated with different tiers of hierarchical complexity) and lines (localized cultural patterns).

At the outset, I stress that the contrast of corporate and exclusionary modes of power is not presented as an alternative or a critique of theoretical frameworks that focus on hierarchical complexity and cultural traditions/practices as two key axes to account for societal variation and change. Over the last five decades of comparative archaeological research, these two axes effectively have made sense of important patterns in societal variation. So, the perspective advanced here (as well as in Feinman 1995 and Blanton et al. 1996) should be viewed as a significant, and perhaps necessary, expansion to such theoretical frames, especially more current approaches (e.g., Spencer 1997), in order to account for systematic patterns of variation in the modes of integration that bind leaders to followers and visa versa.

As laid out initially (Blanton et al. 1996:2–3), the corporate/exclusionary axis was proposed in recognition that political actors make use of differing strategies and that the relative emphasis on one or the other of these strategies has political-economic implications for other aspects of societal variation. Or to state it another way, building on prior research (Blanton et al. 1996:3; Feinman 1995:263–264), marked variability was noted in the ways that power was wielded, legitimized, and funded even for societies of comparable scale and hierarchical complexity. Significantly, analogous or similar patterns of variation have been noted in these two different modes of power (corporate and exclusionary) that crosscut different degrees or tiers of hierarchical complexity (e.g., Feinman 1995, 2000, 2001; Feinman et al. 2000). The corporate/exclusionary continuum in the way power is underpinned and implemented is, in a sense, orthogonal to the vertical dimension of hierarchical complexity (Feinman et al. 2000:454).

To get to the theoretical crux of the matter, I strongly support Drennan and Peterson's (2006:3960) recognition that "early chiefdom communities did not all take the same form and did not all emerge in the same way." The same point can be made for preindustrial states (e.g., Bondarenko et al. 2002; Claessen and Skalník eds. 1978; Grinin 2003, 2004; Feinman and Marcus eds. 1998) and early empires (Alcock et al. eds. 2001). Likewise, when it comes to complex societies, I concur with their observation (Drennan and Peterson 2006:3960) that there are "indications that this variation is not just idiosyncratic detail, and that comparative study of its patterning can provide insight into the developmental dynamics of institutionalized social hierarchy." In my opinion, archaeologists and other historical/social scientists indeed may find a number of different, yet productive axes of variation that can be employed to probe (and endeavor to account for) these patterns of variation in complex societies. The effort to explain patterns of variation that are neither bound to a specific cultural or ethnic tradition nor seen as explicable by the degree of hierarchical political complexity is a relatively under-problematized comparative enterprise in our discipline. The dual-processual theory, which was spurred by earlier comparative efforts (e.g., Lehman 1969; Renfrew 1974) that had noted similar patterning, has already provided avenues for understanding aspects of this diversity in regard to the bases and strategies that political actors use to wield power.

It is therefore necessary to position the aforementioned questions regarding the corporate/exclusionary continuum in this broader theoretical context. To begin with, it is important to assess whether the patterned variation associated with these strategies is (or is not) simply a product of specific cultural traditions. If it is, then the two traditional axes of variation (hierarchical complexity and cultural practice) might be considered adequate on their own. But, if within a specific cultural context, changes in power, legitimation, and inequality shift significantly over time, then these practices could not be considered as immutable within a specific cultural tradition, and a broader interpretive frame would be justified. Likewise, what conditions might prompt and/or allow political actors to change the strategies and funding of their power, and the means by which leaders and commoners interrelate and interconnect (e.g., Lohse 2007; Lohse and Gonlin 2007:xxii–xxiii). Societal transitions in the ways that power is wielded or wealth is distributed are important to explicate even if they do not involve shifts from one tier of hierarchical complexity to another. As Trigger (1996:63–64) wrote, "a general theory of sociocultural evolution would seek not to account for specific transitions from one level of complexity to another but to define processes that explain sociocultural change under any and all conditions."

Why the Contemporary United States?

My decision to focus on the political economy of the contemporary United States was not made lightly. Obviously, I am not a trained expert on this time period, and so I have to depend heavily on secondary and sometimes even journalistic sources. But the available data are both quantitatively and qualitatively rich, including summary statistics, insightful synthetic essays, and expressed statements of motivation. Despite the fullness of the empirical record, there are, of course, marked differences of opinion and interpretation concerning what these data mean. Yet, because of the wealth of data and precise chronological control, interpretive arguments regarding political-economic change are grounded more firmly than they would be for any archaeological case. Of course, in the archaeological past, it is exceedingly rare for researchers to have a chance to see the words of political actors.

At times, when I have discussed the corporate/exclusionary continuum with colleagues, they have questioned why or how political actors would shift the way they fund or wield power, whether such shifts could be implemented, and if such changes would effect or vary in concert with other societal changes. By focusing on the present, this analysis illustrates not only change along this continuum over the last 50–75 years, but also how these changes can take place in a non-revolutionary context. That is, these shifts in power and inequality occurred in a context in which cultural and legal traditions have remained largely intact. Of course, given the short time frame that is in focus, the documented changes would not be expected to move variation from one pole of the corporate/exclusionary continuum to the other. However, the assessment and utility of this frame should be monitored by the directionality and timing of observed changes along several political-economic dimensions. More specifically, do the documented changes fit the expected patterns of variation?

Political Economy: Power, Legitimation, Wealth, and Their Underpinnings

Given the wealth of data and opinions on recent history, the analysis here has to be both selective and in a sense superficial. There are entire shelves of books and reams of papers that probe the analyses and trends that are treated in a few short paragraphs here. For a fuller examination of the patterns under discussion, the reader is asked to pursue the sources cited in this analysis.

The focus is primarily on five key dimensions, which I suspect are at the core of the corporate/exclusionary continuum (Blanton et al. 1996; Feinman 2000:212). This narrowed focus decouples some of the descriptive characteristics outlined in our original formulations (Blanton et al. 1996; Feinman 2000) and stems from both the recognized importance of these dimensions and the desire to explore the patterned relationships between these five dimensions with other extant theoretical constructs.

First, I examine the balance of power or shifts in the ways that political power is divided or shared. Then, attention turns to the associated strategies of legitimation (and its relation to broader aspects of societal values and ethos), the relative importance of personal networks (individual ties) in the wielding, use, and maintenance of power, and the broader economic underpinnings of power. Because this volume's principal thematic emphasis is placed on inequality, the greatest attention is devoted to the fifth dimension, shifts in the distribution of wealth and economic manifestations of this increasing inequality. The discussion of these dimensions is followed by a consideration of some of the factors, strategies, and global conditions that are reasoned to have fostered and/or prompted the observed shifts. Finally, I return to the issues raised at the outset of the paper, including comparative implications for this investigation and the theoretical conceptualization of change and inequality in the deeper archaeological past.

The Balance of Governing Power

The foundation of the United States governmental structure was a reaction against monarchy. Thus a clear power-sharing arrangement was instituted with intended checks and balances between the executive, legislative, and judicial branches of government. The military was embedded within this governing structure, with the legislative branch charged with the power to both declare war and appropriate resources. Although this core constitutional structure remains largely in place, significant changes in practice and the actual balance of power have occurred over the course of more than two centuries.

The tussle for power has been part and parcel of governing in the United States from the outset. The famous debate over the scope of presidential authority occurred between Treasury Secretary Alexander Hamilton and Congressman James Madison during the administration of George Washington, the first president (Rudalevige 2006). Most political scientists recognize that for roughly the next 150 years there was a slow shifting of powers from the legislative to the executive branch. The ebbs and flows in this slow trend toward a greater centralization of power were affected by the nature of the specific partisan relations between the two branches, the personal qualities of the president (Neustadt 1960), and whether the nation was at war (in which case power generally tilted to the executive branch) (Owens 2006; Rudalevige 2006). Nevertheless, the checks built into the structure were sufficient that, despite the small but steady increase in presidential power over generations, overreach by the executive branch was not a regular theme even through the mid-twentieth century.

Such is not the case today, when a cottage industry of books and articles catalog the rapidly increasing concentration of power in the presidency/executive branch (e.g., Conason 2007; Crenson and Ginsberg 2007; Gellman 2008; Goldsmith 2007; Johnson 2007; Mayer 2008; Owens 2006; Rudalevige 2005, 2006; Savage 2007; Schwarz and Huq 2006) during the past four decades (with rapid expansion in recent years during the George W. Bush administration). Appropriately, the acceleration of this power concentration was closely timed with the era detailed in the analysis of the *Imperial Presidency* (Schlesinger 1973). Those who have discussed this recent aggregation of power come from both sides of the political spectrum. Generally, these accounts describe a marked increment in executive power that was accelerated during the Nixon presidency, with a second increase during the Reagan years, and a third even more pronounced expansion occurring since 2000 (e.g., Crenson and Ginsberg 2006; Rudalevige 2006). Some scholars argue that the aggrandizement of presidential powers has been so great in recent years that we may have gone past a "tipping point," reaching a new power-sharing equation between the different branches of government (Owens 2006).

The increasing concentration of power in the office of the President and the executive branch over the last 40 years is documented in detail in the sources cited above. Schlesinger (1973) focused on "the rise of presidential war," embattlement free of congressional authorization. In point of fact, Congress has not exercised its power to declare war since December 8, 1941! However, following the Nixon years, the Church Commission enumerated widespread abuses of executive power during this era, including unauthorized surveillance and implicit orders from high officials to violate the law (such as the targeted infliction of tax audits) (Schwarz and Huq 2006). Schlesinger (1973) also cataloged the efforts of the Nixon administration to centralize both budgeting powers and the shaping of policy (through impoundment, by refusing to spend congressionally allotted funds). The concept of executive privilege was broadened at that time, and there was a dramatic growth in both the size of the presidential staff and its politicization.

Although reforms to rebalance governmental powers were initiated in the years immediately following Watergate, most of these measures had limited lasting effect, remained unused, or were subverted in the subsequent quarter century (Rudalevige 2006:510). Starting with Ronald Reagan, presidents eagerly resumed power-grabbing strategies, ranging from the initiation (and increasing use) of presidential signing statements to mandated regulatory review by the executive branch, in order to avoid legislative dictation and/or oversight (Crenson and Ginsberg 2006). Such signing statements are written comments issued by a President at the time they sign legislation. The more controversial of these statements issue dictums by the President that they intend to ignore or implement selectively elements of the legislation.

There is widespread recognition that the George W. Bush administration has aggressively argued for and implemented presidential unilateralism to new heights (Crenson and Ginsberg 2006; Owens 2006; Rudalevige 2006; Warshaw 2006). Secrecy, surveillance, the treatment of prisoners (the parsing of what it means to torture), the circumvention of habeas corpus, the politicization of the government are all cataloged in recent newspapers and elaborated step-by-step in the sources cited herein. These efforts began prior to September 11, 2001, with unilateral decisions to shield information (Rudalevige 2006:511–515) from the public and other actions; however, the pace of these strategic initiatives to concentrate power picked up after that tragic day, often aided and abetted by the legislative branch. Yet, when statutes were inadequate, signing statement opinions were employed and used more frequently by George W. Bush than by all previous presidents combined, and, compared to earlier Presidents, his statements have made blunter claims to unfettered unitary executive power as well (see Sonnett 2006).

According to the latest figures (2005), the executive branch has mushroomed in size from its modest beginnings at the birth of the nation. It is presently composed of 2.6 million people as compared to 30,000 and 34,000 in the judicial and legislative branches, respectively (US OPM 2006). In addition, we recently have seen a blurring of the line between partisanship and the military, with use of a military man as a spokesman for presidential policy. This unusual step was preceded by the expansion of private security forces (such as Blackwater) that engage in security and military activities outside the rules and constraints of government (or legislative oversight) and with direct loyalties to those who elect to employ/contract them. Significantly, despite the ballooning of the executive branch, the governmental oversight of corporate activities that effect public welfare (agricultural inspection, banking and commerce oversight, corporate leasing of federal lands, the contracting of governmental duties to private industry, environmental protection) has been greatly curtailed.

During the first 150 years of US history, treaties (which require Senate ratification) generally outnumbered executive agreements (which do not); during the last 50 years the latter are roughly ten times more frequent (Howell 2005). Overall, the presidency has assembled more powers today than ever before, and they are being used more unilaterally. There is no doubt that we have moved a long way from the more collective or corporately organized forms of government that mandated the sharing of power across the institutions of government, as envisioned by the framers of the Constitution. But the shifting of this balance over the last 40 years has been accelerated, and never before have the use of the title "Commander-in-Chief" and the claims of "unitary executive" or exclusionary power been so explicit (e.g., Crenson and Ginsberg 2006; Wills 2007).

Legitimation

Throughout this nation's history, the balance of powers generally shifted to the president in times of war or major, yet short-term, international dealings (such as the Louisiana Purchase) (Crenson and Ginsberg 2006:213). Post-9/11, efforts to justify and legitimize claims for a unitary executive (and the associated concentration of power) have been tied to the creation of a perpetual war-time presidency, backed by a well-honed message dissemination and propaganda machine (Rich 2006). To quell debate and dissent, such rhetoric is reinforced by a frame of the president as a commander-in-chief over all of the people, not just the armed forces (Wills 2007). This image is fostered through staged and costumed militarized photo-ops ("Mission Accomplished") and the intentional use of macho, aggressive language by the president and his immediate team (Goldstein 2003; Guerlain 2006; Nelson 2006:5–7). Machismo speech is employed not merely in response to military enemies and reluctant foreign allies, but to members of the opposition party and the legislative branch, creating a highly charged, partisan political atmosphere. Not since the turn of the twentieth century, and the "big stick" presidency of Theodore Roosevelt, has the role of a combative, war-leader president been used so facilely (Guerlain 2006). In fact by 2004, the presidential mission was not merely defined as a battle against the "axis of evil" but as a fight against oppressors, terrorists, and tyrants worldwide (Reich 2008).

The calculated use of such confrontational and militarized rhetoric serves to help undermine the larger societal ethos of democracy, both by fostering the concentration of power and by lionizing a chief executive beyond reproach. After all, democracy is by definition a system based on broad participation, differing opinions, discussion, and compromise. Of course, these relationships are synergistic and must be considered in a broader time frame. In the United States of the late twentieth and early twenty-first centuries, the patrimonial rhetoric of an aggrandizing and all-powerful ruler, who will exchange protection for obedience, resonated in a context in which more people identified with individualizing behavior, cults of celebrity (Street 2004), machismo (Goldstein 2003), charismatic chief executives (Khurana 2002), and a fragmented array of highly partisan and internally homogenous groups and networks (Bishop and Cushing 2008; McPherson et al. 2001; Putnam 1995). Personal and political affiliations revolve around identity and polarization (a winner-take-all social Darwinism) rather than wider, more encompassing class interests (Abramowitz and Stone 2006; Frank and Cook 1995; Michaels 2006), contributing to the notion that affiliation and loyalty is to the man and not the Constitution/government or corporate whole of the citizenry (as typified by the verbal exchange that begins this chapter).

The unifying national ethos of the middle of the twentieth century associated with broad corporate/organizational affiliations (Whyte 1956), shared national experiences (such as watching Walter Cronkite), and reluctant, understated leaders no longer resonates. As Goldstein (2003:18) notes, gone for the most part are the icons of mid-century, "lonely lawmen, reluctant warriors, and world-weary survivors with a decent streak." Today, attention and financial reward accrue to individualizing pop culture idols. The point here is that not only has there been a shift since mid-century in the dominant political rhetoric and strategies of legitimation, but that such changes may recursively mirror (be reinforced by) broader societal trends in ideological practice and behavior. The "Triumphant Individual" has always been a potent tale of the American ethos, but in recent years the image has been recast to the property owner getting rich from his assets, who is part of the "ownership society" and who, like "Joe the Plumber" eschews national benevolence (such as Social Security) (Reich 2008; Sirota 2008).

Yet, at the same time, the process through which presidents are made is in transition. Seemingly gone also are the compromise candidates of brokered conventions, who rose through party support. Today, presidential prospects seem to be in preparation to run for years, if not longer, their quests fostered by raising large amounts of cash and building personal constituencies rather than accruing broad party loyalty. On reaching office, the ambitions of (and debts owed) these powerful constituencies become central to the agenda for and implementation of power by the new leader (Crenson and Ginsberg 2006:215).

The Growing Importance of Personal Networks

As noted above, a key feature of exclusionary (or network) power strategy is an emphasis on personal ties or connections, as contrasted with those who hold power having an orientation to the codes or beliefs of the group as a whole, which is more characteristic of corporate social formations. In line with the shifts toward more exclusionary power and associated legitimation, once again, transitions over the last four decades illustrate that personalized ties and networks are assuming a greater role in United States governance, power, and wealth than was evident in the mid-twentieth century (Domhoff 2005). These networks and loyalties play a significant role in the rise to power (and its maintenance), but they also are becoming a key to the workings of governance, in setting priorities and staffing subordinate positions (Lewis 2005), to ensure that personal debts and political loyalties are acted upon and not forgotten.

For the first time in history, a father and son have served as president (Bush) (Phillips 2004). And while the presidential sample size is small, there is a similar trend toward this practice throughout (elected) government (Millbank 2005). Although the familial succession to office has occurred throughout American history, name recognition and the access to money and connections has made the dynastic dynamic more important in recent years (Hertzberg 2007).

The process of getting elected to the presidency today requires raising huge amounts of money. The pursuit of funds in turn necessitates building networks of loyal supporters and contributors. Over the last two decades, the establishment of leadership PACs (political action committees) in addition to more standard campaign committees has allowed individual donors and lobbyists to circumvent contribution limits to the campaigns of specific candidates (Goff 2004). At the same time, prospective presidential aspirants donate funds from their leadership PACs to candidates running for lower legislative and local offices, thus building indebted networks of loyal political supporters. Campaign funds, of course, also are employed to build staffs of advisors and assistants. Through these and myriad other means, candidates today come to office with a large rolodex of personal connections, most of whom are either "patrons or clients."

Once a candidate is in office, loyal supporters are placed in government positions. Although partisan appointments are not new, they occur at greater frequency now than during the mid-twentieth century (Lewis 2008), with loyalties more apt to be to an individual than a party. Partisan appointments generally are less competent than non-partisan ones (Lewis 2007), and the officeholder is likely more interested in loyalty and responsiveness to political needs than effectiveness (Moe 1985). The harsh realities of these practices have never been more apparent than in the "reconstruction" of Iraq (Chandrasekaran 2006) or the response to hurricane Katrina (Dreier 2006; Frank 2008; Krugman 2006a); where the hiring of incompetent cronies instead of more qualified individuals severely diminished the ability of government to respond effectively to critical challenges.

But the importance of personal ties and affiliations extend beyond appointments to the crafting of agendas and the awarding of no-bid contracts that directly benefit individuals and corporations with close ties to the president. In recent memory, Iraq and Katrina exemplify this practice of "crony capitalism" (or using the power and largesse of government to benefit political associates and supporters) as noted in the sources cited above and numerous others, some of which see it as practically a guiding principle of the latter Bush administration (Frank 2008; Krugman 2002a, 2006a). As noted above, these contracts are awarded and then subsequently receive inadequate oversight. At the same time, over the last decades, wealthy individuals (often former government officials or donors to those who possess political power) establish well-supported media outlets, think tanks, and interest groups (Krugman 2006b). These groups use their hefty bankrolls to promote the policies and guiding principles of those same government officials (and politicians) whose views and interests closely align with theirs. These seemingly independent, but often tightly interconnected groups can be readily mobilized to influence (and even impersonate) the media, sway public opinion, and promote specific agendas when called to action by those in power.

Economic Underpinnings and Trends

Over the last four decades, a shift has been documented in the balance of powers (or how power is implemented). This growth in presidential powers has occurred in concert with changes in legitimation strategies and the increasing importance of personal networks and ties, often at the expense of broader affiliations such as to political party or the civil service. The remaining two dimensions to be explored are more in the economic realm. The consideration of these dimensions is decidedly not to imply or propose that any single individual, regardless how powerful, can play a major role in shaping an economy as complex and multifaceted as that in the United States. Nor do I mean to infer that these economic dimensions are simply or even directly correlated to how power is shared. Rather, the suggested hypothesis is that shifts in how power is funded, shared, and implemented may foster or enhance the likelihood of specific economic transitions or practices and vice versa. In fact, increasing flows of currencies, capital, and even people across borders may weaken governmental abilities to control basic economic processes (Rothkopf 2008), while enhancing the likelihood of success for some political arrangements and strategies over others. Given the shift toward a more exclusionary exercise of power, the expectations of dual-processual theory would be for a shift away from basic production toward a more exchange/"wealth"-focused economy (*sensu* D'Altroy and Earle 1985).

At the outset of the twentieth century, advances in transport and communication technologies (O'Rourke and Williamson 2002:35–37), as well as other factors, spurred international flows of goods, services, and capital to unprecedented levels (at that point) in the world's history. Yet, following two World Wars and the Great Depression, the world economy, including that in the United States, was far less interconnected than it had been four decades earlier (Krueger 2006). Although the importance of agrarian production for the United States economy had declined significantly since the dawn of the twentieth century (Lobao and Meyer 2001), basic manufacturing had increased significantly over that same period. Thus basic production, farm, and factory, remained the mainstay of the nation's economy prior to and immediately after World War II (Fig. 9.1) (Maddison 1997:333). The largest company in the United States (and the world) in that era was General Motors, which focused on the manufacture of automobiles.

The mid-twentieth century in the United States also was a time marked by significant governmental expenditures in infrastructure, including the interstate highway network, the expansion of public universities across the country, and increased funding for science. Nationally, labor organizations were strong, and employment was far more stable than is the case today (Reich 2007; Whyte 1956). Capital

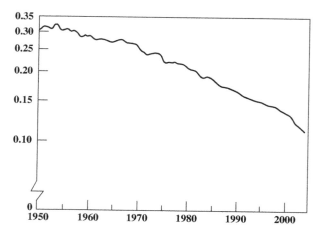

Fig. 9.1 Manufacturing employment as a share of total employment (Maddison 1997)

investments also tended to be longer term, enabling greater corporate commitments to labor and infrastructure. Reich (2007) refers to the immediate post-war era as the "Not Quite Golden Age," referencing, in part, a broadened commitment to national interests and a widespread belief that the country's democratic institutions would reflect public interests.

Today, the basic underpinnings of the national economy have markedly changed. Employment in the service sector now far surpasses basic production-related industries, in both manufacturing and agriculture combined. In fact, by the middle of the first decade of the twenty-first century, only roughly a tenth of United States employment remained in manufacturing jobs. The net number of jobs in these production industries has declined so that the total is now comparable to 1950, although both the size of the overall population and the economy are much larger.

Forbes magazine (2007) ranks the five largest United States public companies (based on sales, market value, assets, and profits) as Citigroup, Bank of America, General Electric, JP Morgan Chase, and American International Group. All of these corporations, with the exception of General Electric, are principally involved in finance and the international flow of capital. Even the conglomerate General Electric, which is the only one of the five firms with a manufacturing focus, has diversified into communications and capital services so that three of its six core divisions are finance, healthcare, and NBC Universal. The sixth United States-based company in the world's corporate top ten is Exxon Mobil, which is involved in the extraction and marketing of resources, primarily from overseas.

As typified by the aforementioned companies, there is no doubt that we are in an era of economic globalization. The movement of portfolio capital and the international transfer of goods, capital, and information across national borders have reached levels that likely are unprecedented in the history of the world (Berger 2000; Brady et al. 2007; Chase-Dunn et al. 2000:86). In the United States between 1960 and 2000, the percentage of the Gross Domestic Product made up by exports and imports more than doubled (Brady et al. 2007:314–315). Membership in labor affiliations has markedly declined from the mid-twentieth century, and job security is reduced (Alderson 2004; Gosselin 2008). Capital flows rapidly in and out of wealth-making opportunities, so that longer-term infrastructural investments become harder to afford and risk. The increasing mobility of capital, people, and goods across borders appears to have a negative impact on labor (wages and stability) while spurring intra-country inequality, although the effects vary across nations (Alderson and Nielsen 2002; Brady et al. 2007:318–325; Brady and Wallace 2000). In the United States, broad popular belief in the institutions of power and the prospects for the economy are at low ebbs (Reich 2007).

The sociopolitical consequences of economic internationalization and higher rates of capital mobility at the national level are not uniformly agreed upon (Berger 2000:56). So, to evaluate its effects, it is important to consider variation in the broader political economies in each national context. In cross-nation comparisons, when social corporatism (broad, shared concerns for the society at large) is diminished, collective interests and identities are fragmented, democratic institutions are weakened, and those holding political power are not heavily invested in the principles of the welfare state, increasing capital mobility tends to dampen governmental investments in social expenditures and associated programs (Berger 2000:56; Swank 2001:138, 2005) with implications for patterns of intra-national inequality. The apparent diminishment of funding for infrastructural improvements and necessary upgrades (ASCE 2005) also would seem to be a consequence of a government that favors narrow class interests in the context of an increasingly internationalized economy.

Economic Inequality

In line with the trends outlined for the four previous dimensions above, increasing economic inequality and growing tendencies toward more ostentatious displays of wealth would be expected over the past four decades, beginning in the 1970s, with marked acceleration since 2000. According to the expectations of dual-processual theory, disparities in wealth should be more marked today than in the mid-twentieth century. Economic inequality can be manifested in diverse ways, and various metrics can be used to assess its manifestation in any specific space–time context. Nevertheless, for the contemporary United States, a range of measures all point to a time-series pattern in which wealth and income have become increasingly concentrated at the very top during the last 30–40 years. This bifurcating trend in income and wealth disparities was noted earlier on (Thurow 1987), but it has received recent in-depth scholarly focus (e.g., Piketty and Saez 2003, 2006; Wolff 2006) as well as serious popular (Krugman 1996, 2006b) attention in recent years.

In the United States, wealth always has been unequally distributed. A long-term examination (Lindert 2000) indicates that the degree or extent of economic concentration has not been uniform over time. After an extended period of increasing inequality, there was a shift toward greater economic equality during the first half of the twentieth century. However, as noted above, this trend was reversed in the 1970s. By 2004 (Fig. 9.2), the top 1% of households held 34.3% of the total wealth, while the next 9% collectively owned 36.9%, and the remaining 90% had 28.7% (Wolff 2006). In other words, based on these figures, 10% of the population owned more than 70% of the nation's wealth (see also Mishel et al. 2007).

Fig. 9.2 The distribution of wealth in the United States in 2004 (Wolff 2006)

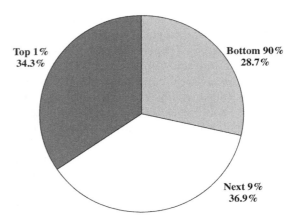

In regard to household wealth, the pattern over the last 30 years reverses a trend that began with the Great Depression and continued with the implementation of the New Deal policies of the Roosevelt administration and during the immediate post-war era (Fig. 9.3). Today, the present wealth disparities are more in line with the distributional pattern during the Gilded Age and the Roaring Twenties than the mid-twentieth century. From 1989 to 2004, the concentration of wealth at the very top increased (Kennickell 2006), with the greatest growth having occurred amongst the Forbes 400, those people representing the top 0.0002% in terms of wealth (Kopczuk and Saez 2004:479–483). The proportion of the nation's wealth controlled by this

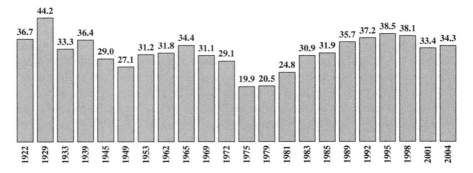

Fig. 9.3 Percentage share of household wealth held by the top 1%, 1922–2004 (Wolff 2006)

group roughly tripled from the early 1980s, when these individuals accounted for just over 1%, to a 3.5% share in 2002. Furthermore, three-quarters of the Top 400's gain between 1983 and 2000 was accounted for by the top quarter of Forbes's list (the top 100). Given these figures, it is not surprising to read headlines that the "very rich are leaving the merely rich behind" (Uchitelle 2006). With the corresponding trends in income differentials and socioeconomic mobility, the prospects for further bifurcation in the distribution of America's wealth appear highly likely.

Over the last century in the United States, income disparities have followed a similar temporal pattern, creating a U-shaped curve in the overall proportion of income received by the top income earners (Figs. 9.4 and 9.5). The proportion of total income, excluding capital gains, accrued by the top .01 % income earners (Fig. 9.5) has increased sixfold since the mid-twentieth century (Piketty and Saez 2003, 2006). Whereas, the bottom fifth of the population by income has had incredibly stagnant earnings (in inflation adjusted dollars) since 1979 (Fig. 9.6), income for the top 1% has soared. Significantly, while the share of income going to the highest quintile also has grown some during this period, that increase is much more modest and largely subsumed by the expansion at the top (Figs. 9.6 and 9.7). Clearly, income concentration in recent years is not just a broad-based economic skew of returns toward the college educated (or technologically skilled), since a much smaller fraction of the overall population (than the college trained) is benefiting significantly from gains in economic productivity (Dew-Becker and Gordon 2005). The gains in income were distributed very differently in the United States between 1947 and 1979 (Fig. 9.8) (Goldin and Katz 2001).

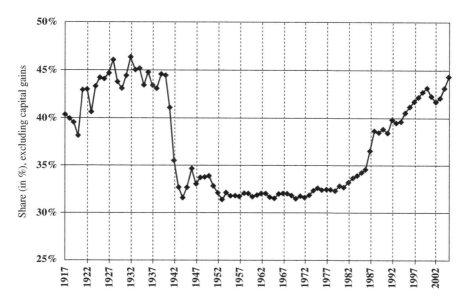

Fig. 9.4 The top decile income share, 1917–2005 (Piketty and Saez 2003, updated through 2005 in August 2007 [http://elsa.berkeley.edu/~saez])

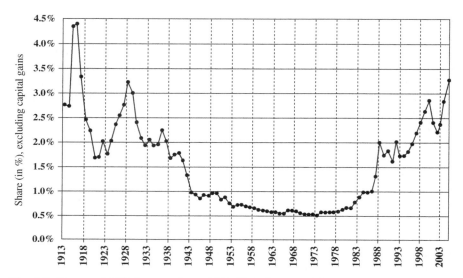

Fig. 9.5 The top 0.01% income share, 1913–2004 (income defined as market income but excludes capital gains; source: Piketty and Saez 2003, updated through 2005 in August 2007 [http://elsa.berkeley.edu/~saez])

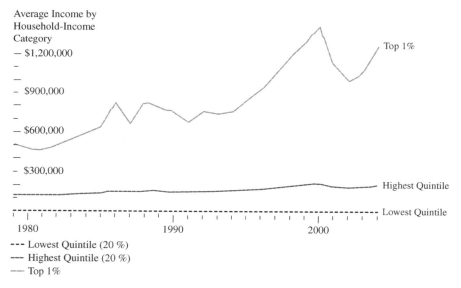

Fig. 9.6 Since 1979, the bottom fifth of the population by income have had remarkably stagnant earnings (adjusted for inflation). Meanwhile, income for the top 1% of earners has soared (New York Times, June 10, 2007; source: Congressional Budget Office)

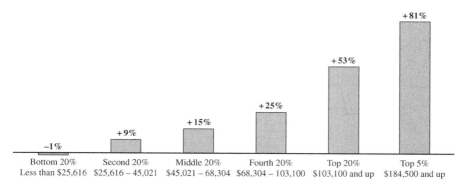

Fig. 9.7 Change in real family income by quintile and top 5%, 1979–2005 (http://www.demos.org/inequality/images/charts/changesrealfamily7905.tif)

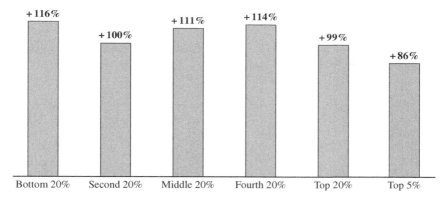

Fig. 9.8 Change in real family income by quintile and top 5%, 1947–1979 (http://demos.org/inequality/images/charts/changesrealfamily4779.tif)

This concentration of income among the wealthiest Americans has not been driven primarily by capital income, but by wage and entrepreneurial earnings (Piketty and Saez 2003). In 2006, the buying power of the minimum wage (adjusted for inflation) reached a 51-year low (Bernstein and Shapiro 2006) (Fig. 9.9). At the same time, CEOs of large United States companies made as much money in a day on the job as average workers took home in a year (Anderson et al. 2007). In 2006, CEOs made in a year 364 times what an average worker took home (Fig. 9.10). Although this figure was down from an even larger multiplier in 2000 (525 times), it was more than three times greater than the differential (107 times) in 1990. Based on a longer time-series analysis (Frydman and Saks 2007), and in contrast to the remarkable upward trajectory of CEO pay during the last two decades, the median real value of CEO compensation was relatively flat from the end of World War II to the mid-1970s. These differentials would be even greater if full annual compensation packages, rather than just salary were considered (Anderson et al. 2007).

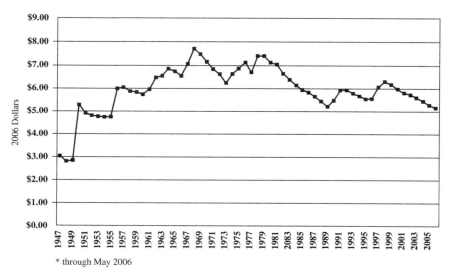

Fig. 9.9 Real value of the minimum wage, 1947 to May 2006 (Economic Policy Institute, Bernstein and Shapiro 2006)

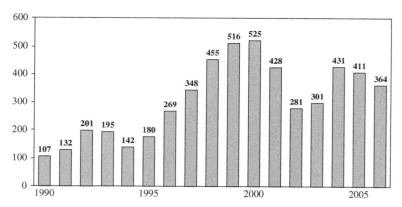

Fig. 9.10 CEO pay as a multiple of average worker pay, 1990–2006 (Executive excess, Anderson et al. 2007)

Meanwhile, unlike the trend in CEO compensation, from 1970 to 1999 the average annual salary in America, expressed in 1998 dollars barely increased from $35,522 to $35,864 (Krugman 2002b).

In his 1967 book, *The New Industrial State*, John Kenneth Galbraith (1967:129–132) opined that the days of the robber barons were over, and that it was practically unimaginable that the managers of large corporations would personally profit from their positions at the helm of America's great corporate institutions. Clearly, the ethos is different today, with the 20 highest-paid individuals at publicly traded corporations in 2006 taking home, on average, \$36.4 million dollars (Anderson et al. 2007). That figure is 38 times more than for the highest-paid leaders in the non-profit sector and 204 times more than for the best-paid generals in the United States army. At the same time, in this decade, executives of such companies as Enron, Countrywide, AIG, and others sold off their own sizable accumulations of company stock prior to (and to avoid) significant declines in share price. Furthermore, CEO salaries have grown much beyond the increase that could be explained by changes in firm size, performance, and industry type. Had the relationship of compensation to size, performance, and industry type remained constant from 1993 to 2003, mean 2003 CEO compensation would only have been half as large as it actually was (Bebchuk and Grinstein 2005).

The widening synchronic disparities in wealth and income have been solidified by a decline in socioeconomic mobility (Fig. 9.11), particularly over the last 20 years (Bradbury and Katz 2002; Neckerman and Torche 2007:339–340). The expansion in economic inequality during the 1980s (in the absence of greater opportunities for social mobility) led to economic differences between households that persisted for longer durations (Beller and Hout 2006). At the same time, a longitudinal survey (Mazumder and Levine 2003) that compared the salaries of brothers found that the correlations in wages and family incomes among brothers rose substantially between those who entered the labor market in the 1970s and the cohort who joined the work force in the 1980s – to – early 1990s. In other words, the family and community influences shared by siblings had a significantly greater role in determining economic outcomes for those who began working more recently.

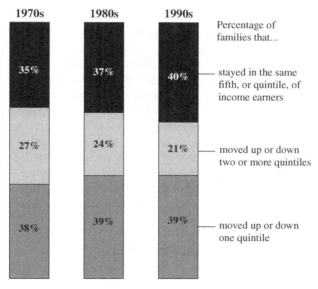

Fig. 9.11 Income mobility (New York Times, adapted from Katherine Bradbury and Jane Katz 2002)

In America today, the resilience to such domestic risks is greatly reduced compared to decades ago, due to the shrinking social safety nets and the greater proportion of households that already depend on more than one adult income (Bernstein 2007a; Gosselin 2008; Hacker 2006). Bernstein (2007a) has categorized these program and policy shifts as the rise of extreme individualism, and the emergence of a YOYO (you're on your own) philosophy at the expense of a value system that emphasizes WITT (we're in this together). As poignantly illustrated through specific cases (Gosselin 2004), the growing risks to family wealth and income are often setoff by job losses, health emergencies, divorce, or other domestic crises, which have impeded upward mobility and further concentrated wealth during the last decades. Today the odds of getting rich are not merely long for children of low-income households, but also for the scions of middle-class families as well (Hertz 2006), and these odds (at least for men) have seemingly become more stacked against upward mobility since the 1930s (Beller and Hout 2006). Furthermore, compared to most other industrial democracies, intergenerational socioeconomic mobility is lower in the contemporary United States (Hertz 2006). Increasing income disparities, especially over the last few decades, have been associated with a comparable bifurcation in the retail market, where low- and high-end stores thrive, but the traditional department store, catering to those in the economic middle, has a tough challenge making ends meet. Likewise, the US sales of diamonds, luxury cars, palatial homes, and extravagant weddings are doing rather well (Frank 2007; Mead 2007; Twitchell 2002).

The twentieth century U-shaped trend in US wealth and income discrepancies has become an important focus for socioeconomic time-series analysis, especially given the keen public and scholarly attention focused on the causes and consequences of economic inequality today. The era of less pronounced income differences during the mid-century, particularly following the depression of the 1930s, has been referred to as "The Great Compression" (Goldin and Margo 1992), while the marked reversal that took place in the late 1970s/early 1980s has been called "The Great U-Turn" (Bluestone and Harrison 1982; Harrison and Bluestone 1988). Many hypotheses have been advanced to account for the rising economic disparities in income and wealth that took off roughly four decades ago in the United States (Dew-Becker and Gordon 2008). Likewise, in previous sections, I referred to a number of published perspectives that have been advanced regarding the factors behind the concentration of political power over roughly the same period. Focusing more heavily on inequality, I now not only consider and evaluate some of these interpretations, but also point to links between the patterned variation in the means and concentration of wealth and the funding and implementation of power.

Correlation, Causality, and Comparison

The previous discussion has outlined how over the last four decades in the United States there has been a shift in the funding and wielding of power from more corporate to more exclusionary modes. These temporally correlated changes, which conform to the expectations of dual-processual theory, have been tracked along five dimensions. Significantly, if we expand the time horizon to roughly a century, we see that changes along most of these dimensions did not occur in a linear or unidirectional manner, but rather in a more cyclic or U-shaped way. That is, in some respects (but clearly not all) the wielding of power and the nature of economic inequality today pattern more like the Gilded Age than with the mid-century, Great Compression. Furthermore, over the past 40 years the important, and seemingly ongoing, transitions outlined above have taken place without any marked shift in hierarchical complexity or any major break in the ethnic/historical tradition most prevalent in United States society. Although some laws and practices certainly have been amended, modified, or overwritten, the basic legal system and underlying governmental structure has remained intact through this period.

Here, with an initial and heavy focus on the changing patterns of economic inequality, I consider some of the factors (and associated discussions) that have been advanced to account for both the mid-century Great Compression and the subsequent U-turn. In examining change along these dimensions, it is important to stress that there is no one causal factor, "grand design," or "great man" (but see Savage 2007) behind what should be seen as more complex, recursive processes and episodes of transition.

Efforts to explain the flattening of income distributions at mid-century reflect in part the loss of fortunes during the earlier Great Depression and the progressive tax and social welfare policies that were put in place as a response to this economic collapse. Yet, during the post-World War II era, broad participation in unions, low volumes of cross-border exchange in capital and goods (particularly imports), and diminished levels of in-migration also are broadly recognized as factors that tended to keep wage disparities in check (at least in a relative sense) (Alderson and Nielsen 2002; Krugman 1996; Neckerman and Torche 2007). In contrast, by the late 1970s–1980s, when economic differences began to rise, the clout and participation in the labor movement was declining, rates of in-migration were rising, and global flows were accelerating. The long-term trends in these factors have continued to the present day. In addition to "globalization," the changing nature of the labor force is another factor frequently proposed as a cause for this economic U-turn. This transformation from heavier production tasks to more knowledge-based jobs that incorporate new information technologies has led to declines in employment, particularly at larger firms where low-skill workers are replaced by a smaller number of higher-skill ones.

The aforementioned factors related to the increased global circulation of goods, services, and people (the importation of inexpensive goods, the lowering of trade barriers, outsourcing of jobs, in-migration) as well as the rise of information technologies have certainly had an important role in The Great U-Turn and the rapid growth in United States economic inequality over the past four decades. Yet, despite their intuitive appeal, they are not the most significant causal factors. For one thing, these factors mostly have contributed to stagnating salaries and the loss of jobs near the base of the income pyramid, but they do not account for the accelerated growth in wealth and incomes at the top. Likewise, the shift from factory to more service-oriented employment also has weakened union density and clout (Clawson and Clawson 1999), but that shift has been promoted by other factors as well and has its own recursive effects. Furthermore, the rapid rise of information technologies actually post-dates the outset of The Great U-Turn in the 1970s, so it could not have been an instigating factor in that reversal from relative income/wealth compression. Perhaps, most tellingly, the same shifts toward information technologies and a more interconnected world have affected the economies of all industrial democracies across the globe, but the extent of subsequent income/wealth bifurcation is far from uniform (Alderson and Nielsen 2002; Bernstein 2007b; Brady et al. 2007; Gangl 2005; Johnston 2007; Mann and Riley 2007).

Compared to other nations, the United States had greater inequalities in its standard of living soon after The Great U-Turn (see Atkinson et al. 1995 for the 1980s), but these disparities have expanded rapidly (and relatively continuously) in recent decades (Gangl 2005) at rates unparalleled in other countries where globalization, the explosion of information technologies, and in-migration all have increased. Like the United States, Great Britain also has experienced increased economic inequality over recent decades, but to a lesser degree and in somewhat more episodic fashion. In the rest of western Europe, there have been more minimal increases in economic inequities (Alderson and Nielsen 2002; Gottschalk and Smeeding 1997). In other words, the shifts toward information and internationalization (as well as the shift away from agrarian production) (see Alderson and Nielsen 2002:1286–1287) all tend to have a positive relationship with increasing income inequality, but through cross-national comparison, the critical role of institutional factors in either mediating or exaggerating these stresses and trends is evident (Harjes 2007).

An array of studies (e.g., Alderson and Nielsen 2002:1280–1281; Brady et al. 2007:324) have illustrated that where unions are strong and policies are implemented that benefit labor (so labor is included in wage-setting decisions and unemployment benefits are good), the expansion in wage and income disparities can be held in check or slowed. In this regard, the declining voice of unions as part of the national conversation in the United States may be as great a loss as the specific role of these institutions in negotiating particular contracts or the proportion of the work force that they cover (Freeman 1993; Wallerstein 1999). Distinctions in the policies established by government and business institutions, and their guiding hand behind how social welfare, redistributive, and social safety net programs are defined, constitute a growing distinction between the United States and many of the other industrial democracies where such programs have been strengthened in response to growing economic inequities (Stiglitz 2007). The differences in these practices have impacted the varying extents of wealth disparities cross-nationally. In the 1970s, in the United States, those in power rejected mediating policies, such as permanent wage and price controls and broader business/labor planning (Domhoff 2006). Subsequently, tactics and policies have been implemented (fostered by consistent efforts to sway broader societal values and the public) that weakened unionization, tightened unemployment and welfare benefits, cut social security and private retirement benefits, curtailed health coverage for many employees, let the minimum wage stagnate, de-investing in public education and national infrastructure while passing highly regressive income, estate, and other tax/transfer policy changes (Gramlich et al. 1993; Gross 1995; Hacker 2006; Krugman 2007). Whether always by explicit design (or not), these policies promoted relative economic inequities in the United States (from a pattern of relative cross-national equality during The Great Compression) at the same time that distinct programs and philosophies (an emphasis on redistributive social welfare programs) were ameliorating the forces of economic disparity in other industrial nations (Gustafsson and Johansson 1999).

Furthermore, none of the aforementioned factors can adequately account for sky-rocketing incomes and wealth at the very apex of the economic pyramid. Clearly, returns to education or skill alone cannot explain these trends (Dew-Becker and Gordon 2005) since they benefit so few. Likewise, the post-war mid-twentieth century was a time of relative economic prosperity in the United States, yet this economic prosperity did not translate into wealth concentration to near the degree that it does now. For today's CEOs, great economic gain does not even necessarily reflect past financial success for the company bottom line or returns to its sharehold-ers. At the same time, something akin to superstar aura and legitimation (valuations) and the drive toward exclusionary power would seem to be the factors behind the swelling gap between chief executives and the next rung of top corporate executives in the same firms (Porter 2007). A few decades ago, chief executives running the largest American companies earned 80% more, on average, than the third highest-paid executives. By the early part of this decade that differential had ballooned to 260% (Frydman and Saks 2007).

So while history and long-standing national laws/values do matter, the particular positions and programs of specific governments and power holders can and do have critical effects on accelerating or mediating change from certain patterns and degrees of inequality to others (Bartels 2008; Gilens 2005; Mann and Riley 2007; Stiglitz 2007). Increasing inequality is not just the product of economic forces, but also the product of political actions. These strategies can be particularly significant in the face of other strong forces and factors of change.

Summarizing Thoughts and Implications for the Diachronic Study of Inequality

In this paper, I have considered the present in order to enhance our perspective on inequality in the past. Others are also beginning to bridge this gulf of time (e.g., Milanovic et al. 2007) to compare the cross-cultural manifestation of inequality in diverse historical contexts. What have we learned and what are the implications, most importantly for how we theorize and frame the archaeological/diachronic investigations of past systems of inequality, and how do these observations relate to broad theoretical issues in the social and behavioral sciences?

At the outset, and to address the two queries that we begin with, we have seen that strategies of power and economic inequality can indeed shift in important ways, even in brief periods of time (at least relative to the lion's share of archaeological investigations). These recent shifts correspond broadly to the expectations of dual-processual theory, marking an increasing trend to exclusionary modes of power and the concentration of economic gain. This shift over the last four decades toward more concentrated political power and wealth in the contemporary United States has occurred without comparable increases in societal scale or hierarchical complexity. They also reverse a trend (in many of these same societal dimensions) during the first half of the twentieth century, indicating that the recent 40-year trend is neither exclusively bound or tied to a specific society/culture or legal system nor is it irreversible. That is, the shift toward more exclusionary manifestations of power occurred within a specific cultural/societal context, the contemporary United States.

Through this example, we also have seen that this recent shift cannot be explained by any one stimuli or cause. Rather, these changes are an outcome that involves the interplay of factors that are recursively interconnected and operate at several spatial scales. Shifts in these factors provide opportunities and challenges for individual and institutional agents. And these responsive strategies and policies in turn lead to changes in other societal spheres. The explanatory webs behind these recent shifts are undoubtedly far more complex than can be provisionally outlined here. But causal links may be inferred between the concentration of wealth, the consolidation of power in the hands of a narrowing few, the systemic importance of those individuals' cross-generational and interpersonal networks (both national and international), the growing significance and breadth of capital, people, and information transfers, along with popular ideologies of legitimacy that promote and reify individualizing behavior, excess, and exclusionary power (at the expense of more collective values and institutions of shared governance that endeavor to competently serve the welfare of society at large) (see also Ember et al. 1997; Russett 1964). Correspondingly, mathematical modeling directed principally at contemporary societies illustrates how strong unitary executives reliant on personal networks to enhance their own power (through economic transactions) are advantaged in contexts already characterized by marked income inequities (Acemoglu 2005; Acemoglu and Robinson 2006).

Nevertheless, the skeptical archaeologists might ask, "how does this analysis inform diachronic studies of inequality and power in the deeper past?" Although time does not permit the in-depth examination of an archaeological case, I briefly consider a major episode of transition in the prehispanic Valley of Oaxaca, Mexico (Feinman 1999). The Classic–Postclassic transition in the Valley of Oaxaca has been the focus of scholarly debate for decades (e.g., Blomster ed. 2008; Feinman 2007: 8–11; Marcus and Flannery 1983). It was marked by the depopulation and political collapse of the early and long-lived city of Monte Albán (and other large centers) at the end of the Classic period and a reorganization of the Valley population into more balkanized and small polities during the subsequent Late Postclassic era.

In the Valley of Oaxaca, the transition from the Classic to Late Postclassic period also involved a shift in the nature of rule from a more faceless rule focused on monumental temple-plaza complexes to a very different Late Postclassic political system that featured large palatial/residential architectural complexes and deer skin books that traced the lives (marriage, military victories) of powerful leaders. Although elements of these shifts began at the end of the Classic period with the erection of genealogical registers (e.g., Marcus 1983), featuring a sequence of named, married couples, at a number of valley sites, they found more detailed expression in the Late Postclassic through murals painted on palatial buildings (and other venues) that describe marriage as well as political alliances (Pohl 1999, 2003).

At the top of the social order, Postclassic rulers were marked by rich burials, laden with labor intensive and exotic goods, such as the re-use of an earlier tomb at Monte Albán, Tomb 7 (Caso 1982; see also Gallegos 1978 for another elaborate Postclassic burial at Zaachila). The accumulation of goods interred in Tomb 7 (excavated in 1931–1932) was so astounding that archaeologists have subsequently probed many burial features from Monte Albán. Yet none of these Classic-era tombs have yielded anything close to the wealth found in the tomb re-used to bury a lord during the Late Postclassic (Winter 1995). In line with this distinction in burial treatment, artifact distributions indicate greater wealth disparities within the regional population during the Late Postclassic period (Kowalewski and Finsten 1983). Thus the more individualizing Late Postclassic rulership was timed with greater disparities in access to wealth during that phase in contrast with more corporate poltical economy earlier in the Classic period.

Originally, this important episode of transition was interpreted to coincide with a population replacement of Zapotec by Mixtec peoples (e.g., Caso et al. 1967). Yet basic ways of commoner domestic life changed little during this era of organizational restructuring (Markens et al. 2008), and most contemporary peoples in the valley still speak and trace their cultural roots to Zapotec traditions. Although an explication of this Valley of Oaxaca shift requires new data and concerted research efforts, it is constructive to find that, as in the contemporary American example reviewed above, the Classic–Late Postclassic transition in the Valley of Oaxaca from a more corporate to more exclusionary mode of organization coincided with an intensified flow of goods and wealth (Blanton and Feinman 1984; Kowalewski et al. 1983; Smith and Berdan eds. 2003) across the cultural and geographic regions of Mesoamerica. Thus the breakdown of the Monte Albán polity (and the reconfiguration into small political units) in conjunction with shifts in the nature and intensified volume of pan-Mesoamerican exchange and alliance networks provide productive avenues through which this organizational transition should be examined and explicated. At the same time, the specific sequence of changes and their interconnections over more than six centuries remains to be documented and refined.

Bridging Theoretical Constructs to Chart Future Directions

The dual-processual perspective was never intended to inject another set of static types into comparative discussions of societal variation and pathways of change (e.g., Blanton et al. 1996:1). Rather, the goal has been to elucidate a behavioral theory rooted in political economy. Although our early presentations sometimes introduced or emphasized empirical patterns that appeared to conform or illustrate these contrasting modes, our aim has been to explain why these patterns of variation

are found cross-culturally, and what that might inform us about different strategies of power and structures of inequality. In this concluding section, I endeavor
to link the dual-processual approach to two bodies of behavioral theory that might
ultimately help account for and provide broader intellectual underpinnings for the
contrastive dynamic of the corporate-exclusionary modes.

At the most foundational level, it is becoming clearer that social hierarchies guide
behavior in many animal species, including humans (Chase et al. 2002). No known
human society is strictly egalitarian so that status distinctions for even age or gender differences are completely absent (Cashdan 1980; Flanagan 1989). Although the
human brain is seemingly hard-wired for hierarchical organization (Sapolsky 2005;
Zink et al. 2008), the manifestation of such group interactions can take a diversity
of forms, as they also can in chimpanzees (Lycett et al. 2007). Yet, at the same time,
the social learning skills and cooperative behaviors that facilitate the formation and
duration of groups has been argued to be a defining feature that early in our evolutionary history distinguished humans from other primates (Gavrilets et al. 2008;
Herrmann et al. 2007; Tomasello 1999). These social practices helped keep overtly
hierarchical behaviors largely in check for a long era of human history as well as
in more contemporary small-scale societies (e.g., Boehm 1993). Therefore, it is not
surprising that both of these deeply rooted, but seemingly contradictory practices,
hierarchy and cooperation, recombine in a range of ways in human social groupings, and that the different outcomes of these behavioral strategies might pattern in
certain repetitive ways. One strategy emphasizes autocratic decision making, display, and unequal access to valued resources (exclusionary) while the other tends
toward a more consensual and participatory structure that also may feature different
manifestations of coercion or the "tyranny of the majority" (corporate).

A second productive avenue for theoretical boot strapping and development
already has been advanced by Richard Blanton (Blanton and Fargher 2008; Fargher
and Blanton 2007), who has drawn on contrasts in political strategies discussed
by the political scientist, Margaret Levi (1988), who, in turn, built upon collective
action theory (Olsen 1965). These ideas explore the extent to which individuals
who share common goals may find it in their personal interest to carry some of
the organizational costs. As Lichbach (1996:32) states, a collective action problem
or the "cooperator's dilemma" "arises whenever mutually beneficial cooperation is
threatened by individual strategic behavior." In other words, like the dual-processual
approach, this conceptual approach is concerned with the kinds of integrative strategies and practices that keep social groups together and why different societal
compacts are favored in certain contexts as opposed to others.

Levi's (1988:2) treatise views variation in governing regimes through the examination of the link between the ways managerial institutions are financed and the
dispersal of political power/voice. The focus is on ruling strategies, political integration, revenue, and resources – particularly how the latter two finance power. In
most respects, these core features are directly parallel to the unpacked core dimensions of the dual-processual perspective utilized above. Levi's thesis is that the more
leaders depend on the extraction of localized resources from their immediate populace, the more voice and so checks on the rulers the ruled will have. Alternatively,

the more external and monopolized a ruler's financial base, the more concentrated power is apt to be. This model is in line with the somewhat counterintuitive findings from the contemporary United States in which reduced basic production and lowered rates of direct taxation on much of the population has been timed over the last four decades with an expansion/concentration of presidential and executive branch power.

Not too long ago, the late social scientist, Charles Tilly (2001:299), decried that anthropology's interest in inequality (and particularly its relationship to leadership and power) was on the descent. This essay serves as a response to Tilly's important call, making the case that more dialogue on this topic is necessary across social and historical disciplines, including archaeologists studying the deeper past. Such scholarly communication not only expands our horizon of cases in time and space, but it forces researchers to consider both the diversity between different levels of organizational complexity as well as variation across those societies with similar tiers of decision-making structure (in line with Trigger's [1996] directive above). In this respect, the past with its longtime perspective can inform the present just as the present can enlighten the past (e.g., Jones 2004), but, of course, neither entirely nor completely. By expanding our temporal lens, we may enlighten both.

Finally, with specific focus on the overarching theme of this collection, economic and power inequities may be practically inevitable in societies of larger scale and marked hierarchical complexity. Yet the precise ways and degrees to which such inequalities are manifest across human socioeconomic groupings are neither uniform nor immutable in time and space. Thus the analysis and arguments made here reaffirm my previous proposition (e.g., Feinman 1995) that there is more than one pathway to political and economic power, and that the alternatives (and changes in specific societal paths) are likely patterned in ways that are recognizable and explicable across the human career.

Acknowledgments I very much appreciate the thoughtful and constructive comments that I received on earlier versions of this manuscript from Richard E. Blanton, Stephen A. Kowalewski, Linda M. Nicholas, and T. Douglas Price. I also owe a debt of gratitude to Linda M. Nicholas for her editorial help in the preparation of this essay. Finally, I express my deepest thanks to Jill Seagard and Linda M. Nicholas for drafting the graphics that supplement this text

References

Abramowitz, A.I., and Stone, W.J. 2006. The Bush Effect: Polarization, Turnout, and Activism in the 2004 Presidential Election. *Presidential Studies Quarterly* 36:141–154.

Acemoglu, D. 2005. Constitutions, Politics, and Economics: A Review Essay on Persson and Tabellini's the Economic Effects of Constitutions. *Journal of Economic Literature* 18: 1025–1048.

Acemoglu, D., and Robinson, J.A. 2006. *Economic Origins of Dictatorship and Democracy*. New York, NY: Cambridge University Press.

Alcock, S.E., D'Altroy, T.N., Morrison, K.D., and Sinopoli, C.M. (eds.). 2001. *Empires: Perspectives from Archaeology and History*. Cambridge: Cambridge University Press.

Alderson, A.S. 2004. Explaining the Upswing in Direct Investment: A Test of Mainstream and Heterodox Theories of Globalization. *Social Forces* 83:81–122.

Alderson, A.S., and Nielsen, F. 2002. Globalization and the Great U-Turn: Income Inequality Trends in 16 OECD Countries. *American Journal of Sociology* 107:1244–1299.

American Society of Civil Engineers (ASCE). 2005. Report Card for America's Infrastructure. http://www.asce.org/reportcard/2005/index/efm

Anderson, S., Cavanagh, J., Collins, C., Pizzigati, S., and Lapham, M. 2007. Executive Excess: The Staggering Cost of U.S. Business Leadership. *Institute for Policy Studies, 14th Annual CEO Compensation Survey.* http://www.ips-dc.org

Ashmore, W. 1996. Comment. *Current Anthropology* 37:47–48.

Atkinson, A.B., Rainwater, L., and Smeeding, T.M. 1995. *Income Distribution in OECD Countries: Evidence from the Luxembourg Income Study (LIS).* Social Policy Studies 18. Organization for Economic Cooperation and Development, Paris.

Bartels, L.M. 2008. *Unequal Democracy: The Political Economy of the New Guided Age.* Princeton, NJ: Princeton University Press.

Bebchuk, L., and Grinstein, Y. 2005. The Growth of Executive Pay. *Oxford Review of Economic Policy* 21:283–303.

Beller, E., and Hout, M. 2006. Intergenerational Social Mobility: The United States in Comparative Perspective. *Future of Children* 16(2):19–36.

Berger, S. 2000. Globalization and Politics. *Annual Review of Political Science* 3:43–62.

Bernstein, J. 2007a. Work, Work Supports, and Safety Nets: Reducing the Burden of Low-Incomes in America. *Economic Policy Institute, Briefing Paper* 200, October 2. http://www.sharedprosperity.org/bp200.html

Bernstein, J. 2007b. Updated CBO Data Reveal Unprecedented Increase in Inequality. *Economic Policy Institute, Issue Brief* 239, December 13. http://www.epi.org/content.cfm/ib239

Bernstein, J., and Shapiro, I. 2006. Buying Power of the Minimum Wage at 51-Year Low. *Economic Policy Institute, Issue Brief* 224, June 20. http://www.epi.org/content.cfm/ib224

Bishop, B., and Cushing, R.G. 2008. *The Big Sort: Why the Clustering of Like-Minded America Is Tearing Us Apart.* New York, NY: Houghton Mifflin Company.

Blanton, R.E., and Fargher, L. 2008. *Collective Action in the Formation of Pre-Modern States.* New York, NY: Springer.

Blanton, R.E., and Feinman, G.M. 1984. The Mesoamerican World System. *American Anthropologist* 86:673–682.

Blanton, R.E., Feinman, G.M., Kowalewski, S.A., and Peregrine, P.N. 1996. A Dual-Processual Theory for the Evolution of Mesoamerican Civilization. *Current Anthropology* 37:1–14.

Blomster, J.P. (ed.). 2008. *After Monte Albán: Transformation and Negotiation in Oaxaca, Mexico.* Boulder, CO: University Press of Colorado.

Bluestone, B., and Harrison, B. 1982. *The De-Industrialization of America: Plant Closings, Community Abandonment, and the Dismantling of Basic Industry.* New York, NY: Basic Books.

Boehm, C. 1993. Egalitarian Society and Reverse Dominance Hierarchy. *Current Anthropology* 34:227–254.

Bondarenko, D.M., Grinin, L.E., and Korotayev, A.V. 2002. Alternative Pathways of Social Evolution. *Social Evolution & History* 1:54–79.

Bradbury, K., and Katz, J. 2002. Are Lifetimes Growing More Unequal? Looking at New Evidence on Family Income Mobility. *Federal Reserve Bank of Boston Regional Review* Q4:2002.

Brady, D., Beckfield, J., and Zhao, W. 2007. The Consequences of Economic Globalization for Affluent Democracies. *Annual Review of Sociology* 33:313–334.

Brady, D., and Wallace, M. 2000. Spatialization, Foreign Direct Investment, and Labor Outcomes in the American States 1978–1996. *Social Forces* 79:67–105.

Brumfiel, E.M. 1996. Comment. *Current Anthropology* 37:48–50.

Cashdan, E.A. 1980. Egalitarianism among Hunters and Gatherers. *American Anthropologist* 82:116–120.

Caso, A. 1982. *El Tesoro de Monte Albán.* Memorias, Instituto Nacional de Antropología e Historia, 3, Mexico.

Caso, A., Bernal, I., and Acosta, J.R. 1967. La Cerámica de Monte Albán. Memorias, Instituto Nacional de Antropología e Historia, 13, Mexico.

Chandrasekaran, R. 2006. *Imperial Life in the Emerald City*. New York, NY: Alfred A. Knopf.

Chase, I.D., Tovey, C., Spangler-Martin, D., and Manfredonia, M. 2002. Individual Differences Versus Social Dynamics in the Formation of Animal Dominance Hierarchies. *Proceedings of the National Academy of Sciences* 99:5744–5749.

Chase-Dunn, C., Kawano, Y., and Brewer, B.D. 2000. Trade Globalization since 1795: Waves of Integration in the World-System. *American Sociological Review* 65:77–95.

Claessen, H.J.M., and Skalník, P. (eds.). 1978. *The Early State*. The Hague: Mouton Publishers.

Clawson, D., and Clawson, M.A. 1999. What Has Happened to the US Labor Movement? Union Decline and Renewal. *Annual Review of Sociology* 25:95–119.

Conason, J. 2007. *It Can Happen Here: Authoritarian Peril in the Age of Bush*. New York, NY: Thomas Dunne Books.

Crenson, M.A., and Ginsberg, B. 2006. Downsizing Democracy, Upsizing the Presidency. *The South Atlantic Quarterly* 105:207–216.

Crenson, M.A., and Ginsberg, B. 2007. *Presidential Power: Unchecked and Unbalanced*. New York, NY: W.W. Norton and Company.

D'Altroy, T.N., and Earle, T. 1985. Staple Finance, Wealth Finance, and Storage in the Inka Political Economy. *Current Anthropology* 26:187–206.

Dew-Becker, I., and Gordon, R.J. 2005. Where Did the Productivity Growth Go? Inflation Dynamics and the Distribution of Income. *National Bureau of Economic Research, Working Paper* 11842. http://www.nber.org/papers/w11842

Dew-Becker, I., and Gordon, R.J. 2008. The Rise in American Inequality. Vox, June 19. http://www.voxeu.org/index.php?q=node/1245

Domhoff, G.W. 2005. Interlocking Directorates in the Corporate Community. http://sociology.ucsc.edu/whorulesamerica/power/corporate_community.html

Domhoff, G.W. 2006. C. Wright Mills 50 Years Later. *Contemporary Sociology* 35:547–550.

Dreier, P. 2006. Katrina and Power in America. *Urban Affairs Review* 41:528–549.

Drennan, R.D., and Peterson, C.E. 2006. Patterned Variation in Prehistoric Chiefdoms. *Proceedings of the National Academy of Sciences* 103:3960–3967.

Ember, M., Ember, C.R., and Russett, B. 1997. Inequality and Democracy in the Anthropological Record. In Midlarsky, M.I. (ed.) *Inequality, Democracy, and Economic Development*, pp. 110–130. Cambridge: Cambridge University Press.

Fargher, L.F., and Blanton, R.E. 2007. Revenue, Voice, and Public Goods in Three Pre-Modern States. *Comparative Studies in Society and History* 49:848–882.

Feinman, G.M. 1995. The Emergence of Inequality: A Focus on Strategies and Processes. In Price, T.D. and Feinman, G.M. (eds.), *Foundations of Social Inequality*, pp. 255–279. New York, NY: Plenum Press.

Feinman, G.M. 1999. The Changing Structure of Macroregional Mesoamerica: The Classic-Postclassic Transition in the Valley of Oaxaca. In Kardulias, P.N. (ed.) *World-Systems Theory in Practice: Leadership, Production, and Exchange*, pp. 53–62. Lanham: Rowman and Littlefield Publishers.

Feinman, G.M. 2000. Dual-Processual Theory and Social Formations in the Southwest. In Mills, B.J. (ed.), *Alternative Leadership Strategies in the Prehispanic Southwest*, pp. 207–224. Tucson, AZ: University of Arizona Press.

Feinman, G.M. 2001. Mesoamerican Political Complexity: The Corporate-Network Dimension. In Haas, J. (ed.), *From Leaders to Rulers*, pp. 151–175. New York, NY: Kluwer Academic/Plenum Publishers.

Feinman, G.M. 2007. The Last Quarter Century of Archaeological Research in the Central Valleys of Oaxaca. *Mexicon* 29:3–14.

Feinman, G.M., Lightfoot, K.G., and Upham, S. 2000. Political Hierarchies and Organizational Strategies in the Puebloan Southwest. *American Antiquity* 65:449–470.

Feinman, G.M., and Marcus, J. (eds.). 1998. *Archaic States*. Santa Fe, NM: School of American Research Press.

Flanagan, J.G. 1989. Hierarchy in Simple "Egalitarian" Societies. *Annual Review of Anthropology* 18:245–266.

Flannery, K.V. 1983. Divergent Evolution. In Flannery, K.V. and Marcus, J. (eds.), *The Cloud People: Divergent Evolution of the Zapotec and Mixtec Civilizations*, pp. 1–4. New York, NY: Academic Press.

Forbes. 2007. The Global 2000. http://www.forbes.com/lists/2007/18/biz_07forbes2000-The-Global-2000_Rank.html

Frank, R.H. 2007. *Richistan: A Journey Through the American Wealth Boom and the Lives of the New Rich*. New York, NY: Crown Publishers.

Frank, R.H., and Cook, P.H. 1995. *The Winner-Take-All Society: Why the Few at the Top Get So Much More than the Rest of Us*. New York, NY: Free Press.

Frank, T. 2008. *The Wrecking Crew: How Conservatives Rule*. New York, NY: Metropolitan Books.

Freeman, R.B. 1993. How Much Has De-Unionization Contributed to the Rise in Male Earnings Inequality? In Danzinger, S. and Gottschalk, P. (eds.), *Uneven Tides: Rising Inequalities in America*, pp. 133–163. New York, NY: Russell Sage Foundation.

Frydman, C., and Saks, R.E. 2007. Executive Compensation: A New View from a Long-Term Perspective. http://web.mit.edu/www.frydmansaks_trends_0707.pdf

Galbraith, J.K. 1967. *The New Industrial State*. New York, NY: A Signet Book.

Gallegos, R. 1978. *El Señor 9 Flor en Zaachila*. Mexico: Universidad Nacional Autonóma de México.

Gangl, M. 2005. Income Inequality, Permanent Incomes, and Income Dynamics. *Work and Occupations* 32:140–162.

Gavrilets, S., Duanez-Guzman, E.A., and Vose, M.D. 2008. Dynamics of Alliance Formation and the Egalitarian Revolution. Plos One 3(10):e3293.

Gellman, B. 2008. *Angler: The Cheney Vice Presidency*. New York, NY: The Penguin Press.

Gilens, M. 2005. Inequality and Democratic Responsiveness. *Public Opinion Quarterly* 69: 778–796.

Goff, M.J. 2004. *The Money Primary: The New Politics of the Early Presidential Nomination Process*. Lanham, MD: Rowman & Littlefield.

Goldin, C., and Katz, L.F. 2001. Decreasing (and Then Increasing) Inequality in America: A Tale of Two Half-Centuries. In Welch, F. (ed.), *The Causes and Consequences of Increasing Inequality*, pp. 37–82. Chicago, IL: University of Chicago Press.

Goldin, C., and Margo, R.A. 1992. The Great Compression: The Wage Structure in the United States at Mid-Century. *The Quarterly Journal of Economics* 107:1–34.

Goldsmith, J.L. 2007. *The Terror Presidency: Law and Judgment Inside the Bush Administration*. New York, NY: W.W. Norton and Company.

Goldstein, R. 2003. Neo-macho Man: Pop Culture and Post 9/11 Politics. *The Nation* 276(11): 16–19.

Gosselin, P.G. 2004. The New Deal: How Just a Handful of Setbacks Sent the Ryans Tumbling Out of Prosperity. *Los Angeles Times*, December 30.

Gosselin, P.G. 2008. *High Wire: The Precarious Lives of American Families*. New York, NY: Basic Books.

Gottschalk, P., and Smeeding, T.M. 1997. Cross National Comparisons of Earnings and Income Inequality. *Journal of Economic Literature* 35:633–687.

Gramlich, E.M., Kasten, R., and Sammartino, F. 1993. Growing Inequality in the 1980s: The Role of Federal Taxes and Cash Transfers. In Danzinger, S. and Gottschalk, P. (eds.), *Uneven Tides: Rising Inequalities in America*, , pp. 225–249. New York, NY: Russell Sage Foundation.

Grinin, L. 2003. The Early State and Its Analogues. *Social Evolution & History* 2:131–176.

Grinin, L. 2004. Democracy and Early State. *Social Evolution & History* 3:93–149.

Gross, J.A. 1995. *Broken Promise: The Subversion of US Labor Relations Policy, 1947–1994.* Philadelphia, PA: Temple University Press.

Guerlain, P. 2006. New Warriors among American Foreign Policy Theorists. *The South Atlantic Quarterly* 105:109–124.

Gustafsson, B., and Johansson, M. 1999. In Search of Smoking Guns: What Makes Income Inequality Vary Over Time in Different Countries? *American Sociological Review* 64:585–605.

Hacker, J.S. 2006. *The Great Risk-Shift: The Assault on American Jobs, Families, Health Care, and Retirement, and How You Can Fight Back.* Oxford: Oxford University Press.

Harjes, T. 2007. Globalization and Income Inequality: A European Perspective. *International Monetary Fund, Working Papers* 07/169.

Harrison, B., and Bluestone, B. 1988. *The Great U-Turn: Corporate Restructuring and the Polarizing of America.* New York, NY: Basic Books.

Harvey, D. 1990. Between Space and Time: Reflections on the Geographical Imagination. *Annals of the Association of American Geographers* 80:418–434.

Herrmann, E., Call, J., Victoria-Lloreda, M., Hare, B., and Tomasello, M. 2007. Humans Have Evolved Specialized Skills of Social Cognition: The Cultural Intelligence Hypothesis. *Science* 317:1360–1366.

Hertz, T. 2006. Understanding Mobility in America. Center for American Progress http://www.americanprogress.org/kf/hertz_mobility_analysis.pdf

Hertzberg, H. 2007. Dynastic Voyage. *The New Yorker* 83(33):33–34.

Howell, W.G. 2005. Unilateral Powers: A Brief Overview. *Presidential Studies Quarterly* 35: 417–439.

Johnson, C. 2007. *Nemesis: The Last Days of the American Republic.* New York, NY: Metropolitan Books.

Johnston, D.C. 2007. Report Says That the Rich Are Getting Richer Faster, Much Faster. *New York Times*, December 15.

Jones, R. 2004. What Time Human Geography? *Progress in Human Geography* 28:287–304.

Kennickell, A.B. 2006. Currents and Undercurrents: Changes in the Distribution of Wealth, 1989–2004. In Wolff, E.N. (ed.), *International Perspectives on Household Wealth*, pp. 19–88. Cheltenham: Edward Elgar Publishing.

Khurana, R. 2002. Good Charisma, Bad Business. *New York Times*, September 13, 2002.

Kopczuk, W., and Saez, E. 2004. Top Wealth Shares in the United States, 1916–2000: Evidence from Estate Tax Returns. *National Tax Journal* 57:445–487.

Kowalewski, S.A., Blanton, R.E., Feinman, G.M., and Finsten, L. 1983. Boundaries, Scale, and Internal Organization. *Journal of Anthropological Archaeology* 2:32–56.

Kowalewski, S.A., and Finsten, L. 1983. The Economic Systems of Ancient Oaxaca: A Regional Perspective. *Current Anthropology* 24:413–441.

Krueger, A.O. 2006. The World Economy at the Start of the twenty-first Century. Remarks at the Annual Gilbert Lecture, Rochester University, New York. http://www.imf.org/external/np/speeches/2006/040606.htm

Krugman, P. 1996. The Spiral of Inequality. *Mother Jones* 21(Nov.–Dec.):44–49.

Krugman, P. 2002a. Crony Capitalism, U.S.A. *New York Times*, January 15.

Krugman, P. 2002b. For Richer. *New York Times*, October 20.

Krugman, P. 2006a. The Crony Fairy. *New York Times*, April 28.

Krugman, P. 2006b. The Great Wealth Transfer. *Rolling Stone* 1015:44–50.

Krugman, P. 2007. Same Old Party. *New York Times*, October 8, 2007.

Lehman, E.H. 1969. Toward a Macrosociology of Power. *American Sociological Review* 34: 453–465.

Levi, M. 1988. *Of Rule and Revenue.* Berkeley, CA: University of California Press.

Lewis, D.E. 2005. Staffing Alone: Unilateral Action and the Politicization of the Executive Office of the President, 1988–2004. *Presidential Studies Quarterly* 35:496–514.

Lewis, D.E. 2007. Testing Pendleton's Premise: Do Political Appointees Make Worse Bureaucrats? *The Journal of Politics* 69:1073–1088.

Lewis, D.E. 2008. *The Politics of Presidential Appointments: Political Control and Bureaucratic Performance.* Princeton, NJ: Princeton University Press.

Lichbach, M.I. 1996. *The Cooperator's Dilemma.* Ann Arbor, MI: University of Michigan Press.

Lindert, P.H. 2000. Three Centuries of Inequality in Britain and America. In Atkinson, A.B. and Bourguignon, F. (eds.), *Handbook of Income Distribution, Volume I,* pp. 167–216. Amsterdam: Elsevier Science.

Lobao, L., and Meyer, K. 2001. The Great Agricultural Transition: Crisis, Change, and Social Consequences of Twentieth Century US Farming. *Annual Review of Sociology* 27:103–124.

Lohse, J.C. 2007. Commoner Ritual, Commoner Ideology: (Sub-) Alternate Views of Complexity in Prehispanic Mesoamerica. In Gonlin, N. and Lohse, J.C. (eds.), *Commoner Ritual and Ideology in Ancient Mesoamerica,* pp. 1–32. Boulder, CO: University Press of Colorado.

Lohse, J.C., and Gonlin, N. 2007. Preface. In Gonlin, N. and Lohse, J.C. (eds.), *Commoner Ritual and Ideology in Ancient Mesoamerica,* pp. xvii–xxxix. Boulder, CO: University Press of Colorado.

Lycett, S.J., Collard, M., and McGrew, W.C. 2007. Phylogenetic Analyses of Behavior Support Existence of Culture among Wild Chimpanzees. *Proceedings of the National Academy of Sciences* 104:17588–17592.

Maddison, A. 1997. Causal Influences on Productivity Performance 1820–1992: A Global Perspective. *Journal of Productivity Analysis* 8:325–359.

Mann, M., and Riley, D. 2007. Explaining Macro-regional Trends in Global Income Inequalities, 1950–2000. *Socio-Economic Review* 5:81–115.

Marcus, J. 1983. Changing Patterns of Stone Monuments after the Fall of Monte Albán, A.D. 600–900. In Flannery, K.V. and Marcus, J. (eds.), *The Cloud People: Divergent Evolution of the Zapotec and Mixtec Civilizations,* pp. 191–197. New York, NY: Academic Press.

Marcus, J., and Flannery, K.V. 1983. The Postclassic Balkanization of Oaxaca: An Introduction to the Late Postclassic. In Flannery, K.V. and Marcus, J. (eds.), *The Cloud People: Divergent Evolution of the Zapotec and Mixtec Civilizations,* pp. 217–226. New York, NY: Academic Press.

Markens, R., Winter, M., and López, C.M. 2008. Ethnohistory, Oral History, and Archaeology at Macuilxochitl: Perspectives on the Postclassic Period (800–1521 CE) in the Valley of Oaxaca. In Blomster, J.P. (ed.), *After Monte Albán: Transformation and Negotiation in Oaxaca, Mexico,* pp. 193–215. Boulder, CO: University Press of Colorado.

Mayer, J. 2008. *The Dark Side.* New York, NY: Doubleday.

Mazumder, B., and Levine, D.I. 2003. The Growing Importance of Family and Community: An Analysis of Changes in Sibling Correlation in Earnings. *Federal Reserve Bank of Chicago, Working Paper* 2003–24. http://papers.ssrn.com/sol3/papers.cfm?abstract_id=483023

McPherson, M., Smith-Lovin, L., and Cook, J.M. 2001. Birds of a Feather: Homophily in Social Networks. *Annual Review of Sociology* 27:415–444.

Mead, R. 2007. *One Perfect Day: The Selling of the American Wedding.* New York, NY: Penguin Press.

Michaels, W.B. 2006. *The Trouble with Diversity: How We Learned to Love Identity and Ignore Inequality.* New York, NY: Metropolitan Books.

Milanovic, B., Lindert, P., and Williamson, J. 2007. Measuring Ancient Inequality. *Munich Personal RePEc Archive,* Paper 5388. http://mpra.ub.uni-muenchen.de/5388/

Millbank, D. 2005. Family Ties Playing a Big Role on the Hill. *Washington Post,* January 23, p. 1.

Mishel, L.R., Bernstein, J., and Allegretto, S. 2007. *The State of Working America 2006/2007,* 10th edn. Ithaca: ILR Press.

Moe, T.M. 1985. The Politicized Presidency. In Chubb, J.E. and Peterson, P.E. (eds.), *The New Direction in American Politics,* pp. 235–271. Washington, DC: Brookings Institution.

Neckerman, K.M., and Torche, F. 2007. Inequality: Causes and Consequences. *Annual Review of Sociology* 33:335–357.

Nelson, D.D. 2006. The President and Presidentialism. *The South Atlantic Quarterly* 105:1–17.

Neustadt, R.E. 1960. *Presidential Power and the Modern Presidencies.* New York, NY: Free Press.

Olsen, M. 1965. *The Logic of Collective Action: Public Goods and the Theory of Groups.* Cambridge: Harvard University Press.

O'Rourke, K.H., and Williamson, J.G. 2002. When Did Globalization Begin? *European Review of Economic History* 6:23–50.

Owens, J.E. 2006. Presidential Power and Congressional Acquiescence in the "War" on Terrorism: A New Constitutional Equilibrium? *Politics & Policy* 34:258–303.

Phillips, K. 2004. *American Dynasty: Aristocracy, Fortune, and the Politics of Deceit in the House of Bush.* New York, NY: Penguin Books.

Piketty, T., and Saez, E. 2003. Income Inequality in the United States, 1913–1998. *The Quarterly Journal of Economics* 118:1–39.

Piketty, T., and Saez, E. 2006. The Evolution of Top Incomes: A Historical and International Perspective. *National Bureau of Economic Research, Working Paper Series* 11955, Cambridge.

Pohl, J.M.D. 1999. The Lintel Paintings of Mitla and the Function of the Mitla Palaces. In Kowalski, J.K. (ed.), *Mesoamerican Architecture as a Cultural Symbol*, pp. 176–197. Oxford: Oxford University Press.

Pohl, J.M.D. 2003. Creation Stories, Hero Cults, and Alliance Building: Confederacies of Central and Southern Mexico. In Smith, M.E. and Berdan, F.F. (eds.), *The Postclassic Mesoamerican World*, pp. 61–66. Salt Lake City: The University of Utah Press.

Porter, E. 2007. More than Ever, It Pays to Be the Top Executive. *New York Times*, May 25.

Price, T.D., and Feinman, G.M. (eds.). 1995. *Foundations of Social Inequality.* New York, NY: Plenum Press.

Putnam, R. 1995. Bowling Alone: America's Declining Social Capital. *Journal of Democracy* 6:65–78.

Reich, R.B. 2007. *Supercapitalism: The Transformation of Business, Democracy, and Everyday Life.* New York, NY: Alfred A. Knopf.

Reich, R.B. 2008. Obama vs. McCain, and the Four Stories of American Life. Robert Reich's Blog, February 12. http://robertreich.blogspot.com/2008/02/obama-vs-mccain-and-four-stories-of.html

Renfrew, C. 1974. Beyond a Subsistence Economy: The Evolution of Social Organization in Prehistoric Europe. In Moore, C.B. (ed.), *Reconstructing Complex Societies: An Archaeological Colloquium*, pp. 69–95. Bulletin No. 20. Cambridge, MA: American Schools of Oriental Research.

Rich, F. 2006. *The Greatest Story Ever Sold.* New York, NY: Penguin Books.

Rothkopf, D.J. 2008. *Superclass: The Global Power Elite and the World They Are Making.* New York, NY: Farrar Straus and Giroux.

Rudalevige, A. 2005. *The New Imperial Presidency: Renewing Presidential Power after Watergate.* Ann Arbor, MI: University of Michigan Press.

Rudalevige, A. 2006. The Contemporary Presidency: The Decline and Resurgence and Decline (and Resurgence?) of Congress: Charting a New Imperial Presidency. *Presidential Studies Quarterly* 36:506–524.

Russett, B.M. 1964. Inequality and Instability: The Relation of Land Tenure to Politics. *World Politics* 16(3):442–454.

Sahlins, M.D., and Service, E.R. (eds.). 1960. *Evolution and Culture.* Ann Arbor, MI: University of Michigan Press.

Sanders, W.T., and Price, B.J. 1968. *Mesoamerica: The Evolution of a Civilization.* New York, NY: Random House.

Sapolsky, R.M. 2005. The Influence of Social Hierarchy on Primate Health. *Science* 308:648–652.

Savage, C. 2007. *Takeover: The Return of the Imperial Presidency and the Subversion of American Democracy.* New York, NY: Little Brown.

Schlesinger, A.M. 1973. *The Imperial Presidency.* Boston, MA: Houghton Mifflin.

Schwarz, F.A.O., Jr., and Huq, A.Z. 2006. *Unchecked and Unbalanced: Presidential Power in a Time of Terror.* New York, NY: The New Press.

Service, E.R. 1971. *Primitive Social Organization: An Evolutionary Perspective*. New York, NY: Random House.

Sirota, D. 2008. The Real Meaning of Joe the Plumber. Campaign for American's Future, October 16. http://www.ourfuture.org/blog-entry/2008104216/real-meaning-joe-plumber

Smith, M.E., and Berdan, F.F. (eds.). 2003. *The Postclassic Mesoamerican World*. Salt Lake City: University of Utah Press.

Sonnett, N.R. 2006. Task Force on Presidential Signing Statements and the Separation of Powers Doctrine: Recommendation. American Bar Association, http://www.abanet.org/op/signingstatements/aba_final_signing_statements_recommendation-report_7-24-06.pdf

Spencer, C.S. 1997. Evolutionary Approaches in Archaeology. *Journal of Archaeological Research* 5:209–264.

Steward, J.H. 1949. Cultural Causality and Law: A Trial Formulation of the Development of Early Civilizations. *American Anthropologist* 51:1–27.

Stiglitz, J.E. 2007. The Economic Consequences of Mr. Bush. *Vanity Fair* 49 (12):312–315.

Street, J. 2004. Celebrity Politicians: Popular Culture and Political Representation. *British Journal of Politics and International Relations* 6:435–452.

Swank, D. 2001. Mobile Capital, Democratic Institutions, and the Public Economy in Advanced Industrial Societies. *Journal of Comparative Policy Analysis: Research and Practice* 3: 133–162.

Swank, D. 2005. Globalisation, Domestic Politics, and the Welfare State: Retrenchment in Capitalist Democracies. *Social Policy & Society* 4:183–195.

Thurow, L.C. 1987. A Surge in Inequality. *Scientific American* 256(5):30–37.

Tilly, C. 2001. Introduction: Anthropology Confronts Inequality. *Anthropological Theory* 1: 299–306.

Tomasello, M. 1999. Human Adaptation for Culture. *Annual Review of Anthropology* 28:509–529.

Trigger, B.G. 1996. Comment. *Current Anthropology* 37:63–64.

Twitchell, J.B. 2002. *Living It Up: Our Love Affair with Luxury*. New York, NY: Columbia University Press.

Uchitelle, L. 2006. Very Rich Are Leaving the Merely Rich Behind. *New York Times*, November 27.

United States Office of Personnel Management (US OPM). 2006. *Federal Civilian Workforce Statistics: The Fact Book 2005 Edition*. http://www.opm.gov/feddata/factbook/2005/factbook2005.pdf

Wallerstein, M. 1999. Wage-Setting Institutions and Pay Inequality in Advanced Industrial Societies. *American Journal of Political Science* 43:649–680.

Warshaw, S.A. 2006. The Administrative Strategies of President George W. Bush. *Extensions* Spring. http://www.ou.edu/special/albertctr/extensions/spring2006/Warshaw.pdf

Whyte, W.H. 1956. *The Organization Man*. New York, NY: Doubleday.

Wills, G. 2007. At Ease, Mr. President. *New York Times,* January 27. http://www.nytimes.com/2007/01/27/opinion/27wills.html?

Winter, M. (ed.). 1995. *Entierros Humanos de Monte Albán: Dos Estudios*. Proyecto Especial de Monte Albán 1992–1994, Contribución 7. Centro INAH Oaxaca, Oaxaca.

Wolff, E.N. 2006. Changes in Household Wealth in the 1980s and 1990s in the United States. In Wolff, E.N. (ed.), *International Perspectives on Household Wealth*, pp. 107–150. Cheltenham: Edward Elgar Publishing.

Zink, C.F., Tong, Y., Chen, Q., Bassett, D.S., Stein, J.L., and Meyer-Lindenberg, A. 2008. Know Your Place: Neural Processing of Social Hierarchy in Humans. *Neuron* 58:273–283.

Subject Index

Note: The letter 'f' following the locators refers to figures.

T.D. Price, G.M. Feinman (eds.), *Pathways to Power*, Fundamental
Issues in Archaeology, DOI 10.1007/978-1-4419-6300-0,
© Springer Science+Business Media, LLC 2010

CPSIA information can be obtained at www.ICGtesting.com
Printed in the USA
LVOW010058121212

311241LV00003B/97/P